Machine Learning for Human Motion Analysis:
Theory and Practice

Liang Wang
University of Bath, UK

Li Cheng
TTI–Chicago, USA

Guoying Zhao
University of Oulu, Finland

MEDICAL INFORMATION SCIENCE REFERENCE

Hershey · New York

Director of Editorial Content: Kristin Klinger
Senior Managing Editor: Jamie Snavely
Assistant Managing Editor: Michael Brehm
Publishing Assistant: Sean Woznicki
Typesetter: Michael Brehm, Carole Coulson
Cover Design: Lisa Tosheff
Printed at: Yurchak Printing Inc.

Published in the United States of America by
    Medical Information Science Reference (an imprint of IGI Global)
    701 E. Chocolate Avenue
    Hershey PA 17033
    Tel: 717-533-8845
    Fax: 717-533-8661
    E-mail: cust@igi-global.com
    Web site: http://www.igi-global.com/reference

Library of Congress Cataloging-in-Publication Data

Machine learning for human motion analysis : theory and practice / Liang Wang,
Li Cheng, and Guoying Zhao, editors.
       p. cm.
   Includes bibliographical references and index.
   Summary: "This book highlights the development of robust and effective
vision-based motion understanding systems, addressing specific vision
applications such as surveillance, sport event analysis, healthcare, video
conferencing, and motion video indexing and retrieval"--Provided by publisher.
   ISBN 978-1-60566-900-7 (hardcover) -- ISBN 978-1-60566-901-4 (ebook) 1.
Computer vision. 2. Machine learning. 3. Image analysis. 4. Motion
perception (Vision) 5. Human locomotion. I. Wang, Liang, 1975- II. Cheng,
Li, 1974- III. Zhao, Guoying, 1977-
   TA1634.M3153 2010
   006.3'7--dc22
                                          2009047277

British Cataloguing in Publication Data
A Cataloguing in Publication record for this book is available from the British Library.

Table of Contents

Detailed Table of Contents

    Tony Tung, Kyoto University, Japan
    Takashi Matsuyama, Kyoto University, Japan

This chapter presents a new formulation for the problem of human motion tracking in video. Tracking is still a challenging problem when strong appearance changes occur as in videos of humans in motion. Most trackers rely on a predefined template or on a training dataset to achieve detection and tracking. Therefore they are not efficient to track objects whose appearance is not known in advance. A solution is to use an online method that updates iteratively a subspace of reference target models. In addition, we propose to integrate color and motion cues in a particle filter framework to track human body parts. The algorithm process consists of two modes, switching between detection and tracking. The detection steps involve trained classifiers to update estimated positions of the tracking windows, whereas tracking steps rely on an adaptive color-based particle filter coupled with optical flow estimations. The Earth Mover distance is used to compare color models in a global fashion, and constraints on flow features avoid drifting effects. The proposed method has revealed its efficiency to track body parts in motion and can cope with full appearance changes. Experiments were performed on challenging real world videos with poorly textured models and non-linear motions.

    Olusegun T. Oshin, University of Surrey, UK
    Andrew Gilbert, University of Surrey, UK
    John Illingworth, University of Surrey, UK
    Richard Bowden, University of Surrey, UK

In this chapter, we present a generic classifier for detecting spatio-temporal interest points within video. The premise being that, given an interest point detector, we can learn a classifier that duplicates its functionality, which is both accurate and computationally efficient. This means that interest point detection can be achieved independent of the complexity of the original interest point formulation. We extend the naive Bayesian classifier of Ferns to the spatio-temporal domain and learn classifiers that duplicate the functionality of common spatio-temporal interest point detectors. Results demonstrate accurate reproduction of results with a classifier that can be applied exhaustively to video at frame-rate, without optimisation, in a scanning window approach.

Chapter 3

Pradeep Natarajan, BBN Technologies, USA
Ramakant Nevatia, The University of South California, USA

Building a system for recognition of human actions from video involves two key problems - 1) Designing suitable low-level features that are both efficient to extract from videos and are capable of distinguishing between events 2) Developing a suitable representation scheme that can bridge the large gap between lowlevel features and high-level event concepts, and also handle the uncertainty and errors inherent in any low-level video processing. Graphical models provide a natural framework for representing state transitions in events and also the spatio-temporal constraints between the actors and events. Hidden Markov Models (HMMs) have been widely used in several action recognition applications but the basic representation has three key deficiencies: These include unrealistic models for the duration of a sub-event, not encoding interactions among multiple agents directly and not modeling the inherent hierarchical organization of these activities. Several extensions have been proposed to address one or more of these issues and have been successfully applied in various gesture and action recognition domains. More recently, Conditional Random Fields (CRF) are becoming increasingly popular since they allow complex potential functions for modeling observations and state transitions, and also produce superior performance to HMMs when sufficient training data is available. We will first review the various extension of these graphical models, then present the theory of inference and learning in them and finally discuss their applications in various domains.

Chapter 4

Ronald Poppe, University of Twente, The Netherlands

We present a discriminative approach to human action recognition. At the heart of our approach is the use of common spatial patterns (CSP), a spatial filter technique that transforms temporal feature data by using differences in variance between two classes. Such a transformation focuses on differences between classes, rather than on modeling each class individually. As a result, to distinguish between two classes, we can use simple distance metrics in the low-dimensional transformed space. The most likely class is found by pairwise evaluation of all discriminant functions, which can be done in real-time. Our image representations are silhouette boundary gradients, spatially binned into cells. We achieve scores of approximately 96% on the Weizmann human action dataset, and show that reasonable results can be obtained when training on only a single subject. We further compare our results with a recent examplar-based approach. Future work is aimed at combining our approach with automatic human detection.

Chapter 5

A marker-less motion capture system, based on machine learning, is proposed and tested. Pose information is inferred from images captured from multiple (as few as two) synchronized cameras. The central concept of which, we call: Kernel Subspace Mapping (KSM). The images-to-pose learning could be done with large numbers of images of a large variety of people (and with the ground truth poses accurately known). Of course, obtaining the ground-truth poses could be problematic. Here we choose to use synthetic data (both for learning and for, at least some of, testing). The system needs to generalizes well to novel inputs: unseen poses (not in the training database) and unseen actors. For the learning we use a generic and relatively low fidelity computer graphic model and for testing we sometimes use a more accurate model (made to resemble the first author). What makes machine learning viable for human motion capture is that a high percentage of human motion is coordinated. Indeed, it is now relatively well known that there is large redundancy in the set of possible images of a human (these images form som sort of relatively smooth lower dimensional manifold in the huge dimensional space of all possible images) and in the set of pose angles (again, a low dimensional and smooth sub-manifold of the moderately high dimensional space of all possible joint angles). KSM, is based on the KPCA (Kernel PCA) algorithm, which is costly. We show that the Greedy Kernel PCA (GKPCA) algorithm can be used to speed up KSM, with relatively minor modifications. At the core, then, is two KPCA's (or two GKPCA's) - one for the learning of pose manifold and one for the learning image manifold. Then we use a modification of Local Linear Embedding (LLE) to bridge between pose and image manifolds.

Chapter 6

Visual processing of people, including detection, tracking, recognition, and behavior interpretation, is a key component of intelligent video surveillance systems. Computer vision algorithms with the capability of "looking at people" at multiple scales can be applied in different surveillance scenarios, such as far-field people detection for wide-area perimeter protection, midfield people detection for retail/banking applications or parking lot monitoring, and near-field people/face detection for facility security and access. In this chapter, we address the people detection problem in different scales as well as human tracking and motion analysis for real video surveillance applications including people search, retail loss prevention, people counting, and display effectiveness.

Chapter 7

Lei Zhang, Rensselaer Polytechnic Institute, USA
Jixu Chen, Rensselaer Polytechnic Institute, USA
Zhi Zeng, Rensselaer Polytechnic Institute, USA
Qiang Ji, Rensselaer Polytechnic Institute, USA

Upper body tracking is a problem to track the pose of human body from video sequences. It is difficult due to such problems as the high dimensionality of the state space, the self-occlusion, the appearance changes, etc. In this paper, we propose a generic framework that can be used for both 2D and 3D upper body tracking and can be easily parameterized without heavily depending on supervised training. We first construct a Bayesian Network (BN) to represent the human upper body structure and then incorporate into the BN various generic physical and anatomical constraints on the parts of the upper body. Unlike the existing upper body models, we aim at handling physically feasible body motions rather than only some typical motions. We also explicitly model part occlusion in the model, which allows to automatically detect the occurrence of self-occlusion and to minimize the effect of measurement errors on the tracking accuracy due to occlusion. Using the proposed model, upper body tracking can be performed through probabilistic inference over time. A series of experiments were performed on both monocular and stereo video sequences to demonstrate the effectiveness and capability of the model in improving upper body tracking accuracy and robustness.

Chapter 8

Vassilis Syrris, Aristotle University of Thessaloniki, Greece

This work describes a simple and computationally efficient, appearance-based approach for real-time recognition of basic human actions. We apply a technique that depicts the differences between two or more successive frames accompanied by a threshold filter to detect the regions of the video frames where some type of human motion is observed. From each frame difference, the algorithm extracts an incomplete and unformed human body shape and generates a skeleton model which represents it in an abstract way. Eventually, the recognition process is formulated as a time-series problem and handled by a very robust and accurate prediction method (Support Vector Regression). The proposed technique could be employed in applications such as vision-based autonomous robots and surveillance systems.

Chapter 9

Konrad Schindler, TU Darmstadt, Germany
Luc van Gool, ETH Zürich, Switzerland ESAT/PSI-IBBT, K. U. Leuven, Belgium

Visual categorisation of human motion in video clips has been an active field of research in recent years. However, most published methods either analyse an entire video and assign it a single category label, or use relatively large look-ahead to classify each frame. Contrary to these strategies, the human visual system proves that simple categories can be recognised almost instantaneously. Here we present a system for categorisation from very short sequences ("snippets") of 1–10 frames, and systematically evaluate it on several data sets. It turns out that even local shape and optic flow for a single frame are enough to achieve 80-90% correct classification, and snippets of 5-7 frames (0.2-0.3 seconds of video) yield results on par with the ones state-of-the-art methods obtain on entire video sequences.

Chapter 10

Wanqing Li, University of Wollongong, Australia
Zhengyou Zhang, Microsoft Research, Redmond, USA
Zicheng Liu, Microsoft Research, Redmond, USA
Philip Ogunbona, University of Wollongong, Australia

An action recognition system is desired to be independent of the subjects who perform the actions, independent of the speed at which the actions are performed, robust against noisy extraction of features used to characterize the actions, scalable to large number of actions and expandable with new actions. Despite the considerable research in the past few years, such a system is yet to be developed. In this chapter, we describe a recently proposed expandable graphical model of human actions that has the promise to realize such a system. This chapter first presents a brief review of the recent development in human action recognition. The principle of modeling actions based on conventional Hidden Markov Model (HMM) and its variants will be described. Then, the expandable graphical model is presented in detail and a system that learns and recognizes human actions from sequences of silhouettes using the expandable graphical model is developed. Conclusion and discussion on future challenges are made in the last section.

Chapter 11

Scott Blunsden, European Commission Joint Research Centre, Italy
Robert Fisher, University of Edinburgh, UK

This chapter presents a way to classify interactions between people. Examples of the interactions we investigate are; people meeting one another, walking together and fighting. A new feature set is proposed along with a corresponding classification method. Results are presented which show the new method performing significantly better than the previous state of the art method as proposed by Oliver et al.

Chapter 12

Qingdi Wei, National Laboratory of Pattern Recognition, Institute of Automation, CAS, Beijing, China
Xiaoqin Zhang, National Laboratory of Pattern Recognition, Institute of Automation, CAS, Beijing, China
Weiming Hu, National Laboratory of Pattern Recognition, Institute of Automation, CAS, Beijing, China

Action recognition is one of the most active research fields in computer vision. This chapter first reviews the current action recognition methods from the following two aspects: action representation and recognition strategy. Then, a novel method for classifying human actions from image sequences is investigated. In this method, the human action is represented by a set of shape context features of human silhouette, and a dominant sets-based approach is employed to classify the predefined actions. The comparison between the dominant sets-based approach with K-means, mean shift, and Fuzzy-Cmean is also discussed.

Dong Seon Cheng, University of Verona, Italy
Marco Cristani, University of Verona, Italy
Vittorio Murino, University of Verona, Italy

Image super-resolution is one of the most appealing applications of image processing, capable of retrieving a high resolution image by fusing several registered low resolution images depicting an object of interest. However, employing super-resolution in video data is challenging: a video sequence generally contains a lot of scattered information regarding several objects of interest in cluttered scenes. Especially with hand-held cameras, the overall quality may be poor due to low resolution or unsteadiness. The objective of this chapter is to demonstrate why standard image super-resolution fails in video data, which are the problems that arise, and how we can overcome these problems. In our first contribution, we propose a novel Bayesian framework for super-resolution of persistent objects of interest in video sequences. We call this process Distillation. In the traditional formulation of the image super-resolution problem, the observed target is (1) always the same, (2) acquired using a camera making small movements, and (3) found in a number of low resolution images sufficient to recover high-frequency information. These assumptions are usually unsatisfied in real world video acquisitions and often beyond the control of the video operator. With Distillation, we aim to extend and to generalize the image super-resolution task, embedding it in a structured framework that accurately distills all the informative bits of an object of interest. In practice, the Distillation process: i) individuates, in a semi supervised way, a set of objects of interest, clustering the related video frames and registering them with respect to global rigid transformations; ii) for each one, produces a high resolution image, by weighting each pixel according to the information retrieved about the object of interest. As a second contribution, we extend the Distillation process to deal with objects of interest whose transformations in the appearance are not (only) rigid. Such process, built on top of the Distillation, is hierarchical, in the sense that a process of clustering is applied recursively, beginning with the analysis of whole frames, and selectively focusing on smaller sub-regions whose isolated motion can be reasonably assumed as rigid. The ultimate product of the overall process is a strip of images that describe at high resolution the dynamics of the video, switching between alternative local descriptions in response to visual changes. Our approach is first tested on synthetic data, obtaining encouraging comparative results with respect to known super-resolution techniques, and a good robustness against noise. Second, real data coming from different videos are considered, trying to solve the major details of the objects in motion.

Preface

The goal of vision-based motion analysis is to provide computers with intelligent perception capacities so they can sense the objects and understand their behaviors from video sequences. With the ubiquitous presence of video data and the increasing importance in a wide range of applications such as visual surveillance, human-machine interfaces, and sport event interpretation, it is becoming increasingly demanding to automatically analyze and understand object motions from large amount of video footage.

Not surprisingly, this exciting research area has received growing interest in recent years. Although there has been significant progress in the past decades, many challenging problems remain unsolved, e.g., robust object detection and tracking, unconstrained object activity recognition, etc. The field of machine learning, on the other hand, is driven by the idea that the essential rules or patterns behind data can be *automatically* learned by a computer or a system. Statistical learning approach is one major frontier for computer vision research. We have evidenced in recent years a growing number of successes of machine learning applications to certain vision problems. It is fully believed that machine learning technologies is going to significantly contribute to the development of practical systems for vision-based motion analysis.

This edited book presents and highlights a collection of recent developments along this direction. A brief summary of each chapter is presented as follow:

Chapter 1, *Human Motion Tracking in Video: A Practical Approach*, presents a new formulation for the problem of human motion tracking in video. Tracking is still a challenging problem when strong appearance changes occur as in videos of humans in motion. A solution is to use an online method that updates iteratively a subspace of reference target models, integrating color and motion cues in a particle filter framework to track human body parts. The algorithm process consists of two modes, switching between detection and tracking. The detection steps involve trained classifiers to update estimated positions of the tracking windows, whereas tracking steps rely on an adaptive color-based particle filter coupled with optical flow estimations. The Earth Mover distance is used to compare color models in a global fashion, and constraints on flow features avoid drifting effects. The proposed method has revealed its efficiency to track body parts in motion and can cope with full appearance changes.

Chapter 2, *Learning to Recognise Spatio-Temporal Interest Points*, presents a generic classifier for detecting spatio-temporal interest points within video. The premise being that, given an interest point detector, a classifier is learnt that duplicates its functionality, which is both accurate and computationally efficient. This means that interest point detection can be achieved independent of the complexity of the original interest point formulation. The naive Bayesian classifier of Ferns is extended to the spatio-temporal domain and learn classifiers that duplicate the functionality of common spatio-temporal interest point detectors. Results demonstrate accurate reproduction of results with a classifier that can be applied exhaustively to video at frame-rate, without optimisation, in a scanning window approach.

Chapter 3, *Graphical Models for Representation and Recognition of Human Actions*, reviews graphical models that provide a natural framework for representing state transitions in events and also the spatio-temporal constraints between the actors and events. Hidden Markov Models (HMMs) have been widely used in several action recognition applications but the basic representation has three key deficiencies: These include unrealistic models for the duration of a sub-event, not encoding interactions among multiple agents directly and not modeling the inherent hierarchical organization of these activities. Several extensions have been proposed to address one or more of these issues and have been successfully applied in various gesture and action recognition domains. More recently, Conditional Random Fields (CRF) are becoming increasingly popular since they allow complex potential functions for modeling observations and state transitions, and also produce superior performance to HMMs when sufficient training data is available. This chapter first reviews the various extensions of these graphical models, then presents the theory of inference and learning in them and finally discusses their applications in various domains.

Chapter 4, *Common Spatial Patterns for Real-Time Classification of Human Actions*, presents a discriminative approach to human action recognition. At the heart of the approach is the use of common spatial patterns (CSP), a spatial filter technique that transforms temporal feature data by using differences in variance between two classes. Such a transformation focuses on differences between classes, rather than on modeling each class individually. The most likely class is found by pairwise evaluation of all discriminate functions, which can be done in real-time. Image representations are silhouette boundary gradients, spatially binned into cells. The method achieves scores of approximately 96% on the Weizmann human action dataset, and shows that reasonable results can be obtained when training on only a single subject.

Chapter 5, *KSM Based Machine Learning for Markless Motion Capture*, proposes a marker-less motion capture system, based on machine learning. Pose information is inferred from images captured from multiple (as few as two) synchronized cameras. The central concept of which, they call: Kernel Subspace Mapping (KSM). The images-to-pose learning could be done with large numbers of images of a large variety of people (and with the ground truth poses accurately known). What makes machine learning viable for human motion capture is that a high percentage of human motion is coordinated. Indeed, it is now relatively well known that there is large redundancy in the set of possible images of a human (these images form some sort of relatively smooth lower dimensional manifold in the huge dimensional space of all possible images) and in the set of pose angles (again, a low dimensional and smooth sub-manifold of the moderately high dimensional space of all possible joint angles). KSM, is based on the KPCA (Kernel PCA) algorithm, which is costly. They show that the Greedy Kernel PCA (GKPCA) algorithm can be used to speed up KSM, with relatively minor modifications. At the core, then, is two KPCA's (or two GKPCA's) - one for the learning of pose manifold and one for the learning image manifold. Then they use a modification of Local Linear Embedding (LLE) to bridge between pose and image manifolds.

Chapter 6, *Multi-Scale People Detection and Motion Analysis for Video Surveillance*, addresses visual processing of people, including detection, tracking, recognition, and behavior interpretation, a key component of intelligent video surveillance systems. Computer vision algorithms with the capability of "looking at people" at multiple scales can be applied in different surveillance scenarios, such as far-field people detection for wide-area perimeter protection, midfield people detection for retail/banking applications or parking lot monitoring, and near-field people/face detection for facility security and access. In this chapter, they address the people detection problem in different scales as well as human tracking and motion analysis for real video surveillance applications including people search, retail loss prevention, people counting, and display effectiveness.

Chapter 7, *A Generic Framework for 2D and 3D Upper Body Tracking*, targets upper body tracking, a problem to track the pose of human body from video sequences. It is difficult due to such problems as the high dimensionality of the state space, the self-occlusion, the appearance changes, etc. In this chapter, they propose a generic framework that can be used for both 2D and 3D upper body tracking and can be easily parameterized without heavily depending on supervised training. They first construct a Bayesian Network (BN) to represent the human upper body structure and then incorporate into the BN various generic physical and anatomical constraints on the parts of the upper body. They also explicitly model part occlusion in the model, which allows to automatically detect the occurrence of self-occlusion and to minimize the effect of measurement errors on the tracking accuracy due to occlusion. Using the proposed model, upper body tracking can be performed through probabilistic inference over time. A series of experiments were performed on both monocular and stereo video sequences to demonstrate the effectiveness and capability of the model in improving upper body tracking accuracy and robustness.

Chapter 8, *Real-Time Recognition of Basic Human Actions*, describes a simple and computationally efficient, appearance-based approach for real-time recognition of basic human actions. They apply a technique that depicts the differences between two or more successive frames accompanied by a threshold filter to detect the regions of the video frames where some type of human motion is observed. From each frame difference, the algorithm extracts an incomplete and unformed human body shape and generates a skeleton model which represents it in an abstract way. Eventually, the recognition process is formulated as a time-series problem and handled by a very robust and accurate prediction method (Support Vector Regression). The proposed technique could be employed in applications such as vision-based autonomous robots and surveillance systems.

Chapter 9, *Fast Categorisation of Articulated Human Motion*, exploits the problem of visual categorisation of human motion in video clips. Most published methods either analyse an entire video and assign it a single category label, or use relatively large look-ahead to classify each frame. Contrary to these strategies, the human visual system proves that simple categories can be recognised almost instantaneously. Here they present a system for categorisation from very short sequences ("snippets") of 1–10 frames, and systematically evaluate it on several data sets. It turns out that even local shape and optic flow for a single frame are enough to achieve 80-90% correct classification, and snippets of 5-7 frames (0.2-0.3 seconds of video) yield results on par with the ones state-of-the-art methods obtain on entire video sequences.

Chapter 10, *Human Action Recognition with Expandable Graphical Models*, proposes an action recognition system that is independent of the subjects who perform the actions, independent of the speed at which the actions are performed, robust against noisy extraction of features used to characterize the actions, scalable to large number of actions and expandable with new actions. In this chapter, they describe a recently proposed expandable graphical model of human actions that has the promise to realize such a system. This chapter first presents a brief review of the recent development in human action recognition. Then, the expandable graphical model is presented in detail and a system that learns and recognizes human actions from sequences of silhouettes using the expandable graphical model is developed.

Chapter 11, *Detection and Classification of Interacting Persons*, presents a way to classify interactions between people. Examples of the interactions they investigate are; people meeting one another, walking together and fighting. A new feature set is proposed along with a corresponding classification method. Results are presented which show the new method performing significantly better than the previous state of the art method as proposed by Oliver et al.

Chapter 12, *Action Recognition*, first reviews the current action recognition methods from the following two aspects: action representation and recognition strategy. Then, a novel method for classifying human actions from image sequences is investigated. In this method, the human action is represented by a set of shape context features of human silhouette, and a dominant sets-based approach is employed to classify the predefined actions. The comparison between the dominant sets-based approach with K-means, mean shift, and Fuzzy-Cmean is also discussed.

Chapter 13, *Distillation: A Super-Resolution Approach for the Selective Analysis of Noisy and Unconstrained Video Sequences*, argues that image super-resolution is one of the most appealing applications of image processing, capable of retrieving a high resolution image by fusing several registered low resolution images depicting an object of interest. However, employing super-resolution in video data is challenging: a video sequence generally contains a lot of scattered information regarding several objects of interest in cluttered scenes. The objective of this chapter is to demonstrate why standard image super-resolution fails in video data, which are the problems that arise, and how they can overcome these problems. They propose a novel Bayesian framework for super-resolution of persistent objects of interest in video sequences, called *Distillation*. With Distillation, they extend and generalize the image super-resolution task, embedding it in a structured framework that accurately distills all the informative bits of an object of interest. They also extend the Distillation process to deal with objects of interest whose transformations in the appearance are not (only) rigid. The ultimate product of the overall process is a strip of images that describe at high resolution the dynamics of the video, switching between alternative local descriptions in response to visual changes. The approach is first tested on synthetic data, obtaining encouraging comparative results with respect to known super-resolution techniques, and a good robustness against noise. Second, real data coming from different videos are considered, trying to solve the major details of the objects in motion.

In summary, this book contains an excellent collection of theoretical and technical chapters written by different authors who are worldwide-recognized researchers on various aspects of human motion understanding using machine learning methods. The targeted audiences are mainly researchers, engineers as well as graduate students in the areas of computer vision and machine learning. The book is also intend to be accessible to a broader audience including practicing professionals working with specific vision applications such as video surveillance, sport event analysis, healthcare, video conferencing, motion video indexing and retrieval. We wish this book would help toward the development of robust yet flexible vision systems.

Liang Wang
University of Bath, UK

Li Cheng
TTI-Chicago, USA

Guoying Zhao
University of Oulu, Finland

May 20, 2009

Acknowledgment

Human motion analysis and understanding is fundamental in many real applications including surveillance and monitoring, human-machine interface, sport event analysis, medical motion analysis and diagnosis, motion kinematics modeling, etc. Statistical learning approach is one major frontier for computer vision research. In recent years, machine learning, and especially, statistical learning theories and techniques, have evidenced rapid and fruitful developments, and are under the way to make significant contributions to the area of vision-based human motion understanding. This edited book provides a comprehensive treatment of recent developments in the application of modern statistical machine learning approaches for modeling, analyzing and understanding human motions from video data. We would like to express our sincere thanks to IGI Global to offer us the opportunity to edit such a book on this exciting area.

During the edition of this book, we received much help and support. First of all, we would like to thank all of the authors for submitting their wonderful works and apologize that not all chapter submissions could be accepted. We are also grateful to all of the chapter reviewers for their remarkable efforts on providing timely reviews of high quality. It was a great honor to have those worldwide leading experts to join the Editorial Advisory Board of this book. They are Prof. Richard Hartley (Australian National University, Australia), Prof. Terry Caelli (National ICT Australian, Australia), Prof. Weiming Hu (Chinese Academy of Sciences, China), Prof. Matti Pietikäinen (University of Oulu, Finland), Prof. Greg Mori (Simon Fraser University, Canada), and Prof. Dit-Yan Yeung (Hong Kong University of Science and Technology, China). We appreciate their valuable suggestions to strengthen the overall quality of this book and help to promote this publication.

This book could not be possible without the help of the people involved in the IGI Global. As a full-service publishing company, IGI Global staff handles all tasks related to production, registration, marketing and promotion, overseas distribution and so on. As well as thanking the financial and technical support from IGI Global, special thanks go to Tyler Heath (Assistant Development Editor), for his assistance in guiding us each step of the way.

Liang Wang
University of Bath, UK

Li Cheng
TTI-Chicago, USA

Guoying Zhao
University of Oulu, Finland

May 20, 2009

Chapter 1
Human Motion Tracking in Video:
A Practical Approach

Tony Tung
Kyoto University, Japan

Takashi Matsuyama
Kyoto University, Japan

ABSTRACT

This chapter presents a new formulation for the problem of human motion tracking in video. Tracking is still a challenging problem when strong appearance changes occur as in videos of humans in motion. Most trackers rely on a predefined template or on a training dataset to achieve detection and tracking. Therefore they are not efficient to track objects whose appearance is not known in advance. A solution is to use an online method that updates iteratively a subspace of reference target models. In addition, we propose to integrate color and motion cues in a particle filter framework to track human body parts. The algorithm process consists of two modes, switching between detection and tracking. The detection steps involve trained classifiers to update estimated positions of the tracking windows, whereas tracking steps rely on an adaptive color-based particle filter coupled with optical flow estimations. The Earth Mover distance is used to compare color models in a global fashion, and constraints on flow features avoid drifting effects. The proposed method has revealed its efficiency to track body parts in motion and can cope with full appearance changes. Experiments were performed on challenging real world videos with poorly textured models and non-linear motions.

1. INTRODUCTION

Human motion tracking is a common requirement for many real world applications, such as video surveillance, games, cultural and medical applications (e.g. for motion and behavior study).

The literature has provided successful algorithms to detect and track objects of a predefined class in image streams or videos. Simple object can be detected and tracked using various image features such as color regions, edges, contours, or texture. On the other hand, complex objects such as human faces require more sophisticated features to handle the multiple possible instances of the object

DOI: 10.4018/978-1-60566-900-7.ch001

class. For this purpose, statistical methods are a good alternative. First, a statistical model (or classifier) learns different patterns related to the object of interest (e.g. different views of human faces), including good and bad samples. And then the system is able to estimate whether a region contains an object of interest or not. This kind of approach has become very popular. For example, the face detector of (Viola, & Jones, 2001) is well known for its efficiency. The main drawback is the dependence to prior knowledge on the object class. As the system is trained on a finite dataset, the detection is somehow constrained to it. As a matter of fact, most of the tracking methods were not designed to keep the track of an object whose appearance could strongly change. If there is no a priori knowledge on its multiple possible appearances, then the detection fails and the track is lost. Hence, tracking a head which turns completely, or tracking a hand in action remain challenging problems, as appearance changes occur quite frequently for human body parts in motion.

We introduce a new formulation dedicated to the problem of appearance changes for object tracking in video. Our approach integrates color cues and motion cues to establish a robust tracking. As well, an online iterative process updates a subspace of reference templates so that the tracking

system remains robust to occlusions. The method workflow contains two modes, switching between detection and tracking. The detection steps involve trained classifiers to update estimated positions of the tracking windows. In particular, we use the cascade of boosted classifiers of Haar-like features by (Viola, & Jones, 2001) to perform head detection. Other body parts can be either detected using this technique with ad-hoc training samples, or chosen by users at the initialization step, or as well can be deduced based on prior knowledge on human shape features and constraints. The tracking steps rely on an adaptive color-based particle filter (Isard, & Blake, 1998) coupled with optical flow estimations (Lucas, & Kanade, 1981; Tomasi, & Kanade, 1991). The Earth Mover distance (Rubner, Tomasi, & Guibas, 1998) has been chosen to compare color models due to its robustness to small color variations. Drift effects inherent to adaptive tracking methods are handled using optical flow estimations (motion features).

Our experiments show the accuracy and robustness of the proposed method on challenging video sequences of human in motion. For example, videos of yoga performances (stretching exercises at various speed) with poorly textured models and non-linear motions were used for testing (cf. Figure 1).

Figure 1. Body part tracking with color-based particle filter driven by optical flow. The proposed approach is robust to strong occlusion and full appearance change. Detected regions are denoted by dark gray squares, and tracked regions by light gray squares.

  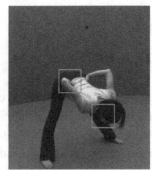

#1   #30   #70

The rest of the chapter is organized as follows. The next section gives a recap of work related to the techniques presented in this chapter. Section 3 presents an overview of the algorithm (initialization step and workflow). Section 4 describes the tracking process based on our color-based particle filter driven by optical flow. Section 5 presents experimental results. Section 6 concludes with a discussion on our contributions.

2. STATE OF THE ART

In the last decade, acquisition devices have become even more accurate and accessible for non-expert users. This has lead to a rapid growth of various imaging applications. In particular, the scientific community has shown a real interest to human body part detection and tracking. For example, face detection in images is nowadays a popular and well explored topic (Viola, & Jones, 2001; Hjelmas, & Low, 2002; Choudhury, Schmid, & Mikolajczyk, 2003). In (Viola, & Jones, 2001), the authors proposed a cascade of boosted tree classifiers of Haar-like features. The classifier is first trained on positive and negative samples, and then the detection is performed by sliding a search window through candidate images and checking whether a region contains an object of interest or not. The technique is known to be fast and efficient, and can be tuned to detect any kind of object class if the classifier is trained on good samples.

Tracking in video is a popular field of research as well. Recognition from video is still challenging because frames are often of low quality, and details can be small (e.g. in video surveillance). Various approaches were proposed to track image features (Lucas, & Kanade, 1981; Tomasi, & Kanade, 1991; Lowe, 2004; Lucena, Fuertes, & de la Blanca, 2004; Tola, Lepetit, & Fua, 2008). Lucas, Tomasi and Kanade first select the good features which are optimal for tracking, and then keep the tracks of these features in consecutive

frames. The KLT feature tracker is often used for optical flow estimation to estimate the deformations between two frames. As a differential method, it assumes that the pixel intensity of objects is not significantly different between two frames.

Techniques based on prediction and correction as Kalman filter, and more recently particle filters have become widely used (Isard, & Blake, 1998; Doucet, Godsill, & Andrieu, 2000; Perez, Hue, Vermaak, & Gangnet, 2002; Sugimoto, Yachi, & Matsuyama, 2003; Okuma, Taleghani, de Freitas, Kakade, Little, & Lowe, 2004; Dornaika, & Davoine, 2005; Wang, Chen, & Gao, 2005; Li, Ai, Yamashita, Lao, & Kawade, 2007; Ross, Lim, Lin, & Yang, 2007; Kim, Kumar, Pavlovic, & Rowley, 2008). Particle filters (or sequential Monte Carlo or Condensation) are Bayesian model estimation techniques based on simulation. The basic idea is to approximate a sequence of probability distributions using a large set of random samples (called particles). Then the particles are propagated through the frames based on importance sampling and resampling mechanisms. Usually, the particles converge rapidly to the distributions of interest. The algorithm allows robust tracking of objects in cluttered scene, and can handle non-linear motion models more complex than those commonly used in Kalman filters. The major differences between the different particle filter based approaches rely on the design of the sampling strategies, which make particles having higher probability mass in regions of interest.

In (Black, & Jepson, 1998; Collins, Liu, & Leordeanu, 2005 ; Wang, Chen, & Gao, 2005; Ross, Lim, Lin, & Yang, 2007; Kim, Kumar, Pavlovic, & Rowley, 2008), linear dimension reduction methods (PCA, LDA) are used to extract feature vectors from the regions of interest. These approaches suit well for adaptive face tracking and can be formulated in the particle filtering framework as well. Nevertheless they require a big training data set to be efficient (Martinez, & Kak, 2001), and still cannot cope with unpredicted change of appearance. On the other hand, color-based models of regions can capture larger appearance variations (Bradski, 1998; Comaniciu, Ramesh, & Meeh, 2000). In (Perez, Hue, Vermaak, & Gangnet, 2002), the authors integrate a color-based model tracker (as in the Meanshift technique of Comaniciu, Ramesh, and Meeh) within a particle filter framework. The model uses color histograms in the HSV space and the Bhattacharyya distance for color distribution comparisons. Nevertheless these methods usually fail to track objects in motion or have an increasing drift on long video sequences due to strong appearance changes or important lighting variations (Matthews, Ishikawa, & Baker, 2004). Indeed most algorithms assume that the model of the target object does not change significantly over time. To adapt the model to appearance changes and lighting variations, subspace of the target object features are extracted (Collins, Liu, & Leordeanu, 2005; Wang, Chen, & Gao, 2005; Ross, Lim, Lin, & Yang, 2007; Kim, Kumar, Pavlovic, & Rowley, 2008). In (Ross, Lim, Lin, & Yang, 2007), a subspace of eigenvectors representing the target object is incrementally updated through the tracking process. Thus, offline learning step is not required and tracking of unknown objects is possible. Recently, (Kim, Kumar, Pavlovic, & Rowley, 2008) proposed to extend this approach with additional terms in the data likelihood definition. In particular, the drift error is handled using an additional dataset of images. However, these approaches are particularly tuned for face tracking, and still require training datasets for every different view of faces.

The core of our approach divides into two steps which are detection and tracking, as (Sugimoto, Yachi, & Matsuyama, 2003; Li, Ai, Yamashita, Lao, & Kawade, 2007). Switching between the two modes allows to dynamically update the search window to an accurate position whenever the detection is positive. In this work, we propose to run a color-based particle filter to achieve the tracking process. Our tracker uses a subspace of color models of regions of interest extracted from the previous frames, and relies on them to estimate the position of the object in the current frame. The subspace is iteratively updated through the video sequence, and dynamically updated by the detection process. The detection is performed by a cascade of boosted classifiers (Viola, & Jones, 2001) and thus can be trained to detect any object class. We also propose to use the Earth Mover distance to improve the robustness of tracking with lighting variations, and constraints based on optical flow estimations to cope with drift effects.

3. ALGORITHM OVERVIEW

This section describes the algorithm workflow. The proposed approach combines two modes, switching between detection mode and tracking mode. The tracking process can be run independently if no detector is available for the class of the object of interest. Besides the tracking process, the detection improves the response accuracy online, and is used as well as initialization step. A subspace of color-based models is used to infer the object of interest location.

3.1. Initialization

The initialization step consists in defining the objects to track. In our framework, we focused on human body parts because of the wide range of possible applications. Basically, there are three straightforward ways to define the regions of interest:

1. **Automatic:** This can be achieved by a detection process using statistical machine learning method (e.g. the face detector of Viola and Jones).
2. **Manual:** Regions of interest are defined by the user (e.g. by picking regions in the first frame). This allows to track any body part without having any prior knowledge.

3. **Deduction:** As the human body has self-constrained motions, its structure can be deduced using a priori knowledge and fuzzy rules. For example, a detected face gives some hints to deduce the torso position, etc.

In some of our experiments (cf. Sect. 5), we have combined the three approaches (e.g. head is automatically detected, torso is deduced, and hands are picked). Afterwards, the regions of interest are used as reference templates on which the tracker relies on to process the next frames.

3.2. Workflow

Assuming the initialization occurs at time y_t, then for every frame at z_t, the tracker estimates the positions of S_t objects of interest y_t based on the color-model subspace z_t, where S_t denotes the color-model of x_t at time S_t, and x_t is the size of the subspaces (which in fact can be different for every object). Assuming a Bayesian framework (cf. Sect. 4), the hidden state t_0 corresponding to the estimated position of $t, t > t_0$ at time M by the tracker, is inferred by $\{A_i\}_{i=1...M}$ and $S_t^i = \{h_{t-k}^i, ..., h_{t-1}^i\}$. We denote by h_j^i the data corresponding to the detection of A_i at time j, and k the response of the algorithm. Thus, if the detection of x_t^i at A_i is positive, then t, else S_t^i. Indeed, if the detection of x_{t-1}^i at y_t^i is positive, then A_i will be updated with the color model corresponding to t. And if not, then z_t^i will be updated with the color model corresponding to A_i. The workflow is illustrated on Figure 2 with t and $z_t^i = y_t^i$.

4. PARTICLE FILTERING DRIVEN BY OPTICAL FLOW

In this section we present our algorithm formulation based on color-based particle filtering (Isard, & Blake, 1998; Perez, Hue, Vermaak, & Gang-

Figure 2. Algorithm workflow. If the detection process $z_t^i = x_t^i$ at time t is positive, then the algorithm response A_i and the subspace of color models t are updated with S_{t+1}^i. If the detection fails, then y_t^i and S_{t+1}^i are updated by the tracking process x_t^i. Note that $M = 1$ is used to infer the state $k = 1$.

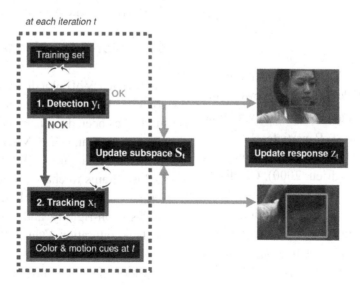

net, 2002] and optical flow estimations (Tomasi, & Kanade, 1991). We propose to use the Earth Mover Distance (Rubner, Tomasi, & Guibas, 1998) to compare color models, and extracted motion features to improve tracking accuracy. Moreover our method updates iteratively a subspace of template models to handle appearance changes and partial occlusions.

4.1. Particle Filtering

We denote by x_t a target state at time t, z_t the observation data at time t, and $Z_t = \{z_1, ..., z_t\}$ all the observations up to time t. Assuming a non-Gaussian state space model, the prior probability $p(x_t \mid Z_{t-1})$ at time t in a Markov process is defined as:

$$p(x_t \mid Z_{t-1}) = \int p(x_t \mid x_{t-1}) p(x_{t-1} \mid Z_{t-1}) dx_{t-1},$$

$$(1)$$

where $p(x_t \mid x_{t-1})$ is a state transition distribution, and $p(x_{t-1} \mid Z_{t-1})$ stands for a posterior probability at time $t-1$. The posterior probability whose the tracking system aims to estimate at each time is defined as:

$$p(x_t \mid Z_t) \propto p(z_t \mid x_t) p(x_t \mid Z_{t-1}),\qquad (2)$$

where $p(z_t \mid x_t)$ is the data likelihood at time t. According to the particle filtering framework, the posterior $p(x_t \mid Z_t)$ is approximated by a Dirac measure on a finite set of P particles $\{x_t^i\}_{i=1...P}$ following a sequential Monte Carlo framework (Doucet, Godsill, & Andrieu, 2000). Candidate particles are sampled by a proposal transition kernel $q(\tilde{x}_t^i \mid x_{t-1}^i, z_{t-1})$. The new filtering distribution is approximated by a new sample set of particles $\{\tilde{x}_t^i\}_{i=1...P}$ having the importance weights $\{w_t^i\}_{i=1...P}$, where

$$w_t^i \propto \frac{p(z_t \mid \tilde{x}_t^i) p(\tilde{x}_t^i \mid x_{t-1}^i)}{q(\tilde{x}_t^i \mid x_{t-1}^i, z_{t-1})} \qquad and \qquad \sum_{i=1}^{P} w_t^i = 1.$$

$$(3)$$

The sample set $\{x_t^i\}_{i=1...P}$ can then be obtained by resampling $\{\tilde{x}_t^i\}_{i=1...P}$ with respect to $\{w_t^i\}_{i=1...P}$. By default, the Bootstrap filter is chosen as proposal distribution: $q(\tilde{x}_t^i \mid x_{t-1}^i, z_{t-1}) = p(\tilde{x}_t^i \mid x_{t-1}^i)$. Hence the weights can be computed by evaluating the corresponding data likelihood. Finally, x_t is estimated upon the Monte Carlo approximation of the expectation $\hat{x}_t = \frac{1}{P} \sum_{i=1}^{P} x_t^i$.

We denote by E, the overall energy function: $E = E_s + E_m + E_d$, where E_s is an energy related to color cues (cf. Sect. 4.2), E_m and E_d are energies related to motion features (cf. Sect. 4.4). E has lower values as the search window is close to the target object. Thus, to favor candidate regions whose color distribution is similar to the reference model at time t, the data likelihood $p(z_t \mid x_t)$ is modeled as a Gaussian function:

$$p(z_t \mid \tilde{x}_t^i) \propto \exp\left(-\frac{E}{\sigma^2}\right), \qquad (4)$$

where σ is a scale factor, and therefore a small E returns a large weight.

4.2. Color-Based Model

The efficiency of color distributions to track color content of regions that match a reference color model has been demonstrated in (Bradski, 2000; Comaniciu, Ramesh, & Meeh, 2000; Perez, Hue, Vermaak, & Gangnet, 2002]. They are represented by histograms to characterize the chromatic information of regions. Hence they are robust against non-rigidity and rotation. In addition, the Hue-Saturation-Value (HSV) color space has been chosen due to its low sensitivity to lighting condition. In our approach, color distributions are discretized into three histograms of N_h, N_s, and N_v bins for the hue, saturation, and value respectively.

Let α be h, s, or v, $q_t(x_t) = \frac{1}{3}\sum_\alpha q_t^\alpha(x_t)$, and $q_t^\alpha(x_t) = \{q_t^\alpha(i,x_t)\}_{i=1...N_\alpha}$. $q_t(x_t)$ denotes the kernel density estimate of the color distribution in the candidate region $R(x_t)$ of the state x_t at time t, and is composed by:

$$q_t^\alpha(i,x_t) = K_\alpha \sum_{u \in R(x_t)} \delta[h_\alpha(u) - i], \qquad (5)$$

where K_α is a normalization constant so that $\sum_{i=1}^{N_\alpha} q_t^\alpha(i,x_t) = 1$, h_α is a function assigning the pixel color at location u to the corresponding histogram bin, and δ is the Kronecker delta function.

At time t, $q_t(x_t)$ is compared to a set of reference color model templates $S_t = \{h_{t-k},...,h_{t-1}\}$, where k is the number of templates. The templates are extracted iteratively from the detected regions at each frame. We recall that color model subspaces help to handle appearance changes and partial occlusions, and we define the energy function:

$$E_s[S_t, q_t(x_t)] = \min_{h \in S_t}(D^2[h, q_t(x_t)]), \qquad (6)$$

where D is a distance between color distributions (cf. Sect. 4.3).

4.3 Earth Mover Distance

We propose to use the Earth Mover distance (EMD) (Hillier, & Lieberman, 1990; Rubner, Tomasi, & Guibas, 1998) to strengthen the property of invariance to lighting of the HSV color space. EMD allows to make global comparison of color distributions relying on a global optimization process. This method is more robust than approaches relying on histogram bin-to-bin distances that are more sensitive to quantization and small color changes. The distributions are represented by sets of weighted features called *signatures*. The EMD is then defined as the minimal amount of *work* needed to match a signature to another one. The notion of work relies on a metric (e.g. a distance) between two features. In our framework we use the L_1 norm as distance, and histogram bins as features.

Assuming two signatures to compare $P = \{(p_1, w_1),...,(p_m, w_m)\}$ and $Q = \{(q_1, u_1),...,(q_n, u_n)\}$, P having m components p_i with weight w_i, and Q having n components q_j with weight u_j. The global optimization process consists in finding the amount of data f_{ij} of a signature to be transported from the component i to the component j that minimizes the work W:

$$W = \min_{f_{ij}}(\sum_{i=1}^m \sum_{j=1}^n d_{ij} f_{ij}), \qquad (7)$$

where d_{ij} is the distance between the components p_i and q_j assuming the following constraints:

$$f_{ij} \geq 0 \qquad 1 \leq i \leq m, 1 \leq j \leq n,$$

$$\sum_{j=1}^n f_{ij} \leq w_i \qquad 1 \leq i \leq m,$$

$$\sum_{i=1}^m f_{ij} \leq u_j \qquad 1 \leq j \leq n,$$

$$\sum_{i=1}^m \sum_{j=1}^n f_{ij} = \min(\sum_{i=1}^m w_i, \sum_{j=1}^n u_j).$$

The first constraint allows only the displacements from P to Q. The two following constraints bound the amount of data transported by P, and the amount of data received by Q to their respective weights. The last constraint sets the maximal amount of data that can be displaced.

The EMD distance D between two signatures P and Q is then defined as:

$$D(P,Q) = \frac{W}{N} = \frac{\sum_{i=1}^{m}\sum_{j=1}^{n} d_{ij} f_{ij}}{\sum_{i=1}^{m}\sum_{j=1}^{n} f_{ij}}, \qquad (8)$$

where the normalization factor N ensures a good balance when comparing signatures of different size (N is the smallest sum of the signature weights). Note that EMD computation can be approximated in linear time with guaranteed error bounds (Shirdhonkar, & Jacobs, 2008).

4.4 Motion Cues

We propose to use motion features to guide the search window through the tracking process. Motion features are extracted using the KLT feature tracker (Lucas, & Kanade, 1981; Tomasi, & Kanade, 1991). The method detects feature windows and matches the similar ones between consecutive frames (cf. Figure 3).

Assuming the set $Y_{t-1} = \{y_{t-1}^j\}_{j=1...m}$ of m motion features detected in the neighborhood region of the state x_{t-1} (cf. Sect. 4) at time $t-1$, and the set $Y_t = \{y_t^j\}_{j=1...m}$ of matching features extracted at time t, then $(Y_{t-1}, Y_t) = \{(y_{t-1}^j, y_t^j)\}_{j=1...m}$ forms

a set of m motion vectors (optical flow field) between the frames at time $t-1$ and t. As well, we denote by $\tilde{Y}_t^i$ the set of features detected in the neighborhood region of the particle $\tilde{x}_t^i$, and $\tilde{y}_t$ the position of the search window estimated by optical flow as: $\tilde{y}_t = x_{t-1} + \text{median}(\{y_{t-1}^j - y_t^j\}_{j=1...m})$. Thus we define the following energy functions:

$$E_m(\tilde{x}_t^i) = \alpha \cdot \left\| \tilde{x}_t^i - \tilde{y}_t \right\|_2 \qquad and \qquad E_d = \beta \cdot C(\tilde{Y}_t^i, Y_t),$$
$$(9)$$

where α and β are two constant values, and C is the following function:

$$C(\tilde{Y}_t^i, Y_t) = 1 - \frac{\text{card}(\tilde{Y}_t^i \cap Y_t)}{\text{card}(Y_t)}. \qquad (10)$$

The data energy E_m aims to favor the particles located around the object target position estimated by optical flows, whereas E_d aims to prevent the drift effect. E_d works as a constraint which attracts the particles near the estimated search window (cf. Figure 4). E_m and E_d are

Figure 3. Feature tracking. The tracking process is driven by motion features. Dark dots denote feature positions in the previous frame. Grey lines show the estimated motion flows.

Figure 4. Motion cues. Motion cues are formulated in term of energy to minimize. (a) E_m measures the distance between the estimated position $\tilde{x}_t^i$ by particles and the estimated position by optical flow $\tilde{y}_t$. (b) E_d maximizes the number of features detected in the previous frame.

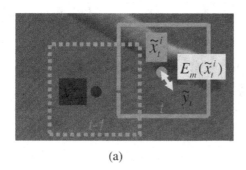 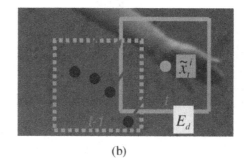

(a)   (b)

introduced in the overall energy formulation as described in Sect. 4.1.

5. EXPERIMENTAL RESULTS

Our algorithm has been tested on various real video sequences. For example, we have tracked the body parts of a lady practicing yoga (head, hands, torso, and feet) in different video sequences and from different viewpoints. The model wears simple clothes with no additional features (cf. Figure 1 and Figure 7). As well, we have tested the tracker on a model wearing traditional Japanese clothes which are more much complex and contain a lot of features (cf. Figure 5). In this study case, the video frame sizes are 640x480 and 720x576 pixels and were acquired at 25 fps. The algorithm was run on a Core2Duo 3.0 GHz with 4GB RAM.

The following parameters were identical for all the experiments: we have used $N_h = 10$, $N_s = 10$ and $N_v = 10$ for the quantization of color models, $P = 200$ particles, $k = 5$ for the color model subspace size, and $\sigma^2 = 0.1$ as scale factor of the likelihood model. The constant values α and β weight the contribution of the motion cues, and are tuned regarding to the frame size. He have defined a square window size of

Figure 5. Using optical flow to improve tracking. The combination of color cues and motion cues allows to perform robust tracking and prevent drift effects. The tracking of hands is efficient even with a changing background.

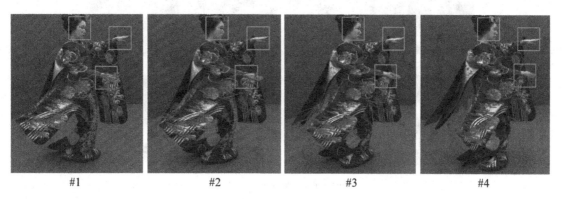

#1   #2   #3   #4

Figure 6. Tracking with appearance change. The proposed approach integrates motion cues and a subspace of color models which is updated online through the video sequence. The system can track objects in motion with appearance change.

Figure 7. Robust body part tracking. (a) Classical Condensation methods (Isard, & Blake, 1998; Perez, Hue, Vermaak, & Gangnet, 2002) are confused by regions with similar color and shape content. (b) In frame #20, both hands are almost included in a same tracking window, but afterwards motion cues have helped to discriminate the different tracks.

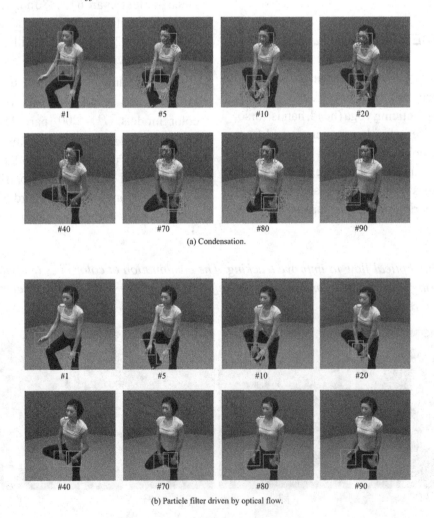

40 pixels to determine the regions of interest. The proposed formulation has shown promising results even in uncontrolled environments. The Figures 1 and 6 illustrate the robustness to appearance changes, lighting variations and partial occlusions, thanks to the online update of the color-based model subspace combined with the Earth Mover distance and motion cues. For example, the system can track a head even if the face is no more visible (e.g. hidden by hair or due to a viewpoint change). Figure 5 illustrates an accurate tracking with free-drift effect of a hand with a varying background under the guidance of optical flow as motion cues. Figure 7 illustrates the robustness of our approach in comparison to a color-based particle filter (Condensation of Perez, Hue, Vermaak, and Gangnet) that does not include our features. We show that the Condensation mixes regions having the same color shape and distribution whereas our tracker is not confused by the similar regions. This is due in particular to the addition of motion cues.

CONCLUSION

Human motion tracking in video is an attractive research field due to the numerous possible applications. The literature has provided powerful algorithms based on statistical methods especially dedicated to face detection and tracking. Nevertheless, it is still challenging to handle complex object classes such as human body parts whose appearance changes occur quite frequently while in motion.

In this work, we propose to integrate color cues and motion cues in a tracking process relying on a particle filter framework. We have used the Earth Mover distance to compare color-based model distribution in the HSV color space in order to strengthen the invariance to lighting condition. Combined with an online iterative update of color-based model subspace, we have obtained robustness to partial occlusion. We have also proposed to integrate extracted motion features

(optical flow) to handle strong appearance changes and prevent drift effect. In addition, our tracking process is run jointly with a detection process that dynamically updates the system response. Our new formulation has been tested on real videos, and results on different sequences were shown. For future work, we believe our approach can be easily extended to handle a online manifold learning process. This would improve both detection and tracking modes.

REFERENCES

Black, M., & Jepson, A. (1998). Eigentracking: Robust matching and tracking of articulated objects using a view-based representation. *International Journal of Computer Vision, 26*, 63–84. doi:10.1023/A:1007939232436

Bradski, G. (1998). Computer vision face tracking as a component of a perceptual user interface. In *Workshop on Applications of Computer Vision* (pp. 214–219).

Verma, R. C., Schmid, C., & Mikolajczyk, K. (2003). Face detection and tracking in a video by propagating detection probabilities. *IEEE Transactions on Pattern Analysis and Machine Intelligence, 25*(10), 1215–1228. doi:10.1109/TPAMI.2003.1233896

Collins, R. T., Liu, Y., & Leordeanu, M. (2005). Online selection of discriminative tracking features. *IEEE Transactions on Pattern Analysis and Machine Intelligence, 27*(10), 1631–1643. doi:10.1109/TPAMI.2005.205

Comaniciu, D., Ramesh, V., & Meeh, P. (2000). Real-time tracking of non-rigid objects using mean shift. *IEEE Conference on Computer Vision and Pattern Recognition, 2*, 142–149.

Dornaika, F., & Davoine, F. (2005). Simultaneous facial action tracking and expression recognition using a particle filter. *IEEE International Conference on Computer Vision*, 1733-1738.

Doucet, A., Godsill, S., & Andrieu, C. (2000). On sequential Monte Carlo sampling methods for bayesian filtering. *Statistics and Computing, 10*(3), 197–208. doi:10.1023/A:1008935410038

Hillier, F. S., & Lieberman, G. J. (1990). Introduction to mathematical programming. New York: McGraw-Hill.

Hjelmas, E., & Low, B. K. (2001). Face detection: a survey. *Computer Vision and Image Understanding, 83*, 236–274. doi:10.1006/cviu.2001.0921

Isard, M., & Blake, A. (1998). Condensation - conditional density propagation for visual tracking. *International Journal of Computer Vision, 29*(1), 5–28. doi:10.1023/A:1008078328650

Kim, M., & Kumar, S. Pavlovic, & Rowley, H. V. (2008). Face tracking and recognition with visual constraints in real-world videos. In *IEEE Conference on Computer Vision and Pattern Recognition.*

Li, Y., Ai, H., Yamashita, T., Lao, S., & Kawade, M. (2007). Tracking in low frame rate video: A cascade particle filter with discriminative observers of different lifespans. In *IEEE Conference on Computer Vision and Pattern Recognition.*

Lowe, D. G. (2004). Distinctive image features from scale-invariant keypoints. *International Journal of Computer Vision, 60*(2), 91–110. doi:10.1023/B:VISI.0000029664.99615.94

Lucas, B., & Kanade, T. (1981). An iterative image registration technique with an application to stereo vision. In *International Joint Conferences on Artificial Intelligence* (pp. 674–679).

Lucena, M., Fuertes, J. M., & de la Blanca, N. P. (2004): Evaluation of three optical flow based observation models for tracking. In *International Conference on Pattern Recognition* (pp. 236–239).

Martinez, A. M., & Kak, A. C. (2001). PCA versus LDA. *IEEE Transactions on Pattern Analysis and Machine Intelligence, 23*(2), 228–233. doi:10.1109/34.908974

Matthews, I., Ishikawa, T., & Baker, S. (2004). The template update problem. *IEEE Transactions on Pattern Analysis and Machine Intelligence, 26*(6), 810–815. doi:10.1109/TPAMI.2004.16

Okuma, K., Taleghani, A., de Freitas, N., Kakade, S., Little, J., & Lowe, D. (2004). A boosted particle filter: multitarget detection and tracking. In *European Conference on Computer Vision* (pp. 28–39).

Perez, P., Hue, C., Vermaak, J., & Gangnet, M. (2002). Color-based probabilistic tracking. In *European Conference on Computer Vision* (pp. 661–675).

Ross, D., Lim, J., Lin, R., & Yang, M. (2008). Incremental learning for robust visual tracking. *International Journal of Computer Vision, 77*(1-3), 125–141. doi:10.1007/s11263-007-0075-7

Rubner, Y., Tomasi, C., & Guibas, L. J. (1998). A metric for distributions with applications to image databases. In *IEEE International Conference on Computer Vision* (pp. 59–66).

Shirdhonkar, S., & Jacobs, D. W. (2008). Approximate Earth mover's distance in linear time. In *IEEE Conference on Computer Vision and Pattern Recognition.*

Sugimoto, A., Yachi, K., & Matsuyama, T. (2003). Tracking human heads based on interaction between hypotheses with certainty. In *The 13th Scandinavian Conference on Image Analysis.*

Tola, E., Lepetit, V., & Fua, P. (2008). A fast local descriptor for dense matching. In *IEEE Conference on Computer Vision and Pattern Recognition.*

Tomasi, C., & Kanade, T. (1991). *Detection and tracking of point features.* Technical Report CMU-CS-91-132, Carnegie Mellon University.

Viola, P., & Jones, M. (2001). Rapid object detection using a boosted cascade of simple features. In *IEEE Conference on Computer Vision and Pattern Recognition* (pp. 511–518).

Wang, J., Chen, X., & Gao, W. (2005). Online selecting discriminative tracking features using particle filter. *IEEE Conference on Computer Vision and Pattern Recognition*, 2, 1037-1042.

Chapter 2
Learning to Recognise Spatio–Temporal Interest Points

Olusegun T. Oshin
University of Surrey, UK

Andrew Gilbert
University of Surrey, UK

John Illingworth
University of Surrey, UK

Richard Bowden
University of Surrey, UK

ABSTRACT

In this chapter, we present a generic classifier for detecting spatio-temporal interest points within video, the premise being that, given an interest point detector, we can learn a classifier that duplicates its functionality and which is both accurate and computationally efficient. This means that interest point detection can be achieved independent of the complexity of the original interest point formulation. We extend the naive Bayesian classifier of Randomised Ferns to the spatio-temporal domain and learn classifiers that duplicate the functionality of common spatio-temporal interest point detectors. Results demonstrate accurate reproduction of results with a classifier that can be applied exhaustively to video at frame-rate, without optimisation, in a scanning window approach.

INTRODUCTION

The recognition of actions in video has gained significant attention in the field of computer vision, partly due to increasing processing and storage capabilities of computers, and the considerable potential of automated action recognition systems to manage modern multimedia content. In order to classify a particular action, it is necessary for such systems to be able to determine and extract characteristics of the action, which distinguish it from other actions. Action recognition can be applied in areas including automated video surveillance, human-computer interaction and behaviour recognition, to name a few.

The task of determining and extracting distinguishable action characteristics is complex, as

DOI: 10.4018/978-1-60566-900-7.ch002

actions are performed under various conditions including occlusion, cluttered backgrounds, camera motion, scale, appearance and illumination variations. Moreover, there can be significant variations within the action classes, and multiple actions performed in a video.

Methods used in action recognition can generally be divided into two classes based on the nature of action characteristics extracted. Methods belonging to the first class are known as local approaches, as they use a number of local interest points to characterise actions (Laptev and Lindeberg, 2003), (Dollar *et al*, 2005), (Niebles *et al*, 2008), etc. Local interest points are regions that possess a high degree of information and are usually areas of large local variations in pixel intensity. The second group of methods are called global or holistic approaches, and they make use of global motion information of the action like optical flow (Ke, 2005), 3D silhouettes (Blank, 2005), Motion Energy Images and Motion History Images (Bobick, 2001), etc.

The use of sparse local interest points as an optimal representation of objects or actions has shown promising results in object and action recognition. Hence, the focus of our work is an approach to learning a classifier capable of accurately and efficiently detecting spatio-temporal interest points in constant time for use in action recognition.

We propose a general framework for training interest point detectors in video, such that, given examples of the types of interest point within a training sequence, we can detect those interest point types at near frame rate in a novel video sequence. We extend a Naive Bayesian classifier called Randomised Ferns (Ozuysal *et al*, 2007) to the spatio-temporal domain allowing for the encoding of temporal information without increasing computational overhead, and it is shown that spatio-temporal interest points can be recognised efficiently and reliably. This method is motivated by the use of Ferns in rapidly classifying keypoints in 2D images while maintaining high classification

rates. The success of our method is measured by its ability to reproduce the results of two popular spatio-temporal interest point detectors proposed by Laptev and Lindeberg (2003) and Dollar *et al* (2005). The method provides a generic approach to recognising spatio-temporal features in constant time regardless of original detector complexity.

BACKGROUND AND PREVIOUS WORK

This section reviews current methods used in action recognition. First, a short description of relevant spatial interest point detectors is given, followed by examples of local spatio-temporal interest point detectors and methods that make use of them. Global approaches to the task of action recognition are also explored along with a brief evaluation of both local and global approaches. This section also examines common interest point descriptors and methods by which interest point representations are used to achieve action recognition.

Spatial Interest Point Detectors

Interest points are local regions in an image or video sequence that possess high information content, such as corners or edges. A simple example of a spatial interest point detector is the corner detector developed by Harris and Stephens (1988), which has been used in many applications involving object matching and tracking. The method involves detecting locations in an image where pixel intensities have significant local variations, obtained by applying a corner/edge response function and selecting its maxima.

Several methods make use of existing methods of interest point detection, but encode interest points using descriptors that are robust to a number of variations in their appearance. Schmid and Mohr (1997) use the Harris corner detector to identify interest points and propose a rotation-invariant local image descriptor at each interest point, using local differential grey value features. This allows for reliable characterisation, which, when coupled with a voting algorithm makes the method robust to mismatches, making it successful in image indexing.

Lowe (1999) introduced the SIFT descriptor, which is invariant to scale as well as rotation and translation, but only partially invariant to affine projection and changes in illumination. Keypoints are detected that are present in all possible scales of an image. They are selected by comparing a pixel with each surrounding pixel in the current scale and both adjacent scales and are assigned a gradient magnitude and orientation. SIFT has proven effective in many areas as its invariance has underpinned recent trends into large scale object recognition.

Mikolajczyk and Schmid (2002) developed an affine invariant interest point detector, which is an affine-adapted version of the Harris detector. Mikolajczyk and Schmid (2005) also carry out an extended evaluation of spatial interest point detectors.

Spatio-Temporal Interest Point Detectors

Akin to spatial interest points used in object recognition, interest points are proving to be important in activity recognition. Laptev and Lindeberg (2003) extended the Harris Corner detector to include temporal corners, where a corner is required to have significant local variations in time. Laptev obtains a sparse set of corners which are used to characterise actions and compute scale-invariant spatio-temporal interest point descriptors.

Similar to the extension of Harris corners by Laptev above, there exist other methods that extend aspects of spatial interest point detectors to their spatio-temporal counterparts. Oikonomopoulos *et al* (2006) extend the salient feature detection in images of Kadir and Brady (2003). In contrast to measuring saliency within a circular neighbour-

hood of pixels, spatio-temporal saliency, based on Shannon entropy is measured within the spherical neighbourhood of pixels in an image sequence. They proceed using the Chamfer distance as a metric between differing classes of salient points and time warping to deal with actions carried out at different speeds.

Also, Scovanner *et al* (2007) extend Lowe's SIFT descriptor (Lowe, 1999) to create a spatio-temporal SIFT descriptor. They obtain 3D gradient magnitudes and orientations for each pixel, then construct weighted histograms and descriptors from these. To classify actions, the video is randomly sampled at different locations, times and scales, and the bag of words classification approach (Csurka *et al*, 2004) is extended to the 3D SIFT descriptors and used to categorise actions.

Dollar *et al* (2005) argue that the direct extension of spatial interest point detectors to the spatio-temporal domain does not provide for an optimal solution and neglects important information, resulting in interest points that are too sparse since they require abrupt changes in motion. Dollar proposed a method that involves convolving the video with a 2D Gaussian smoothing kernel along the spatial dimensions, and applying a pair of 1D Gabor filters along the temporal dimension. Local maxima of this response function are chosen as interest points and 3D windows of pixels surrounding the points, termed cuboids, are extracted.

For the methods outlined above, interest points are designed in such a way as to provide invariance to a number of possible transformations, as dictated by the authors. These top-down approaches make several strong assumptions about the data and detected interest points. Recent work by Gilbert *et al* (2008), Uemura *et al* (2008), and Mikolajczyk and Uemura (2008) deviate from this paradigm. They extract large numbers of low level interest points per frame and build transformation invariant features from them without loss of information. For example, Gilbert *et al* build high level compound features from an over-complete set of simple 2D corners, using data mining. Mikolajczyk and Uemura extract many features of various types along with their motion vectors, and encode them in multiple vocabulary trees. These methods are computational expensive because of the number of interest point detection methods used and the large number of interest points detected.

Global Approaches

This subsection outlines methods in the global domain of action recognition methods. Unlike local methods, global approaches capture and make use of the entire action when distinguishing between actions.

Blank *et al* (2005) define actions as three-dimensional silhouette shapes, which contain spatial and dynamic information. They exploit relevant properties of the Poisson equation, generalising a method developed for the analysis of 2D shapes (Gorelick *et al*, 2006), and apply it to the representation of the spatio-temporal silhouettes. Ke *et al* (2005) also extend a 2D object detection method, directly generalising the real-time object detection method of Viola and Jones (2001). Integral images are extended to integral videos, and volumetric features are employed, building a detector that uses dense optical flow measurements to recognise actions involving smooth motions.

Prior to the work of Ke above, Efros *et al* (2003) introduced a motion descriptor based on optical flow measurements. The approach was developed to recognise actions in low resolution videos, extracting underlying induced motion fields in similar actions. The method requires a consistent tracker so that objects can be stabilised. The approach of Shechtman and Irani (2007) also makes use of the underlying motion fields, measuring the degree of consistency between the implicit patterns in two video fragments. Video template correlation is utilised between spatio-temporal templates and video segments to obtain a measure of behavioural similarity. Fathi and Mori

(2008) build a motion-based classifier by applying Adaboost to low-level, and then mid-level motion features. Motion features at both levels are used as weak classifiers to select a subset of features that can separate between action classes.

An approach that uses global information to extract a set local spatio-temporal interest points is that of Wong and Cipolla (2007), who obtain subspace images and then extract a sparse set of two-dimensional motion components which correspond to moving parts in a sequence. They also detect associated one-dimensional coefficient matrices, which are tip regions of the motion components, essentially the temporal aspect of the motion. Hence the 3D interest point detection problem is decomposed into a 2D spatial interest point detector coupled with its 1D temporal counterpart.

Local vs. Global Approaches

Local methods make use of a number of local interest points in the video. Due to the large local variations in pixel intensity in their local neighbourhoods, these points possess a high degree of information that makes them useful when categorising actions. Hence, actions can be described using the compact representation afforded by spatio-temporal interest points.

It is usually necessary to compare local spatio-temporal neighbourhoods of interest points in order to distinguish between interest point types, regardless of various possible transformations. These neighbourhoods therefore need to be described in such ways as to achieve invariance to these transformations. One example is the gradient descriptor used by Dollar *et al* (2005), Niebles *et al* (2008) and Savarese *et al* (2008). This descriptor involves obtaining the intensity gradient of the neighbourhood and flattening them to form a vector, and has proven effective in encoding local motion information. Based on their descriptors, interest points belonging to an action can be identified, leading to the classification of the action.

Another example is the Scovanner *et al*'s (2007) 3D SIFT descriptor described earlier.

Global methods make use of the action in its entirety. An example of global information is the optical flow (Efros, 2003), (Ke, 2005), where only motion information is used. An alternative is to use shape information (Blank *et al*, 2005). Typically, the action is segmented or tracked throughout the video, and to classify an action, a measure of similarity e.g. template correlation (Shechtman and Irani, 2007), is computed between learnt representations of several actions and the candidate representation.

In general, representations that make use of only motion information often fail when there are discontinuities in motion. On the other hand, shape only representations assume that there is minimal variation in shape information, and fail when this is not the case. Methods that combine both shape and motion information of an action achieve more discriminative results.

Compared to their local counterparts, global approaches require such pre-processing as background segmentation, tracking and object stabilisation, which makes them computationally expensive. Also, most global methods cannot localise actions or recognise multiple actions in a video, and are less robust to global deformations in actions. On the other hand, local approaches make use of interest points that can be too sparse. Sparseness, though desirable, can result in representations that are not invariant to cluttered backgrounds, camera motion, etc.

Interest Point Classification

While most of the above approaches extend spatial recognition methods to the temporal domain, some methods utilise existing spatio-temporal interest point detectors, but extend methods of classification and recognition that have proven successful in object recognition.

Examples of such methods are the works of Schuldt *et al* (2004) and Niebles *et al* (2008).

Schuldt use the interest point detector of Laptev and Lindeberg (2003) and compute jet descriptors of spatio-temporal neighbourhoods. Spatio-temporal jet descriptors are a generalisation of the local jets developed by Koenderink and van Doorn (1987). Schuldt apply Support Vector Machine (SVM) classifiers to descriptors of spatio-temporal neighbourhoods of the interest points and also provide a publicly available human action dataset on which their method is tested.

In object recognition, Sivic *et al* (2005) introduced an unsupervised method of categorising and localising objects in images using a bag of visual words technique. Niebles *et al* generalise this method to recognise human action categories, noting that previous methods use modelling and learning frameworks that are too simple to handle challenging action scenarios such as those involving multiple actions. Niebles make use of the cuboids extracted by the interest point detector of Dollar *et al* (2005) and apply a probabilistic Latent Semantic Analysis (pLSA) model (Hoffman, 1999) with a 'bag of video words' representation to learn action categories in an unsupervised manner and localise multiple actions in a video sequence.

Liu and Shah (2008) also apply bags of video words to Dollar interest points. In addition, they apply Maximization of Mutual Information to discover an optimal number of clusters in an unsupervised manner. They also apply spatial correlogram and spatio-temporal pyramid matching approaches to capture structural information ignored by the bag of words representation.

Lepetit and Fua (2006) extend the randomised trees classifier developed by Amit and Geman (1997). Already widely used in character recognition, Lepetit and Fua apply the method to object recognition and treat the wide baseline matching of feature points in images as a classification problem. They synthesise many new views of each feature point and define a class as the set of all possible views of a particular feature point. To increase the speed of randomised trees, Ozuysal *et al* (2007) proposed the Fern classifier. The Fern classifier is of particular relevance to work presented in this chapter and is fully explained later.

LEARNING METHODOLOGY

We aim to detect trained spatio-temporal interest points accurately and efficiently in video, using a semi-naive Bayesian classifier called Randomised Ferns, which was proposed by Ozuysal (2007) as an alternative to Randomised Trees (Lepetit and Fua, 2006). This section gives an overview of Randomised Trees and Ferns, and describes the extension of the Fern classifier, used in object recognition, to the spatio-temporal domain, allowing for the encoding of temporal information without increasing computational overhead; and a generic approach to recognising spatio-temporal interest points efficiently in novel video sequences, in constant time.

Randomised Trees and Ferns

Randomised Trees are simple yet effective classification structures introduced and applied to handwriting recognition by Amit and Geman (1997), and later used in object recognition by Lepetit and Fua (2006). For a randomised tree, all non-leaf nodes of a randomised tree contain a simple test that splits the space of the data to be classified. Lepetit and Fua used the simple test of comparing pixel intensities, which could be chosen randomly or by a greedy algorithm that gives the best separation based on information gain. After training, the leaf nodes contain estimates of the posterior distributions over the classes for an image that reaches that leaf. Randomised trees are built in a top-down manner and all training examples are passed down through the tree nodes, based on the test. Figure 1 shows a randomised tree that uses a comparison of pixel intensities as the test. If the intensity at point j_1 of the image

patch is greater than that of point j_2, then the patch is passed down the tree via the right child node; otherwise, it traverses the left child node. The process terminates when the node receives too few examples or it reaches a given depth. It would be very difficult to build one tree that performs well for a large number of classes, training examples and possible tests, so multiple trees are grown, and each tree is trained with a random subset of the training examples to obtain weak dependency between the trees.

When classifying, a test patch is passed down each of the trees to a leaf node. The class assigned to the image is found by averaging the posterior distributions at the leaf of each tree where the image terminates, and the class with the maximum value is selected.

Ferns (Ozuysal *et al*, 2007), unlike randomised trees, are non-hierarchical classification structures. Each Fern consists of a set of ordered binary tests and returns probabilities of a patch belonging to each of the classes learnt during training. The structure of Ferns is shown in Figure 2. As with randomised trees above, Ozuysal used the simple binary test of pixel intensity comparisons, with the result f_j being 1 if the intensity at point j_1 is greater than that of point j_2, and 0 otherwise, given that $j=\{1...S\}$ and S is the number of binary tests in a Fern, called nodes. The binary values $\{f_1, f_2, ... f_S\}$, returned from the ordered tests are combined and converted to decimal. Hence, a Fern with S nodes will return a decimal value between 0 and 2^{S-1}. For multiple patches that belong to the same class, the output of a Fern for that class can be modelled with a histogram, with each training patch incrementing the value of a bin in the histogram. More Ferns can be created by generating new nodes and obtaining distributions for all classes within the Ferns. Independence is assumed between Ferns.

During classification, the same set of ordered tests are performed on a test patch and a binary code is obtained, which when converted to decimal is used to select a bin in the class histograms to

Figure 1. A Randomised Tree using pixel intensity comparisons at random points in the image patch. After training, each leaf node contains class probabilities of a new patch arriving at that node.

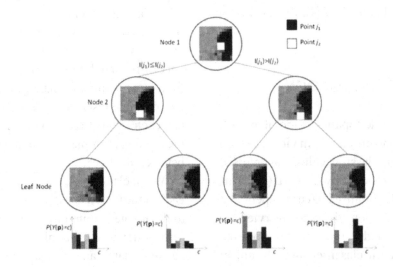

Figure 2. A set of Ferns. The binary digits are results of the comparison between pixels at points j_1 and j_2. During training, an image patch belonging to a particular class is run through all nodes in all Ferns and each Fern updates its distribution for that class based on the results. During classification, the results are used to select bins in the class histograms

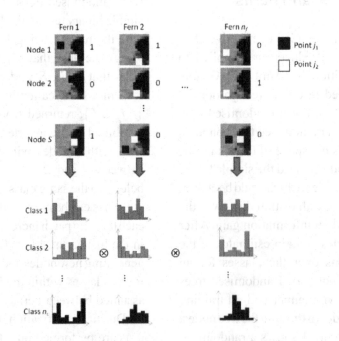

Figure 3. Example of nodes in the spatio-temporal domain. The cuboid is flattened with respect to time to show subpatches (black and white patches within the cuboid frame) at different temporal offsets.

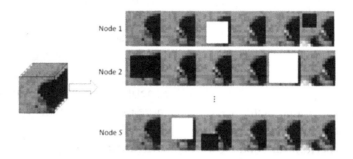

look up. The selected bin gives the likelihood of that patch belonging to each of the classes. The class with the maximum likelihood is chosen as the most probable class. For multiple Ferns, the class with the maximum product of class likelihoods across the Ferns is selected, assuming independence between the Ferns. Performance-memory trade-offs can be made by changing the number of Ferns and the number of nodes within each Fern, allowing for a flexible implementation.

Semi-Naive Bayesian Spatio-temporal Classification

The first major contribution of this research is the extension of Ferns as applied in the spatial domain for object recognition (Ozuysal *et al*, 2007) to the spatio-temporal domain. Building upon the method described in the previous section, Ferns are applied to *cuboids*, which are spatio-temporal neighbourhoods centred at selected interest points.

In contrast to Ferns in the spatial domain, the sets of binary tests performed on the cuboids are not single pixel comparisons. Instead, we define a node as a comparison between the sums of pixels within two *subpatches*. Subpatches are 2-dimensional spatial patches that fit within frames of the spatio-temporal volume of a cuboid. Figure 3 shows a flattened spatio-temporal volume with

subpatches generated on different frames within the volume. These subpatches can be chosen randomly, i.e., located on random frames of the cuboid, at random points on the frame, and have random sizes; or be chosen using a greedy algorithm that would best separate the space of data within the cuboids. Mathematically, for subpatches encoded by a spatial offset x, y, spatial extent x_s, y_s, and temporal offset t, the output of a node f_j is given by:

$$f_j = \begin{cases} 1, & if \ s(x_1, y_1, x_{s_1}, y_{s_1}, t_1) - s(x_2, y_2, x_{s_2}, y_{s_2}, t_2) < T; \\ 0, & otherwise. \end{cases}$$

$$(1)$$

where T is a threshold that can be arbitrarily chosen, and s is the sum of pixels within the subpatch, given by,

$$s(x, y, x_s, y_s, t) = \frac{1}{x_s y_s} \sum_{x'=x}^{x+x_s} \sum_{y'=y}^{y+y_s} I(x', y', t). \qquad (2)$$

The sums are normalised by the number of pixels in the subpatch, $x_s \times y_s$. Sums of subpatch pixel comparisons are used as opposed to pixel comparisons so as to build a classifier that is more robust to scale variations as simple pixel comparisons make the classifier more sensitive to the scale at which it was trained.

EXPERIMENTAL SETUP

Training

Given a cuboid belonging to a particular class, we train a fern classifier by generating S nodes as described above. We perform the node tests and obtain values f_j, where $j = \{1 \dots S\}$, for each fern. The threshold, T, is given the value 0, so equation (1) above simplifies to:

$$f_j = \begin{cases} 1, & if \ s(x_1, y_1, x_{s_1}, y_{s_1}, t_1) < s(x_2, y_2, x_{s_2}, y_{s_2}, t_2); \\ 0, & otherwise. \end{cases}$$

All the node results $\{f_1, f_2, \dots, f_S\}$ are combined to form a binary code, which is then converted to decimal. For all the cuboids belonging to a particular class, we build a histogram of the decimal values, and normalize the histogram by the number of samples to give a probability distribution for that class. For additional classes, the same tests are performed within the fern and separate distributions are obtained for them. Additional ferns are trained by generating new nodes and obtaining distributions for all classes based on the nodes' results.

In order to rapidly determine the difference between the sums of subpatches, we calculate the integral image representation (Viola and Jones, 2001) of each frame in the cuboid. This allows for 8 array dereferences per node and $8 \times S$ array dereferences per fern. The integral image representation of each frame is chosen in favour of an integral volume representation of the cuboid because the volumetric approach includes an additional parameter over which to optimise. Also, this method sufficiently captures temporal information in the cuboids. Laptev and Perez (2007) have shown that applying a space-time classifier to single keyframes of an action can yield good results.

Random selection of nodes was chosen in favour of a greedy algorithm because random selection allows for faster training. The added benefit of a greedy algorithm is offset by using more randomised ferns.

Classification

To classify a new cuboid, we apply the fern classifier by performing the same set of ordered node tests on the cuboid as during training. A decimal value is obtained from the combined binary node results. The decimal value determines the bin of the normalised class distributions within the fern that is selected. For a single fern implementation, the cuboid most likely belongs to the class that has the highest value in the selected bin. For multiple ferns, we combine the selected normalised bin values by adding the logarithms of these values within the classes and across the ferns. The class with the maximum likelihood is selected.

Since the objective is the recognition of interest points, the task becomes a binary classification problem between the classes of *Interest Point* and *Background* - a local spatio-temporal volume either contains an interest point or it does not. For each classification made, likelihood values are obtained for both *Interest Point* and *Background* classes. Using the likelihood ratio of these two values, we can obtain a value of confidence from the classifier, for the classified spatio-temporal volume. A threshold is then set for the likelihood ratio, above which, candidate spatio-temporal volumes can be classified as interest point neighbourhoods. This threshold is selected from the ROC curve to give the desired positive-to-negative response rate, and is normally chosen as the Equal Error Rate.

RESULTS

The performance of the spatio-temporal Ferns classifier is measured by its ability to obtain comparable detection performance to two spatio-temporal interest point detectors. This section presents results of recognition of learnt features in various test videos, using a scanning volume over the entire sequence. Below are descriptions of the dataset on which interest points are learnt and detected. Also described are the two interest point detectors used in training and evaluation. The first is an extension of the Harris corner detector (Harris and Stephens, 1988) to the spatio-temporal domain by Laptev and Lindeberg (2003), selecting local maxima of spatio-temporal corners as features. In the results, this method is labelled *Laptev*. The second method by Dollar *et al* (2005), applies separable linear filters to the video and selects local maxima of the response as features, labelled *Dollar*.

Dataset

The classifier is trained and tested on the KTH human action dataset (Schuldt *et al*, 2004), which contains videos of 25 persons performing six actions in four different scenarios. These actions are boxing, hand waving, walking, running, jogging and hand clapping. One action is performed in each video over static homogeneous backgrounds and are split into four different conditions that include scale variations, appearance variations, and outdoor and indoor lighting conditions. In total, there are 598 videos. Of the 25 subjects, the dataset is split by Schuldt *et al* such that 8 persons are used for training, 9 for testing, and 8 for validation purposes, for all actions. In these experiments, we follow the prescribed Training-Validation-Test split, training with 8 persons and testing with 9 unseen persons. The Validation subset of the dataset was not used. Though it can be argued that the KTH data set is limited in terms of complexity, it is important to note that the goal of this work is to provide comparable interest point segmentation to other detectors and not to classify the actions.

Feature Point Extraction

The method of Laptev and Lindeberg (2003) extend the Harris corner detector (Harris and Stephens, 1988) to the spatio-temporal domain by requiring that image values in space-time have significant variations in both the spatial and temporal dimensions. They compute a windowed 3×3 second moment matrix composed of first order spatial and temporal derivatives, averaged with a Gaussian weighting function. Interest points are then detected by searching for regions that have significant eigenvalues of the matrix.

The second method, proposed by Dollar (Dollar *et al*, 2005), applies separable linear filters to the video sequence. A response function of the form $R = (I * g * h_{ev})^2 + (I * g * h_{od})^2$ is obtained, where $g(x, y : \sigma)$ is the 2D Gaussian kernel applied along the spatial dimensions of the video, and h_{ev} and h_{od} are a quadrature pair of 1D Gabor filters applied in the temporal dimension. The detector responds best to complex motions made by regions that are distinguishable spatially, including spatio-temporal corners as defined by Laptev, but not to pure translational motion or motions involving areas that are not distinct in space. Local maxima of the response function R are selected as interest points.

For both methods, spatio-temporal windowed pixel values around the interest points are set to contain the data that contributed to that interest point being detected. These windows are cubic for the *Dollar* detector, and are called *Cuboids*. For the *Laptev* detector, the spatio-temporal windows are ellipsoidal. For both detectors, the scale at which an event is observed determines the type of event that is detected, and ideally interest points should be detected at various scales. However, we choose one scale for each detection method such that the sizes of the extracted spatio-temporal windows are similar across methods for comparison purposes. For *Dollar*, the size of the cuboids is $13 \times 13 \times 13$ pixels, and for *Laptev*, the ellipsoid diameter is chosen to be as close to 13 pixels as possible. The cuboid size was chosen as it adequately captures local changes for most of the action sizes in the KTH dataset. Figure 4 highlights example interest points detected in videos of boxing, hand waving and walking for both *Laptev* and *Dollar* interest point detectors. It can be seen that *Laptev* interest points are much sparser than dollar interest points for the same action.

During training, the classifier is applied to the extracted $13 \times 13 \times 13$ pixel volumes surrounding each of the spatio-temporal interest points detected, including *Laptev* interest points. Once feature volumes are extracted, additional positive example cuboids are artificially generated by randomly offsetting and scaling the cuboids at the detected feature points by a small amount in all directions, making the classifier robust to slight variations in the feature regions. The maximum noise offset was set as 2 pixels in all dimensions, allowing for at least a 60% overlap between a noisy positive training cuboid and the original cuboid from which it was derived. A class of negative examples (background) are then created by extracting cuboids at randomly selected areas that do not overlap with positive feature cuboids. The number of background cuboids and the number of feature cuboids are equal, to avoid biasing the classifier.

Performance

In order to detect interest points in a test sequence, a spatio-temporal scanning window is employed across the entire video. The applied scanning window is the size of the extracted cuboids used

Figure 4. Example frames from action video sequences highlighting points where spatio-temporal interest points have been detected for the actions Boxing, Walking and Hand Waving. Top: Laptev interest points; Bottom: Dollar interest points on the same frame of the actions. These points are used as positive data during training.

in training ($13 \times 13 \times 13$). This is also necessary to compare with extracted interest points during evaluation. The Fern classifier is applied on the region within the scanning window to determine whether it contains an interest point or background. Subpatch comparisons for each node are carried out efficiently using an integral image representation of the entire video, which is calculated once. This differs from the integral video representation used by Ke (2005), as the integral images are computed on individual frames of the video. The sums of selected subpatches can therefore be computed using 4 array dereferences, giving 8 array dereferences for each node comparison.

To determine whether a windowed volume contains an interest point, likelihoods are obtained from the Ferns for both the classes of interest point and background as described, and a log likelihood ratio of interest point to background is calculated. Receiver Operating Characteristic (ROC) Curves are used to determine how well the classifier is able to emulate learnt detections. Positives are feature cuboids detected by one of the *Dollar* and *Laptev* interest point detectors on test data, and true positives are *Dollar* or *Laptev* positives that have also been labelled a feature by our Fern classifier. ROC curves are obtained by varying the threshold on the log likelihood ratio.

There exists a set of parameters for which the performance of the Ferns classifier is optimal for a particular application. Generally, if the number of nodes in a fern is too small, it would result in over-population of histogram bins and result in poor class separation. On the other hand, a very high number of nodes would result in sparsely populated distributions. For this application, 1-node ferns would result in 2-bin class histograms, which might be adequate, but is not optimal for a 2-class problem; using 10 nodes would result in sparse 1024-bin histograms, making for a memory inefficient solution. We perform tests in order to find an appropriate number of nodes. Figure 5 shows a graph of average classification performance for different numbers of nodes in a

Figure 5. Graph of average classification performance against number of nodes used per fern.

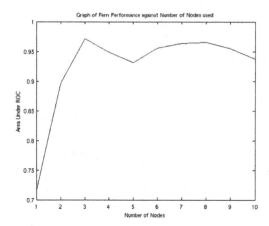

fern. The Area Under ROC measure is used to measure performance. It can be observed that improved class discrimination is obtained for 3 nodes or higher, and that the classifier performs best with 3 nodes per fern.

It is expected, and is shown by Ozuysal *et al* (2007) that, up to a certain limit, the higher the number of ferns, the better the performance of classifier. However, there are limitations on memory and the speed of classification. For this reason, the results presented here are obtained with 50 ferns. The number of ferns, and indeed nodes, can be varied to achieve a trade-off between memory and performance.

The Fern classifier is expected to trigger multiple detections around a *Dollar* or *Laptev* positive. Also, the detections will not always occur at the same points selected by the feature detectors. This is natural as noise was added during training and the classifier is only applied at alternating pixels and frames. To this end, a minimum percentage is chosen, above which a Fern-classified interest point must overlap a *Dollar* or *Laptev* interest point, before it can be labelled a true positive. Figure 6 shows averaged ROC curves obtained for different percentage overlaps. All percentage overlaps perform well, with 100% overlap achieving a surprisingly good Equal Error Rate of 0.67. For our experiments, we used an overlap of 50%, as this is used in most work involving similar comparisons. Consequently, for a particular $13 \times 13 \times 13$-pixel *Dollar/Laptev* interest point, the Fern-classified interest point must overlap that *Dollar/Laptev* interest point by more than $\frac{13 \times 13 \times 13}{2}$ pixels.

To reduce classification time, the scanning window operates over alternate pixels and frames of the video. No loss of accuracy is observed as the noise added during training gives robustness to offsets from the optimal detection position. In contrast, tests carried out without the addition of noise in training show a reduction in average classification performance.

Figure 7 shows how well features are detected in novel video sequences of Boxing, Hand waving and Walking actions, having trained with *Dollar* and *Laptev* feature detectors. Each curve indicates the different scenarios of the KTH video data set (Schuldt *et al*, 2004), where *S1* is static with a homogeneous background, *S2* includes scale variations, *S3* has appearance variations, and *S4* has illumination variations. It can be seen that the spatio-temporal Fern classifier performs extremely well in detecting learnt features. It is able to correctly recognise more than 95% of the *Dollar* features with less than 5% error for all the scenarios. For *Laptev* features, we obtain Equal Error Rates greater than 0.9 for the actions in all scenarios except for Illumination variations (*S4*), where the Equal Error Rates are 0.85 and 0.87 for Boxing and Walking features respectively. This lower performance on the *Laptev* interest points is not surprising as these features are more localised than those of *Dollar – Laptev* interest points are ellipsoidal and the spatial-temporal volume the Ferns operate upon are cubic, incorporating additional surrounding information. The classifier is kept the same between both experiments to allow comparison, but optimising the spatio-temporal support region of the classifier for different interest

Figure 6. Classification of features against background for various percentages of overlap between classified feature cuboids and actual positive feature cuboids.

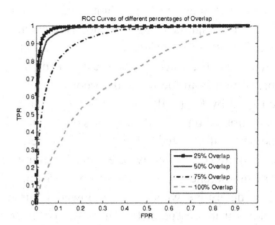

point detectors is likely to increase performance further. It is worth noting that although the classifier was trained at one spatial and temporal scale, the *S2* curves show that performance on different scales is comparable to that of the static homogenous background. This highlights our classifier's ability to cope with changes in scale from the training data.

The *Dollar* detector runs at frame rate on the KTH data set, whereas the *Laptev* detector is considerably slower. The spatio-temporal Fern classifier, implemented in C++, using the scanning window approach proceeds at frame rate, showing that regardless of the complexity of the interest point detector used in training, good classification performance can be achieved in constant time. The speed of the classifier is dependent upon the number of Ferns and nodes used for classification.

DISCUSSION

A spatio-temporal interest point classifier has been developed that extends a semi-naive Bayesian classifier used in object recognition, and a novel

Figure 7. Left: ROC Curves for features detected by the Dollar feature detector against background for Boxing, Handwaving and Walking. Right: ROC Curves for features detected by the Laptev feature detector against background for Boxing, Handwaving and Walking. Each graph shows performance in the four scenarios of the KTH video data set, S1 - S4, where S1 videos have a static homogeneous background, S2 have scale variations, subjects in S3 have different clothes, and S4 have illumination variations.

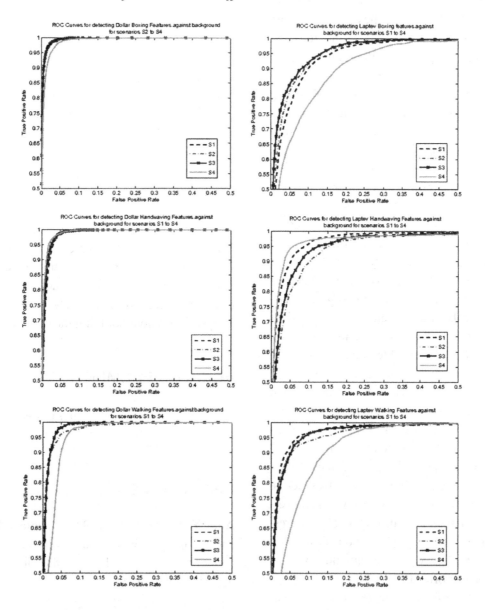

approach to recognising the interest points in videos is proposed. The method is demonstrated on the task of detecting learnt spatio-temporal features on the KTH human action data set. Results of recognition performance are presented,

having trained on interest points selected by two different spatio-temporal interest point detectors, indicating that the classifier is capable of obtaining results comparable to these feature detectors on test data. These high classification rates are achieved in constant time without an increase in computational overhead.

This method generalises to other interest point detection methods including those of Gilbert *et al* (2008), Uemura *et al* (2008) and Mikolajczyk and Uemura (2008) where they detect a large number of interest points. These methods are computationally expensive as they extract a large number of interest points. However, our spatio-temporal Fern classifier is capable of obtaining comparable detection results using much less computational resources. While this method is not limited in applicability to action recognition, it provides for a very efficient way of detecting spatio-temporal interest points where available interest point detection methods are computationally demanding. Our can be employed as part of a larger action recognition framework.

To further assess generality, the ability of the Fern classifier to detect from one action, features learnt from other actions was investigated. This test relies upon the original features being invariant to action type as well as occurring in both activities, which although desirable, might be assumed is not the case. Having trained the classifier on Boxing features, its ability to detect features that occur in a Walking video sequence is tested and the results on *Dollar* interest points are presented in Figure 8. It can be observed that features common to Boxing and Walking are detected with high equal error rates, showing that irrespective of the action, the Fern classifier gives good performance in detecting spatio-temporal features. This also goes some way to demonstrating that the features are indeed consistent and invariant to the action performed.

A single Fern is not expected to separate all classes in an n-class classification problem. However, it is possible to have Ferns that are not able to discriminate between *any* of the classes. While they do not degrade the overall performance of the Ferns, they constitute redundancy. It is also possible to have Ferns that do degrade classification performance. Hence, in continuation of this

Figure 8. ROC curves for features detected in Walking video sequences trained with Boxing features. S1 to S4 are defined as in Figure 7.

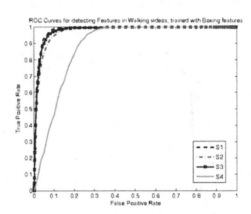

work, an optimisation step is needed after the Ferns are generated to discard poorly performing Ferns, making the classifier even more efficient. Furthermore, Ferns can be structured so that a low cumulative likelihood early in classification is rejected without applying the entire classifier

ACKNOWLEDGMENT

This work is supported by the EU FP6 Project, URUS.

REFERENCES

Amit, Y., & Geman, D. (1997). Shape quantization and recognition with randomized trees. *Neural Computation*, 9(7), 1545–1588. doi:10.1162/neco.1997.9.7.1545

Blank, M., Gorelick, L., Shechtman, E., Irani, M., & Basri, R. (2005). Actions as space-time shapes. In *Proceedings IEEE Intl. Conf. on Computer Vision (ICCV '05)* (pp. 1395–1402).

Bobick, A. F., & Davis, J. W. (2001). The recognition of human movement using temporal templates. [PAMI]. *IEEE Transactions on Pattern Analysis and Machine Intelligence, 23*(3), 257–267. doi:10.1109/34.910878

Csurka, G., Dance, C., Fan, L., Willamowski, J., & Bray, C. (2004). Visual categorization with bags of keypoints. In *Proceedings ECCV Intl. Workshop on Statistical Learning in Computer Vision* (pp. 1–22).

Dollar, P., Rabaud, V., Cottrell, G., & Belongie, S. (2005). Behavior recognition via sparse spatio-temporal features. In *Proceedings IEEE Intl. Workshop on Visual Surveillance and Performance Evaluation of Tracking and Surveillance (VS-PETS '05)* (pp. 65–72).

Efros, A., Berg, A., Mori, G., & Malik, J. (2003). Recognizing action at a distance. In *Proceedings Intl. Conf. on Computer Vision (ICCV '03)* (pp. 726–733).

Fathi, A., & Mori, G. (2008). Action Recognition by Learning Mid-Level Motion Features. In *Proceedings IEEE Conf. on Computer Vision and Pattern Recognition (CVPR '08)* (pp. 1–8).

Gilbert, A., Illingworth, J., & Bowden, R. (2008). Scale Invariant Action Recognition Using Compound Features Mined from Dense Spatio-temporal Corners. In *Proceedings European Conf. on Computer Vision (ECCV '08)* (pp. 222–233).

Gorelick, L., Galun, M., & Brandt, A. (2006). Shape representation and classification using the poisson equation. [PAMI]. *IEEE Transactions on Pattern Analysis and Machine Intelligence, 28*(12), 1991–2005. doi:10.1109/TPAMI.2006.253

Harris, C., & Stephens, M. (1988). A combined corner and edge detection. In Proceedings *Alvey Vision Conf.* (pp. 147–151).

Hofmann, T. (1999). Probabilistic latent semantic indexing. In *Proceedings Intl. ACM SIGIR Conf. on Research and Development in Information Retrieval* (pp. 50–57).

Kadir, T., & Brady, M. (2003). Scale saliency: a novel approach to salient feature and scale selection. In *Proceedings Intl. Conf. on Visual Information Engineering (VIE '03)* (pp. 25–28).

Ke, Y., Sukthankar, R., & Hebert, M. (2005). Efficient visual event detection using volumetric features. In *Proceedings IEEE Intl. Conf. on Computer Vision (ICCV '05)*, (Vol. 1, pp. 166–173).

Koenderink, J. J., & van Doom, A. J. (1987). Representation of local geometry in the visual system. *Biological Cybernetics, 55*(6), 367–375. doi:10.1007/BF00318371

Laptev, I., & Lindeberg, T. (2003). Space-time interest points. In Proceedings *IEEE Intl. Conf. on Computer Vision (ICCV '03)*, (Vol. 2, pp. 432–439).

Laptev, I., & Perez, P. (2007). Retrieving Actions in Movies. In *Proceedings Intl. Conf. on Computer Vision (ICCV '07)* (pp 1-8).

Lepetit, V., & Fua, P. (2006). Keypoint recognition using randomized trees. [PAMI]. *IEEE Transactions on Pattern Analysis and Machine Intelligence, 28*(9), 1465–1479. doi:10.1109/TPAMI.2006.188

Liu, J., & Shah, M. (2008). Learning Human Actions via Information Maximization. In *Proceedings IEEE Conf. on Computer Vision and Pattern Recognition (CVPR '08)* (pp. 1–8).

Lowe, D. G. (1999). Object recognition from local scale-invariant features. In *Proceedings IEEE Intl. Conf. on Computer Vision (ICCV '99)* (pp. 1150–1157).

Mikolajczyk, K., & Schmid, C. (2002). An affine invariant interest point detector. In *Proceedings European Conf. on Computer Vision (ECCV '02)* (pp. 128–142).

Mikolajczyk, K., & Schmid, C. (2005). A performance evaluation of local descriptors. [PAMI]. *IEEE Transactions on Pattern Analysis and Machine Intelligence*, *27*(10), 1615–1630. doi:10.1109/TPAMI.2005.188

Mikolajczyk, K., & Uemura, H. (2008). Action Recognition with Motion-Appearance Vocabulary Forest. In *Proceedings IEEE Conf. on Computer Vision and Pattern Recognition (CVPR '08)* (pp. 1–8).

Niebles, J., Wang, H., & Fei-Fei, L. (2008). Unsupervised learning of human action categories using spatial-temporal words. *International Journal of Computer Vision*, *79*(3), 299–318. doi:10.1007/s11263-007-0122-4

Oikonomopoulos, A., Patras, I., & Pantic, M. (2006). Spatiotemporal salient points for visual recognition of human actions. *IEEE Transactions on Systems, Man, and Cybernetics . Part B*, *36*(3), 710–719.

Oshin, O., Gilbert, A., Illingworth, J., & Bowden, R. (2008). Spatio-temporal Feature Recogntion using Randomised Ferns. In *Proceedings Intl. Workshop on Machine Learning for Vision-based Motion Analysis (MLVMA '08)* (pp. 1-12).

Ozuysal, M., Fua, P., & Lepetit, V. (2007). Fast keypoint recognition in ten lines of code. In *Proceedings IEEE Conf. on Computer Vision and Pattern Recognition (CVPR '07)* (pp. 1–8).

Savarese, S., DelPozo, A., Niebles, J. C., & Fei-Fei, L. (2008). Spatial-Temporal Correlations for Unsupervised Action Classification. In *Proceedings IEEE Workshop on Motion and Video Computing (WMVC '08)* (pp. 1-8).

Schmid, C., & Mohr, R. (1997). Local grayvalue invariants for image retrieval. [PAMI]. *IEEE Transactions on Pattern Analysis and Machine Intelligence*, *19*(5), 530–534. doi:10.1109/34.589215

Schuldt, C., Laptev, I., & Caputo, B. (2004). Recognizing human actions: A local SVM approach. In *Proceedings Intl. Conf. on Pattern Recognition (ICPR '04)* (pp. 32–36).

Scovanner, P., Ali, S., & Shah, M. (2007). A 3-dimensional sift descriptor and its application to action recognition. In *Proceedings Intl. Conf. on Multimedia* (pp. 357–360).

Shechtman, E., & Irani, M. (2007). Space-time behavior-based correlation. [PAMI]. *IEEE Transactions on Pattern Analysis and Machine Intelligence*, *29*(11), 2045–2056. doi:10.1109/TPAMI.2007.1119

Sivic, J., Russell, B. C., Efros, A. A., Zisserman, A., & Freeman, W. T. (2005). Discovering objects and their location in images. In *Proceedings IEEE Intl. Conf. on Computer Vision (ICCV '05)* (pp. 370–377).

Uemura, H., Ishikawa, S., & Mikolajczyk, K. (2008). Feature Tracking and Motion Compensation for Action Recognition. In *Proceedings British Machine Vision Conference (BMVC '08)* (pp 1-10).

Viola, P., & Jones, M. (2001). Rapid object detection using a boosted cascade of simple features. In *Proceedings IEEE Conf. on Computer Vision and Pattern Recognition (CVPR '01)* (pp. 511–518).

Wong, S., & Cipolla, R. (2007). Extracting spatiotemporal interest points using global information. In *Proceedings IEEE Intl. Conf. on Computer Vision (ICCV '07)* (pp. 1–8).

Chapter 3
Graphical Models for Representation and Recognition of Human Actions

Pradeep Natarajan
BBN Technologies, USA

Ramakant Nevatia
University of Southern California, USA

ABSTRACT

*Building a system for recognition of human actions from video involves two key problems - 1) designing suitable low-level features that are both efficient to extract from videos and are capable of distinguishing between events 2) developing a suitable representation scheme that can bridge the large gap between low-level features and high-level event concepts, and also handle the uncertainty and errors inherent in any low-level video processing. Graphical models provide a natural framework for representing state transitions in events and also the spatio-temporal constraints between the actors and events. **Hidden Markov models**(HMMs) have been widely used in several action recognition applications but the basic representation has three key deficiencies: These include unrealistic models for the duration of a sub-event, not encoding interactions among multiple agents directly and not modeling the inherent hierarchical organization of these activities. Several extensions have been proposed to address one or more of these issues and have been successfully applied in various gesture and action recognition domains. More recently, conditionalrandomfields (CRF) are becoming increasingly popular since they allow complex potential functions for modeling observations and state transitions, and also produce superior performance to HMMs when sufficient training data is available. The authors will first review the various extension of these graphical models, then present the theory of inference and learning in them and finally discuss their applications in various domains.*

DOI: 10.4018/978-1-60566-900-7.ch003

INTRODUCTION

Systems for automated recognition of human gestures and actions are needed for a number of applications in human computer interaction, including assistive technologies and intelligent environments. While the vision of semantic analysis and recognition of actions is compelling there are several difficult challenges to overcome. These include bridging the gap between the low-level sensor readings and high-level semantic concepts, modeling the uncertainties in the observed data, minimizing the requirement for large training sets which are difficult to obtain, and accurately segmenting and recognizing actions from a continuous stream of observations in real time.

Several probabilistic models have been proposed over the years in various communities for activity recognition. (Intille & Bobick, 2001) demonstrates recognition of structured, multi-person actions by integrating goal-based primitives and temporal relationships into a Bayesian network (BN). (Chan et al., 2006) uses dynamic Bayesian networks (DBNs) to simultaneously link broken trajectories and recognize complex events. (Moore & Essa, 2002) uses stochastic context-free grammars (SCFGs) for activity representation and demonstrates the approach for recognizing player strategies in multi-player card games. (Ryoo & Aggarwal, 2006) also uses context-free grammars (CFGs) and presents a layered approach which first recognizes pose, then gestures and finally the atomic and complex events with the output of the lower levels fed to the higher levels.

While each of these formalisms have been successfully applied in various domains, hidden Markov models (HMM) and their extensions have by far been the most popular in activity recognition. Besides their simplicity, they also have well understood learning and inference algorithms making them well suited for a wide range of applications. For example, (Starner, Weaver, & Pentland, 1998) recognizes complex gestures in American sign language (ASL) by modeling the actions of each hand with HMMs. (Vogler & Metaxas, 1999) introduces parallel hidden Markov models (PaHMM), also for recognizing ASL gestures by modeling each hand's action as an independent HMM. In contrast, (Brand, Oliver, & Pentland, 1997) introduces coupled hidden Markov models (CHMM) to explicitly model multiple interacting processes and demonstrated them for recognizing tai-chi gestures. (Bui, Phung, & Venkatesh, 2004) adopt the hierarchial hidden Markov model (HHMM) for monitoring daily activities at multiple levels of abstraction. The abstract hidden Markov model (AHMM) (Bui, Venkatesh, & West, 2002) describes a related extension where a hierarchy of policies decide the action at any instant. (Hongeng & Nevatia, 2003) explores the use of explicit duration models using hidden semi-Markov models (HSMMs) to recognize video events and also presented an algorithm to reduce inference complexity under certain assumptions. (Duong, Bui, Phung, & Venkatesh, 2005) presents the switching hidden semi-Markov model (S-HSMM) which is a two-layered extension of HSMM and applied to activity recognition and abnormality detection. More recently, (Natarajan & Nevatia, 2007a) combines these various extensions in a unified framework to simultaneously model hierarchy, duration and multi-channel interactions.

In contrast to the *generative* HMMs, *discriminative* models like conditional random fields (CRFs) are becoming increasingly popular due to their flexibility and improved performance especially when a large amount of labeled training data is available. (Sminchisescu, Kanaujia, Li, & Metaxas, 2005) applies CRFs for contextual motion recognition and showed encouraging results. (Wang, Quattoni, Morency, Demirdjian, & Darrell, 2006) uses the hidden conditional random fields (HCRFs) introduced a 2-layer extension to the basic CRF framework for recognizing segmented gestures. The latent dynamic conditional random fields (LDCRF)(Morency, Quattoni, & Darrell, 2007) extend HCRFs further for recognizing gestures from a continuous unsegmented stream. More recently, (Natarajan & Nevatia, 2008a) embeds complex shape and flow features into a CRF and demonstrated encouraging results for recognizing human actions in cluttered scenes with dynamic backgrounds.

In this chapter, we present the different models explored in previous work in a unified way, and discuss the relationships between these models. We will then discuss algorithms for learning and inference in these models, and show how the various algorithms presented in earlier papers are special cases. Finally we will present experimental results from various domains in which the models have been applied. Here we will also discuss the low-level features used in these methods.

GRAPHICAL MODELS REPRESENTATION

A *graphical Model* is a graph that represents the dependence and independence assumptions among a set of random variables $\{V_1,...,V_n\}$. The value of each variable V_i depends only its neighbors. More formally, a graphical model factorizes the joint probability $P(V_1,...,V_n)$ into a product of conditional probabilities for each node:

$$P(V_1,...,V_n)=\prod_{i=1}^{n}P(V_u\,\big|\,\mathrm{Pa}(V_i))\qquad(1)$$

where $\mathrm{Pa}(V_i)$ denotes the set of nodes that are parents of V_i. The graph in this factorization is restricted to be a *directed acyclic graph* (*DAG*) and is commonly called as Bayesian networks (*BN*). Instead of restricting the factors $P(V_i\mid \mathrm{Pa}(V_i))$ to be probabilities, we can generalize them to be *potential functions* $\phi_k\{v_{\{c\}}\}$ with arbitrary structure, where c is a clique in the set of possible cliques of nodes C that are connected to each other:

$$P(V_1,...,V_n)=\frac{1}{Z}\prod_{c\in C}\phi_k\{\nu_{\{c\}}\}\qquad(2)$$

where Z is a normalization constant. It is customary to express the potentials in the exponential form as:

$$P(V_1,...,V_n)=\frac{1}{Z}\prod_{c\in C}\exp\left(\sum_k w_k f_k(\nu_{\{c\}})\right)\qquad(3)$$

where w_k is a weight and $f_k(v_{\{c\}})$ is a feature. In this form, the log-likelihood of the joint distribution is simply a weighted sum of the features $f_k(v_{\{c\}})$. The graph in this factorization is undirected and is generally referred to as *Markov random fields* (*MRF*).

In action recognition and many other applications, we have a set of random variables **X** called *observations* whose values are known, and variables **Y** called *states* whose values need to be inferred. This can be done by calculating the joint probability $P(\mathbf{X},\mathbf{Y})$ between the states and observations which are called *generative* models. Alternatively, we can calculate the conditional probability $P(\mathbf{Y}|\mathbf{X})$ which are *discriminative* models. *Hidden Markov models* (*HMM*) and *dynamic Bayesian networks* (*DBN*) are examples of generative models which generalize BNs in (1). *Conditional random fields* (*CRF*) are discriminative models which generalize MRFs in (2). We will now discuss the representation of DBNs, CRFs and their extensions in detail. Figure 1 illustrates the relationships between the graphical models that are discussed in this section.

Dynamic Bayesian Networks (DBN)

A *dynamic Bayesian network* (*DBN*) extends *Bayesian networks* (*BN*) to model the temporal evolution of random variables $Z_t=(U_t,X_t,Y_t)$, where U_t,X_t,Y_t correspond to the input, hidden and output variables respectively. A DBN is defined by the pair $(B_1,B_\rightarrow)$, where B_1 is a BN that defines the

Figure 1. Relationships between various graphical models discussed

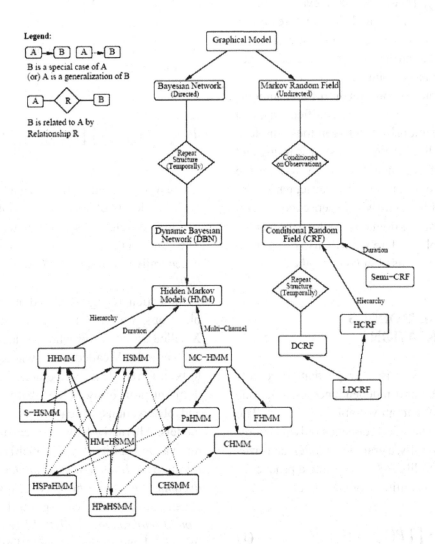

prior probability distribution, and $B_\rightarrow$ is also a BN over two time slices that defines $P(Z_t|Z_{t-1})$ as:

$$P(Z_t|Z_{t-1}) = \prod_{i=1}^{n} P(Z_u^i | \text{Pa}(Z_u^i)) \qquad (4)$$

where Z_t^i is the ith node at time t and can correspond to the input, hidden or output variables. $Pa(Z_t^i)$ are the parents of Z_t^i in the graph and $P(Z_t|Z_{t-1})$ is calculated using the parameters that

define the conditional probability distributions (CPDs) in $B_\rightarrow$.

The nodes in $Pa(Z_t^i)$ can be in the current time slice or the previous one since we make the first-order Markov assumption. This model can however be generalized to allow current state to depend on states from earlier time slices. The parameters of the CPDs are constant and do not vary with time. Thus the structure of $B_\rightarrow$ repeats over time. The probability distribution over time T is obtained by unrolling $B_\rightarrow$

$$P(Z_{1:T}) = \prod_{t=1}^{T} \prod_{i=1}^{n} P(Z_t^i \mid \mathrm{Pa}(Z_t^i)) \qquad (5)$$

Equation (5) represents the probability of a state sequence in a DBN.

Hidden Markov Models (HMM)

Hidden Markov models (HMM) are a special case of DBN, where a single variable represents the hidden state at each instant. The HMM model Λ is defined by the tuple-

$$\Lambda = (Q, O, A, B, \pi) \qquad (6)$$

where,

- Q = the set of possible states
- O = the set of observation symbols
- A = the state transition probability matrix with $a_{ij} = P(q_{t+1} = j \mid q_t = i)$
- B = the observation probability distribution with $b_j(k) = P(o_t = k \mid q_t = j)$ and
- π = the initial state distribution.

It is straightforward to generalize this model to continuous (like *Gaussian*) output models. The parameter π correspond to the prior probability distribution B_1 in DBN, and A, B correspond to the parameters B_{\rightarrow}.

Hierarchical Hidden Markov Models

(Fine, Singer, & Tishby, 1998) introduced the hierarchical hidden Markov model (HHMM) to model complex multi-scale structure by including a hierarchy of hidden states, and (Bui et al., 2004) applied for activity recognition. Formally a HHMM with H levels can be represented by the tuples (Λ')-

$$\Lambda'_h = (Q_h, O_h, A_h, B_h, \pi_h) \qquad h = 1...H \qquad (7)$$

where Λ'$_h$ corresponds to the parameters at level h in the hierarchy. The parameters Q_h, O_h, A_h, B_h, π_h have similar interpretations as in HMMs, but the state transition at each level can also depend on the parent state at level (h-1) and the child state at level (h+1).

Hidden Semi-Markov Models

In traditional HMMs the first order Markov assumption implies that the duration probability of a state decays exponentially. The hidden semi-Markov models (HSMM) were proposed to alleviate this problem by introducing explicit state duration models. The HSMM model (Λ'') is specified by the tuple-

$$\Lambda''_h = (Q, O, A, B, D, \pi) \qquad (8)$$

Here D is the set of parameters representing the duration models. Variable transition hidden Markov models (VTHMM) (called Inhomogeneous HMM in (Ramesh & Wilpon, 1992)) provide an alternate method to model durations by making the transition probability A dependent on the duration:

$$a_{ij}(d) = P(q_{t+1} \mid q_t = i, d_t(i) = d) \qquad (9)$$

where, $1 <= i,j <= n$, $1 <= d <= D$. Inference in VTHMM is has lower complexity than HSMM due to this factorization, but the number of parameters to be learned is potentially higher than for HSMM.

Multichannel Hidden Markov Models

In the basic HMM, a single variable represents the state of the system at any instant. However, many interesting processes have multiple interacting processes and several multi-channel HMMs have been proposed to model these. These extensions basically generalize the HMM state to be a collection of state variables ($S_t = S_t^1, ..., S_t^C$). In their most general form, such extensions can be represented as-

$$\Lambda''' = (Q^C, O^C, A^C, B^C, \pi^C) \qquad (10)$$

where Q^C and O^C are the possible states and observations at channel c respectively and π^C represents the initial probability of channel c's states. A^C contains the transition probabilities over the composite states ($P([q_{t+1}^1, .., q_{t+1}^C] \| [q_t^1, .., q_t^C])$), and B^C contains the observation probabilities over the composite states ($P([o_t^1, .., o_t^C] \| [q_t^1, .., q_t^C])$). In this form, the learning as well as inferencing algorithms are exponential in C, and also result in poor performance due to over-fitting and large number of parameters to learn. The various multi-channel extensions typically introduce simplifying assumptions that help in factorizing the transition and observation probabilities.

Factorial hidden Markov models (FHMM) (Ghahramani & Jordan, 1996) factor the hidden state into multiple variables which are nominally coupled at the output. This allows factorizing A^C into C independent n*n matrices (n=number of states in each channel)-

$$P([q_{t+1}^1, ..., q_{t+1}^C] \| q_t^1, ..., q_t^C) = \prod_{c=1}^{C} P(q_{t+1}^C | q_t^C)$$

while the observation probabilities B^C are left unfactorized.

Parallel hidden Markov models (PaHMM) (Vogler & Metaxas, 1999) factor the HMM into multiple independent chains and hence allow factorizing both A^C and B^C. Thus we have,

$$P([q_{t+1}^1, ..., q_{t+1}^C] \| [q_t^1, ..., q_t^C]) = \prod_{c=1}^{C} P(q_{t+1}^C | q_t^C)$$

$$P([o_t^1, ..., o_t^C] \| [q_t^1, ..., q_t^C]) = \prod_{c=1}^{C} P(o_t^C | q_t^C) \qquad (11)$$

Coupled hidden Markov models (CHMM) (Brand et al., 1997) on the other hand factor the HMM into multiple chains where the current state of a chain depends on the previous state of all the chains. In CHMMs, each channel has its own observation sequence and hence B^C can be factorized. Like FHMM and PaHMM, they allow each channel to evolve independently and hence we have,

$$P([q_{t+1}^1, ..., q_{t+1}^C] \| [q_t^1, ..., q_t^C]) = \prod_{i=1}^{C} P(q_{t+1}^i | [q_t^1, ..., q_t^C])$$

$$(12)$$

Further, they assume that the interaction between channels i and j is independent of the interaction between i and k. Hence we can further simplify the transition probabilities-

$$P(q_{t+1}^i | [q_t^1, ..., q_t^C]) = \prod_{j=1}^{C} P(q_{t+1}^i | q_t^j) \qquad (13)$$

With this simplification, we can have a n*n transition matrix for each pair of channels i and j and hence factorize A^C into C^2 n*n matrices. One issue with this formulation is that the RHS does not sum to 1 over all q_{t+1}^c and needs to be normalized. Alternate methods (Zhong, 2002) (Saul, 1999) for factoring replace the joint probability with a weighted sum of the marginal probabilities-

$$P(q_{t+1}^c | [q_t^1, ..., q_t^C]) = \prod_{c'=1}^{C} \theta_{c,c'} P(q_{t+1}^c | q_t^{c'}) \qquad (14)$$

This introduces C^2 additional parameters to learn/set. The original formulation in equation (13) however has been successfully used in many applications since it provides a "score" that can approximate the log-likelihood well in many domains.

Hierarchical Multichannel Hidden Semi-Markov Models

The hierarchical multi-channel hidden semi-Markov models (HM-HSMM) combine duration modeling, multi-channel interactions and hierarchical structure into a single model structure. In the most general form, they can be described by a set of parameters of the form-

$$\Lambda_h'''' = (Q_h^C, O_h^C, A_h^C, B_h^C, D_h^C, \pi_h^C) \quad h \in 1... H$$

$$(15)$$

where, h is the hierarchy index, c is the number of channels at level h, and the parameters have interpretations similar to before. Each channel at a higher level can be formed by a combination of channels at the lower level. Also, the duration models at each level are optional. Further, the channels at each level in the hierarchy maybe factorized using any of the methods discussed above (PaHMM, CHMM etc). It can be seen that Λ'''' presents a synthesis of Λ', Λ'' and Λ'''.

(Duong et al., 2005) introduced the Switching-HSMM (S-HSMM) which simultaneously addresses duration modeling and hierarchical organization. S-HSMM represents activities in 2-layers with the lower layer containing a HSMM and the upper layer containing a Markov model. Thus we have,

$$\Lambda_{lower}^{S-HSMM} = (Q_{lower}, O_{lower}, A_{lower}, B_{lower}, D_{lower}, \pi_{lower})$$
$$\Lambda_{upper}^{S-HSMM} = (Q_{upper}, O_{upper}, A_{upper}, B_{upper}, \pi_{upper})$$

$$(16)$$

CHSMM (Natarajan & Nevatia, 2007b) is a multi-channel HMM similar to CHMM where each channel has states with explicitly specified duration models. This can be specified by the tuple-

$$\Lambda^{CHSMM} = (Q^C, O^C, A^C, B^C, D^C, \pi^C) \qquad (17)$$

where the parameters Q^C, O^C, A^C, B^C, Π^C are defined as before. D^C contains a set of parameters of the form $P(d_i^c = k | q_t^c = i)$, i.e the probability of state i in channel c having a duration k. Further, A^C and B^C can be factorized in any of the methods discussed before.

HSPaHMM (Natarajan & Nevatia, 2007a) has 2 layers with multiple HMMs at the lower layer and HSMM at the upper layer and has the following set of parameters-

$$\Lambda_{lower}^{HSPaHMM} = (Q_{lower}^C, O_{lower}^C, A_{lower}^C, B_{lower}^C, \pi_{lower}^C)$$

$$\Lambda_{upper}^{HSPaHMM} = (Q_{upper}, O_{upper}, A_{upper}, B_{upper}, D_{upper}, \pi_{upper})$$

$$(18)$$

HPaHSMM (Natarajan & Nevatia, 2007a) contains multiple HSMMs at the lower layer and a single Markov chain at the upper layer and hence has the following set of parameters-

$$\Lambda_{lower}^{HPaHSMM} = (Q_{lower}^C, O_{lower}^C, A_{lower}^C, B_{lower}^C, D_{lower}^C, \pi_{lower}^C)$$
$$\Lambda_{upper}^{HPaHSMM} = (Q_{upper}, O_{upper}, A_{upper}, B_{upper}, \pi_{upper})$$

$$(19)$$

Figure 2 illustrates the graphical structure of the HMM extensions discussed, unrolled over time.

Conditional Random Fields (CRF)

A *conditional random field (CRF)* (Lafferty, McCallum, & Pereira, 2001) is an undirected graphical model similar to MRF in equation (2), conditioned on a set of observations. Thus, if the random variable Y denotes the states/labels and X denotes the observations, a graph $G=(V,E)$ is a CRF factorizes the conditional probability $P(\mathbf{Y}|\mathbf{X})$ as-

$$P(\mathbf{Y}|\mathbf{X}) = \frac{1}{Z(X)} \prod_{c \in C} \exp\left(\sum_k \lambda_k f_k(y_{\{c\}}, \mathbf{X}) \right) \quad (20)$$

Figure 2. Structure of a) HMM b) HSMM c) PaHMM d) PaHSMM e) CHMM f) CHSMM g) HSPaHMM h) HPaHSMM - squares are observations, circles states, rounded rectangles are states over some duration

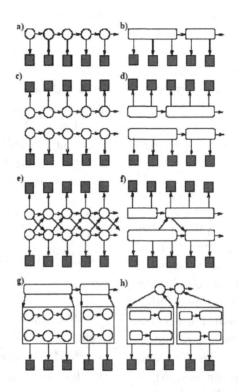

Here V is the set of vertices and E is the set of edges in G, $f_k(y_{\{c\}}, \mathbf{X})$ are features and λ_k are their corresponding weights. The features $f_k(y_{\{c\}}, \mathbf{X})$ are typically classified into observation features $f_k(y_i, \mathbf{X})$ and transition features $g_k(y_i, y_j, \mathbf{X})$-

$$P(\mathbf{Y}|\mathbf{X}) = \frac{1}{Z(X)} \exp\left(\sum_{k \in V} \lambda_k f_k(y_{\{c\}}, \mathbf{X}) + \sum_{i,j \in E} \mu_{i,j} g_k(y_i, y_j, \mathbf{X}) \right)$$

(21)

As the names suggest, $f_k(y_i, \mathbf{X})$ corresponds to the affinity between the state y_i and the observations $\mathbf{X}$, while $g_k(y_i, y_j, \mathbf{X})$ corresponds to the affinity between neighboring nodes having values y_i and y_j given the observations $\mathbf{X}$. λ and μ are the corresponding weights. CRF is also an undirected version of HMM which generalizes the observation and transition probabilities to potentials.

Dynamic Conditional Random Fields (DCRF)

A *dynamic conditional random field (DCRF)* (Sutton, Rohanimanesh, & McCallum, 2004) is an undirected graphical model where the structure and parameters repeat over time. If C denotes a set of cliques in a graph G, $F=\{f_k(y_{t,c}, \mathbf{X}, t)\}$ be a set of features and λ the set of weights, (C, F, λ) defines DCRF as-

$$P(\mathbf{Y}|\mathbf{X}) = \frac{1}{Z(X)} \prod_t \prod_{c \in C} \exp\left(\sum_k \lambda_k f_k(y_{t,c}, \mathbf{X}, t) \right)$$

(22)

Note that the primary difference between (20) and (22) is in the product over time t.

Hidden Conditional Random Fields (HCRF)

Hidden conditional random fields (HCRF) (Quattoni, Collins, & Darrell, 2004) learn a mapping between the observations **X** and class labels $y\varepsilon Y$ by introducing an additional set of hidden states $\mathbf{h}=\{h_1..h_m\}$. It models the conditional probability $P(y|x)$ as-

$$P_\lambda(y|x)=\sum_h P(y,h|x)=\frac{\sum_h \exp(\Psi(y,h,x))}{\sum_{h,y'\in\mathbf{Y}} \exp(\Psi(y',h,x))}$$

(23)

The hidden states h allow us to model underlying structure of each class, while the potential function $\psi(y,h,x)$ captures the affinity between the label, observations and the hidden states.

Latent Dynamic Conditional Random Fields (LDCRF)

The *latent dynamic conditional random fields* (*LDCRF*) (Morency et al., 2007) combine DCRF and HCRF and allow recognizing a continuous stream of gestures (or other labels), while simultaneously modeling the hidden structure of each class. It is defined as-

$$P(y|x)=\sum_h P(y|h,x)P(h|x)$$

(24)

If the classes y_i do not share the hidden states h_j, then each y will have a distinct set of hidden states H_{yi}. Thus we have,

$$P(y|h,x)=1, \quad \text{if } h \in H_y$$
$$= 0, \quad \text{otherwise}$$

(25)

Figure 3. Structure of a) CRF b) semi-CRF c) HCRF d) LDCRF

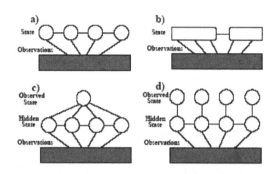

and $P(h|x)$ is defined using the CRF formulation as:

$$P(h|x)=\frac{1}{Z(X)}\prod_{c\in C}\exp\left(\sum_k \lambda_k f_k(h_{\{k\}},\mathbf{X})\right)$$

(26)

Figure 3 illustrates the graphical structure of the CRF extensions discussed in this section.

INFERENCE IN GRAPHICAL MODELS

We will now discuss algorithms for inference in the graphical models discussed. The content of this section is intended to give the reader a general idea of the algorithms without focusing on the details for the individual models. We refer interested readers to the individual papers, as well as the tutorial on DBNs presented in (Murphy, 2002) for a detailed review of various inference algorithms.

Let $\mathbf{X}=\{x_1,..,x_m\}$ denote the set of observed variables and $\mathbf{Y}=\{y_1,..,y_n\}$ denote the set of *hidden* variables whose values need to be computed in a graphical model. Inference in graphical models involves computing the following quantities:

Marginal Probability:

$$P(X) = \sum_Y P(Y, X) \qquad (27)$$

Conditional Probability:

$$P(Y|X) = \frac{P(Y, X)}{\sum_Y P(Y, X)} \qquad (28)$$

Maximum a posteriori (MAP) probability:

$$P^*(X) = \max_Y P(Y, X) \qquad (29)$$

In action recognition and other time-series analysis problems, we have a series of observations $\mathbf{X} = \{x_1, .., x_T\}$ and we need to compute the *state sequence* $\mathbf{Y} = \{y_1, .., y_T\}$, where each y_t can be a multi-dimensional vector of values representing the state at time t. Further, we are interested in computing the quantities $P(y_t|X_{1:t})$, $P(y_t|X_{1:T})$ and $max_{y\{1:T\}} P(Y_{1:T}, X_{1:T})$, which are instances or special cases of the quantities in equations (27)-(28).

Forward-Backward Algorithm

The simplest algorithm for exact inference in HMM, DBN, CRF and other graphical models is the *forward-backward* algorithm used commonly in HMMs. This involves recursively computing forward variables $\alpha(y_t)$:

$$\alpha(y_t) = \left\{ \sum_{y_{t-1}} \alpha(y_{t-1}) \psi(y_{t-1}, y_t, X) \right\} \varphi(y_t, X) \quad (30)$$

and backward variables $\beta(y_t)$:

$$\beta(y_t) = \sum_{y_{t+1}} \psi(y_t, y_{t+1}, X) \varphi(y_{t+1}, X) \beta(y_{t+1}) \quad (31)$$

where $\psi(y_{t-1}, y_t, \mathbf{X})$ corresponds to the transition potential in undirected graphical models like CRFs and the transition probability $P(y_t| y_{t-1})$ in directed graphical models, and $\phi(y_t, \mathbf{X})$ is the local evidence for state y_t at time t in undirected graphical models and the observation probability $P(x_t| y_t)$ in directed graphical models.

The forward variables $\alpha(y_t)$ correspond to the probability $P(x_{1:t}|y_t)$ of being in state y_t at time t based on the observations upto time t, while the backward variables $\beta(y_t)$ correspond to the probability $P(x_{t+1:T}|y_t)$ and correspond to the probability of generating the observations from time $(t+1)$ to T, given state that the state at time t is y_t. From the forward and backward variables the marginal probability $P(y_t)$ can be computed as:

$$P(y_t) = \frac{\alpha(y_t)\beta(y_t)}{\sum_{y_t} \alpha(y_t)\beta(y_t)} \qquad (32)$$

The MAP probability can be obtained by computing variables $\delta(y_t)$ obtained by replacing the sum in equation (30) with *max*:

$$\delta(y_t) = \left\{ \max_{y_{t-1}} \delta(y_{t-1}) \psi(y_{t-1}, y_t, X) \right\} \varphi(y_t, X)$$

$$(33)$$

This corresponds to the *Viterbi* algorithm used for computing the MAP path in HMMs. If there are $|Y|$ possible states, a sequence of T observations takes $O(T|Y|^2)$ time for inference.

In simple HMMs and CRFs, the state y_t corresponds to the value assigned to a *single* variable with discrete, finite domain. In DBNs in general and the various multi-channel HMMs as well as DCRFs, the state is represented by the values assigned to a variable vector with C channels $\{s_t\}_{c=1..C}$. In hierarchical HMMs (HHMM) and HCRFs with H levels, the state y_t is represented by the vector $\{y_t^h\}_{h=1..H}$. In semi-Markov models that explicitly model durations, the state y_t is represented by the tuple $[s_t, d_t]$ where s_t is the value assigned to the state and d_t corresponds to the time left to be in state s_t. The transition potential $\psi(y_t, y_{t+1}, \mathbf{X})$ is then defined as:

$$\psi(y_t, y_{t+1}, X) = \psi(s_t, s_{t+1}, X)\psi(s_{t+1}, d_{t+1})$$
$$= 1$$
$$= 0$$

$d_t = 1$

$d_t \neq 1, s_t = s_{t+1}$

otherwise (34)

Thus, in each of the basic extensions of HMMs and CRFs, the forward-backward algorithm can be directly applied for inference by enhancing the state representation appropriately. For CHSMM (Natarajan & Nevatia, 2007b) which combines CHMM with HSMM, the state is a combination of the multi-channel and HSMM representations - $[\{s_t\}_{c=1..C}, d_t]$ and for the more general HM-HSMMs (Natarajan & Nevatia, 2007a) the state is represented as $[\{ s_t \}_c, d_t]^h$ for *c=1..C* and *h=1..H*.

Belief Propagation (BP)

We showed so far how the basic forward-backward algorithm in equations (30)-(31) can be applied for inference in various graphical models by extending the state representation appropriately. While these extensions are intuitive, the resulting inference complexity is exponential in H (the number of levels) in HHMMs and C in multi-channel HMMs. This is addressed by factorizing the general α and β variables by taking advantage of the specific structure of the models. These algorithms are typically special cases of the *belief propagation* (Pearl, 1988) algorithm, also called as the *sum-product* algorithm. Each of the factorizations define the *neighbors* for each hidden node y_i and compute messages m_{ij} from hidden node y_i to node y_j:

$$m(y_i, y_j) = \sum_{y_i} \psi_{ij}(y_i, y_j, X) \prod_{k \in N(i) \backslash j} m(y_k, y_i) \quad (35)$$

where $N(i)$ is the set of neighbors of node i, and $\psi_{ij}(y_i, y_j, \mathbf{X})$ corresponds to the transition potential

in undirected graphical models and the transition probability $P(y_j \mid y_i)$ in directed graphical models.

The message m_{ij} in effect accumulates the messages from all neighbors of node i except j and then sends it to node j. The marginal probability at node i is proportional to the product of all incoming messages to node i:

$$P(y_i) = k\varphi_i(y_i, X) \prod_{j \in N(i)} m_{ji}(y_i) \quad (36)$$

where k is a normalization constant and $\phi_i(y_i, \mathbf{X})$ is the local evidence at node i in undirected graphical models and the observation probability $P(x_i|y_i)$ in directed graphical models. The MAP probabilities can be computed by replacing the sum in equation (35) with *max*.

The belief propagation algorithm is guaranteed to converge to the correct MAP probabilities in graphical models with tree-like structures, and also shows good empirical performance in graphs with cycles (Murphy, Weiss, & Jordan, 1999). For example (Wainwright, Jaakkola, & Willsky, 2001) presents a *tree-based reparameterization* (*TRP*) approach for inference in such graphical models with cycles by repeatedly sending messages on different spanning trees of the original graphical model, until convergence and (Sutton et al., 2004) successfully used belief propagation with TRP for inference in DCRFs.

Generalized Belief Propagation (GBP)

(Yedidia, Freeman, & Weiss, 2000) explains the surprisingly good performance of belief propagation even in graphical models with cycles, by showing that BP converges to a stationary point of an approximate free energy, known as *Bethe free energy* in statistical physics. The authors build on their insight to present a generalization of BP called *generalized belief propagation* (*GBP*), whose convergence point corresponds to a stationary point in the more general *Kikuchi free energy*. GBP works by sending messages between *cliques* of hidden nodes instead of between single nodes:

$$m(r,s) = \left[\sum_{y_{r\backslash s}} \psi_{r\backslash s}(y_{r\backslash s}, X) \prod_{m(r'',s'') \in M(r)\backslash M(s)} m(r'',s'') \right] \Big/ \prod_{m(r',s') \in M(r,s)} m(r',s')$$

(37)

where,

- *r,s,r',s',r'',s''* are *regions* or *cliques* of nodes.
- *m(r,s)* is a message between a region *r* and its *direct sub-region s*, i.e. s\subset r, and \ neg\exists s' s.t. s\subset s'.
- r\ s indicates all nodes that are in region *r* but not in *s*.
- *M(r)* denotes the set of messages *m(r',s')* that start outside region *r* and goes inside *r*, i.e. r \s \cap r=\emptyset, s \subseteq r.
- *M(r,s)* is the set of messages that start in a subregion of *r* and also belong to *M(s)*.
- *M(r)\M(s)* is the set of messages that are in *M(r)* but not in *M(s)*.

The belief *b(r)* in a region *r* is computed as:

$$b(r) = k\varphi_r(r) \prod_{m(r',s') \in M(r)} m(r',s')$$

(38)

where *k* is a normalization constant. The messages are updated starting with the messages into the smallest regions first. It is easy to see that equations (37), (38) generalize (35), (36) by using cliques of nodes instead of single nodes. The GBP algorithm can give significantly more accurate marginal probabilities than BP based on the choice of regions, with a potentially higher computational cost.

LEARNING IN GRAPHICAL MODELS

We will now turn our attention to learning in graphical models, which involves two problems:

1. **Structure learning** which involves learning the structure of the graphical model such as number of states, number of levels of hierarchy, number of channels, etc.
2. **Parameter learning** which involves learning model parameters including the weights or probabilities of the observation and transition potentials, assuming that the basic structure of the model is known.

Structure learning is complex and requires a large training set, which is difficult to get in activity recognition applications. We will focus only on parameter learning in graphical models.

The choice of the learning algorithm depends on the nature of the training data as well as the model:

- **Supervised vs. unsupervised:** If training data contains only the observation sequence *unsupervised* learning algorithms, typically based on *expectation-maximization* (*EM*) are used. If full or partial annotations of the state sequence are also available *supervised* learning algorithms, typically based on *gradient-descent* are used.
- **Generative vs. discriminative:** Generative models compute the *joint* probability $P(\mathbf{Y},\mathbf{X})$ between the observations $\mathbf{X}$ and state sequence $\mathbf{Y}$, while discriminative models compute the *conditional* probability $P(\mathbf{Y}|\mathbf{X})$.

While not necessary, the generative models, namely HMMs and their extensions are typically trained using the unsupervised EM-based algorithms while the discriminative CRFs are trained using supervised gradient-descent methods. We will now discuss these methods in the following subsections.

Expectation Maximization (EM)

Expectation maximization (*EM*) is a well known iterative algorithm for learning parameters in probabilistic models with hidden or *latent* variables. The EM procedure consists of the following steps:

a. Initialize parameters.
b. Repeat until convergence:
    1. **E-Step:** Estimate the expected value of the latent variables given the current parameter values.
    2. **M-Step:** Given estimates of latent variables, re-estimate parameters to maximize the likelihood of training data.

The time taken to converge as well as the quality of the convergence point (local *vs.* global maximum) depends on the parameter initialization. We will now specify the EM algorithm formally. Let **X** denote the observed variables, **Y** denote the hidden variables and θ denote the parameter vector for the probability distribution. During the *E-step* in the algorithm above, we compute the expected value of the log-likelihood of the joint probability $P(\mathbf{X},\mathbf{Y}|\theta)$, given the current parameter assignment θ_n:

$$Q(\theta) = \sum_{Y} p(Y|X,\theta_n) \log p(X,Y|\theta) \qquad (39)$$

We then re-estimate the parameter assignment θ_{n+1} in the *M-Step* as:

$$\theta_{n+1} = \arg\max_{\theta} Q(\theta) \qquad (40)$$

The estimation of the joint probability $P(\mathbf{X},\mathbf{Y}|\theta)$ depends on the structure of the individual probability distributions. The *Baum-Welch* algorithm

used for parameter re-estimation in HMMs is a special case of the EM algorithm. This works by first computing the forward and backward variables α and β as in equations (30) and (31) respectively. From these, we compute variables χ and ξ:

$$\gamma(y_t = i) = \frac{\alpha(y_t = i)\beta(y_t = i)}{\sum_{y_t} \alpha(y_t)\beta(y_t)} \qquad (41)$$

$$\xi(y_t = i, y_{t+1} = j) = \frac{\alpha(y_t = i)\psi(y_t = i, y_{t+1} = j, X)\varphi(y_{t+1} = j, X)\beta(y_{t+1} = j)}{\sum_{y_t}\sum_{y_{t+1}} \alpha(y_t)\psi(y_t, y_{t+1}, X)\varphi(y_{t+1}, X)\beta(y_{t+1})}$$

$$(42)$$

where χ ($y_t=i$) is the probability of being in state i at time t and ξ ($y_t=i,y_{t+1}=j$) is the probability of being in state i at time t and state j at time ($t+1$). In HMMs, the observation potential $\phi(y_t=i,\mathbf{X})$ corresponds to the *observation probability* $P(O_t|y_t=i)$ and the transition potential $\psi(y_t=i,y_{t+1}=j,\mathbf{X})$ corresponds to the *transition probability* $P(y_{t+1}=j|y_t=i)$. $P(O_t=o|y_t=i)$ and $P(y_{t+1}=j|y_t=i)$ in addition to the probability of starting in state i - $P(y_1=i)$ are the parameters that define the HMM. These can be re-estimated using EM as (Rabiner, 1989):

Observation Probability:

$$P(o|i) = \left\{ \sum_{\substack{t=1 \\ s.t.O_t=o}}^{T} \gamma(y_t = i) \right\} / \left\{ \sum_{t=1}^{T} \gamma(y_t = i) \right\}$$

$$(43)$$

Transition Probability:

$$P(j|i) = \left\{ \sum_{t=1}^{T-1} \xi(y_t = i, y_{t+1} = j) \right\} / \left\{ \sum_{t=1}^{T} \gamma(y_t = i) \right\}$$

$$(44)$$

Initial Probability:

$$P(y_1 = i) = \gamma(y_1 = i) \qquad (45)$$

Equations (43)-(45) is for HMMs where the state is represented by a single value, and the possible observations are from a discrete, finite domain. It is straightforward to generalize these equations for continuous observations. In case of more complex HMM extensions and DBNs, the specific re-estimation equations can be quite complex, but they are similar to the equations above in concept, that sum out the free-variables. (Fine et al., 1998),(Bui et al., 2004) use a generalization of the forward-backward algorithm called the *inside-outside* algorithm, typically used in *stochastic context free grammars* (*SCFG*), for parameter estimation in HHMMs. This has a complexity of $O(T^3)$, but (Murphy & Paskin, 2001) presents an $O(T)$ algorithm for HHMMs that is based on the forward-backward algorithm presented here.

Learning by Gradient Descent

Gradient Descent algorithms are typically used for parameter learning in *discriminative* models, primarily CRFs. Let us first consider training the parameters of $\lambda = \{\lambda_k\}$ of a CRF, given training data $D = \{\mathbf{x}^{(d)}, \mathbf{y}^{(d)}\}_{d=1}^{N}$, where $\mathbf{x}^{(d)}$ is the observation sequence and $\mathbf{y}^{(d)}$ is the label sequence. This is done by optimizing the conditional log-likelihood:

$$L(\lambda) = \sum_d \log p_\gamma \left(y^{(d)} \middle| x^{(d)} \right) \qquad (46)$$

This function is convex when the values $\mathbf{y}^{(d)}$ are available in the training data. Hence the local optimum obtained by gradient descent optimization of $L(\lambda)$ is also the global optimum. The derivative of $L(\lambda)$ with respect to a parameter λ_k is given by:

$$\frac{\partial L}{\partial \lambda_k} = \sum_d \sum_c f_k \left(y_c^{(d)} \middle| x^{(d)} \right) - \sum_d \sum_c \sum_{y_c^{(d)}} p_\lambda \left(y_c^{(d)} \middle| x^{(d)} \right) f_k \left(y_c^{(d)} \middle| x^{(d)} \right) \qquad (47)$$

Here, $y_c^{(d)}$ is an assignment to clique $\mathbf{y}_c$ in $\mathbf{y}^{(d)}$ and $\mathbf{y}_c$ ranges over possible assignments to clique $\mathbf{y}_c$. The factor $p_\lambda(y_c^{(d)}|\mathbf{x}^{(d)})$ requires computing marginal probabilities as specified in equation (32). There are several techniques for optimizing L, but L-BFGS (Lu, Nocedal, Zhu, & Byrd, 1995) has been shown to outperform others in several previous works.

It is straightforward to extend this approach for parameter learning in DCRFs in the fully observed case where $\mathbf{y}$ include observed values for all variables in the state representation as the function $L(\lambda)$ is still convex. The derivative of $L(\lambda)$ is given by:

$$\frac{\partial L}{\partial \lambda_k} = \sum_d \sum_c f_k (y_{t,c}^{(d)}, x^{(d)}, t) - \sum_d \sum_c \sum_{y_{t,c}} p_\lambda \left(y_{t,c}^{(d)} \middle| x^{(d)} \right) f_k (y_{t,c}^{(d)}, x^{(d)}, t)$$

$$(48)$$

The gradient descent algorithm for parameter re-estimation in CRFs and DCRFs is well understood and optimal when annotations for all variables in the state representation are available. However, in most action recognition scenarios only partial annotations of the state are available. HCRFs (Quattoni et al., 2004)(Wang et al., 2006) are applicable under such conditions and learn a mapping of observations $\mathbf{x} = \{x_1, x_2, \dots x_m\}$ to class labels $y \backslash \mathrm{in} \mathbf{Y}$ as follows:

$$P_\lambda \left(y \middle| x \right) = \sum_h P_\lambda \left(y, h \middle| x \right) = \frac{\sum_h e^{\Psi(y,h,\mathbf{X};\lambda)}}{\sum_{y' \in \mathbf{Y}, h \in \mathbf{h}} e^{\Psi(y',h,\mathbf{X};\lambda)}} \qquad (49)$$

where $\mathbf{h} = \{h_1, h_2, \dots h_m\}$, each $h_i \backslash \mathrm{in} \mathbf{h}$ are set of hidden variables which are not annotated. The parameters λ can then be re-estimated by substituting for $P_\lambda(y|\mathbf{x})$ from equation (49) in (46).

LDCRFs (Morency et al., 2007) generalize HCRFs by learning a mapping between an observation sequence $\mathbf{x} = \{x_1, x_2, \dots x_m\}$ to a label sequence $\mathbf{y} = \{y_1, y_2, \dots y_m\}$, given a set of hidden variables $\mathbf{h} = \{h_1, h_2, \dots h_m\}$:

$$P_\lambda(\mathbf{y}|\mathbf{x}) = \sum_{\mathbf{h}} P_\lambda(\mathbf{y}|\mathbf{h},\mathbf{x})P_\lambda(\mathbf{h}|\mathbf{x}) \qquad (50)$$

If the set of possible hidden states H_{yj} corresponding to a class label y_j are disjoint, we have by definition $P_\Lambda(\mathbf{y}|\mathbf{h},\mathbf{x})$ for sequences which have any $h_j \notin H_{y\_j}$. Thus we can simplify (50):

$$P_\lambda(\mathbf{y}|\mathbf{x}) = \sum_{\mathbf{h}:\forall h_j \in H_{y_j}} P_\lambda(\mathbf{h}|\mathbf{x}) \qquad (51)$$

The parameters of the LDCRF can then be re-estimated by substituting (51) in (46). The training of HCRF and LDCRF are intuitive extensions of CRF training. However, the log-likelihood L(Λ) in equation (46) is no longer convex under the partially observed case, and hence gradient descent converges only to a local minimum.

So far we discussed training CRFs using the traditional gradient descent approaches. While such discriminative models have shown improved performance over the generative models in several domains, they require a large training set before the improvements are observed (Ng & Jordan, 2001). It is difficult to obtain such large sets in many action recognition applications. However, CRFs provide a more flexible representation that allow complex potentials while HMMs restrict the parameters to be probabilities. In recent work, (Taycher, Demirdjian, Darrell, & Shakhnarovich, 2006)(Natarajan & Nevatia, 2008a) take advantage of domain constraints and train the transition and observation potentials *independently*} from suitable training data. This requires much smaller training set sizes, but still takes advantage of the representational flexibility of CRFs.

APPLICATIONS OF GRAPHICAL MODELS IN ACTIVITY RECOGNITION

So far in this chapter, we have discussed representation, inference and learning of various graphical models from a theoretical standpoint. We will now discuss specific applications of these models in-

cluding the features used as well as the application domain. A direct quantitative comparison of the models is difficult since the results are published in widely varying datasets. We will instead present a qualitative comparison of the models based on the results presented in the papers.

Generative Models (HMMs)

(Yamato, Ohya, & Ishii, 1992) presents one of the earliest applications of using graphical models for human action recognition in videos, by using a feature based bottom-up approach with HMMs. They first extract image features using 2D meshes in each video and and assign a codeword to them, to obtain the observation sequence. Then, they recognize the action by computing the log-likelihood for each of a set of pre-learned action HMMs and recognize the action corresponding to the HMM with the highest log-likelihood. They show impressive performance in distinguishing among 6 tennis strokes. (Schlenzig, Hunter, & Ishii, 1994) presents another early application of HMMs for recognizing gestures by updating a recursive filter based on extracted hand pose information.

While impressive, these early works applied HMMs for recognizing actions in a *temporally segmented* video sequence - i.e. the input sequences contained only one action. (Starner & Pentland, 1995) demonstrates HMMs for recognizing sentences from American Sign Language (ASL) from hand tracks obtained by tracking colored gloves in video. This is particularly impressive since their algorithm does not require costly "datagloves" or explicit modeling of fingers, and has high accuracy rates on sentences from a large 40 word lexicon. Further, both the inference and training were done using unsegmented ASL sentences. (Starner et al., 1998) built on this work and showed impressive results with explicit high-level grammar constraints as well as in unrestricted experiments.

The states of the HMMs in (Starner & Pentland, 1995)(Starner et al., 1998) correspond to the state of both hands, without explicitly modeling the fact that ASL gestures involve two, interacting hands. (Vogler & Metaxas, 1999) addressed this by introducing an extension of HMM called PaHMM for modeling processes occurring independently, in parallel. They apply it for ASL recognition by modeling the actions of each hand as parallel streams and trained the parameters appropriately. The independence assumption reduces the number of parameters in the model compared to HMMs, making it potentially more scalable for large vocabularies and their results demonstrate improved robustness for ASL recognition. (Vogler, Sun, & Metaxas, 2001) incorporates linguistic constraints from the *Movement-Hold* (Liddel & Johnson, 1989) model of ASL into the PaHMM framework and shows improved performance. (Vogler et al., 2001) also demonstrates the generality of the PaHMM framework by incorporating high-level constraints for gait recognition. The explicit use of high-level models and constraints in (Vogler et al., 2001) is in contrast to most other approaches using HMMs and other graphical models that focus on bottom-up learning from image features. (Brand et al., 1997) introduces the coupled HMM (CHMM) for modeling multiple *interacting* processes, in contrast to PaHMM which assumes that the processes are independent. (Brand, 1996) presents an "N-heads" dynamic programming algorithm for efficient inference and learning in CHMMs. (Brand et al., 1997)(Brand, 1996) demonstrate the advantages of CHMM over HMMs by rigorous testing in simulated data, and also for recognizing tai-chi gestures in video. The results also demonstrate that CHMM training is insensitive to parameter initialization in contrast to HMMs. (Rosario, Oliver, & Pentland, 1999) applied CHMMs for recognizing human interactions by training them first using synthetic data and then using the trained models for recognition in real videos, with no additional training or tuning.

Actions in most real world applications occur at multiple levels of abstraction and have a natural hierarchical structure. For example, a *walking* action by a person involves simultaneous limb motions, which in turn involves muscle motions and so on. This gap between the observations and higher-level semantic concepts has been addressed using variants of the hierarchical HMMs (HHMM). (Hongeng & Nevatia, 2003) recognizes events in video by first detecting simpler *primitive* events using Bayesian networks in each frame and then recognizes more complex *composite* from the primitive events using a hidden semi-Markov model (HSMM). This work is one of the earliest demonstrations of using explicit duration models for event recognition. Further, (Hongeng & Nevatia, 2003) also presents an algorithm for linear time inference in HSMM, if the duration model is uniform or Gaussian, and presents recognition results for monitoring vehicles in videos collected from an unmanned aerial vehicle (UAV), as well as in actions involving multiple interacting people like stealing. Action recognition at multiple levels has been addressed in several other works as well. (Oliver, Garg, & Horvitz, 2004) introduces the layered hidden Markov model (LHMM) to recognize actions at multiple temporal scales and abstraction levels. The activities at each level are classified using a HMM for that level. Further, only the lower-level actions can influence inference at the higher levels. (Oliver et al., 2004) applied LHMMs to recognize common office actions from multiple real-time streams including video, audio and computer interactions. (Bui et al., 2004) introduces an extension of hierarchical HMM (HHMM) that allows lower level states to share parents, making the hierarchical structure a lattice instead of a tree. (Nguyen, Phung, Venkatesh, & Bui, 2005) applied this extension of HHMM for recognizing actions in a typical indoor office environment, similar to (Oliver et al., 2004).

There has been recent work to combine the representational advantages of these different models in a single formalism. The switching hidden semi-Markov model (S-HSMM) (Duong et al., 2005) presents a two layer extension of HSMM and recognizes actions at different abstractions and also models action durations. (Duong et al., 2005) consider two possible duration models: the multinomial and the discrete Coxian distribution and demonstrate S-HSMM for recognizing human actions of daily living. (Natarajan & Nevatia, 2007b) presents the coupled hidden semi-Markov model (CHSMM) which combines HSMM and CHMM to simultaneously model multiple interacting processes as well as action durations. (Natarajan & Nevatia, 2007a) on the other hand introduce the hierarchical multi-channel hidden semi-Markov models (HM-HSMM) which simultaneously model action hierarchy, state durations and multi-channel interactions. (Natarajan & Nevatia, 2007a)(Natarajan & Nevatia, 2007b) present efficient algorithms for learning and inference in the combined models and demonstrate them for sign language recognition in a domain similar to (Vogler & Metaxas, 1999)(Vogler et al., 2001). They show good performance even with a small training set and simple features. Further, they incorporate high-level language constraints into their models similar to (Vogler et al., 2001).

In the models we discussed so far, the states are represented by variables with discrete, finite domains. In human motion analysis however, the joint locations of the human pose have continuous domains. This is typically addressed by discretizing the state space, but there have also been work done to use continuous state variables. (Pavlovic, Rehg, & MacCormick, 2000) learn models for human dynamics from *Mocap* data using switching linear dynamic systems (SLDS), and demonstrate their superiority over HMMs for visual tracking. More recently, (Turaga, Veeraraghavan, & Chellappa, 2007) also use linear dynamic systems (LDS) for clustering video sequences into activities. They do this by using a cascade of dynamical systems to represent a diverse class of actions. (Caillette, Galata, & Howard, 2008) introduce a 3D human body tracker that uses *variable length Markov model* (VLMM) to explain high-level behaviors over long intervals. This is done by automatically partitioning the parameter space into Gaussian

clusters, each of which representing an elementary motion. (Fossati, Dimitrijevic, Lepetit, & Fua, 2007) also use generative models to recover 3D motion of people seen from arbitrary viewpoints by a single camera. They do this by detecting key poses and then using a motion model to infer poses between consecutive detections.

Discriminative Models (CRF)

The various HMM extensions discussed so far model the joint probability $P(\mathbf{X}, \mathbf{Y})$ between the observations $\mathbf{X}$ and states $\mathbf{Y}$. This assumes that the observations $x_t \backslash in \mathbf{X}$ are independent of each other, which is unrealistic in many applications and the conditional random fields (CRF) (Lafferty et al., 2001) were introduced to directly model the conditional probability $P(\mathbf{Y}|\mathbf{X})$. CRFs have been successfully applied in a wide range of domains including natural language processing (e.g.(Lafferty et al., 2001)), document processing (e.g.(Sutton et al., 2004)), image classification (e.g.(Kumar & Hebert, 2003)), object segmentation (e.g.(Wang & Ji, 2005)), pose tracking (e.g.(Taycher et al., 2006)) among others. There has been several recent works in action recognition as well that attempt to replicate this success.

(Sminchisescu et al., 2005) presents one of the earliest applications of CRFs for action recognition, and demonstrates the effectiveness of CRFs for classifying not only distinct actions but also among subtle variations in a single action class. They train their models from synthetic data generated by rendering motion capture data for various actions, and recognize actions in videos by extracting shape context features (Belongie, Malik, & Puzicha, 2002) from silhouettes. Their results show that CRFs outperform HMMs as well as the maximum entropy Markov models(MEMM) (Mccallum, Freitag, & Pereira, 2000).

One key disadvantage of CRFs is that they need annotations of the entire state for training models, which is costly or even impractical for most action recognition applications. (Wang et al., 2006) introduce a discriminative hidden state approach for action recognition using hidden CRF (HCRF). HCRFs were originally introduced in (Quattoni et al., 2004) for object recognition, and (Wang et al., 2006) adapted them for recognition of human gestures. Each action/gesture in the HCRF contains a set of unobserved hidden states and the training data contains annotations only for the actions. They show superior performance of HCRFs over CRF and HMM for recognition of human arm gestures and head gestures. They also show that the performance improves significantly by using observations from window around the current frame instead of only the current frame.

While HCRFs capture the internal dynamics of gestures, they require pre-segmented sequences for training and inference. Thus they do not capture dynamics that involve transitions between different gestures. The latent dynamic CRF (LDCRF) (Morency et al., 2007) addresses this issue by combining HCRF with DCRF. LDCRF incorporates hidden state variables for each action and also learn the dynamics between the actions. (Morency et al., 2007) evaluated LDCRFs for recognizing human gestures from unsegmented video streams in the domains of head and eye gesture recognition. Their results demonstrate the advantages of LDCRFs over HMMs, CRFs as well as support vector machines (SVMs).

There has also been multi-channel CRF models explored in literature, similar to the HMM extensions discussed. (Wang & Suter, 2007) combines kernel principal component analysis (KPCA) based feature extraction with factorial CRF (FCRF) based motion modeling. The features are extracted from silhouette data, and FCRF models temporal sequences in multiple, interacting ways. They demonstrate their approach to recognize human actions robustly, with temporal, intra- and inter-person variations.

Discriminative continuous state models have also been developed in recent literature, similar to the generative LDS models discussed earlier. (Kim & Pavlovic, 2007) introduced conditional

state space models (CSSM) as a discriminative alternative to the generative state space models (SSM). They also present an efficient inference algorithm for CSSM and evaluate their method on synthetic data as well as for 3D pose tracking on *Mocap* data.

Combined Tracking and Action Recognition

The various applications that we discussed so far take a *bottom-up* approach to recognition where suitable image features are first extracted and then the graphical models are used for action recognition. Such approaches rely heavily on accurate extraction of low-level features such as silhouettes or tracks, which is unrealistic in many applications. In contrast, several *top-down* approaches have been proposed in recent work, which use high-level action models to guide low-level tracking and then use the feedback from the lower levels to recognize the action sequence. Such approaches are robust to low-level errors, but assume that only a known set of actions can take place in the domain.

(Zhao & Nevatia, 2002) presents a *tracking-as-recognition* approach where a hierarchical finite state machine is constructed from 3D motion capture data for each action. Actions in video sequences are then recognized by comparing the prior models with motion templates extracted from the video. (Zhao & Nevatia, 2002) shows very promising results in several difficult sequence, demonstrating the utility of the top-down approach. (Elgammal, Shet, Yacoob, & Davis, 2003) presents a related approach where the states of an HMM are represented with a set of pose exemplars and gestures in video are recognized by comparing the exemplars with image edge maps, using the *Hausdorff* distance. More recently, (Peursum, Venkatesh, & West, 2007) also takes a tracking-as-recognition approach for analyzing actions involving articulated motion. Here the actions are represented by a variant of HHMM known as the factored state HHMM (FS-HHMM) which represents possible transitions of the actor pose, which in turn is represented by a 3D body model with 29 degrees of freedom (for the joint angles). At each frame, the score for each pose is computed based on the overlap between the projected pose and the silhouette, and track poses and recognize actions by accumulating the scores.

(Natarajan & Nevatia, 2008b) combines ideas from (Zhao & Nevatia, 2002) and (Peursum et al., 2007) to present a top-down approach to simultaneously track and recognize articulated full-body human motion using learned action models. (Natarajan & Nevatia, 2008b) introduces the hierarchical variable transition hidden Markov model (HVT-HMM) that is a three-layered extension of the variable transition hidden Markov model

(VTHMM). The top-most layer of the HVT-HMM represents the composite actions and contains a single Markov chain, the middle layer represents the primitive actions which are modeled using a VTHMM whose state transition probability varies with time and the bottom-most layer represents the body pose transitions using a HMM. Figure 4 illustrates the HVT-HMM graphical structure. They represent the pose using a 23D body model similar to the 29D model used in (Peursum et al., 2007) and demonstrate their methods in the domain of two-handed military signals and in a domain with actions involving articulated motion of the entire body.

Each of the top-down approaches presented so far use fairly simple features extracted from silhouettes obtained by background subtraction.

Figure 4. Graphical structure of HVT-HMM

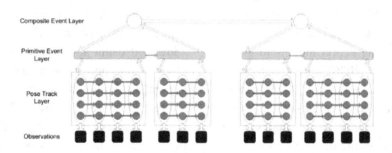

Figure 5. Unrolled graphical model of the SFD-CRF for pose tracking and recognition

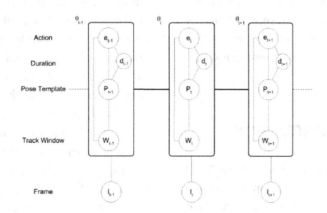

Actions in real world on the other hand, typically take place in cluttered environments with large variations in the orientation and scale of the actor. (Natarajan & Nevatia, 2008a) presents an approach to simultaneously track the actor, estimate the approximate pose and recognize actions that is robust to such variations, starting from a person detection in the standing pose. This approach first renders synthetic poses from multiple viewpoints using Mocap data for known actions and represent them in a Conditional Random Field (CRF) called the shape, flow, duration-conditional random field (SFD-CRF). Figure 5 illustrates the graphical structure of SFD-CRF. The observation potential of the SFD-CRF is computed using shape similarity and the transition potentials are computed using optical flow and these basic potentials are enhanced with terms to represent spatial and temporal constraints. The best sequence of actions using Viterbi search in the SFD-CRF and (Natarajan & Nevatia, 2008a) demonstrate the approach on videos from multiple viewpoints and in the presence of background clutter.

In contrast to using action models to guide tracking, (Chan et al., 2006) present a method for jointly recognizing events and also link fragmented tracklets into long duration tracks. Actions are represented with a DBN, which supplies data driven constraints for estimating the likelihood of possible tracklet matches. The event constraints are then combined with appearance and kinematic constraints, and the event model with the highest event score is recognized to have occurred if the likelihood score exceeds a threshold. (Chan et al., 2006) demonstrate the approach in a scene with airplane servicing actions with many non event actors.

SUMMARY AND CONCLUSION

In this chapter, we discussed a range of graphical models that have been used in action recognition applications, starting from the simplest HMMs to more complex models that address deficiencies inherent in the basic model. These extend HMMs to address a specific deficiency or combine earlier models and have shown promising results in action and gesture recognition. We presented these models in a unified way and discussed the relationships between them in terms of representational ability. We also discussed conditional random fields (CRF) which offer a discriminative alternative to HMMs and presented various CRF extensions. We then discussed inference and learning in both HMMs and CRFs, and the issues involved in training these models. We finally presented applications of these models in a range of domains as well as the features used to represent observations.

While graphical models provide a natural framework for representing high-level event constraints and model the uncertainty inherent in processing visual information, several open questions remain. The various HMM and CRF extensions discussed result in increased inference and learning complexity, which are typically addressed using approximations specific to the models and application domain which may not generalize to other models and domains. Further, the features used in many of the existing works are fairly simple and are typically dependent on fairly clean silhouettes. More work needs to be done to include more sophisticated and robust features in the graphical models. Further, current approaches are either top-down or bottom-up, but robust and scalable systems need to combine both approaches with feedback between different layers. Also, most of the published results are in fairly simple videos with static background and camera. A suitable standard action recognition dataset need to be collected that allow action recognition algorithms to be tested in a wide range of conditions and also allow for a quantitative comparison of their performance. Despite these deficiencies, graphical models have shown a lot of promise for action recognition and have been demonstrated to be robust in several domains.

REFERENCES

Belongie, S., Malik, J., & Puzicha, J. (2002). Shape matching and object recognition using shape contexts. *PAMI, 24*, 509–522.

Brand, M. (1996). *Coupled hidden Markov models for modeling interacting processes* (Tech. Rep. 405). MIT Media Lab Vision and Modeling.

Brand, M., Oliver, N., & Pentland, A. (1997). Coupled hidden markov models for complex action recognition. In *Proceedings of the CVPR* (pp. 994-999).

Bui, H., Phung, D., & Venkatesh, S. (2004). Hierarchical hidden markov models with general state hierarchy. In *Proceedings of the National Conference in Artificial Intelligence* (pp. 324-329).

Bui, H., Venkatesh, S., & West, G. (2002). Policy recognition in the abstract hidden markov model. *Journal of Artificial Intelligence Research, 17*, 451–499.

Caillette, F., Galata, A., & Howard, T. (2008). Real-time 3-d human body tracking using learnt models of behavior. *Computer Vision and Image Understanding, 109*(2), 112–125. doi:10.1016/j.cviu.2007.05.005

Chan, M., Hoogs, A., Bhotika, R., Perera, A., Schmiederer, J., & Doretto, G. (2006). Joint recognition of complex events and track matching. In *Proceedings of the 2006 IEEE Computer Society Conference on Computer Vision and Pattern Recognition - Volume 2 (CVPR'06)* (pp. 1615-1622).

Duong, T., Bui, H., Phung, D., & Venkatesh, S. (2005). Activity recognition and abnormality detection with the switching hidden semi-Markov model. In . *Proceedings of the CVPR, 1*, 838–845.

Elgammal, A., Shet, V., Yacoob, Y., & Davis, L. (2003). Learning dynamics for exemplar-based gesture recognition. In *Proceedings of the CVPR* (pp. 571-578).

Fine, S., Singer, Y., & Tishby, N. (1998). The hierarchical hidden markov model: Analysis and applications. *Machine Learning, 32*(1), 41–62. doi:10.1023/A:1007469218079

Fossati, A., Dimitrijevic, M., Lepetit, V., & Fua, P. (2007). Bridging the gap between detection and tracking for 3d monocular video-based motion capture. In *Proceedings of the CVPR*.

Ghahramani, Z., & Jordan, M. (1996). Factorial hidden markove models. In *Advances in Neural Information Processing Systems* (Vol. 8).

Hongeng, S., & Nevatia, R. (2003). Large-scale event detection using semi-hidden markov models. In *International Conference on Computer Vision* (Vol. 2, pp. 1455).

Intille, S., & Bobick, A. (2001). Recognizing planned, multi-person action. *Computer Vision and Image Understanding, 81*(3), 414–445. doi:10.1006/cviu.2000.0896

Kim, M., & Pavlovic, V. (2007). Conditional state space models for discriminative motion estimation. In . *Proceedings of the, ICCV*, 1–8.

Kumar, S., & Hebert, M. (2003). Discriminative random fields: A discriminative framework for contextual interaction in classification. In . *Proceedings of the, ICCV*, 1150–1157.

Lafferty, J., McCallum, A., & Pereira, F. (2001). Conditional random fields: Probabilistic models for segmenting and labeling sequence data. In *Proceedings of the ICML* (pp. 282-289).

Liddell, S., & Johnson, R. (1989). American Sign Language: The phonological base. *Sign Language Studies, 64*, 195–277.

Lu, P., Nocedal, J., Zhu, C., & Byrd, R. H. (1995). A limited memory algorithm for bound constrained optimization. *SIAM Journal on Scientific Computing, 16*, 1190–1208. doi:10.1137/0916011

Mccallum, A., Freitag, D., & Pereira, F. (2000). Maximum entropy markov models for information extraction and segmentation. In *Proceedings of the ICML* (pp. 591-598).

Moore, D., & Essa, I. (2002). Recognizing multitasked activities from video using recognizing multitasked activities from video using stochastic context-free grammar. In *American Association of Artificial Intelligence (AAAI) Conference.*

Morency, L.-P., Quattoni, A., & Darrell, T. (2007). Latent-dynamic discriminative models for continuous gesture recognition. In *Proceedings of the CVPR.*

Murphy, K. P. (2002). Dynamic Bayesian networks. In *Probabilistic Graphical Models.*

Murphy, K. P., & Paskin, M. A. (2001). Linear time inference in hierarchical HMMs. In *Proceedings of the NIPS.*

Murphy, K. P., Weiss, Y., & Jordan, M. I. (1999). "Loopy belief propagation for approximate inference: An empirical study," in *In Proceedings of Uncertainty in AI*, 467–475.

Natarajan, P., & Nevatia, R. (2007a). Hierarchical multi-channel hidden semi markov models. In *Proceedings of the IJCAI* (pp. 2562-2567).

Natarajan, P., & Nevatia, R. (2007b). Coupled hidden semi markov models for activity recognition. In *Proceedings of the WMVC.*

Natarajan, P., & Nevatia, R. (2008a). View and scale invariant action recognition using multiview shape-flow models. In *Proceedings of the CVPR.*

Natarajan, P., & Nevatia, R. (2008b). Online, real-time tracking and recognition of human actions. In *Proceedings of the WMVC.*

Ng, A. Y., & Jordan, M. I. (2001). On discriminative vs. generative classifiers: A comparison of logistic regression and naive bayes. In *Proceedings of the NIPS* (pp. 841-848).

Nguyen, N. T., Phung, D. Q., Venkatesh, S., & Bui, H. H. (2005). Learning and detecting activities from movement trajectories using the hierarchical hidden markov models. In *Proceedings of the CVPR (2)* (pp. 955-960).

Oliver, N., Garg, A., & Horvitz, E. (2004). Layered representations for learning and inferring office activity from multiple sensory channels. *Computer Vision and Image Understanding, 96*(2), 163–180. doi:10.1016/j.cviu.2004.02.004

Oliver, N. M., Rosario, B., & Pentland, A. (1998). Graphical models for recognizing human interactions. In *Proc. of Intl. Conference on Neural Information and Processing Systems (NIPS).*

Pavlovic, V., Rehg, J. M., & MacCormick, J. (2000). Learning switching linear models of human motion. In *Proceedings of the NIPS* (pp. 981-987).

Pearl, J. (1988). *Probabilistic Reasoning in Intelligent Systems: Networks of Plausible Inference.* San Francisco: Morgan Kaufmann.

Peursum, P., Venkatesh, S., & West, G. A. W. (2007). Tracking-as-recognition for articulated full-body human motion analysis. In *Proceedings of the CVPR.*

Quattoni, A., Collins, M., & Darrell, T. (2004). Conditional random fields for object recognition. In *Proceedings of the NIPS.*

Rabiner, L. R. (1989). A tutorial on hidden Markov models and selected applications in speech recognition. *Proceedings of the IEEE, 77*(2), 257–286. doi:10.1109/5.18626

Ramesh, P., & Wilpon, J. G. (1992). Modeling state durations in hidden markov models for automatic speech recognition. In *Proceedings of the ICASSP* (pp. 381-384).

Rosario, B., Oliver, N., & Pentland, A. (1999). A synthetic agent system for Bayesian modeling human interactions. In *Proceedings of the Third International Conference on Autonomous Agents (Agents'99)* (pp. 342-343).

Ryoo, M., & Aggarwal, J. (2006). Recognition of composite human activities through context-free grammar based representation. In *Proceedings of the 2006 IEEE Computer Society Conference on Computer Vision and Pattern Recognition - Volume 2 (CVPR'06)* (pp. 1709-1718).

Saul, M. J. L. (1999). Mixed memory markov models: decomposing complex stochastic processes as mixtures of simpler ones. *Machine Learning*, *37*(1), 75–87. doi:10.1023/A:1007649326333

Schlenzig, J., Hunter, E., & Ishii, K. (1994). Recursive identification of gesture inputs using hidden Markov models. In *Proc. Second Annual Conference on Applications Computer Vision* (pp. 187-104).

Sminchisescu, C., Kanaujia, A., Li, Z., & Metaxas, D. (2005). Conditional random fields for contextual human motion recognition. In . *Proceedings of the, ICCV*, 1808–1815.

Starner, T., & Pentland, A. (1995). Real-time american sign language recognition from video using hidden Markov models. In *Proceedings of the ISCV*.

Starner, T., Weaver, J., & Pentland, A. (1998). Real-time american sign language recognition using desk and wearable computer based video. *IEEE Transactions on Pattern Analysis and Machine Intelligence*, *20*(12), 1371–1375. doi:10.1109/34.735811

Sutton, C., Rohanimanesh, K., & McCallum, A. (2004). Dynamic conditional random fields: factorized probabilistic models for labeling and segmenting sequence data. In *Proceedings of the ICML* (p. 99).

Taycher, L., Demirdjian, D., Darrell, T., & Shakhnarovich, G. (2006). Conditional random people: Tracking humans with crfs and grid filters. In *Proceedings of the CVPR (1)* (pp. 222-229).

Turaga, P. K., Veeraraghavan, A., & Chellappa, R. (2007). From videos to verbs: Mining videos for activities using a cascade of dynamical systems. In *Proceedings of the CVPR*.

Vogler, C., & Metaxas, D. (1999). Parallel hidden markov models for american sign language recognition. In *International Conference on Computer Vision* (pp. 116-122).

Vogler, C., Sun, H., & Metaxas, D. (2001). A framework for motion recognition with applications to American Sign Language and gait recognition. In *Proc. Workshop on Human Motion*.

Wainwright, M. J., Jaakkola, T., & Willsky, A. S. (2001). Tree-based reparameterization for approximate inference on loopy graphs, In *Proceedings of the NIPS* (pp. 1001-1008).

Wang, L., & Suter, D. (2007). Recognizing human activities from silhouettes: Motion subspace and factorial discriminative graphical model. In *Proceedings of the CVPR*.

Wang, S. B., Quattoni, A., Morency, L.-P., Demirdjian, D., & Darrell, T. (2006). Hidden conditional random fields for gesture recognition. In *Proceedings of the CVPR (2)* (pp. 1521-1527).

Wang, Y., & Ji, Q. (2005). A dynamic conditional random field model for object segmentation in image sequences. In *Proceedings of the CVPR (1)* (pp. 264-270).

Yamato, J., Ohya, J., & Ishii, K. (1992). Recognizing human action in time-sequential images using hidden Markov model. In *Proceedings of the CVPR* (pp. 379-385).

Yedidia, J. S., Freeman, W. T., & Weiss, Y. (2000). Generalized belief propagation. In *Proceedings of the NIPS* (pp. 689-695).

Zhao, T., & Nevatia, R. (2002). 3d tracking of human locomotion: A tracking as recognition approach. *ICPR, 1*, 541–556.

Zhong, J. G. S. (2002). HMMs and coupled HMMs for multi-channel eeg classification. In *IEEE Int. Joint Conf. on Neural Networks* (pp. 1154-1159).

Chapter 4
Common Spatial Patterns for Real–Time Classification of Human Actions

Ronald Poppe
University of Twente, The Netherlands

ABSTRACT

We present a discriminative approach to human action recognition. At the heart of our approach is the use of common spatial patterns (CSP), a spatial filter technique that transforms temporal feature data by using differences in variance between two classes. Such a transformation focuses on differences between classes, rather than on modeling each class individually. As a result, to distinguish between two classes, we can use simple distance metrics in the low-dimensional transformed space. The most likely class is found by pairwise evaluation of all discriminant functions, which can be done in real-time. Our image representations are silhouette boundary gradients, spatially binned into cells. We achieve scores of approximately 96% on the Weizmann human action dataset, and show that reasonable results can be obtained when training on only a single subject. We further compare our results with a recent examplar-based approach. Future work is aimed at combining our approach with automatic human detection.

INTRODUCTION

Automatic recognition of human actions from video is an important step towards the goal of automatic understanding of human behavior. This understanding has many potential applications, including improved human-computer interaction, video surveillance and automatic annotation and retrieval of stored video footage. In general, these applications demand

classification of human movement into several broad categories. Real-time and robust processing is often an important requirement, while there is still some control over the recording conditions. For example, human-computer interfaces require direct interaction. Another example is surveillance in the area of domotica, where elderly people are monitored to enable them to live independently for a longer period of time.

In the development of a human action recognition algorithm, one issue is the type of image representa-

DOI: 10.4018/978-1-60566-900-7.ch004

tion that is used. At the one extreme, bag-of-word approaches (Batra et al., 2007, Niebles and Fei-Fei, 2007) have been used. At the other extreme, pose information is used (e.g. Ali et al. (2007)). In this chapter, we assume that the location of a human figure in the image is known. While this might seem unrealistic, related work by Thurau (2007) and Zhu et al. (2006) shows that this detection can be performed reliably and within reasonable time. Recent work on human detection by Wu and Nevatia (2007) and Lin et al. (2008) even deals with partial observations, but we do not consider these here. To encode the observation of the human figure, we use a grid-based silhouette descriptor, where each cell is a histogram of oriented boundary points. This representation resembles the concept of histograms of oriented gradients (HOG, Dalal and Triggs (2005)), as it models the spatial relations, yet is able to generalize about local variations.

For classification, we learn simple functions that can discriminate between two classes. Our main contribution is the application of common spatial patterns (CSP), a spatial filter technique that transforms temporal feature data by using differences in variance between two classes. After applying CSP, the first components of the transformed feature space contain high temporal variance for one class, and low variance for the other class. This effect is opposite for the last components. For an unseen sequence, we calculate the histogram over time, using only a fraction – the first and last components – of the transformed space. Each action is represented by the mean of the histograms of all corresponding training sequences, which is a very compact but somewhat naive representation. A simple classifier distinguishes between the two classes. All discriminant functions are evaluated pairwise to find the most likely action class. This introduces a significant amount of noise over class labels but works well for the given task. Note that CSP can be used with any image descriptor that is

encoded as a vector of a fixed size, for example a histogram of codeword frequencies.

We obtained competitive results on the publicly available Weizmann action dataset introduced in Blank et al. (2005). One advantage of our method is that we require relatively few training samples. In fact, despite considerable variation in action performance between persons, we obtain reasonable results when training on data from a single subject. Also, we avoid retraining all functions when adding a new class, as the discriminative functions are learned pairwise, instead of jointly over all classes. Another advantage is that our approach is fast. Training of our classification scheme takes well under 1 second for all actions, with unoptimized Matlab code on a standard PC. After calculating the image descriptors, which can be done efficiently using the integral image (Zhu et al. 2006), classification can be performed in real-time as only a moderate number of simple functions have to be evaluated.

In the next section, we discuss related work on action recognition from monocular video. Common spatial patterns, and the construction of the CSP classifiers, are discussed subsequently. We evaluate our approach on the Weizmann dataset and perform additional experiments to gain more insight into the strengths and limitations of our approach. Finally, we summarize our approach and compare our results to those that have previously been reported in literature. An early version of this chapter appeared as Poppe and Poel (2008).

RELATED WORK ON HUMAN ACTION RECOGNITION

There has been a considerate amount of research into the recognition and understanding of human actions and activities from video and motion capture data. We discuss related work on action recognition, obtained from segmented monocular video sequences. More comprehensive overviews appear in Hu et al. (2004) and Turaga et al. (2008).

Action recognition can be thought of as the process of classifying arbitrary feature streams obtained from video sequences. This reveals the two main components of the problem: the feature representation and the classification. There have been many variations of both.

The choice of feature representation is important as it partly captures the variation in human pose, body dimension, appearance, clothing, and environmental factors such as lighting conditions. An ideal representation would be able to discriminate between poses, while at the same time being able to generalize over other factors. Since it is difficult to robustly obtain rich descriptors from video, often a compromise is sought in the complexity of the representation. At the one end, many approaches use retinotopic representations where the person is localized in the image. The image observations, such as silhouette or edge representations, are conveniently encoded into a feature vector. At the other end, there is the bag-of-words approach, where the spatial dimension is ignored altogether. Feature representations that are somewhere in between these concepts, such as grid-based descriptors (e.g. Ikizler and Duygulu (2007), Wang and Suter (2007)), are currently popular. These encode the image observation locally as a bag-of-words, but preserve the spatial arrangement of these local descriptors.

Regarding classifiers, we can generally distinguish two large classes of action recognition approaches. Spatio-temporal templates match unseen sequences to known action templates. These templates can take many forms. A key frame or the mean of a sequence of silhouettes over time can be used as templates. Slightly more advanced is the concept of Motion History Images, introduced by Bobick and Davis (2001). Here, the differences between subsequent silhouettes are used, and stored in a two-dimensional histogram. Recent work by Blank et al. (2005) concatenates silhouettes over time to form a space-time shape.

Special shape properties are extracted from the Poisson solution, and used for shape representation and classification.

The time dimension plays an important role in the recognition of actions, since there is often variation in the timing and speed with which an action is performed. Spatio-temporal templates can be considered as prototypes for a given action. The temporal aspect is often poorly modeled, especially when using histograms.

State-based representations, the second class of action classifiers, model the temporal aspect more accurately. These methods are often represented as a graphical model, where inference is used to perform the classification. Temporal relations between different states are encoded as transition probabilities. Hidden Markov Models (HMM) have been used initially (Brand, 1997). HMMs are also used by Weinland et al. (2007) for action recognition from arbitrary, monocular views. A similar approach using Action Nets was taken by Lv and Nevatia (2007).

Generative models try to maximize the likelihood of observing any example of a given class. For different actions that show many similarities yet have significant intra-class variance in performance (e.g. walking and jogging), generative models do a poor job in the classification task. Another drawback of generative models is the assumption that observations are independent. Discriminative models such as conditional random fields (CRF) condition on the observation, which makes this independence assumption unnecessary. Such models can model long-range dependencies between observations, as well as overlapping features.

Recently, discriminative alternatives have been proposed, based on CRFs. Sminchisescu et al. (2006) use CRFs and Maximum Entropy Markov Models (MEMM) to learn models for different actions simultaneously from image observations or motion capture data. Wang and Suter (2007) employ factorial conditional random fields (FCRF). Quattoni et al. (2007) use hidden conditional random fields (HCRF) that model the substructure of an action in hidden states. State-based approaches usually have a large number of parameters that need to be determined during training. This requires a large amount of training data, which is not always available.

In our approach, we learn functions that discriminate between two classes. Yet we avoid having to estimate a large number of parameters by representing actions as single prototypes. These prototypes lie in a space that is transformed by applying common spatial patterns on the feature data which are HOG-like representations of silhouette boundaries. We reduce the dimensionality of the feature representation and select the components that maximize the variance between the two classes. For an unseen action, we evaluate all pairwise discriminant functions, where each function softly votes into the two classes. Our estimated class label corresponds to the action that received most of the votes. Even though such an approach inherently generates a lot of noise in the classification, we show that we can recognize actions accurately, even when few training sequences are used. We explain common spatial patterns in the next section.

COMMON SPATIAL PATTERNS

Common Spatial Patterns (CSP) is a spatial filter technique that is often used in classifying brain signals (Müller-Gerking et al., 1999). It transforms temporal feature data by using differences in variance between two classes. After applying the CSP, the first components of the transformed data have high temporal variance for one class and low temporal variance for the other. For the last data components, this effect is opposite. When transforming the feature data of an unseen sequence, the temporal variance in the first and last components can be used to discriminate between the two classes. Consider the case where we have training sequences for two actions, a and b. Each

training sequence can be seen as $n \times m_p$ matrix, where n is the number of features and m_p is number of time samples. We assume that the data is normalized in such a way that the mean of each feature is 0. Let C_a be the concatenation of the examples of action a, C_a is an $n \times m_a$ matrix. We do the same for action b to construct the matrix C_b. Now consider the matrix:

$$C = C_a C_a^T + C_b C_b^T \qquad (1)$$

C is the variance of the union of the two data sets. Since C is symmetric, there exists a orthogonal linear transformation U such that $\Lambda = UCU^T$, a positive diagonal matrix. The next step is to apply the whitening transformation $\Psi = \Lambda^{-1/2}$, which gives us $(\Psi U)C(\Psi U)^T = I$, and thus:

$$S_a = (\Psi U)C_a C_a^T (\Psi U)^T \qquad (2)$$

$$S_b = (\Psi U)C_b C_b^T (\Psi U)^T \qquad (3)$$

$$S_a + S_b = \qquad I \qquad (4)$$

Since S_a is symmetric, there is an orthogonal transformation D such that $DS_a D^T$ is a diagonal matrix with decreasing eigenvalues on the diagonal. Hence, $DS_b D^T$ is also a diagonal matrix but with increasing eigenvalues on the diagonal. The CSP is the spatial transform $W = D\Psi U$ which transforms a data sequence into a sequence of dimension $2k$ such that a vector belonging to one action has high values in the first k components. For a vector of the other action, the situation is opposite. Hence, the temporal variance in these first and last components can be used to discriminate between action a and b.

CSP Classifiers

Based on the CSP technique, we designed discriminating functions $g_{a,b}$ for every action a and b with $a \neq b$. First we calculated the CSP transformation $W_{a,b}$ as described above. Then we applied $W_{a,b}$ to each action sequence of class a and b. Afterwards, the variance was taken over the entire sequence. This resulted in a single n-dimensional vector which can be considered a histogram, normalized for the length of the sequence. Next, we calculated the means a' and b' of these training vectors for action a and b, respectively. In order to compute $g_{a'b}(x)$ for an unseen action sequence x, we used the same procedure and first apply $W_{a'b}$ to x. We then calculate the variance over time over all components, which gives a vector x' of length n. Finally, $g_{a'b}(x)$ is defined as:

$$g_{a,b}(x) = \frac{\left\| b' - x' \right\| - \left\| a' - x' \right\|}{\left\| b' - x' \right\| + \left\| a' - x' \right\|} \qquad (5)$$

Here, $\| x \|$ denotes the vector length, or norm, of x. Evaluation of a this function gives a continuous output in the [-1, 1] interval. Note that $g_{a'b}$ + $g_{b'a}$ = 0. With a rescaling and transform into the [0, 1] domain, we could interpret these outputs as probabilities. However, since we assume equal prior probabilities for each class, we use our voting scheme for clarity. Also, we could have used different discriminative functions. For example, we could have kept the individual training vectors, instead of the mean. This would allow to better model intra-class variance. In this case, one could use Mahalanobis distance, or use a margin classifier such as Support Vector Machine (SVM). These alternatives are, however, sensitive to outliers in the data.

We combined our pairwise classifiers into a multi-class classifier using voting. Such a scheme has been proposed by Friedman (1996) for binary outputs, i.e. $g'_{a'b}(x) = sgn(g_{a'b})$. We applied their work for continuous outputs, without loss of generality. In such a scheme, an action sequence is classified by evaluating all discriminant functions between pairs of a and b over all actions, and summing their votes:

$$g_a(x) = \sum_{a \neq b} g_{a,b}(x) \qquad (6)$$

Since each action class appears in the exact same number of discriminative functions, the classification of x is the action η for which $g_a(x)$ is maximal. This is the class that received most of the voting mass:

$$\eta(x) = \arg \max_a g_a(x) \qquad (7)$$

Note that we also evaluate the discriminant functions in which the actual class does not appear. This introduces a large component of noise into the voting. However, actions that show more similarities with the unseen sequence will receive more mass in the voting. Hastie and Tibshirani (1998) remark that such a voting approach tends to favor classes that are closer to the average value in feature space. Such an effect would be larger for weaker pairwise discriminative functions. In our experiments, the dimensionality is relatively high compared to the number of classes and we expect that the effect of this bias is small.

More complex classification schemes are also possible. For example, Hastie and Tibshirani (1998) take into account all individual pairwise probability estimates and minimize a Kullback-Leibler criterion to find the optimal decision boundaries. The advantage is that the decision boundaries are determined jointly for all pairs of classes. Works by Allwein et al. (2000) and Dietterich and Bakiri (1995) use error-correcting codes, where each 'bit' in the code corresponds to a pairwise decision. While these approaches are better at dealing with noise caused by incidental erroneous decisions, their added value in performance over voting is limited (Allwein et al., 2000). Moreover, we prefer the straightforward interpretation of the voting outcome.

Our multi-class classifier requires $m(m - 1)/2$ functions, with m being the number of classes. Note that we could alternatively have used a one-versus-all classification scheme. In this case, we would have needed to learn a discriminative function for each class. While the complexity of such an approach is linear in the number of classes, instead of quadratic as in our scheme, the discriminative functions need to be more complex.

HISTOGRAMS OF ORIENTED SILHOUETTE GRADIENTS

To encode our image observations, we used a grid-based approach. For action recognition, grids were used as an image representation by Ikizler and Duygulu (2007), Thurau (2007) and Wang and Suter (2007). Our image representation is a variant of histogram of oriented gradients (HOG, Dalal and Triggs (2005)). For completeness, we summarize the processing steps used to obtain these descriptors.

The different steps in our approach are shown in Figure 1. Given an extracted silhouette, we determine the enclosing bounding box, which determines the region of interest (ROI). We add space to make sure the height is 2.5 times the width. Next, we divide the ROI into a grid of 4 × 4 cells. Within each cell, we calculate the distribution of silhouette gradients, which we divide over 8 bins that each cover a 45° range. Pixels that are not on silhouette boundaries are ignored.

This idea is similar to that of histogram of oriented gradients (HOG) but our implementation is a simplification at a number of levels. First, we do not apply a Gaussian filter to enhance the edges.

Second, we do not use overlapping cells, which significantly reduces the size of our descriptor. Third, and most important, we only take into account the silhouette outline thus discarding the internal edges. The fact that the gradient of binary silhouettes can only be vertical, horizontal or diagonal motivates the use of 45° orientation ranges. The final 128-dimensional descriptor is a concatenation of the histograms of all cells, normalized to unit length to accommodate variations in scale. We will refer to this representation as histograms of oriented silhouette gradients (HOSG). We will, however, also report the performance of our algorithm on different HOG and HOSG settings in our additional experiments.

Due to the normalization of the descriptor to unit length, and the relatively high dimensionality compared to the number of data points in a sequence, the covariance over a sequence may be nearly singular in some cases. We avoid this by applying PCA and select the 50 first components. These explain approximately 75% of the variance, depending on the subject that is left out. See the next section for details regarding this process.

EXPERIMENT RESULTS

We evaluated our approach on the publicly available Weizmann human action dataset which is briefly described in the next section. We then

Figure 1. Silhouette descriptor, (left) image, (center) mask and (right) the boundary orientations, spatially binned into cells. Normal vectors are shown for clarity.

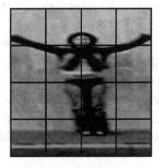 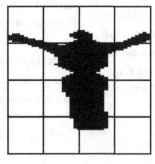 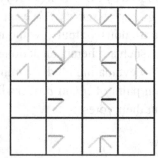

present the setup of our experiments and our obtained results. Additional experiments are described subsequently. A discussion of our results and a comparison with related work are given in the "Discussion" section.

Weizmann Human Action Dataset

For the evaluation of our approach, we used the Weizmann action dataset (Blank et al., 2005, Gorelick et al., 2007). This set consists of 10 different actions, each performed by 9 different subjects (see also Figure 2). For subject Lena, additional sequences appear for the run, skip and walk action. We decided to leave these out in order to obtain a balanced set. This also allows for direct comparison of our results to those previously reported on the dataset. Note that our approach also works for unbalanced sets. The skip action was not originally present in the set and we present results both with and without the skip action.

Each sequence is approximately 2.5 seconds long. There is considerable intra-class variation due to different performances of the same action by different subjects. Most notably, the jump, run, side, skip and walk actions are performed either from left to right, or in the opposite direction. Since the actions were performed on a slight slope, the direction of movement also results in slightly different movement style. Despite these differences, we treated performances in different

directions as belonging to the same class. The sequences were recorded from a single camera view, against a static background, with minimal lighting differences. Binary silhouette masks are provided with the dataset. These masks contain a considerable amount of noise due to inaccurate background segmentation (see also Figure 6).

Experiment Setup

We evaluated our method using leave-one-out cross-validation (LOOCV), where each of the 9 folds corresponds to all sequences of the corresponding subject. Specifically, this gave us 80 training sequences per fold, 8 for each of the 10 actions. First, we calculated the PCA transformation over all training sequences and projected the silhouette descriptors onto the first 50 components. Next, we learned all discriminant functions $g_{a,b}$, between all pairs of actions a and b ($1 \leq a, b \leq 10, a \neq b$). Specifically, we used the first and last $k = 5$ components in the transformation, which gave us action prototypes vectors of dimension 10. We experimented with other values for k but found no improvement for $k > 5$. For each of the sequences of the subject whose sequences were left out, we evaluated all discriminant functions. Each of these evaluations softly votes over class a and b. In our final classification, we selected the class that received the highest voting mass.

Figure 2. Example frames from the Weizmann dataset. Different subjects performing actions bend, jack, jump, pjump, run, side, skip, walk, wave1 and wave2.

Results

We performed the LOOCV experiment and obtained a performance of 95.56%. In total, 4 sequences were misclassified. The skip action of subject Daria was classified as jumping, the skip action of subject Ido was classified as running. Also, the jump action of subject Eli and the run action of subject Shahar were both classified as walking. The confusion matrix for this experiment is shown in Table 1.

In order to be able to compare our results with those reported in previous studies, we also left out the skip class. This resulted in a performance of 96.30%. Again, the jump action of subject Eli and the run action of subject Shahar were classified as walking. In addition, the wave1 action of subject Lyova was misclassified as wave2.

Table 1. Confusion matrix for Weizmann dataset including skip action with CSP (performance 95.56%). See text for explanation

Actual	Guessed									
	Bend	Jack	Jump	Pjump	Run	Side	Skip	Walk	Wave1	Wave2
Bend	9									
Jack		9								
Jump			8					1		
Pjump				9						
Run					8			1		
Side						9				
Skip		1			1		7			
Wl								9		
Wave1									9	
Wave2										9

Table 2. Confusion matrix for Weizmann dataset including skip action without CSP (performance 77.78%). See text for explanation

Actual	Guessed									
	Bend	Jack	Jump	Pjump	Run	Side	Skip	Walk	Wave1	Wave2
Bend	7	1							1	
Jack		9								
Jump		1	5			1	1		1	
Pjump				9						
Run					6			2	1	
Side						9				
Skip		1			3		2	3		
Walk					1		1	7		
Wave1									8	1
Wave2		1								8

In line with Friedman (1996), we also evaluated the performance when using binary outputs for the discriminative functions (i.e. $g'_{d'b}(x) = sgn(g_{d'b})$). With the skip action, 3 additional errors were made which resulted in a performance of 92.22%. Without skip, the performance was similar to the soft vote case at 96.30%.

Both the feature representation and the classifier had an important impact on the performance. To measure the added value of using CSP, we performed an additional experiment where we did not transform the feature space. Instead, we took the first 10 components of the PCA. For each training sequence, we calculated the histogram by taking the mean of the feature vector over time which resulted in a 10-dimensional vector. We determined the prototype for each action by averaging these histograms. Again, we used Equations (5) and (7) to determine the class estimate. We achieved a performance of 77.78% for all actions, and 85.19% with the skip action omitted. The confusion matrix for all 10 actions is shown in Table 2. When we used the first 50 PCA components, the performance slightly increased to 80.00% for all actions, while the performance without skip remained the same. A closer look at the misclassifications shows confusion between run, skip and walk, along with some incidental confusions. It thus becomes clear that the use of CSP is advantageous over a feature representation without CSP transform.

The baseline for the full dataset is 10.00%, and 11.11% when the skip action is left out. Obviously, our results are well above these baselines and show that we can achieve good recognition, even when single action prototypes of dimension 10 are used. Also, it shows that intra-class variations can be handled without modeling the variance between different subjects. To gain insight in the characteristics of our method, we conducted additional experiments. These are described in the next section.

ADDITIONAL EXPERIMENTS

In addition to the evaluations described above, we conducted several additional experiments to see how our approach performs with different settings and under different conditions. We used our HOSG descriptors with the settings as described previously, unless stated otherwise. Also, we used the standard Weizmann dataset, except for the robustness experiment.

First, we present our experiment with different image representations. Next, we describe our experiments where we used only part of the available training data. Evaluations on sequences with different deformations and viewpoints are then discussed. Finally, we describe our experiment with recognition from a smaller number of frames.

Results Using Different Image Representations

In this section, we evaluate the effect of descriptor size and type on the classification performance. Specifically, we used 2 descriptor types: HOG and HOSG. The former uses edges extracted within a silhouette mask. We also used three different grid sizes: 3×3, 4×4 and 5×6. HOSG-4×4 was used

Table 3. Classification performance using HOSG and HOG for different grid sizes

	HOSG			HOG		
	3×3	4×4	5×5	3×3	4×4	5×5
All actions	84.44%	95.56%	85.56%	83.33%	90.00%	87.78%
Skip omitted	88.89%	96.30%	91.36%	90.12%	92.59%	90.12%

in the previous section. Descriptor sizes for HOG are 81, 144 and 270 for the grid sizes respectively. For HOSG, these sizes are 72, 128 and 240. We kept the number of CSP components constant. Unseen sequences and action prototypes were both points in 10-dimensional space ($k = 5$).

We used the LOOCV approach for evaluation, with the data of 8 subjects for training and the data of the remaining subject for testing. The results are summarized in Table 3. HOSG performed slightly better than HOG. We can see that 4×4 outperformed both smaller and bigger grids. We expect that 3×3 grids do not capture enough detail to distinguish between classes. For 5×6 grids, we contribute the lower performance to the smaller cell sizes. This causes the histograms to become sparse which results in higher similarity scores when small variations between performances of an action occur.

Results Using Less Training Data

The fact that our approach is able to perform well, even though intra-class variation is not modeled, gives the impression that we can train our classifiers with less training data. Note here that training for all actions and all training subjects takes well under 1 second. To verify this hypothesis, we evaluated the performance of our approach using different numbers of subjects in the train-

ing set. Again, we used the LOOCV scheme. For each number of training subjects k, we present the results as averages over all $8!/(k!(8-k)!)$ combinations of training subjects. Table 4 summarizes these results, both using all actions, and with the skip action omitted.

Clearly, performance decreases with a decreasing amount of training data. But, even when only a few subjects are used for training, the results are reasonable. We expect that the variation in the direction of movement of the jump, run, side, skip and walk sequences will have a significant impact on the results, especially for the evaluations with very few training subjects. Even though we do not model the movement in the image, changing the direction of movement results in mirrored image observations. In turn, this results in very different silhouette descriptors. We look at this issue further in the next section. Nevertheless, our approach can cope with these variations to some extent.

Results on Robustness Sequences

The Weizmann dataset contains additional robustness sequences that can be used to investigate how well an approach performs with more challenging data. There are two types of sets, each of which contain 10 additional walking sequences. In the deformation sequences, different variations of walking are viewed from the side (see Figure 3

Table 4. Classification performance of our CSP classifier on the Weizmann dataset, using different numbers of training subjects. Combinations is the evaluated number of subsets of subjects.

Number of subjects	Number of combinations	All actions	Skip omitted
1	8	64.72%	69.14%
2	28	77.82%	83.82%
3	56	81.83%	88.98%
4	70	84.60%	90.85%
5	56	86.63%	92.44%
6	28	89.01%	93.87%
7	8	91.39%	94.91%
8	1	95.56%	96.30%

Figure 3. Example frames from the Weizmann robustness sequences. (top) Deformations, images and silhouettes for bag, briefcase, dog, kneesup, limp, moonwalk, nofeet, normwalk, pole and skirt. (bottom) Different viewpoints, images and silhouettes, 0° - 81° in increments of 9°.

(top row)). These sequences include walking with objects (bag, briefcase, dog), different walking styles (kneesup, limp, moonwalk), different clothing styles (skirt) and occlusion settings (nofeet, pole). It is arguable whether the different styles should be classified as walking since they show many similarities with the skip action. The viewpoint sequences show one walking subject, viewed from 0° (side view) to 81° (near-front view), in increments of 9°. Figure 1 (bottom row) shows example frames.

Our experimental setup was similar to the one used earlier but we used training data of all 9 subjects. We performed the experiments on the deformation and viewpoint sequences separately. We used the HOSG-4 × 4 descriptors. Our results are averaged over the 10 sequences of each set. For the deformation sequences, we obtained 80.00% correct estimates. The incorrectly classified sequences were moonwalk and pole, both of which were classified as running. For the viewpoints sequences, 80.00% were also classified correctly. The most challenging trials corresponding to viewpoints 72° and 81° were both classified as pjump.

When we reduced the number of subjects in our training set, we obtained lower results. Specifically, for 5 subjects, we score 79.60% correctly on the deformations, and 70.16% on the viewpoints. For training on a single subject,

these numbers decrease to 58.89% and 48.89%, respectively. These percentages are averages of all combinations of training subjects. For the condition where we test only on a single subject, we can evaluate the influence on walking direction on the performance, as the sequences in both the deformations and viewpoints sets show walking from left to right. When the training subject is walking in the same direction as the test subject, the scores are respectively 80.00% and 74.00% on the deformations and viewpoints sets. For the opposite direction, these numbers are significantly lower at 32.50% and 17.50%, respectively. Here, we did not look at the direction of related classes such as run and skip but it shows that it is important to take the direction of movement into account during training. Alternatively, different directions can be treated as different action classes.

Results on Subsequences

So far, we have used the entire sequence for classification. We assumed that temporal segmentation was performed previously. This raises the question as to how well our approach would perform when such accurate segmentation is not available. Since the Weizmann dataset contains only sequences with a single action, we focus on subsequences instead. We repeated our main LOOCV experiment but varied the length of the test sequences.

Figure 4. Classification performance for different subsequence lengths (left) and at different relative times (percentages given) within the sequence (right).

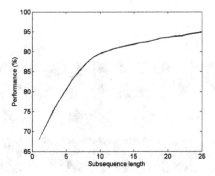 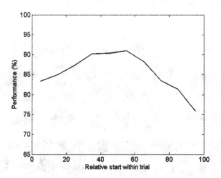

The training phase was exactly the same, so we used the entire sequences. For testing, we used a sliding window with a length in the range [1, 25]. The minimum sequence length is 28 frames. We slid the window through the sequence with steps of 1 frame. Average performance results over all sequences for different subsequence lengths are given in Figure 4 (left). It is clear that increasing subsequence length results in an increased performance. This can be explained by the additional information that is available as the sequence becomes longer.

We expect that the relative progress within the sequence influences these results. Most action performances start and end in a resting pose. Also, for moving actions (e.g. walking and running), the start and end of the sequence take place partly outside the viewing window. Therefore, we looked at the classification performance at different relative times within the sequence. We calculated the relative start of the subsequence as the starting frame divided by the sequence length. To compare sequences of different lengths, we binned these values into a 10-dimensional histogram. Each cell contains the average classification performance. Figure 4 (right) shows these results, averaged over all sequence lengths. It immediately becomes clear that performance is indeed lower at the start and at the end of the sequence.

DISCUSSION

In this section, we compare our results with those reported previously in literature. In the first sub-section, we present an in-depth comparison with recent exemplar-based holistic work. Next, we compare our approach with other results on the Weizmann human action dataset. Finally, we summarize our approach and present directions for future research.

Comparison with Exemplar-Based Holistic Work

In many cases, humans can recognize human actions from only a single prototypical pose. Motivated by this observation, we explored the use of such key poses. Recently, Weinland and Boyer (2008) presented an approach where they described sequences as a vector of minimum distances to selected exemplars. There are several approaches to select these exemplars. Unsupervised clustering algorithms such as k-means and expectation-maximization (Dempster et al., 1977) are likely to select as exemplars those frames that are common among all classes. As such, they are not discriminative. Alternatively, the exemplar selection problem can be regarded as a feature subset selection problem, where each frame is a feature. There are three types of supervised approach (Blum and Langley, 1997, Guyon and Elisseeff, 2003). Filters select subsets as a preprocessing step, without taking into account the induction algorithm (classifier). Wilson and Martinez (2000) present an overview of filter approaches. In contrast, wrapper approaches (Kohavi and John, 1997) explicitly use the induction algorithm in the subset selection scheme. A third approach is that of embedding methods, which perform subset selection within the training process. Usually, these methods are specifically designed for a given classifier and we do not consider them here.

In this section, we describe our implementation of the approach of Weinland and Boyer (2008), using either k-medoids (k-means where cluster centra correspond to the closest exemplar) or the wrapper approach to select exemplars. We used a Bayes classifier where each class is described as a multivariate Gaussian. Given the conceptual advantages of the wrapper approach over the unsupervised k-medoids, we expect to achieve higher accuracies for a smaller number of exemplars.

We used a LOOCV approach where each fold corresponds to one of the 9 test subjects. Our settings corresponded to those in Weinland and Boyer, (2008), which we summarize here for completeness. Specifically, we used a forward selection scheme. We started with an empty set of exemplars $E = \emptyset$, and a full set of candidates $C = \{c_i \mid 1 \leq i \leq n\}$ with n the total number of candidates. We sampled $n = 300$ frames from the training sequences. At each iteration, an exemplar from the candidate set was moved to the exemplar set. This was the exemplar that resulted in the largest performance increase on the validation set. To make sure exemplar selection was not based on a single subject, we used cross-validation within this exemplar-selection step. Since a perfect performance score on the validation set is easily obtained, we temporarily and randomly removed exemplars until the validation score was below 100%. In the validation step, we used the Bayes classifier where each class was described as a multivariate Gaussian.

To avoid singularity problems in the inversion, we used an axis-aligned covariance matrix, in which all off-diagonal covariance elements are zero. We used Mahalanobis distance D to determine the distance of each unseen trial to all classes: $D = (x - \mu)^T \Sigma^{-1} (x - \mu)$, where x is the k-dimensional vector of minimum distances to the k selected exemplars, and μ and Σ are the mean and covariance of the given class, respectively.

When multiple frames resulted in the highest performance increase on the validation set, we randomly selected one of them. Also, the selection of the candidate set was random. Therefore, we present our results as averages over 3 repetitions. Again, we used the HOSG-4 × 4 descriptor as our image representation, and performed our experiments with all 10 action classes.

The results for different numbers of k are presented in Figure 5, with either k-medoids or the wrapper approach for exemplar selection. The graphs show that for the wrapper approach, performance increases more rapidly. This can be understood by the discriminative selection in the wrapper approach. Also, the performance with the wrapper approach is slightly higher. For one repetition, the exemplars for $k = 10$ are shown in Figure 6. The exemplars that are selected in the wrapper approach correspond more clearly to different classes, whereas k-medoids selects exemplars that are more common among classes. Confusion matrices for $k = 50$ are presented in Table 5. It is clear that run and skip are often guessed, which can be explained by the large within-variance. Remarkably, the two wave actions are both often classified as bend. This is probably due to scaling the bounding box to a fixed ratio. Notice the perfect recognition for the walk action when the wrapper approach is used. This shows the discriminative effect of the selected exemplars (see exemplar 1 and 7 in the bottom row of Figure 6).

Both the exemplar-based approach and our CSP classifiers are discriminative but their strengths are different. The results of the exemplar-based approach are easily interpretable and arbitrary distance measures between frames and exemplars can be used. For example, Weinland and Boyer (2008) use Chamfer distance and achieve 100% accuracy when at least 120 exemplars are used. The CSP classifiers are limited in that they require a vector representation. However, the CSP classifiers can be trained very efficiently and have been shown to yield good results even for small subsets or when limited training data is available. In a direct comparison using the HOSG descriptors our CSP classifier outperforms the exemplar-based approach with over 10%. Differences between our results on the wrapper approach and those reported in Weinland and Boyer (2008) can be explained by the different image representation and matching. The Chamfer matching is more robust at the cost of being more computationally expensive.

Comparison with Other Related Research

There have been several other reports of results on the Weizmann set. We review these and point out differences with our work. Such comparisons reveal the relative advantages of one method over the other. We selected works that are representative of a class of approaches.

Niebles and Fei-Fei (2007) achieved a 72.80% score over 9 actions. Spatial and spatiotemporal interest points were sampled, and combined into a constellation. Action classification was performed by taking a majority vote over all individually classified frames. No background segmentation or localization was needed. This makes their approach more robust than ours. Recent work by Thurau (2007) used HOG-descriptors for both

Figure 5. Classification performance for different numbers of exemplars k for k-medoids (left) and the wrapper approach (right)

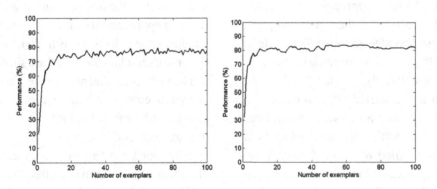

Figure 6. Exemplars selected using k-medoids (top), and the wrapper approach (bottom), both with the number of exemplars k = 10. Test subject is Daria.

Table 5. Confusion matrix for exemplar-based experiment with HOSG descriptors, with k = 50. Exemplars are selected using k-medoids (top, performance 74.81%) or the wrapper approach (bottom, performance 83.70%). The numbers are accumulated for 3 repetitions.

Actual	Guessed									
	Bend	Jack	Jump	Pjump	Run	Side	Skip	Walk	Wave1	Wave2
Bend	23				3		1			
Jack		25			2					
Jump	2		15		6		4			
Pjump				24	3					
Run					24		3			
Side					3	24				
Skip					18		9			
Walk					10		1	16		
Wave1	6				1				20	
Wave2	4				1					22

Actual	Guessed									
	Bend	Jack	Jump	Pjump	Run	Side	Skip	Walk	Wave1	Wave2
Bend	24						3			
Jack		27								
Jump			18				9			
Pjump				25	2					
Run					24		3			
Sid					3	24				
Skip					1		13			
Walk								27		
Wave1	6								21	
Wave2	3					1				23

detection and action classification. No background segmentation was used, but centered and aligned training data was needed. For classification, n-grams of action snippets were used. With all 10 actions and 90 bi-grams, performance was 86.66%.

In theory, the work of Ikizler and Duygulu (2007) did not require background segmentation but localization was assumed. A large number of rotated rectangular patches were extracted, and divided over a 3 × 3 grid, forming a histogram of oriented rectangles. A number of settings and classification methods was evaluated on the dataset without the skip action. All actions were classified correctly when using Dynamic Time Warping. This requires the temporal alignment of each unseen sequence to all sequences in the training set, which is computationally expensive. Using one histogram per sequence, 96.30% was scored. Again, this required comparison to all training sequences. For comparison, we calculated the performance of our descriptor using a length-normalized histogram over the entire sequence and 1-nearest neighbor using Euclidian distance, and with the skip action left out. This resulted in 96.30% performance, a similar score.

Other works require background subtraction and use the masks that are provided with the dataset. Wang and Suter (2007) score 97.78% over all 10 actions. Raw silhouette values were used, and long-term dependencies between observations were modeled in their FCRF. When small blocks of pixels were regarded, thus effectively reducing the resolution, performance decreased. For 4×4 blocks and 8×8 blocks, scores were obtained of 92.22% and 77.78%, with descriptor sizes 192 and 48, respectively. Kernel PCA was used to reduce the dimensionality, but the dimension of the projected space was not reported. In contrast, we started with a 128-dimensional silhouette descriptor, and performed the classification using only 10 components. Moreover, our training requirements were much lower. On the other hand, FCRFs are able to model complex temporal dynamics.

There are several reports of subsequence classifications. For example, Blank et al. (2005) used subsequences of 10 frames, and obtained a performance of 99.64%. They used local features, extracted from a space-time volume that was constructed by concatenating silhouettes over time. Schindler and Van Gool (2007) used local shape and optical flow, and evaluated their approach using subsequences between one and 10 frames. Their performance of 93.5% for a single frame increased to 99.60% when 10 frames were used. In contrast to these works, we used a holistic representation and no motion information. Such a representation can be obtained much faster. The downside is our lower performance of 89.56% using 10-frame subsequences.

CONCLUSION

We have shown that the application of common spatial patterns (CSP) to increase the margin between pairs of classes, increases classification performance. We demonstrated our approach on the Weizmann dataset and obtained approximately 96% accuracy. Confusions that remain are between related classes such as walking and running. These results are competitive, and we have shown that we can obtain reasonable results with only a few training subjects. Moreover, training and evaluation complexity are low. In fact, we can perform human action recognition in real-time. CSP can take sequences of any fixed-size vector representation as input. Here, we have used histograms of oriented silhouette gradients (HOSG), calculated within a grid. Such a holistic representation can be calculated fast but requires background segmentation and the determination of the region of interest. To assess the performance of our method on more realistic scenes reliably, our work should be combined with a preprocessing step to automatic human detection, such as in Zhu et al. (2006). In situations where silhouettes cannot be obtained reliably, histograms of codeword frequencies, for example from interest point detectors, can be used.

For the classification, we used simple pairwise discriminative functions, where each class was represented by the average of all training sequences of the class. Such an approach is simple, but does not model intra-class variance. Each prototype is likely to be an average of multiple modes, especially when there are large differences within the class, such as different directions of movement. To overcome this issue, multiple classes for different direction of movement for a single action could be introduced. Moreover, the temporal aspect in our action prototypes is, to a large extent, ignored. Performance could be increased by including temporal characteristics.

We have evaluated our work on entire sequences and subsequences. We did not explicitly address the temporal segmentation. Also, current datasets for human action recognition do not contain an "other" class. Instead of selecting the class with the highest voting mass, this would also require an approach to decide whether the chosen class is really observed. Generally, this is a harder problem since there is more variation in the "other" class and the prior probabilities for the classes can vary significantly.

ACKNOWLEDGMENT

The author would like to thank Mannes Poel and Daniel Weinland for insightful discussions on parts of this chapter, and the authors of Blank et al. (2005) for making their dataset available. This work was supported by the European IST Programme Project FP6-033812 (Augmented Multi-party Interaction with Distant Access), and is part of the ICIS program. ICIS is sponsored by the Dutch government under contract BSIK03024.

REFERENCES

Ali, S., Basharat, A., & Shah, M. (2007). Chaotic invariants for human action recognition. In *Proceedings of the International Conference On Computer Vision (ICCV'07)*, Rio de Janeiro, Brazil (pp. 1–8).

Allwein, E. L., Schapire, R. E., & Singer, Y. (2000). Reducing multiclass to binary: a unifying approach for margin classifiers. *Journal of Machine Learning Research, 1*, 113–141. doi:10.1162/15324430152733133

Batra, D., Chen, T., & Sukthankar, R. (2008). Space-time shapelets for action recognition. In *Proceedings of the Workshop on Motion and Video Computing (WMVC'08)*, Copper Mountain, CO (pp. 1–6).

Blank, M., Gorelick, L., Shechtman, E., Irani, M., & Basri, R. (2005). Actions as space-time shapes. In *Proceedings of the International Conference on Computer Vision (ICCV'05)*, Beijing, China (Vol. 2, pp. 1395–1402).

Blum, A. L., & Langley, P. (1997). Selection of relevant features and examples in machine learning. *Artificial Intelligence, 97*(1), 245–271. doi:10.1016/S0004-3702(97)00063-5

Bobick, A. F., & Davis, J. W. (2001). The recognition of human movement using temporal templates. [PAMI]. *IEEE Transactions on Pattern Analysis and Machine Intelligence, 23*(3), 257–267. doi:10.1109/34.910878

Brand, M., Oliver, N., & Pentland, A. P. (1997). Coupled hidden Markov models for complex action recognition. In *Proceedings of the Conference on Computer Vision and Pattern Recognition (CVPR'97)*, San Juan, Puerto Rico (pp. 994–999).

Dalal, N., & Triggs, B. (2005). Histograms of oriented gradients for human detection. In *Proceedings of the Conference on Computer Vision and Pattern Recognition (CVPR'05)*, San Diego, CA (Vol. 1, pp. 886–893).

Dempster, A. P., Laird, N. M., & Rubin, D. B. (1977). Maximum likelihood from incomplete data via the EM algorithm. *Journal of the Royal Statistical Society. Series B. Methodological, 39*(1), 1–38.

Dietterich, T. G., & Bakiri, G. (1995). Solving multiclass learning problems via errorcorrecting output codes. *Journal of Artificial Intelligence Research, 2*, 263–286.

Friedman, J. H. (1996). *Another approach to polychotomous classification.* Statistics department, Stanford University, Stanford, CA.

Gorelick, L., Blank, M., Shechtman, E., Irani, M., & Basri, R. (2007). Actions as space-time shapes. [PAMI]. *IEEE Transactions on Pattern Analysis and Machine Intelligence, 29*(12), 2247–2253. doi:10.1109/TPAMI.2007.70711

Guyon, I., & Elisseeff, A. (2003). An introduction to variable and feature selection. [JMLR]. *Journal of Machine Learning Research*, *3*, 1157–1182. doi:10.1162/153244303322753616

Hastie, T., & Tibshirani, R. (1998). Classification by pairwise coupling. *Annals of Statistics*, *26*(2), 451–471. doi:10.1214/aos/1028144844

Hu, W., Tan, T., Wang, L., & Maybank, S. (2004). A survey on visual surveillance of object motion and behaviors. *IEEE Transactions On Systems, Man, & Cybernetics (SMC) - . Part C: Applications And Reviews*, *34*(3), 334–352.

Ikizler, N., & Duygulu, P. (2007). Human action recognition using distribution of oriented rectangular patches. In *Human Motion: Understanding, Modeling, Capture and Animation (HUMO'07)*, Rio de Janeiro, Brazil (LNCS 4814, pp. 271–284).

Kohavi, R., & John, G. H. (1997). Wrappers for feature selection. *Artificial Intelligence*, *97*(1), 273–324. doi:10.1016/S0004-3702(97)00043-X

Lin, Z., & Davis, L. S. (2008). A pose-invariant descriptor for human detection and segmentation. In *Proceedings of the European Conference on Computer Vision (ECCV'08) - part 4*, Marseille France (LNCS 5305, pp. 423–436).

Lv, F., & Nevatia, R. (2007). Single view human action recognition using key pose matching and Viterbi path searching. In *Proceedings of the Conference on Computer Vision and Pattern Recognition (CVPR'07)*, Minneapolis, MN (pp. 1–8).

Müller-Gerking, J., Pfurtscheller, G., & Flyvbjerg, H. (1999). Designing optimal spatial filters for single-trial EEG classification in a movement task. *Clinical Neurophysiology*, *110*(5), 787–798. doi:10.1016/S1388-2457(98)00038-8

Niebles, J. C., & Fei-Fei, L. (2007). A hierarchical model of shape and appearance for human action classification. In *Proceedings of the Conference on Computer Vision and Pattern Recognition (CVPR'07)*, Minneapolis, MN (pp. 1–8).

Poppe, R., & Poel, M. (2008). Discriminative human action recognition using pairwise CSP classifiers. In *Proceedings of the International Conference on Automatic Face and Gesture Recognition (FGR'08)*, Amsterdam, The Netherlands.

Quattoni, A., Wang, S. B., Morency, L.-P., Collins, M., & Darrell, T. (2007). Hidden conditional random fields. [PAMI]. *IEEE Transactions on Pattern Analysis and Machine Intelligence*, *29*(10), 1848–1852. doi:10.1109/TPAMI.2007.1124

Schindler, K., & van Gool, L. J. (2008). Action snippets: How many frames does human action recognition require? In *Proceedings of the Conference on Computer Vision and Pattern Recognition (CVPR'08)*, Anchorage, AK (pp. 1–8).

Sminchisescu, C., Kanaujia, A., & Metaxas, D. N. (2006). Conditional models for contextual human motion recognition. [CVIU]. *Computer Vision and Image Understanding*, *104*(2-3), 210–220. doi:10.1016/j.cviu.2006.07.014

Thurau, C. (2007). Behavior histograms for action recognition and human detection. In *Human Motion: Understanding, Modeling, Capture and Animation (HUMO'07)*, Rio de Janeiro, Brazil (LNCS 4814, pp. 271–284).

Turaga, P., Chellappa, R., Subrahmanian, V., & Udrea, O. (2008). Machine recognition of human activities: A survey. *IEEE Transactions on Circuits and Systems for Video Technology*, *18*(11), 1473–1488. doi:10.1109/TCSVT.2008.2005594

Wang, L., & Suter, D. (2007). Recognizing human activities from silhouettes: Motion subspace and factorial discriminative graphical model. In *Proceedings of the Conference on Computer Vision and Pattern Recognition (CVPR'07)*, Minneapolis, MN (pp. 1–8).

Weinland, D., & Boyer, E. (2008). Action recognition using exemplar-based embedding. In *Proceedings of the Conference on Computer Vision and Pattern Recognition (CVPR'08)*, Anchorage, AK (pp. 1–7).

Weinland, D., Boyer, E., & Ronfard, R. (2007). Action recognition from arbitrary views using 3D exemplars. In *Proceedings of the International Conference On Computer Vision (ICCV'07)*, Rio de Janeiro, Brazil (pp. 1–8).

Wilson, D., & Martinez, T. R. (2000). Reduction techniques for instance-based learning algorithms. *Machine Learning, 38*(3), 257–286. doi:10.1023/A:1007626913721

Wu, B., & Nevatia, R. (2007). Detection and tracking of multiple, partially occluded humans by bayesian combination of edgelet based part detectors. [IJCV]. *International Journal of Computer Vision, 75*(2), 247–266. doi:10.1007/s11263-006-0027-7

Zhu, Q., Avidan, S., Yeh, M.-C., & Cheng, K.-T. (2006). Fast human detection using a cascade of histograms of oriented gradients. In *Proceedings of the Conference on Computer Vision and Pattern Recognition (CVPR'06)*, New York, NY (Vol. 2, pp. 1491–1498).

Chapter 5
KSM Based Machine Learning for Markerless Motion Capture

Therdsak Tangkuampien
Monash University, Australia

David Suter
Monash University, Australia

ABSTRACT

A marker-less motion capture system, based on machine learning, is proposed and tested. Pose informa-tion is inferred from images captured from multiple (as few as two) synchronized cameras. The central concept of which, we call: Kernel Subspace Mapping (KSM). The images-to-pose learning could be done with large numbers of images of a large variety of people (and with the ground truth poses accurately known). Of course, obtaining the ground-truth poses could be problematic. Here we choose to use syn-thetic data (both for learning and for, at least some of, testing). The system needs to generalizes well to novel inputs:unseen poses (not in the training database) and unseen actors. For the learning we use a generic and relatively low fidelity computer graphic model and for testing we sometimes use a more accurate model (made to resemble the first author). What makes machine learning viable for human motion capture is that a high percentage of human motion is coordinated. Indeed, it is now relatively well known that there is large redundancy in the set of possible images of a human (these images form som sort of relatively smooth lower dimensional manifold in the huge dimensional space of all possible images) and in the set of pose angles (again, a low dimensional and smooth sub-manifold of the mod-erately high dimensional space of all possible joint angles). KSM, is based on the KPCA (Kernel PCA) algorithm, which is costly. We show that the Greedy Kernel PCA (GKPCA) algorithm can be used to speed up KSM, with relatively minor modifications. At the core, then, is two KPCA's (or two GKPCA's) - one for the learning of pose manifold and one for the learning image manifold. Then we use a modification of Local Linear Embedding (LLE) to bridge between pose and image manifolds.

DOI: 10.4018/978-1-60566-900-7.ch005

1. OVERVIEW

Humans can look at an image of a human and "see" what pose they are in (i.e., can infer, to some accuracy, the joint angles). We have built a system to do something similar: pose information is inferred from images captured from multiple (as few as two) synchronized cameras. The central concept of which, we call: Kernel Subspace Mapping (KSM)(Section 5).

The concept can be seen in Figure 1. The image (we extract silhouettes) to pose mapping is to be learnt (left hand side) and then used (right hand side). The learning could be done with large numbers of images of a large variety of people (and with the ground truth poses accurately known). Of course, obtaining the ground-truth poses could be problematic: In principle, this could be done using a commercial (expensive) motion capture system but we choose to use *synthetic* data (both for learning and for, at least some of, testing). Of course, the system needs to generalizes well to novel inputs. That is *unseen* poses (not in the training database) and unseen actors. For the learning we use a generic and relatively low fidelity computer graphic model (left of the figure) and for testing we sometimes use a more accurate model (made to resemble the first author).

What makes machine learning viable for human motion capture is that a high percentage of human motion is coordinated [Safonova *et al*, 2004; Char and Hodgins, 2005]. Indeed, it is now relatively well known that there is large redundancy in the set of possible images of a human (these images form som sort of relatively smooth lower dimensional manifold in the hug dimensional space of all possible images) and in the set of pose angles (again, a lowdimensional and smooth sub-manifold of the moderately high dimensional space of all possible joint angles). Figure 7 shows these subspaces.

There have been many experiments on the application of learning algorithms (such as Principal Components Analysis (PCA) [Jolliffe, 1986; Smith, 2002] and Locally Linear Embedding (LLE) [Saul and Roweis, 2000]) in learning low

Figure 1. Diagram to summarize the training and testing process of Kernel Subspace Mapping, which learns the mapping from image to the normalized Relative Joint Centers (RJC) Pose space (section 1.3.1). Note that different mesh models are used in training and testing. The generic model [top left] is used to generate training images, whereas the accurate mesh model of the author (Appendix 3) is used to generate synthetic test images.

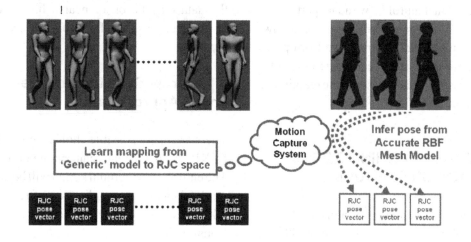

dimensional embedding of human motion [Elgammal and Lee, 2004; Bowden, 2000; Safonova *et al*, 2004]. Similarly, there have been many markerless motion capture techniques based on machine learning [Elgammal and Lee, 2004; Urtasun *et al*, 2005; Grauman *et al*, 2003; Agarwal and Triggs, 2006; Ren at al, 2005].

Note: in contrast to [Grauman *et al*, 2003; Elgammal and Lee, 2004], KSM can estimate pose using training silhouettes generated from a *single* generic model (Figure 1 [top left]). To ensure the robustness of the technique and test that it generalizes well to previously unseen[1] poses from a different actor, a different model is used in testing (Figure 1 [top right]). Results are presented in section 5.3, which shows that KSM can refer accurate human pose and direction, without the need for 3D processing (*e.g.* voxel carving, shape form silhouettes), and that KSM works robustly in poor segmentation environments as well.

KSM, is based on the KPCA algorithm [Schölkopf *et al*, 1997], which is costly. We show that the Greedy Kernel PCA (GKPCA) algorithm [Franc and Hlavac, 2003] (section 6). can be used to speed up KSM, with relatively minor modifications. At the core, then, is two KPCA's (or two GKPCA's) - one for the pose manifold and one for the image manifold. However, there are several issues to be addressed to turn this into a complete system. These include: selection of kernels, selection of the number of KPCA components, mapping between the learnt manifolds (we adapt part of the LLE algorithm) - see centre of Figure 7, and how to invert the right hand mapping (we learn pose to manifold but the system requires manifold to pose). These issues are addressed in the remainder of the chapter.

2. SUBSPACE LEARNING FOR HUMAN MOTION CAPTURE

The inference of full human pose and orientation (57 degrees of freedom) from silhouettes without the need of real world 3D processing is a complex and ill conditioned problem. When inferring from silhouettes, ambiguities arise due to the loss of depth cues (when projecting from 3D onto the 2D image plane) and the loss of foreground photometric information. Another complication to overcome is the high dimensionality of both the input and output spaces, which also leads to poor scalability of learning based algorithms. To avoid confusion it is important to note that, visually, an image as a whole is considered to exist in 2D. However, low level analysis of the pixels of an image (as applied in KSM) is considered high dimensional (more than 2D) as each pixel intensity represents a possible dimension for processing. Specifically in our work, the input is the vectorized pixel intensities of concatenated images from synchronized cameras.

Principal Components Analysis (PCA) [Jolliffe, 1986] has been shown to be successful in learning human subspaces for the synthesis of novel human motion [Safonova *et al*, 2004; Bowden, 2000]. However, PCA, being a linear technique is limited by its inability to effectively model non-linear data.

Kernel Principal Components Analysis (KPCA) [Schölkopf *et al*, 1997; Schölkopf *et al*, 1999; Schölkopf *et al*, 1998] is a non-linear extension of PCA. Geometrically speaking, KPCA implicitly maps non-linear data to a (potentially infinite) higher dimensional feature space where the data may lie on or near a linear subspace. In this feature space, PCA might work more effectively.

2.1. Kernel Selection for Pre-Image Approximation

There are many possible choices of valid kernels for KPCA, such as Gaussian or polynomial kernels. The choice of the optimal kernel will be dependent on the data and the application of KPCA. From a KPCA de-noising perspective, the radial basis Gaussian kernel

$$k(\mathrm{x}_i, \mathrm{x}) = \exp^{-\gamma\{(\mathrm{x}_i - \mathrm{x})^T (\mathrm{x}_i - \mathrm{x})\}} \qquad (1)$$

is selected due to the availability of well estab-lished and tested 'pre-image' approximation algorithms [Schölkopf *et al*, 1999; Kwok and Tsang, 2003]. The pre-image (which exists in the original input space) is an approximation of the KPCA projected vector (which exists in the de-noised feature space). Approximating the pre-image of a projected vector (in feature space) is an extremely complex problem and for some kernels, this still remains an open question. Since the projected (de-noised) vector exists in a higher (possibly infinite) feature space, not all vectors in this space may have pre-images in the original (lower dimensional) input space. Specifically for the case of Gaussian kernels, however, the fixed point algorithm [Schölkopf *et al*, 1998], gradient optimization [Franc, 2000] or the Kwok-Tsang algorithm [Kwok and Tsang, 2003], have been shown to be successful in approximating pre-images. For more information regarding the approximation of pre-images, the reader should refer to [Schölkopf and Smola, 2002]. Note that there are two free parameters that requires tuning for the Gaussian kernel (equation 1), these being γ, the Euclidian distance scale factor, and K^+, the optimal number of principal axis projections to retain in the feature space. To do so, tuning for de-noising can be implemented. By letting $\mathcal{P}_{K^+}^{\gamma}$ define the KPCA de-noising function (projection and pre-image approximation with the Euclidian scale factor of γ and an optimal principal axes number of K^+), the optimal parameters will be chosen such as to minimize the error function

$$\varepsilon(\gamma, K^+) = \sum_{i=1}^{N} \mathrm{P} \mathrm{x}_i - \mathcal{P}_{K^+}^{\gamma}(\mathrm{x}_i + \Delta n_i^{\sigma}) \mathrm{P}^2 \qquad (2)$$

Note that this can be improved to generalize to unseen inputs by using cross validation in tuning, hence resulting in the following form:

$$\varepsilon(\gamma, K^+) = \sum_{k=1}^{\kappa} \sum_{i=1}^{card(\mathcal{X}_{tr}^k)} \mathrm{P} \mathrm{x}_i^k - \mathcal{P}_{K_k^+}^{\gamma}(\mathrm{x}_i^k + \Delta n_i^{\sigma}) \mathrm{P}^2$$

$$(3)$$

where $\mathcal{X}_{tr}^k$ denotes the k-th subset for cross validation and $\mathcal{P}_{K_k^+}^{\gamma}(\bullet)$ represents the KPCA de-noising function using the principal components learnt from the remaining $\kappa - 1$ subsets (*i.e.* not inclusive of data in subset k).

3. KPCA SUBSPACE LEARNING FOR MOTION CAPTURE

The concept of motion subspace learning via KPCA is to use (Gaussian) kernels to model the non-linearity of joint rotation, such that computationally efficient pose 'distance' can be calculated, hence, allowing practical human motion de-noising. Clean human motion captured via a marker-based system [Carnegie Mellon University, 2007] are converted to the normalized Relative Joint Center (RJC) encoding (section 3.1) and used as training data. The optimal de-noising subspace is learnt by mapping the concatenated joint rotation (pose) vector via a Gaussian kernel and tuning its parameters to minimize error in pre-image approximations (section 2.1).

3.1. Normalized Relative Joint Center (RJC) Encoding

Generally, human pose can be encoded using a variety of mathematical forms, ranging from Euler angles (Appendix A.1.1) to homogeneous matrices (Appendix A.1.2). In terms of pose reconstruction and interpolation [Alexa, 2002; Kovar *et al*, 2002], problems usually encountered (when using Euler angles and matrices) include how to overcome the non-linearity and non-commutative structure of rotation encoding. Specifically for markerless motion capture using Euler angles, we do not try to map from input to Euler space as in [Agarwal and Triggs, 2006] because Euler angles also suffer from singularities and gimbal locks. Instead we model (3D) joint rotation as a point on a unit sphere.

We then use a Gaussian "kernel" type mapping of angle differences (dot products of unit vectors) to allow us to combine individiual joint angle differences into a complete measure of pose difference. A similar concept of applying non-linear exponential maps to model human joint rotations has been proposed by Bregler and Malik (1998). To illustrate, consider the simple case of defining the 'distance' between two different orientations of the same joint (*e.g.* the shoulder joint). In this case, the two rotations can be modelled as two points on a unit sphere, with a logical 'distance' being the geodesic (surface) distance between the two surface points. If we denote the two *normalized* points on the unit sphere as p and q respectively, the 'distance' between two orientations of the i-th joint will be defined as $k(p_i, q_i)$, with

$$k(p_i, q_i) = \exp^{-\gamma\{(p_i - q_i)^T (p_i - q_i)\}} \qquad \forall \ k(\cdot, \cdot) \in [0, 1],$$

(4)

The reader should note that the Gaussian kernel is an inverse encoding (*i.e.* a complete alignment of the two orientations is indicated by the maximum value of $k(p_i, q_i) = 1$). Any misalignment of the specific joint will tend to reduce the kernel function's output towards zero.

Now, if two different pose vector x and y for a human model of M joints is encoded as

$$x = [p_1, p_2, \cdots \quad p_M]^T, \quad x \in R^{3M}, \qquad and$$
$$y = [q_1, q_2, \cdots \quad q_M]^T, \quad y \in R^{3M},$$

(5)

then the distance between these pose vectors, is

$$k(x, y) = k(p_1, q_1) \times k(p_2, q_2) \times \cdots \quad k(p_M, q_M)$$
$$= \exp^{-\gamma\{(x-y)^T(x-y)\}}.$$

(6)

This results in (another) Gaussian kernel.

A disadvantage of encoding a rotation using a normalized spherical surface point is that it loses a degree of rotation for any ball & socket joint (Figure 2). This is because a surface point on a sphere cannot encode the rotation about the axis

Figure 2. Diagram to illustrate the missing rotation in a ball & socket joint using the RJC encoding. The missing rotation of the ball & socket joint (shoulder) can be inferred from the hinge joint (elbow) below it in the skeletal hierarchy (provided that the limb is not fully extended).

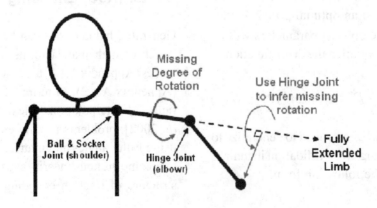

defined by the sphere's center and the surface point itself. However, as highlighted in the phase space representation of Moeslund [Moeslund and Granum, 2000], for the main limbs of the human body (*e.g.* arms and legs), the ball & socket joints (*e.g.* shoulder or pelvis) are directly linked to hinge joints (*e.g.* elbow or knee), which only has one degree of freedom. Provided that the limb is not fully extended, it is possible to rediscover the missing degree of freedom (for a ball & socket joint) by analyzing the orientation of the corresponding hinge joint. If the limb is fully extended, then temporal constraints can be used to select the most probable missing rotation of the ball & socket joint.

4. EXPERIMENTS AND RESULTS

To compare PCA and KPCA for the de-noising of human motion, various motion sequences were downloaded from the CMU motion capture database. All motions were captured via the VICON marker-based motion capture system [Vicon Peak, 2007], and were originally downloaded in AMC format (Appendix A.1.1). To avoid the singularities and non-linearity of Euler angles (AMC format), the data is converted to its RJC equivalent (section 3.1) for training. All experiments were performed on a Pentium™ 4 with a 2.8

GHz processor. Synthetic Gaussian white noise are added to motion sequence $\mathcal{X}^{tr}$ in normalized RJC format, and the de-noising qualities compared quantitatively (Figure 20) and qualitatively in 3D animation playback.

Figure 20 highlights the superiority of KPCA over linear PCA in human motion de-noising. Specifically for the walking and running motion sequences (Figure 3 and Figure 4 respectively), the frame by frame comparison further emphasizes the superiority of KPCA (blue line) over PCA (black line). Furthermore, the KPCA algorithm was able to generate realistic and smooth animation when the de-noised motion is mapped to a skeleton model and play-backed in real time. PCA de-noising, on the other hand, was unsuccessful due to its linear limitation and resulted in jittery unrealistic motions similar to the original noisy sequences. A repeat of this experiment (motivated by our work) has also been conducted by Schraudolph *et al* (2007) with the fast iterative Kernel PCA algorithm, and similar de-noising results are confirmed.

Figure 5 [top] shows the correlation (though erratic) between feature space noise and pose (RJC) space noise (in mean square error [*mse*]) for KPCA de-noising of a walk sequence. As expected, smaller noise level in feature space is an indication of smaller noise level in the original space, and vice versa.

Figure 3. Frame by frame error comparison between PCA and KPCA de-noising of a walk sequence

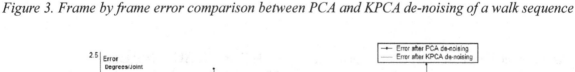

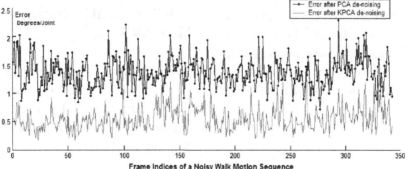

Figure 4. Frame by frame error comparison between PCA and KPCA de-noising of a run sequence

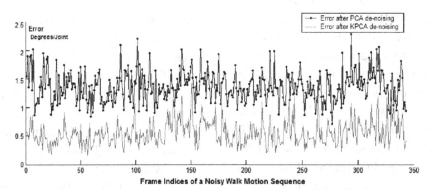

Figure 5. Feature and pose space mean square error [mse] relationship for KPCA [top]. Average computational de-noising cost for KPCA [bottom]

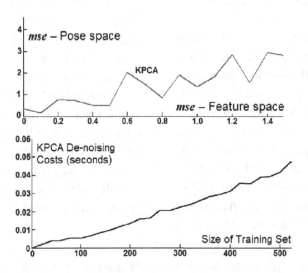

As the processing cost of KPCA is dependent on the training size, an analysis of this cost with respect to the training size was also investigated. Figure 5 [bottom] confirms the linear relationship between the de-noising cost of KPCA and its training size.

5. KERNEL SUBSPACE MAPPING (KSM)[2]

This section integrates human motion de-noising via KPCA (section 2) and the Pyramid Match Kernel [Grauman and Darrell, 2005] into a novel markerless motion capture technique called Kernel Subspace Mapping.

Previous silhouette based techniques, such as [Agarwal and Triggs, 2006; Caillette *et al*, 2005; Chen *et al*, 2005; Elgammal and Lee; 2004, Grauman *et al*, 2003; Mori and Malik, 2002; Navaratnam and Thayananthan, 2005], involve complex and expensive schemes to disambiguate between the multi-valued silhouette and pose pairs.

For mapping from silhouettes to the pose subspace, instead of using standard or robust regression (which was found to be both slower and less accurate in our experiments), non-parametric LLE mapping [Saul and Roweis, 2000] is applied. The silhouette kernel parameters are tuned to optimize the silhouette-to-pose mapping by minimizing the LLE mapping error (section 5.2). By mapping silhouettes to the pose feature subspace, the search space can be implicitly constrained to a set of valid poses, whilst taking advantage of well established and optimized pre-image (inverse mapping) approximation techniques, such as the fixed-point algorithm of [Schölkopf *et al*, 1998] or the gradient optimization technique [Franc, 2000].

5.1 Markerless Motion Capture: A Mapping Problem

In our work, the static pose of a person (in the pose space) is encoded using the normalized relative joint centers (RJC) format (section 3.1), where a pose (at a time instance) is denoted by

$$\mathrm{x} = [\mathrm{p}_1, \mathrm{p}_2, \cdots \mathrm{p}_M]^\mathrm{T}, \quad \mathrm{x} \in R^{3M}, \tag{7}$$

and p_k represents normalized spherical surface point encoding of the k-th joint relative to its parent joint in the skeletal's hierarchy (appendix 2.1). Regression is not performed from silhouette to Euler pose vectors as in [Agarwal and Triggs, 2004; Agarwal and Triggs, 2006] because the mapping from pose to Euler joint coordinates is non-linear and multi-valued. Any technique, like KPCA and regression based on standard linear algebra and convex optimization will therefore eventually breakdown when applied to vectors consisting of Euler angles (as it may potentially map the same 3D joint rotation to different loca-

Figure 6. Scatter plot of the RJC projections onto the first 4 kernel principal components in $\mathcal{M}^p$. of a walk motion, which is fully rotated about the vertical axis. The 4th dimension is represented by the intensity of each point.

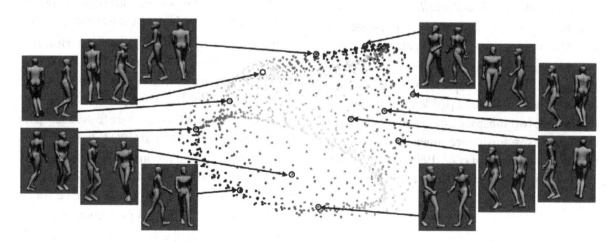

Figure 7. Diagram to highlight the relationship between human motion de-noising (section 1.2), Kernel Principal Components Analysis (KPCA) and Kernel Subspace Mapping (KSM)

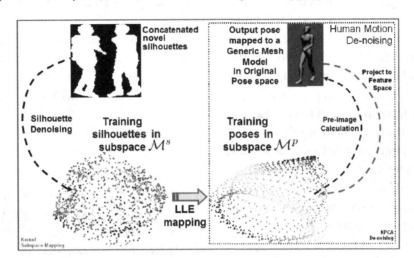

tions in vector space). To avoid these problems, the KPCA de-noising subspace is learnt from (training) pose vectors in the relative joint center format (section 3.1).

The *pose feature subspace* $\mathcal{M}^p$ (Figure 6) is learnt from the set of training poses. Similarly, for the silhouette space, synchronized and concatenated silhouettes (synthesized from the pose x_i) are preprocessed to a hierarchical shape descriptor Ψ_i (Section 5.1) using a technique similar to the pyramid match kernel of [Grauman and Darrell, 2005]. The preprocessed hierarchical training set is embedded into KPCA, and the *silhouette subspace* $\mathcal{M}^s$ learnt (Figure 7 [bottom left]). The system is tuned to minimize the LLE non-parametric mapping [Saul and Roweis, 2000] from $\mathcal{M}^s$ to $\mathcal{M}^p$ (Section 5.2). During Capture, novel silhouettes of unseen actors (Figure 7 [top left]) are projected through the two subspaces, before mapping to the output pose space using pre-image approximation techniques [Schölkopf *et al*, 1998; Franc, 2000]. Crucial steps are explained fully in the remainder of this section.

Learning the Pose Subspace via KPCA

From a motion capture perspective, pose subspace learning is the same as learning the subspace of human motion for de-noising (Section 2). For the latter (motion de-noising), a noisy pose vector is projected onto the (kernel) principal components for de-noising in the feature subspace $\mathcal{M}^p$. Thereafter, the pre-image of the projected vector is approximated, hence mapping back to the original space (Figure 7 [KPCA De-noiser: black rectangle]).

For markerless motion capture (Figure 7 [KSM: red rectangle]), KSM initially learns the projection subspace $\mathcal{M}^p$ as in KPCA de-noising. However, instead of beginning in the normalized RJC (pose) space, the input is derived from concatenated silhouettes (Figure 7 [left]) and mapped (via a silhouette feature subspace $\mathcal{M}^s$) to the pose feature subspace $\mathcal{M}^p$. Thereafter, KSM and KPCA de-noising follow the same path in pre-image approximation.

To update the notations for KSM, for a motion sequence, the training set of RJC pose vectors is denoted as $\mathcal{X}^{tr}$. The KPCA projection of a novel pose vector x onto the k-th principal axis $\mathbf{V}_p^k$ in the pose feature space can be expressed implicitly via the *kernel trick* as

$$\langle \mathbf{V}_p^k \cdot \Phi(\mathbf{x}) \rangle = \sum_{i=1}^{N} \alpha_i^k \langle \Phi(\mathbf{x}_i) \cdot \Phi(\mathbf{x}) \rangle$$

$$= \sum_{i=1}^{N} \alpha_i^k k_p(\mathbf{x}_i, \mathbf{x}) \tag{8}$$

where α refers to the Eigenvectors of the centered RJC kernel matrix. In this case, the radial basis Gaussian kernel

$$k_p(\mathbf{x}_i, \mathbf{x}) = \exp^{-\gamma_p \{(\mathbf{x}_i - \mathbf{x})^{\mathrm{T}} (\mathbf{x}_i - \mathbf{x})\}} \tag{9}$$

is used because of the availability of well established and tested fixed point pre-image approximation algorithm [Schölkopf *et al*, 1998] (The reason for this selection will become clear later in section 5.1). To avoid confusion, the symbol $k_p(\cdot, \cdot)$ will be used explicitly for the pose space kernel and $k_s(\cdot, \cdot)$ for the silhouette kernel [the kernel $k_s(\cdot, \cdot)$ will be discussed in section 5.1]. As in section 2.1, there are two free parameters in need of tuning of $k_p(\cdot, \cdot)$, these being γ_p the Euclidian distance scale factor, and η_p the optimal number of principal axis projections to retain in the pose feature space. The KPCA projection (onto the first η_p principal axis) of $\mathbf{x}_i$ is denoted as $\mathbf{v}_i^p$, where

$$\mathbf{v}_i^p = [\langle \mathbf{V}_p^1 \cdot | (\mathbf{x}_i) \rangle, .., \langle \mathbf{V}_p^{\eta_p} \cdot | (\mathbf{x}_i) \rangle]^{\mathrm{T}}, \quad \forall \ \mathbf{v}^p \in R^{\eta_p}. \tag{10}$$

For novel input pose $\mathbf{x}$, the KPCA projection is simply signified by $\mathbf{v}^p$.

Pose Parameter Tuning via Pre-image Approximation

In order to understand how to optimally tune the KPCA parameters γ_p and η_p for the pose feature subspace $\mathcal{M}^p$, the context of how $\mathcal{M}^p$ is applied in KSM must be highlighted (Figure 7 [bottom right]). Ideally, a tuned system should minimize the inverse mapping error from $\mathcal{M}^p$ to the original pose space in normalized RJC format (Figure 7 [top right]). In the context of KPCA, if we encode each pose as x and its corresponding KPCA projected vector as v^p, the inverse mapping from v^p to x is commonly referred as the pre-image [Schölkopf *et al*, 1998] mapping. Since a novel input will first be mapped from $\mathcal{M}^s$ to $\mathcal{M}^p$, the system needs to determine its inverse mapping (pre-image) from $\mathcal{M}^p$ to the original pose space. Therefore, for this specific case, the Gaussian kernel parameters, γ_p and η_p, are tuned using cross-validation to minimize pre-image reconstruction error (as in equation 3). Cross validation prevents over-fitting and it ensures that the pre-image mapping generalized well to unseen poses, which may be projected from the silhouette subspace $\mathcal{M}^s$.

An interesting advantage of using pre-image approximation for mapping is its implicit ability to *de-noise* if the input vector (which is perturbed by noise) lies outside the learnt subspace $\mathcal{M}^p$. This is relatively the same problem as that encountered by Elgammal and Lee in [Elgammal and Lee, 2004], which they solved by fitting each separate manifold to a spline and re-scaling before performing a one dimensional search (for the closest point) on each separate manifold. For Kernel Subspace Mapping, however, it is usual that the noisy input (from $\mathcal{M}^s$) lies outside the clean subspace, in which case, the corresponding pre-image of v^p usually does not exist [Schölkopf *et al*, 1999]. In such a scenario, the algorithm will implicitly locate the closest point in the clean subspace corresponding

Figure 8. Example of a training pose and its corresponding concatenated synthetic image using 2 synchronized cameras. Each segmented silhouette is first rotated to align the silhouette's principal axis with the vertical axis before cropping and concatenation (Figure 8)

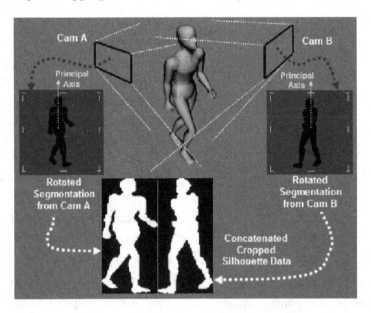

to such an input, without the need to explicitly search for the optimal point.

Learning the Silhouette Subspace

This section shows how to optimally learn the silhouette subspace $\mathcal{M}^s$, which is a more complicated problem than learning the pose subspace $\mathcal{M}^p$ (section 5.1). Efficiently embedding silhouette distance into KPCA is more complex and expensive because the silhouette exists in a much higher dimensional image space. The use of Euclidian distance between vectorized images, which is common but highly inefficient, is therefore avoided. For KPCA, an important factor that must be taken into account when deciding on a silhouette kernel (to define the distance between silhouettes) is if the kernel is positive definite and satisfies Mercer's condition [Schölkopf *et al*, 1998]. In KSM, we use a modified version of the pyramid match kernel [Grauman and Darrell, 2005] (to define silhouette distances), which has already been proven positive definite. The main

difference (between the original pyramid match kernel [Grauman and Darrell, 2005] and the one used in KSM) is that instead of using feature points sampled from the silhouette's edges (as in [Grauman and Darrell, 2005]), KSM consider all the silhouette foreground pixels as feature points. This has the advantage of skipping the edge segmentation and contour sampling step. During training (Figure 8), virtual cameras (with the same extrinsic parameters as the real cameras to be used during capture) are set up to capture synthetic training silhouettes. Note that more cameras can be added by concatenating more silhouettes into the image.

Each segmented silhouette is normalized by first rotating the silhouette's principal axis to align with its vertical axis before cropping and concatenation. Thereafter, a simplified recursive multi-resolution approach is applied to encode the concatenated silhouette (Figure 9). At each resolution (level) the silhouette area ratio is registered in the silhouette descriptor Ψ.

Figure 9. Diagram to summarize the silhouette encoding for 2 synchronized cameras. Each concatenated image is preprocessed to ¨ before projection onto $\mathcal{M}^s$

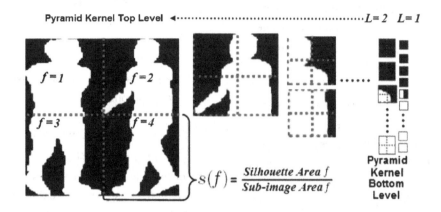

A five level pyramid is implemented, which results in a 341 dimensional silhouette descriptor. (For a five level pyramid, the feature vector dimension is determined by the following formula: $1^2 + 2^2 + 4^2 + 8^2 + 16^2 = 341$). To compare the difference between two concatenated images, their respective silhouette descriptors Ψ_i and Ψ_j are compared using the weighted distance

$$D^\Psi(\Psi_i, \Psi_j) = \sum_{f=1}^{F} \frac{1}{L(f)} \{|\Psi_i(f) - \Psi_j(f) - \gamma_{L(f)+1}\}$$

(11)

The counter $L(f)$ denotes the current level of the sub-image f in the pyramid, with the smallest sub-images located at the bottom of the pyramid and the original image at the top. In order to minimize segmentation and silhouette noise (located mainly at the top levels), the lower resolution images are biased by scaling each level comparison by $1/L(f)$. As the encoding process moves downwards from the top of the pyramid to the bottom, it must continually update the cumulative mean area difference $\gamma_{L(f)+1}$ at each level. This is because at any current level $L(f)$, only the differences in features that have not already been recorded at levels above it is recorded, hence

the subtraction of $\gamma_{L(f)+1}$. To embed $D^\Psi(\Psi_i, \Psi_j)$ into KPCA, the Euclidian distance in k_p is replaced with the weighted distance, resulting in a silhouette kernel

$$k_s(\Psi_i, \Psi) = \exp^{-\gamma_s D^\Psi(\Psi_i, \Psi)^2}.$$

(12)

Using the same implicit technique as that of equation 1.8, KPCA silhouette projection is achieved by using $k_s(\cdot, \cdot)$ and the projection (onto the first η_s principal axis) of Ψ_i is denoted as

$$\mathrm{v}_i^s = [\langle \mathbf{V}_s^1 \cdot \Phi(\Psi_i) \rangle, .., \langle \mathbf{V}_s^{\eta_s} \cdot \Phi(\Psi_i) \rangle]^{\mathrm{T}}, \quad \forall \ \mathrm{v}^s \in R^{\eta_s},$$

(13)

where $\langle \mathbf{V}_s^k \cdot \Phi(\Psi_i) \rangle = \sum_{j=1}^{N} \gamma_j^k k_s(\Psi_j, \Psi_i)$, with γ representing the Eigenvectors of the corresponding centered silhouette kernel matrix.

5.2. Locally Linear Subspace Mapping

Having obtained $\mathcal{M}^s$ and $\mathcal{M}^p$, markerless motion capture can now be viewed as the problem of mapping from the silhouette subspace $\mathcal{M}^s$ to the pose subspace $\mathcal{M}^p$. Using P^{tr} to denote the KPCA projected set of *training* poses (where $P^{tr} = [v_1^p, v_2^p, \ldots, v_M^p]$) and, similarly, letting S^{tr} denote the projected set of *training* silhouettes (where $S^{tr} = [v_1^s, v_2^s, \ldots, v_M^s]$), the subspace mapping can now be summarized as follows:

- Given S^{tr} (the set of training silhouettes projected onto $\mathcal{M}^s$ via KPCA using the pyramid kernel) and its corresponding pose subspace training set P^{tr} in $\mathcal{M}^p$, how do we learn a mapping from $\mathcal{M}^s$ to $\mathcal{M}^p$, such that it generalizes well to previously unseen silhouettes projected onto $\mathcal{M}^s$ at run-time?

Referring to Figure 10, the projection of the (novel) input silhouette during capture (onto $\mathcal{M}^s$) is denoted by s^{in} and the corresponding pose subspace representation (in $\mathcal{M}^p$) is denoted by p^{out}. The captured (output) pose vector x^{out} (representing the joint positions of a generic mesh in normalized RJC format) is approximated by determining the pre-image of p^{out}.

The (non-parametric) LLE mapping [Saul and Roweis, 2000] is used to transfer projected vectors from $\mathcal{M}^s$ to $\mathcal{M}^p$. This only requires the first 2 (efficient) steps of LLE:

1. Neighborhood selection in $\mathcal{M}^s$ and $\mathcal{M}^p$.
2. Computation of the weights for neighborhood reconstruction.

The goal of LLE mapping for KSM is to map s^{in} (in $\mathcal{M}^s$) to p^{out} (in $\mathcal{M}^p$), whilst trying to preserve the local isometry of its nearest $\mathcal{K}$ neighbors in both subspaces. Note that, in this case, we are not trying to learn a complete embedding of the data, which requires the inefficient third step of LLE, which is of complexity $O(dN^2)$, where d is the dimension of the embedding and N is the training size. Crucial details regarding the first two steps of LLE, as used in KSM, are now summarized.

Figure 10. Markerless motion capture re-expressed as the problem of mapping from the silhouette subspace $\mathcal{M}^s$ to the pose subspace $\mathcal{M}^p$. Only the projection of the training set (S^{tr} and P^{tr}) onto the first 4 principal axis in their respective feature spaces are shown (point intensity is the 4th dimension). Note that the subspaces displayed here is that of a walk motion fully rotated about the vertical axis. Different sets of motion will obviously have different subspace samples, however, the underlying concept of KSM remains the same.

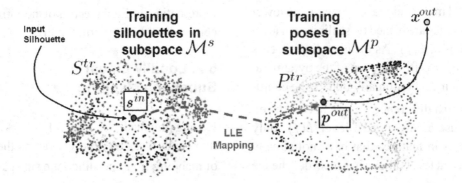

Figure 11. Diagram to summarize the mapping of S^{tr} from silhouette subspace P^{tr} to $\mathcal{K}$ in pose subspace $\mathcal{M}^s$ via non-parametric LLE mapping [Saul and Roweis, 2000]. Note that the reduced subsets $\mathcal{M}^s$ and $\mathcal{M}^p$ are used in mapping novel input silhouette feature vectors

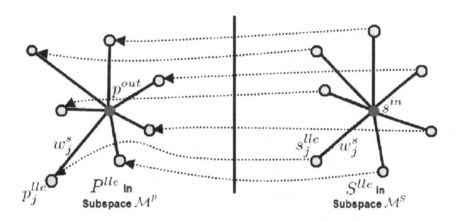

Figure 12. Diagram to show how two different poses p^A and p^B may have similar concatenated silhouettes in image space

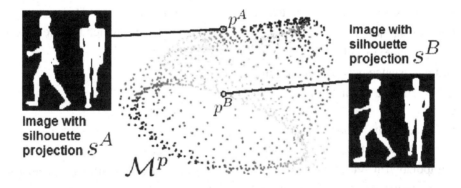

Neighborhood Selection for LLE Mapping

From initial visual inspection of the two projected training sets s^{in} and $\mathcal{M}^s$ in Figure 11, there may not appear to be any similarity. Therefore, the selection of the nearest p^{out} neighbors (of an input silhouette captured at run-time) by simply using Euclidian distances in $\mathcal{M}^p$ is not ideal. This is because the local neighborhood relationships between the training silhouettes themselves do not appear to be preserved between S^{lle} and P^{lle}, let alone trying to preserve the neighborhood relationship for a novel silhouette.

For example to understand how the distortion in $\mathcal{M}^s$ may have been generated, the silhouette kernel k_s is used to embed two different RJC pose subspace vectors p^A and p^B which have similar silhouettes (Figure 12). The silhouette kernel k_s, in this case, will map both silhouettes to positions close together (represented as s^A and s^B) in $\mathcal{M}^s$, even though they are far apart in $\mathcal{M}^p$.

As a result, an extended neighborhood selection criterion, which takes into account temporal constraints, must be enforced. That is, given the unseen silhouette projected onto $\mathcal{M}^s$, training exemplars that are neighbors in *both* $\mathcal{M}^s$ and $\mathcal{M}^p$ must be identified. Euclidian distances between training vectors in S^{tr} and s^{in} can still identify neighbors in $\mathcal{M}^s$. The problem lies in finding local neighbors in P^{tr} , since the system does not yet know the projected output pose vector p^{out} (this is what the KSM is trying to determine in the first place). However, a rough estimation of p^{out} can be predicted by tracking in the subspace $\mathcal{M}^p$ via a predictive tracker, such as the Kalman Filter [Kalman, 1961]. From experiments, it was concluded that tracking using linear extrapolation is sufficient in KSM for motion capture. This is because tracking is only used to eliminate potential neighbors which may be close in $\mathcal{M}^s$, but far apart (from the tracked vector) in $\mathcal{M}^p$. Therefore, no accurate Euclidian distance between the training exemplars in P^{tr} and the predicted pose needs to be calculated.

In summary, to select the $\mathcal{K}$ neighbors needed for LLE mapping, the expected pose is predicted using linear extrapolation in $\mathcal{M}^p$. A subset of training exemplars nearest to the predicted pose is then selected (from P^{tr}) to form a reduced subset P^{lle} (in $\mathcal{M}^p$) and S^{lle} (in $\mathcal{M}^s$). From the reduced subsets (From experiments, subsets consisting from 10% to 40% of the entire training set are usually sufficient in filtering out silhouette outliers. The subset size also does not affect the output pose (as visually determined by the naked eye) whilst in this range, and is therefore not included as a parameter in the tuning process - section 5.2.) the closest $\mathcal{K}$ neighbors to s^{in} (using Euclidian distances in $\mathcal{M}^s$) can be identified and p^{out} reconstructed from the linked neighbors in $\mathcal{M}^p$.

LLE Weight Calculation

Based on the filtered neighbor subset S^{lle} (with $\mathcal{K}$ exemplars identified from the previous section), the weight vector w^s is calculated, such as to minimize the following reconstruction cost function:

$$\varepsilon(s^{in}) = Ps^{in} - \sum_{j=1}^{\kappa} \bar{w}_j^s s_j^{lle} P^2 . \quad (14)$$

LLE mapping also enforces that the $\sum_{j=1}^{\kappa} w_j^s = 1$. Saul and Roweis [Saul and Roweis, 2000] showed that w^s can be determined by initially calculating the symmetrical (and semi-positive definite) "local" Gram matrix $\mathbf{H}$, where

$$\mathbf{H}_{ij} = (s^{in} - s_i^{lle}) \cdot (s^{in} - s_j^{lle}). \quad (15)$$

Solving w_j^s from $\mathbf{H}$ is a constrained least square problem, which has the following closed-form solution:

$$w_j^s = \frac{\pounds_k \mathbf{H}_{jk}^{-1}}{\pounds_{lm} \mathbf{H}_{lm}^{-1}} . \quad (16)$$

To avoid explicit inversion of the Gram matrix $\mathbf{H}$, w_{j^s} can efficiently be determined by solving the linear system of equation, $\pounds_k \mathbf{H}_{jk} w_k^s = 1$ and re-scaling the weights to sum to one [Saul and Roweis, 2003]. From w^s, the projected pose subspace representation can be calculated as,

$$p^{out} = \sum_{j=1}^{\kappa} w_j^s p_j^{lle}, \quad p^{out} \in \mathcal{M}^p \quad (17)$$

where p_j^{lle} is an instance of P^{lle} (the pose subspace representation of S^{lle} in $\mathcal{M}^p$). From p^{out} (which exists in $\mathcal{M}^p$), the captured (pre-image) pose x^{out} (in the normalized RJC pose space) is approximated via the fixed point algorithm of Schölkopf *et al* (1998).

Silhouette Parameter Tuning via LLE Optimization

Similar to $\mathcal{M}^p$, the two free parameters γ_s and η_s (in equation 1.12 and equation 1.13) need to be tuned for the silhouette subspace $\mathcal{M}^s$. In addition, an optimal value for $\mathcal{K}$, the number of neighbors for LLE mapping must also be selected. Referring back to Figure 7, the parameters should be tuned to optimize the non-parametric LLE mapping from $\mathcal{M}^s$ to $\mathcal{M}^p$. The same concept as in section 5.1 is applied, but instead of using pre-image approximations in tuning, the parameters γ_s, η_s and $\mathcal{K}$ are tuned to optimize the LLE silhouette-to-pose mapping. Note that due to the use of an unconventional kernel in silhouette KPCA projection, it is unlikely that a good pre-image can be approximated. However, in KSM for motion capture, there is no need to map back to the silhouette input space, hence, no requirement to determine the pre-image in silhouette space.

The silhouette tuning is achieved by minimizing the LLE reconstruction cost function

$$C_s = \frac{1}{N} \sum_{i=1}^{N} \mathrm{P} \mathbf{v}_i^p - \sum_{j=1}^{\mathcal{K}} w_{ij}^s \mathbf{v}_j^p \mathrm{P}^2 \qquad (18)$$

where j indexes the $\mathcal{K}$ neighbors of $\mathbf{v}_i^p$. The mapping weight w_{ij}^s, in this case, is the weight factor of $\mathbf{v}_i^s$ that can be encoded in $\mathbf{v}_j^s$ (as determined by the first two steps of LLE in [Saul and Roweis, 2000] and the reduced training set from $\mathcal{M}^p$) using the Euclidian distance in $\mathcal{M}^s$. To ensure that the tuned parameters generalizes well to unseen novel inputs, training is again performed using cross validation on the training set. Once the optimal parameters are selected for both

$\mathcal{M}^s$ and $\mathcal{M}^p$, the system is ready for capture by projecting the input silhouettes through the learnt feature subspaces.

5.3 Experiments and Results

Section 5.3 presents experiments which compares the Pyramid Match kernel [Grauman and Darrell, 2005] (adopted in KSM) and the Shape Context [Belongie *et al*, 2002] (which is a popular choice for silhouette-based markerless motion capture [Mori and Malik, 2002; Agarwal and Triggs, 2006]) in defining correspondence between human silhouettes. Motion capture results for Kernel Subspace Mapping (KSM) from real and synthetic data are presented in section 5.3 and section 5.3 respectively. The system is trained with a generic mesh model (Figure 8) using motion captured data from the Carnegie Mellon University motion capture database [Carnegie Mellon University, 2007]. Note that even though the system is trained with a generic model, the technique is still model free as no prior knowledge nor manual labelling of the test model is required. All concatenated silhouettes are preprocessed and resized to 160×160 pixels.

Pyramid Match Kernel for Motion Capture

This section aims to show that the pyramid kernel for human silhouette comparison (section 5.1) is as descriptive as the shape context [Belongie *et al*, 2002] (which has already been shown successful in silhouette-based markerless motion capture techniques such as [Agarwal and Triggs, 2006; Mori and Malik, 2002]). A set of synthetic silhouettes of a generic mesh model walking (Figure 15 [right]) is used to test the efficacy of the modified pyramid Match kernel (section 5.1) on human silhouettes. For comparison, the Shape Context of the silhouettes are also calculated and the silhouette correspondence recorded (Figure 15

Figure 13. Illustration to summarize markerless motion capture and the training and testing procedures. The generic mesh model (Figure 14 [center]) in used in training, whilst a previously unseen mesh model is used for testing

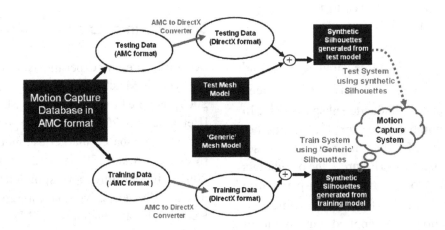

Figure 14. Selected images of the different models used to test Kernel Subspace Mapping (KSM) for markerless motion capture. [left] Biped model used to create deformable meshes for training and testing. [center] Generic model used to generate synthetic training silhouettes. [right] Example of a previously unseen mesh model, which can be used for synthetic testing purposes (Appendix A, Section 3).

[left]). From the experiments, our pyramid kernel is as expressive as the Shape Context for human silhouette comparison [Belongie *et al*, 2002; Mori and Malik, 2002] and its cost is (only) linear in the number of silhouette features (*i.e.* the sets' cardinality).

Quantitative Experiments with Synthetic Data

In order to test KSM quantitatively, novel motions (similar to the training set) are used to animate a previously unseen mesh model of the author (appendix 3) and their corresponding synthetic silhouettes are captured for use as control test images Using a walking training set of 323 ex-

Figure 15. Comparison between the shape context descriptor (341 sample points) and the optimized pyramid match kernel (341 features) for walking human silhouettes. The silhouette distances are given relative to the first silhouette at the bottom left of each silhouette bar.

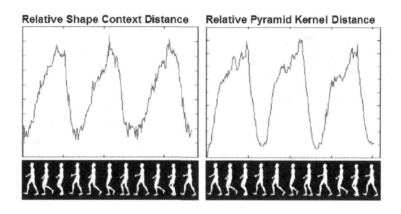

emplars, KSM is able to infer novel poses at an average speed of 0.104 seconds per frame on a Pentium™ 4 with 2.8 GHz processor. The captured pre-image pose is compared with the original pose that was used to generate the synthetic silhouettes (Figure 16). At this point, it should be highlighted that the test mesh model is different to the training mesh model, and all our test images are from an unseen viewing angle or pose (though relative camera-to-camera positions should be the same as was used in training).

For 1260 unseen test silhouettes of a walking sequence, which is captured from different yaw orientations, KSM (with prior knowledge of the starting pose) can achieve accurate pose reconstructions with an average error of $2.78°$ per joint.

For comparison with other related work [Mori and Malik, 2002] the error may reduce down to less than $2°$ of error per each Euler degree of freedom [d.o.f.] (each 3D rotation is represented by a set of 3 Euler rotations Agarwal and Triggs in [Agarwal and Triggs, 2004] were able to achieve a mean angular error of $4.1°$ per d.o.f., but their approach requires only a single camera. We have intentionally recorded our errors in terms of degrees per joint, and not in Euler degree of freedom (as in

[Agarwal and Triggs, 2004]), because for each 3D rotation, there are many possible set of Euler rotations encoding. Therefore, using the Euler degree of freedom to encode error can result in scenarios where the same 3D rotation, can be interpreted as different, hence inducing false positives.

Our technique (which uses a reduced training set of 343 silhouettes and 2 synchronized cameras) also shows visually comparable results to the technique proposed by Grauman *et al* in (2003), which uses a synthetic training set of 20,000 silhouettes and 4 synchronized cameras. In [Grauman *et al*, 2003], the pose error is recorded using the Euclidian distance between the joint centers in real world scale. We believe that this error measurement is not normalized, in the sense, that, for a similar motion sequence, a taller person (with longer limbs) will more likely record larger average error than a shorter person (due to larger variance for the joint located at the end of each limb). Nevertheless, to enable future comparison, we have presented our real world distance results (as in [Grauman *et al*, 2003]) in combination with the test model's height. For a test model with a height of 1.66cm, KSM can estimate pose with a mean (real world) error of approximately 2.02 cm per joint (Figure 18). The technique proposed by Grauman *et al* in (2003) reported an average

Figure 16. Visual comparison of the captured pose (red with `O'joints) and the original ground truth pose (blue with `'joints) used to generate the synthetic test silhouettes.*

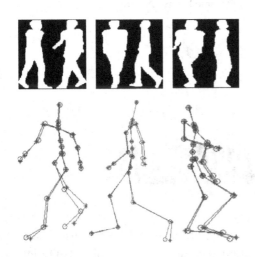

pose error of 3 cm per joint, when using the full system of 4 cameras. A fairer comparison can be achieved when the two approaches (KSM and [Grauman *et al*, 2003]) both use 2 synchronized cameras, in which case, the approach in [Grauman *et al*, 2003] reported an average pose estimation error of over 10 cm per joint.

To further test the robustness of KSM, binary salt & pepper noise with different noise densities are added to the original synthetic data set and the results were detailed in [Tangkuampien,

2007]. Noise densities of 0.2, 0.4 and 0.6 were added to the test silhouettes and the following mean errors of $2.99°$ per joint, $4.45°$ per joint and $10.17°$ per joint were attained respectively. Note that KSM is now being tested for its ability to handle a combination of silhouette noise (*i.e.* the test silhouettes are different to that of the training silhouettes) and pixel noise (which is used to simulate scenarios with poor silhouette segmentation). An interesting point to note is that the increase in noise level does not equally affect the inference error for each silhouette, but rather, the noise increases the error significantly for a minority of the poses. This indicates that the robustness of KSM can be improved substantially by introducing some form of temporal smoothing to minimize these peaks in error.

Qualitative Experiments with Real Data

For testing with real data, silhouettes of a spiral walk sequence were captured using simple background subtraction. Two perpendicular cameras were set up (with the same extrinsic parameters as the training cameras) without precise measurements. Due to the simplicity of the setup, segmentation noise (as a result of shadows and varying light) was prominent in our test sequences. Selected results are shown in Figure 19.

Figure 17. KSM capture error (degrees per joint) for a synthetic walk motion sequence. The entire sequence has a mean error of $2.78°$ per joint

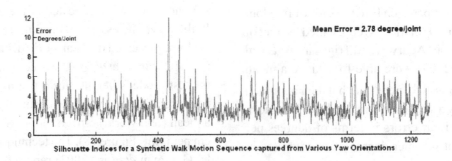

Figure 18. KSM capture error (cm/joint) for a synthetic walk motion sequence. The entire sequence has a mean error of 2.02 cm per joint

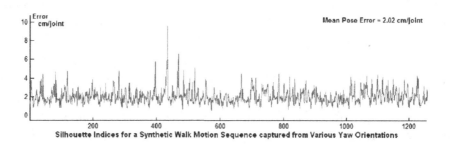

For animation, captured poses were mapped to a generic mesh model and the technique was able to created smooth realistic animation in most parts of the sequence. In other parts ($\cdot$ 12% of the captured animation's time frame), the animation was unrealistic as inaccurate captured poses were being appended, the presence of which is further exaggerated in animation. However, even though an incorrect pose may lead to unrealistic animation, it still remains within the subspace of realistic pose when viewed statically (by itself). This is because all output poses are constrained to lie within the subspace spanned by the set of realistic training poses in the first place.

6 GREEDY KPCA FOR HUMAN MOTION CAPTURE [3]

Greedy KPCA can be applied (GKPCA) [Franc and Hlavac, 2003] as a preprocessing filter (in training set reduction) for Kernel Subspace Mapping (KSM). Greedy KPCA results in relatively similar pose estimation quality (as standard KSM [section 5]) but with lower evaluation cost (due to the reduced training set).

During training, the kernel matrix (which grows quadratically with the number of exemplars in the training set) needs to be calculated before standard PCA can be applied in feature space. As

Figure 19. Kernel subspace mapping motion capture on real data using 2 synchronized un-calibrated cameras. All captured poses are mapped to a generic mesh model and rendered from the same angles as the cameras

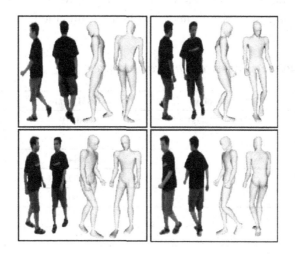

for the de-noising (projection and pre-image approximations [Schölkopf *et al*, 1999]) via KPCA, the cost is linear in the exemplar number because each projection requires a kernel comparison with each vector in the training set. As a result, the cardinality of the training set is vital in any real system incorporating KPCA. The goal of KPCA with greedy filtering (GKPCA) [Franc and Hlavac, 2003] is to filter (from the original motion sequences) a reduced training subset than can optimally represent the original de-noising subspace, given a specific prior constraint (*e.g.* using 70% of the original training data).

6.1 Experiments and Results

There are three factors that should be considered in concluding if Greedy KPCA can filter out a reduced set (in a manner which will enhance the performance of KSM). These are:

1. Does a reduced training size lead to a reduction in motion capture time (*i.e.* an increase in motion capture rate)?
2. What is the effect of a reduced training set on the de-noising qualities of human motion when compared with using the full set?
3. What is the effect of a reduced training set on the quality of pose estimation via KSM?

Figure 5 [bottom] highlights the linear relationship between the de-noising cost of KPCA and the training size. Table 1 summarizes how the current capture rate of KSM for motion capture can be controlled via training size modification. The dominant cost, being the recursive pyramid cost of calculating the silhouette feature vector $\Psi(f)$, which is currently implemented in un-optimized Matlab™ code. This cost is not shown in the table as it is independent of the training size, but can be determined by taking the difference between the KSM total cost and the LLE mapping and pre-image cost.

All experiments were performed on a Pentium™ 4 with a 2.8 GHz processor. In Figure 20, GKPCA selects 30% of the original sequence to build the reduced set subspace. Synthetic gaussian white noise is added to motion sequence $\mathcal{X}$ in pose space, and the de-noising qualities compared quantitatively (Figure 20) and qualitatively in a 3D animation playback.

Figure 20 highlights the superiority of both KPCA and GKPCA over linear PCA in motion de-noising. GKPCA will tend towards the KPCA de-noising limit as a greater percentage of the original sequence is included in the reduced set. Specifically for the walking and running motion sequences, the frame by frame comparison in Figure 21 and Figure 22 further emphasizes the similarity of de-noising qualities between KPCA (blue line) and GKPCA (red line). Both the error plots for GKPCA and KPCA are well below the error plot for PCA de-noising (black line). For human animation, the GKPCA algorithm is able

Table 1. Comparison of capture rate for varying training sizes

Training	LLE mapping	KSM total	Capture
size	and pre-image (s)	cost (s)	rate (*Hz*)
100	0.0065	0.0847	11.81
200	0.0120	0.0902	11.09
300	0.0220	0.1002	9.98
400	0.0310	0.1092	9.16
500	0.0410	0.1192	8.39

to generate realistic and smooth animation comparable with KPCA when the de-noised motion is mapped to a skeleton model and play backed in real time.

To analyze the ability for GKPCA to implicitly de-noise feature subspace noise, we add synthetic noise in the feature space of a walk motion sequence. We are interested in this aspect of de-noising because, in KSM, noise may be induced in the process of mapping from one feature subspace to another (*i.e.* from $\mathcal{M}^s$ to $\mathcal{M}^p$). Figure 23 shows the relationship between feature space noise and pose space noise for both KPCA and GKPCA de-noising for a walk sequence from various yaw orientations (GKPCA uses a reduced set consisting of 30% of the original set). Surprisingly, the ratio of pose space noise to feature subspace noise (*i.e.* pose space noise/feature subspace noise) is lower for GKPCA de-noising when compared to using KPCA de-noising. The lower GKPCA plot indicates its superiority over KPCA at minimizing feature space noise, which may be induced in the process of pose inference

Figure 20. Pose space mse comparison between PCA, KPCA and GKPCA de-noising for walking and boxing sequences

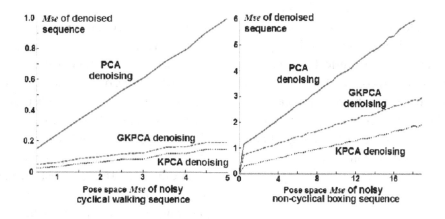

Figure 21. Frame by Frame error comparison between PCA, KPCA and GKPCA de-noising of a human walk sequence. GKPCA selects 30% of the original sequence

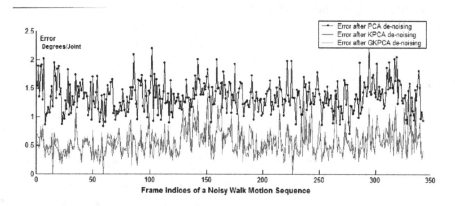

Figure 22. Frame by frame error comparison between PCA, KPCA and GKPCA de-noising of a human run sequence. GKPCA selects 30% of the original sequence

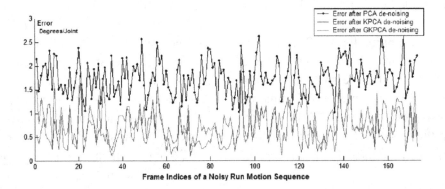

via KSM (*i.e.* the same level of noise in GKPCA feature subspace will more likely map to a lower level of noise [when compared to KPCA] in the RJC pose space). However, it is important to note that the noise analysis presented here is only for human motion de-noising. The effect of a reduced set (filtered via GKPCA) on markerless motion capture has not yet been analyzed. The following section attempts to investigate this relationship between the size of the reduced training set and the quality of pose estimation via KSM.

Greedy KPCA for Kernel Subspace Mapping

To test the efficacy of KSM motion capture with a GKPCA pre-processing filter, the training set of 323 exemplars (as previously applied in section 5.3) is used as the original (starting) set. Using the distance in the pose feature subspace for filtering, the GKPCA algorithm [Franc, 2000; Franc and Hlavac, 2003] is initialized to extract reduced training sets from the original set. The reduced sets are then tuned independently using the process described in section 1.5. For comparison with previous results of motion capture via KSM, the

Figure 23. Comparison of feature and pose space mse relationship for KPCA and GKPCA; GKPCA uses a reduced set consisting of 30% of the original set

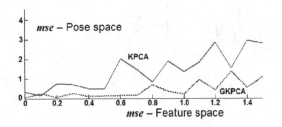

Figure 24. Average errors per joint for the reduced training sets filtered via GKPCA

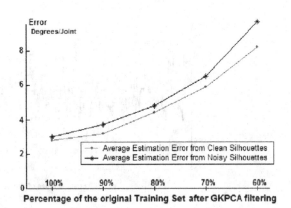

Figure 25. Frame by frame error comparison (degrees per joint) for a clean walk sequence with different level of GKPCA filter in KSM

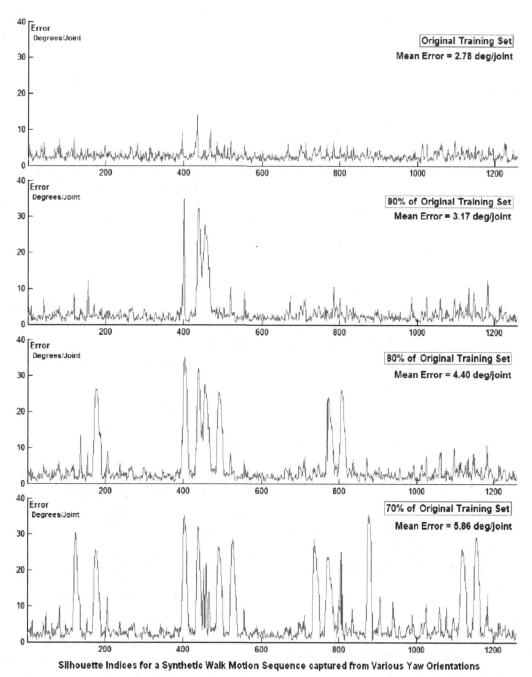

Silhouette Indices for a Synthetic Walk Motion Sequence captured from Various Yaw Orientations

same synthetic set of 1260 unseen silhouettes (as used in section 5.3) is used for testing.

For pose inference from clean silhouettes (*i.e.* clean silhouette segmentation, but still using

silhouettes of different models between testing and training), and using reduced training sets consisting of 90%, 80% and 70% of the original set: KSM can infer pose with average errors of

3.17° per joint, 4.40° per joint and 5.86° degree per joint respectively. The frame by frame error in pose estimation (from clean silhouettes) are plotted in Figure 25.

REFERENCES

Agarwal, A., & Triggs, B. (2004). Learning to track 3D human motion from silhouettes. *International Conference on Machine Learning* (pp. 9-16).

Agarwal, A., & Triggs, B. (2006). Recovering 3D Human Pose from Monocular Images. *IEEE Transactions on Pattern Analysis and Machine Intelligence, 28*(1). doi:10.1109/TPAMI.2006.21

Alexa, M. (2002). Linear combination of transformations. *SIGGRAPH* (pp. 380-387).

Belongie, S., Malik, J., & Puzicha, J. (2002). Shape Matching and Object Recognition Using Shape Contexts. *IEEE Transactions on Pattern Analysis and Machine Intelligence, 24*, 509–522. doi:10.1109/34.993558

Bowden, R. (2000). Learning statistical models of human motion. *IEEE Workshop on Human Modeling, Analysis and Synthesis, Internation Conference on Computer Vision & Pattern Recognition.*

Bregler, C., & Malik, J. (1998). Tracking People with Twists and Exponential Maps. *International Conference on Computer Vision & Pattern Recognition* (pp. 8-15).

Caillette, F., Galata, A., & Howard, T. (2005). Real-Time 3D human body tracking using variable length markov models. *British Machine Vision Conference* (pp. 469-478).

Carr, J.C., Beatson, R.K., Cherrie, J.B., Mitchell, T.J., Fright, W.R., McCallum, B.C., & Evans, T.R. (2001). Reconstruction and Representation of 3D Objects with Radial Basis Functions. *SIGGRAPH*, 67-76.

Carr, J. C., Beatson, R. K., McCallum, B. C., Fright, W. R., McLennan, T. J., & Mitchell, T. J. (2003). Smooth Surface Reconstruction from Noisy Range Data. *Applied Research Associates NZ Ltd.*

Chai, J., & Hodgins, J. K. (2005). Performance animation from low-dimensional control signals. *ACM Transactions on Graphics, 24*(3), 686–696. doi:10.1145/1073204.1073248

Chen, Y., Lee, J., Parent, R., & Machiraju, R. (2005). Markerless monocular motion capture using image features and physical constraints. *Computer Graphincs International*, 36-43. Carnegie Mellon University Graphics Lab Motion Capture Database. (n.d.). Retrieved from http://mocaps.cs.cmu.edu

Elgammal, A., & Lee, C.-S. (2004). Inferring 3D Body Pose from Silhouettes using Activity Manifold Learning. *International Conference on Computer Vision & Pattern Recognition* (pp. 681-688).

Franc, V. (2000). Pattern Recognition Toolbox for Matlab. *Centre for Machine Perception, Czech Technical University.*

Franc, V., & Hlavac, V. (2003). Greedy Algorithm for a Training Set Reduction in the Kernel Methods. *Int. Conf. on Computer Analysis of Images and Patterns* (pp. 426-433).

Grauman, K., & Darrell, T. The Pyramid Match Kernel: Discriminative Classification with Sets of Image Features. *International Conference on Computer Vision* (pp. 1458-1465).

Grauman, K., Shakhnarovich, G., & Darrell, T. (2003). Inferring 3D Structure with a Statistical Image-Based Shape Model. *International Conference on Computer Vision* (pp. 641-648).

Jolliffe, I. T. (1986). *Principal Component Analysis*. New York: Springer-Verlag.

Kalman, R. E. (1961). A New Approach to Linear Filtering and Prediction Problems. *Transactions on the ASME - . Journal of Basic Engineering*, 95–107.

Kovar, L., Gleicher, M., & Pighin, F. (2002). Motion graphs. *SIGGRAPH: Proceedings of the 29th annual conference on Computer graphics and interactive techniques* (pp. 473-482).

Kwok, J. T., & Tsang, I. W. (2003). The pre-image problem in kernel methods. *International Conference on Machine Learning* (pp. 408-415).

Lander, J. (1998). Working with Motion Capture File Formats. *Game Developer*, 30-37.

Luna, F. (2004). Skinned Mesh Character Animation with Direct3D 9.0c. Retreived from http://www.moons-lab.com.

Moeslund, T. B., & Granum, E. (2000). 3D Human Pose Estimation using 2D-Data and An Alternative Phase Space Representation. In *Proceedings of the IEEE Workshop on Human Modeling, Analysis and Synthesis* (pp. 26-33).

Mori, G., & Malik, J. (2002). Estimating Human Body Configurations Using Shape Context Matching. *European Conference on Computer Vision* (pp. 666-680).

Navaratnam, R., Thayananthan, A., Torr, P. H. S., & Cipolla, R. (2005). Heirarchical Part-Based Human Body Pose Estimation. *British Machine Vision Conference* (pp. 479-488).

Ren, L., Shakhnarovich, G., Hodgins, J. K., Pfister, H., & Viola, P. (2005). Learning Silhouette Features for Control of Human Motion. *ACM Transactions on Graphics*, 24(4). doi:10.1145/1095878.1095882

Safonova, A., Hodgins, J. K., & Pollard, N. S. (2004). Synthesizing physically realistic human motion in low-dimensional. *ACM Transactions on Graphics*, 23(3), 514–521. doi:10.1145/1015706.1015754

Saul, L. K., & Roweis, S. T. (2000). Nonlinear dimensionality reduction by locally linear embedding. *Science*, 290, 2323–2269. doi:10.1126/science.290.5500.2323

Saul, L. K., & Roweis, S. T. (2003). Think globally, fit locally: unsupervised learning of low dimensional manifolds. *Journal of Machine Learning Research*, 4, 119–155. doi:10.1162/153244304322972667

Schölkopf, B., Knirsch, P., Smola, C., & Burges, A. (1998). Fast approximation of support vector kernel expansions, and an interpretation of clustering as approximation in feature spaces. *Mustererkennung*, 124-132.

Schölkopf, B., Mika, S., Smola, A. J., Rätsch, G., & Müller, K. R. (1998). Kernel PCA pattern reconstruction via approximate pre-images. *International Conference on Artificial Neural Networks* (pp. 147-152).

Schölkopf, B., & Smola, A. J. (2002). *Learning with Kernels: Support Vector Machines, Regularization, Optimization and Beyond*. Cambridge, MA: MIT Press.

Schölkopf, B., Smola, A. J., & Müller, K. R. (1997). Kernel principal component analysis. *Internation Conference on Artificial Neural Networks* (pp. 583-588).

Schölkopf, B., Smola, A. J., & Müller, K. R. (1999). Kernel PCA and De-noising in feature spaces. *Advances in Neural Information Processing Systems*, 536–542.

Schraudolph, N. N., Günter, S., & Vishwanathan, S. V. N. (2007). Fast Iterative Kernel PCA. *Advances in Neural Information Processing Systems*.

Smith, L. I. (2002). *A Tutorial on Principal Components Analysis*. Vicon Peak: Vicon MX System. (n.d.). Retrieved from http://www.vicon.com/products/systems.html

Tangkuampien, T. (2007). *Kernel subspace mapping: robust human pose and viewpoint inference from high dimensional training sets*. PhD thesis, Monash University.

Tangkuampien, T., & Suter, D. (2006). Human Motion De-noising via Greedy Kernel Principal Component Analysis Filtering. *International Conference on Pattern Recognition* (pp. 457-460).

Tangkuampien, T., & Suter, D. (2006). Real-Time Human Pose Inference using Kernel Principal Components Pre-image Approximations. *British Machine Vision Conference* (pp. 599-608).

Urtasun, R., Fleet, D. J., Hertzmann, A., & Fua, P. (2005). Priors for People Tracking from Small Training Sets. *International Conference on Computer Vision* (pp. 403-410).

ENDNOTES

[1] The term `previously unseen' is used in this chapter to refer to vectors/silhouettes that are not in the training set.

[2] This chapter is based on the conference paper [41] T. Tangkuampien and D. Suter: Real-Time Human Pose Inference using Kernel Principal Component Pre-image Approximations: British Machine Vision Conference (BMVC) 2006, pages 599--608, Edinburgh, UK.

[3] This chapter is based on the conference paper [40] T. Tangkuampien and D. Suter: Human Motion De-noising via Greedy Kernel Principal Component Analysis Filtering: International Conference on Pattern Recognition (ICPR) 2006, pages 457--460, Hong Kong, China.

APPENDIX A: MOTION CAPTURE FORMATS AND CONVERTERS

A.1. Motion Capture Formats in KSM

A deformable mesh model can be animated by simply controlling its inner hierarchical biped/skeleton structure (Figure 26). As a result, most motion formats only encode pose information to animate these structures. For information on how to create a deformable skinned mesh in DirectX (*i.e. attach* a static mesh model to its skeleton), the reader should refer to [Luna, 2004].

In KSM, three different formats are used. These are: the Acclaim Motion Capture (AMC) (section A.1.1) [Lander, 1998], the DirectX format (section A.1.2) [Luna, 2004] and the Relative Joint Center (RJC) format (section 3.1). Figure 27 shows a diagram summarizing the use of these formats in the system. KSM learns the mapping from the synthetic silhouette space to the corresponding RJC space (Figure 27 [right:dotted arrow]) for a specific motion set (*e.g.* walking, running). For training, a database of accurate human motion is required, which can be downloaded in AMC format from the CMU mo-

Figure 26. Diagram to summarize the hierarchical relationship of the bones of inner biped structure

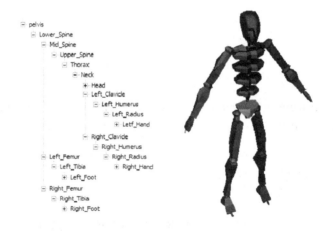

Figure 27. Diagram to summarize the proposed markerless motion capture system and how the reviewed motion formats combine together to create a novel pose inference technique called Kernel Subspace Mapping (KSM)

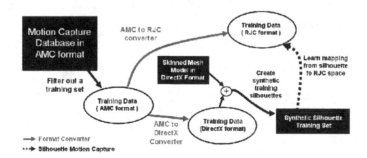

tion capture database [Carnegie Mellon University, 2007]. From this, synthetic silhouettes for machine learning purposes can be generated via the DirectX skinned mesh model [Luna, 2004]. From our experiments, the interpolation and reconstruct (of realistic new poses) is best synthesized in the normalized RJC format (section 3.1).

A.1.1. Acclaim Motion Capture (AMC) Format

The Acclaim motion capture (AMC) format, developed by the game maker Acclaim, stores human motion using concatenated Euler rotations. The full motion capture format consists of two types of file, the Acclaim skeleton file (ASF) and the AMC file [Lander, 1998]. The ASF file stores the attributes of the skeleton such as the number of bones, their geometric dimension, their hierarchical relationships and the base pose, which is usually the `tpose' (Figure 28 [right]). For the case where a single skeletal structure is used, the ASF file can be kept constant and ignored. On the other hand, the AMC file (which encodes human motion using joint rotations over a sequence of frames) is different for every set of motion and is the file generated during motion capture.

The AMC format is the simplest form of joint encoding and is one of the format adopted by the VICON marker based motion capture system [Vicon Peak, 2007].

Figure 28. Example of a Acclaim motion capture (AMC) format with example rotation of the left humerus bone (i.e. the left shoulder joint)

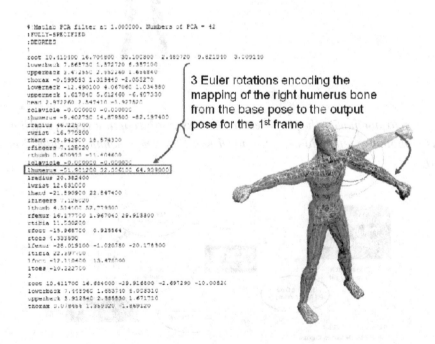

A.1.2. DirectX Animation Format

Human motion capture format in DirectX is similar to the AMC format in that there are two parts to the file structure, the skeleton/mesh attribute section and the human motion section. The skeleton/mesh attribute section encodes the biped hierarchical structure, its geometric attributes and additional information such as its relationship to the mesh model (*i.e.* the weight matrix of the mesh vertices [Luna, 2004]). This information can again be considered constant and can be ignored in the pose inference process. Similar to the AMC format (section A.1.1), we concentrating principally on the file section that encodes the motion data.

Instead of encoding 3D rotations using Euler rotations, the 4×4 homogeneous matrix is adopted. Note that the 4×4 matrix can also encode translation and scaling data (in addition to the rotation). However, for motion capture, where the geometric attributes of the model (*e.g.* length of arms, height, etc) is known and considered constant, pose inference can be constrained to inferring a set of 3×3 rotation matrices, which *only* encodes the rotation information.

The main advantage of the DirectX format is the optimized skinned mesh animation and support for the format [Luna, 2004], which enables the efficient rendering and capture of synthetic silhouettes for training and testing purposes.

A.2. Accurate Mesh Acquisition

Human model acquisition was achieved via a laser scanner integrated with a synchronized high-resolution camera. The surface fitting and re-sampling technique of Carr et al (2003) was applied to the scanned data. Images captured from the digital camera during scanning were textured onto the mesh. See Figure 29.

Figure 29. Selected textured mesh models of the first author in varying boxing poses

A.2.1. Model Acquisition for Surface Fitting and Re-Sampling

The model acquisition was performed using the Riegl LMS-Z420i terrestrial laser scanner equipped with a calibrated Nikon D100 6 mega pixels digital camera. The laser is positioned approximately five metres from the actor and two scans of the front and back of the actor are captured. Two stands are positioned on the left and right of the actor for hand placement in order to ensure ease of biped and mesh alignment. Thereafter, the front and back point cloud data are filtered and merged using the Riscan Pro software and the combined point cloud data exported for surface fitting.

A.2.2. Radial Basis Fitting and Re-Sampling

From the merged point cloud data of the actor (Figure 30 [right]), a radial basis function (RBF) can be fitted to the data set for re-sampling, after which a smooth mesh surface can be attained by joining the sampled points. For the case of 3D point cloud data, the original scanned points (also referred to as *on*-surface points) are each assigned a 4th dimension density value of zero [Carr *et al*, 2003]. By letting *x* denote a 3D vector, a smooth surface in R^3 can be obtained by fitting an RBF function $S(\mathrm{x})$ to the labelled scanned points and re-sampling the function at the same density value of $S(\mathrm{x}) = 0$. It is obvious that if only data points with density values of 0 are available, RBF fitting (to this set) will produce the trivial solution [i.e. $S(\mathrm{x}) = 0$ for all $\mathrm{x} \in R^3$]. To avoid this, a *signed-distance function*, which encodes the relationship between *off*-surface and *on*-surface points, can be adopted (Figure 31).

An *off*-surface point, in this case, is a *synthetic* point x_m^s whose density is assigned the signed value d_m, which is proportional to the distance to its closest *on*-surface point. *Off*-surface points are created along the projected normals, and can be created inside (blue points: $d_m < 0$) or outside (red points: $d_m > 0$) the surface defined by the *on*-surface (green) points. Normals are determined from local patches of *on*-surface points and performed using an evaluation version of the FastRBF ^{TM} Matlab toolbox [Carr *et al*, 2003]. The surface fitting problem can now be re-formulated as the problem of determining an RBF function S(*x*) such that

$$
\begin{aligned}
S(\mathrm{x}_n) &= 0, &\quad for \quad n = 1, 2, ..., N &\quad and \\
S(\mathrm{x}_m^s) &= d_m, &\quad for \quad m = 1, 2, ..., M
\end{aligned}
\tag{19}
$$

where N and M are the number of *on*-surface and *off*-surface points respectively. The RBF function $S(\mathrm{x})$ can be sampled at any point within the range of the *on*-surface and *off*-surface training data. More importantly, it is possible to sample the RBF at $S(\mathrm{x}) = 0$, which corresponds to the surface defined by the *on*-surface points. Furthermore, it is possible to sample this RBF at regular grid interval, adding to the simplicity and efficiency of the mesh construction algorithm.

By applying fast approximation techniques [Carr *et al*, 2003], it is possible to calculate the RBF reasonably efficiently. Figure 32 shows the resultant mesh model of the first author generated via the RBF fast approximation and re-sampling technique.

For increases realism, images of the person captured from the synchronized digital camera can be textured onto the plain model. Selected poses of textured mesh models of the first author (using this simple solution) are shown in Figure 29.

Figure 30. Examples images of the front and back scan of the first author [left] and the merged filtered scan data, which is used for surface fitting and re-sampling purposes

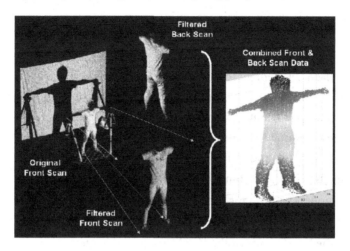

Figure 31. Diagram to illustrate the generation of off-surface points (blue and red) from the input on-surface points (green) before fitting an RBF function

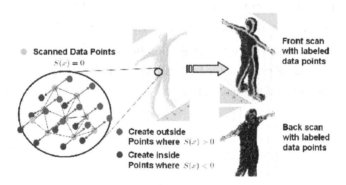

Figure 32. Selected examples of the accurate mesh model of the first author create via the RBF fast approximation & sampling technique of Carr et al (2003)

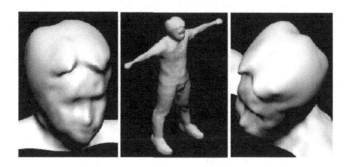

APPENDIX B: COMMONLY USED SYMBOLS

Some commonly used symbols in this thesis are defined here:

- $\mathcal{X}^{tr}$ refers to the training set.
- x_i refers to the i-th element (column vector) of the training set $\mathcal{X}^{tr}$.
- x refers to the novel input (column vector) for the model learnt from $\mathcal{X}^{tr}$.
- $\mathcal{M}^p$ refers to the pose feature subspace.
- $\mathcal{M}^s$ refers to the silhouette feature subspace.
- $k_p(\cdot,\cdot)$ refers to the KPCA kernel function in the pose space.
- $k_s(\cdot,\cdot)$ refers to the KPCA kernel function in the silhouette space.
- Ψ refers the the silhouette descriptor for the silhouette kernel $k_s(\cdot,\cdot)$.
- v^p refers to the coefficients of the KPCA projected vector x via $k_p(\cdot,\cdot)$.
- v^s refers to the coefficients of the KPCA projected vector $\ddot{}$ via $k_s(\cdot,\cdot)$.
- P^{tr} refers to the KPCA projected set of training poses.
- S^{tr} refers to the KPCA projected set of training silhouettes.
- P^{lle} refers to the reduced training subset of P^{tr} used in LLE mapping.
- S^{lle} refers to the reduced training subset of S^{tr} used in LLE mapping.
- s^{in} refers to projection of the the input silhouette in $\mathcal{M}^s$.
- p^{out} refers to the pose subspace representation of s^{in} in $\mathcal{M}^p$.
- x^{out} refers to the output pose vector for KSM (*i.e.* the pre-image of p^{out}).
- $\mathcal{X}^{gk}$ refers to the reduced training subset (of $\mathcal{X}^{tr}$), filtered via Greedy KPCA.n

Chapter 6
Multi–Scale People Detection and Motion Analysis for Video Surveillance

YingLi Tian
The City College of City University of New York, USA

Rogerio Feris
IBM T. J. Watson Research Center, USA

Lisa Brown
IBM T. J. Watson Research Center, USA

Daniel Vaquero
University of California, Santa Barbara, USA

Yun Zhai
IBM T. J. Watson Research Center, USA

Arun Hampapur
IBM T. J. Watson Research Center, USA

ABSTRACT

Visual processing of people, including detection, tracking, recognition, and behavior interpretation, is a key component of intelligent video surveillance systems. Computer vision algorithms with the capability of "looking at people" at multiple scales can be applied in different surveillance scenarios, such as far-field people detection for wide-area perimeter protection, mid-field people detection for retail/banking applications or parking lot monitoring, and near-field people/face detection for facility security and access. In this chapter, we address the people detection problem in different scales as well as human tracking and motion analysis for real video surveillance applications including people search, retail loss prevention, people counting, and display effectiveness.

DOI: 10.4018/978-1-60566-900-7.ch006

1. INTRODUCTION

As the number of cameras deployed for surveillance increases, the challenge of effectively extracting useful information from the torrent of camera data becomes formidable. The inability of human vigilance to effectively monitor surveillance cameras is well recognized in the scientific community [Green 1999]. Additionally, the cost of employing security staff to monitor hundreds of cameras by manually watching videos is prohibitive.

Intelligent (smart) surveillance systems, which are now "watching the video" and providing alerts and content-based search capabilities, make the video monitoring and investigation process scalable and effective. The software algorithms that analyze the video and provide alerts are commonly referred to as video analytics. These are responsible for turning video cameras from a mere data gathering tool into smart surveillance systems for proactive security. Advances in computer vision, video analysis, pattern recognition, and multimedia indexing technologies have enabled smart surveillance systems over the past decade.

People detection, tracking, recognition, and behavior interpretation play very important roles in video surveillance. For different surveillance scenarios, different algorithms are employed to detect people in distinct scales, such as far-field people detection for wide-area perimeter protection, mid-field people detection for retail/banking applications or parking lot monitoring, and near-field people/face detection for facility security and access. People detection and tracking has been an active area of research. The approaches for people detection can be classified as either model-based or learning-based. The latter can use different kinds of features such as edge templates [Gavrila 2000], Haar features [Viola *et al.* 2001, 2003], histogram-of-oriented-gradients descriptors [Dalal & Triggs 2005, Han *et al.* 2006], shapelet features [Sabzmeydani 2007], etc. To deal

with occlusions, some approaches use part-based detectors [Wu & Nevatia 2005, Leibe 2005].

In our system, learning-based methods are employed to detect humans at different scales. For each person entering and leaving the field of view of a surveillance camera, our goal is to detect the person and to store in a database a key frame containing the image of the person, associated with a corresponding video. This allows the user to perform queries such as "Show me all people who entered the facility yesterday from 1pm to 5pm." The retrieved key frames can then be used for recognition, either manually or by an automatic face recognition system (if the face image is available). To achieve this goal, we developed a novel face detector algorithm that uses local feature adaptation prior to Adaboost learning. Local features have been widely used in learning-based object detection systems. As noted by Munder and Gavrila [Munder & Gavrila 2006], they offer advantages over global features such as Principal Component Analysis [Zhang *et al.* 2004] or Fisher Discriminant Analysis [Wang & Ji 2005], which tend to smooth out important details.

In order to detect trajectory anomalies, our system tracks faces and people, analyzes the paths of tracked people, learns a set of repeated patterns that occur frequently, and detects when a person moves in a way inconsistent with these normal patterns. We implement two types of tracking methods: person-detection-based and moving-object-based. The person-detection-based tracking method is used to track faces and people in near-field scenarios. In far-field scenarios, the moving-object-based tracking method is employed because faces are too small to be accurately detected. The moving objects are first detected by an adaptive background subtraction method, and are then tracked by using a tracking method based on appearance. An object classifier further labels each tracked object as a car, person, group of people, animal, etc. To build the model of motion patterns, the trajectories of all tracks with a given start/end location labeling are resampled and clustered together. This gives an average or "prototypical" track along with standard deviations. Most tracks from a given entry location to a given exit will lie close to the prototypical track, with typical normal variation indicated by the length of the crossbars. Tracks that wander outside this normal area can be labeled as anomalous and may warrant further investigation. The principal components of the cluster indicate typical modes of variation or "eigentracks", providing a more accurate model of normal vs. abnormal.

The algorithms for people detection and motion analysis can then be used in several higher-level surveillance applications. Starting from a detected person, we perform clothing color classification based on two body parts (torso and legs), which are segmented from the human silhouette. This enables searching for people based on the color of their clothes. We also present applications of our system in retail loss prevention, people counting and display effectiveness. These have been successfully deployed in commercial establishments.

The rest of this chapter is organized as follows: Section 2 reviews the IBM Smart Surveillance System (SSS). Section 3 presents our learning framework for selecting and combining multiple types of visual features for object detection. The application of this framework to human detection in multiple scales is discussed in Section 4. Section 5 covers human tracking and motion analysis. Several case studies in video surveillance including people search by clothes color, retail loss prevention, people counting, and display effectiveness are demonstrated in Section 6. We conclude our work in Section 7.

2. THE IBM SMART SURVEILLANCE SYSTEM

The IBM Smart Surveillance System (SSS) employs a number of distinct and highly specialized techniques and algorithms [Hampapur *et al.* 2005], which can be summarized as follows:

- **Plug and play analytics frameworks:** Video cameras capture a wide range of information about people, vehicles and events. The type of information captured is dependent on a number of parameters like camera type, angle, field of view, resolution, etc. Automatically detecting each type of information requires specialized sets of algorithms. For example, automatically reading license plates requires specialized OCR algorithms; capturing face images requires face detection algorithms and recognizing behaviors; finding abandoned packages requires detection and tracking algorithms. A smart surveillance system needs to support all of these algorithms, typically through a plug and play framework;

- **Object detection and tracking:** One of the core capabilities of smart surveillance systems is the ability to detect and track moving objects. Object detection algorithms are typically statistical learning algorithms that dynamically learn the scene background model and use the reference model to determine which parts of the scene correspond to moving objects [Tian *et al.* 2005]. Tracking algorithms associate the movement of objects over time generating a trajectory [Senior *et al.* 2001]. These two algorithms together take a video stream and decompose it into objects and events, effectively creating a parse tree for the surveillance video;

- **Object and color classification:** Object classification algorithms classify objects into different classes (such as people, vehicles, animals, etc.), using training data and calibration schemes. Color classification algorithms classify the dominant color of the object into one of the standard colors (red, green, blue, yellow, black and white). These attributes become part of the searchable index, allowing users to query for "red vehicles" or "people wearing blue clothes" [Brown 2008, Chen *et al.* 2008].

- **Alert definition and detection:** Typical smart surveillance systems support a variety of user-defined behavior detection capabilities such as detecting motion within a defined zone, detecting objects that cross a user-defined virtual boundary, detecting abandoned objects, etc. The user uses graphical user interface tools to specify zones of interest, object sizes and other parameters that define the behavior. When the behavior of interest occurs within a camera's field of view, the system automatically generates an alert message that can be transmitted to a workstation, PDA or email reader, depending on the users' preference [Tian *et al.* 2008, Zhai *et al.* 2008].

- **Database event indexing:** The events detected by the video analysis algorithms are indexed by content and stored in a database. This allows events to be cross-referenced across multiple spatially distributed cameras and creates a historical archive of events. The event index information

typically includes time of occurrence, camera identifier, event type, object type, object appearance attributes and an index into the video repository, which allows the user to "play back the relevant video at the touch of a button".

- **Search and retrieval:** Users can use a variety of GUI tools to define complex search criteria to retrieve specific events. Events are typically presented as shown in the middle section of Figure 1. Search criteria include object size, color, location in the scene, velocity, time of occurrence, and several other parameters. The results of a search can also be rendered in a variety of summary views, one of which (called track summary) is shown in the right section of Figure 1.

3. FEATURE ADAPTATION PRIOR TO LEARNING FOR OBJECT DETECTION

In this section, we describe a novel learning framework for selecting and combining multiple types of visual features for object detection [Feris *et al.* 2008]. The application of this framework

Figure 1. (a) The home page, with 1) cameras (bottom right) running a variety of video analysis capabilities, such as license plate recognition, face capture and behavior analysis; 2) Real-time alert panel (top right); 3) Map of the area (top left); 4) Video player (bottom left). (b) The results of searching for a red car. (c) A summary view of all activity in a camera over a selected period, represented as object tracks.

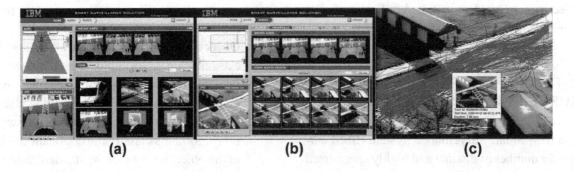

(a)　　　　　(b)　　　　　(c)

to human detection in multiple scales is covered in Section 4.

3.1 Motivation

Current machine learning methods for object detection based on local image features suffer from a scalability problem in the feature selection process. For a specific *feature type* (*e.g.*, Gabor filters), most methods include many feature configurations in a *feature pool* (*e.g.*, Gabor filters uniformly sampled at different positions, orientations and scales), and then use a learning algorithm, such as Adaboost or SVM, to select the features that best discriminate object images from images that do not contain the object. Therefore, as new feature types are considered, the feature pool size increases dramatically, leading to computational problems. This scalability issue has several implications. First, the training time can be excessively long due to the large feature pool and the brute-force strategy for feature selection. Most methods consider a pool with hundreds of thousands of local features, and training can take weeks on conventional machines. Second, the detection/recognition accuracy can be significantly affected, as important feature configurations may not be included in the feature pool due to the sampling process, whereas many features that are less meaningful for discrimination may be present in the pool.

In order to overcome the limitations discussed above, we propose a novel framework to combine and select multiple types of visual features in the learning process. Our approach relies on the observation that the local features selected for discrimination tend to match the local structure of the object. Figure 2 shows the first features selected by Adaboost in the context of face detection [Viola & Jones 2001] and recognition [Yang *et al.* 2004]. In this example, the selected Haar filters capture the local image contrast. In the middle image of the top row, the dark part of the filter coincides with the dark image region (the eyes), while the bright

part of the filter matches the bright image region under the eyes (the cheek and nose). Similarly, in the bottom row, Gabor wavelets capture local structures of the face. In fact, Liu and Shum [Liu & Shum 2003], in their Kullback-Leibler boosting framework, argued that features should resemble the face semantics, matching the face structure either locally or globally.

Based on this observation, we present an approach that pre-selects local image filters based on how well they fit the local image structures of an object, and then use traditional learning techniques such as Adaboost or SVMs to select the final set of features. Our technique can be summarized in two stages. In the first stage, features that adapt to each particular sample in the training set are determined. This is carried out by a non-linear optimization method that determines local image filter parameters (such as position, orientation and scale) that match the geometric structure of each object sample. By combining adaptive features of different types from multiple training samples, a compact and diversified feature pool is generated. Thus, the computational cost of learning is

Figure 2. Features selected by Adaboost in the context of face detection (top) and face recognition (bottom); Note that the features tend to adapt to the local face structure

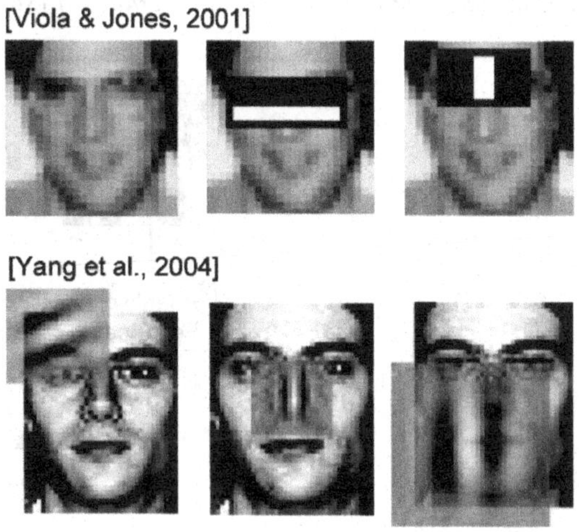

[Viola & Jones, 2001]

[Yang et al., 2004]

reduced, since it is proportional to the feature pool size. The efficiency and the accuracy of the detector are also improved, as the use of adaptive features allows for the design of classifiers composed of fewer features, which better describe the structure of the objects to be detected. In the second stage, Adaboost feature selection is applied to the pool of adaptive features in order to select the final set of discriminative features. As the pool contains features adapted to *individual* object samples, this process selects features which encode common characteristics of *all* training samples, and thus are suitable for detection. Figure 3 illustrates this process for the particular case when the objects to be detected are faces. Throughout the remainder of this chapter, we use the term *adaptive features* to describe features that match the geometric structure of an object in a particular training image and *general features* to describe the final set of discriminative features that encode common characteristics of all training images.

3.2 Learning Using Locally Adapted Features

We now describe our framework to incorporate local feature adaptation in the training process. We begin by presenting the feature adaptation algorithm, which should be applied to each individual training image containing the target object. We then show how to use this adaptation method to create a meaningful feature pool containing multiple types of wavelet features. Lastly, the adapted feature pool is used in Adaboost learning to design a classifier to detect the object present in the training images. Although we have used wavelet filters in our work, the technique is general in the sense that other local image filters could also have been applied in the same settings.

3.2.1 Feature Adaptation

In this section, we address the problem of generating a set of local adaptive features for a given image of the object that we would like to detect. In other words, our goal is to learn the parameters of wavelet features, including position, scale, and orientation, such that the wavelet features match the local structures of the object. This is motivated by the wavelet networks proposed by Zhang [Zhang 1997] and introduced in computer vision by Krueger [Krueger 2001].

Consider a family $\Psi = \{\psi_{n_1}, \ldots, \psi_{n_N}\}$ of N two-dimensional wavelet functions, where $\psi_{n_i}(x, y)$ is a particular mother wavelet (*e.g.*, Haar or Gabor)

Figure 3. Our approach has two stages: first, we compute adaptive features for each training sample; then, we use a feature selection mechanism (such as Adaboost) to obtain general features

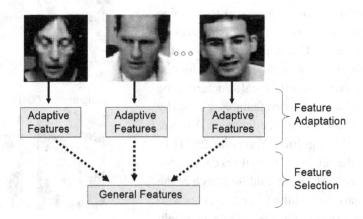

Figure 4. Learning adaptive features for a particular training image. (a) Input training image with wavelets initialized as a grid along the object region, with random orientations and scales. (b-e) Wavelet features being selected one by one, with parameters (position, scale, and orientation) optimized to match the local structure of the input image.

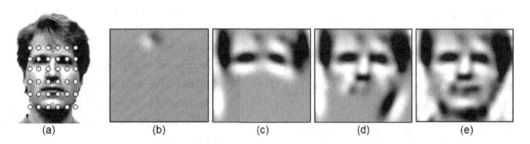

with parameters $n_i = (c_x, c_y, \theta, s_x, s_y)^T$. Here, c_x and c_y denote the translation of the wavelet, s_x and s_y denote the dilation, and θ denotes the orientation. The choice of N depends on the desired degree of precision for the representation.

Let I be an input training image, which contains an instance of the object for which a detector is to be designed. First, we initialize the set of wavelets Ψ along the image in a grid, with the wavelets having random orientations, and scales initialized to a unified value that is related to the density with which the wavelets are distributed. Figure 4(a) illustrates this process, for the specific case when the objects to be detected are faces. Then, assuming I is dc-free, without loss of generality, we minimize the energy function

$$E = \min_{n_i, w_i \forall i} \| I - \sum_i w_i \psi_{n_i} \|^2$$

with respect to the wavelet parameter vectors n_i and their corresponding weights w_i. Figures 4(b-e) show the wavelet features being optimized one by one to match the local image structure of the object. In this example, a Gabor wavelet was adopted as the mother wavelet, and we used the Levenberg-Marquardt method to solve the optimization problem.

Differently from most existing discrete approaches, the parameters n_i are optimized in the *continuous* domain and the wavelets are positioned with sub-pixel accuracy. This assures that a maximum of the image information can be encoded with a small number of wavelets.

Using the optimal wavelets ψ_{n_i} and weights w_i, the image I can be closely reconstructed by a linear combination of the weighted wavelets:

$$\hat{I} = \sum_{i=1}^{N} w_i \psi_{n_i} .$$

There is an alternative procedure to directly compute the wavelet weights w_i once the wavelet parameters n_i have been optimized. This solution is faster and more accurate than using Levenberg-Marquardt optimization. If the wavelet functions are orthogonal, the weights can be calculated by computing the inner products of the image I with each wavelet filter, *i.e.*, $w_i = <I, \psi_{n_i}>$. In the more general cases where the wavelet functions may not be orthogonal, a family of dual wavelets $\tilde{\Psi} = \{\tilde{\psi}_{n_1}, ..., \tilde{\psi}_{n_N}\}$ has to be considered. Recall that the wavelet $\tilde{\psi}_{n_j}$ is the dual wavelet of ψ_{n_i} if it satisfies the bi-orthogonality condition: $<\psi_{n_i}, \tilde{\psi}_{n_j}> = \delta_{i,j}$, where $\delta_{i,j}$ is the Kronecker delta function. Given an image I and a set of wavelets $\Psi = \{\psi_{n_1}, ..., \psi_{n_N}\}$, the optimal weights are given by $w_i = <I, \tilde{\psi}_{n_i}>$. It can be shown that $\tilde{\psi}_{n_i} = \sum_j (A_{i,j}^{-1}) \psi_{n_j}$, where $A_{i,j} = <\psi_{n_i}, \psi_{n_j}>$.

3.2.2 Integrating Multiple Features

We have described how to obtain adaptive features for a single object training image. Now we proceed to generate a pool of adaptive features obtained from multiple training images.

Let $\chi = \{I_1, ..., I_M\}$ be a set of object training images. For each image I_i, we generate a set of adaptive features Ψ_i, using the optimization method described in the previous section.

It is possible to integrate multiple feature types by using different wavelet settings for each training image. More specifically, each set Ψ_i is learned with different parameters, including:

- **Number of wavelets.** The number of wavelets indicates how many wavelet functions will be optimized for a particular object image. From this set, we can further select a subset of functions that have the largest weights, as wavelet filters with larger associated weights in general tend to coincide with more significant local image variations;

- **Wavelet type.** In our system, we used only Haar and Gabor wavelets for the wavelet type parameter, but other feature types could also be considered;

- **Wavelet frequency.** The frequency parameter controls the number of oscillations for the wavelet filters;

- **Group of features treated as a single feature.** We also allow a group of wavelet functions to be treated as a single feature, which is important to encode global object information.

Those parameters can be randomly initialized for each training image in order to allow a variety of different features to be in the pool. This initialization process is fully automatic and allows the creation of a compact and diversified feature pool.

All generated adaptive features for all object images are then put together in a single pool of features Ω, defined as

$$\Omega = \bigcup_{i=1}^{M} \Psi_i .$$

As an example, Figure 5 shows some adaptive features (Haar and Gabor wavelets with differ-

Figure 5. Some examples of features present in the pool of learned adaptive features for a frontal face dataset. A large variety of different wavelet filters are considered. The top row shows local wavelet functions, whereas the bottom row shows global features generated by combining a set of local filters.

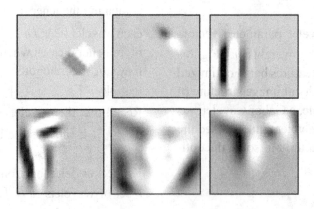

ent frequencies, orientations and aspect ratios) learned from a dataset of frontal face images. In the resulting feature pool, different types of local wavelet filters and global features, which are obtained by grouping individual wavelet functions, are present.

3.2.3 Learning General Features for Detection

In Sections 3.2.1 and 3.2.2, we have described a method to generate a pool of adaptive features from a set of training images. Those features are selected according to how well they match each individual training example. Now, in order to design an object detector, the goal is to select general features, *i.e.*, features from the pool that encode common characteristics to *all* object samples.

We use Adaboost learning for both selecting general features and designing a classifier [Viola & Jones 2001]. A large set of negative examples (*i.e.*, images that do not contain the object to be detected) is used in addition to the previously mentioned training images (which contain instances of the object of interest). The general features are those that best separate the whole set of object samples from non-object (negative) samples during classification. We refer the reader to [Viola & Jones 2001] for more details about the Adaboost

classifier and the feature selection mechanism. It is important to notice that other boosting techniques might be used in this step, such as GentleBoost [Friedman *et al.* 2000], Real Adaboost [Schapire & Singer 1999], and Vector Boosting [Huang *et al.* 2005]. In a more interesting way, our method could be integrated into the learning method recently proposed by Pham and Cham [Pham & Cham 2007], which achieves extremely fast learning time in comparison to previous methods. We believe that this method would have an even larger reduction in computational learning time if locally adapted features are used.

3.2.4 Applying the Classifier and Efficiency Considerations

Once the cascade classifier is designed, we would like to apply it to images in order to find the object of interest. A sliding window is moved pixel by pixel at different image scales. Starting with the original scale, the image is rescaled by a given factor (typically 1.1 or 1.2) in each iteration, and the detector is applied to every window. Overlapping detection results can be merged to produce a single result for each location and scale. However, even using a cascade classifier, real-time performance (25/30Hz) can not be achieved due to the time required to compute our features. We addressed

Figure 6. We use a Haar filter in the first levels of the cascade detector in order to achieve real-time performance

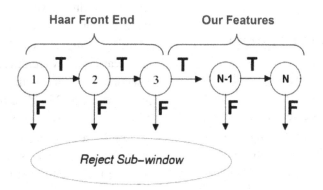

this problem by using traditional Haar-like/rectangle features in the first levels of the cascade. This allows for efficient rejection of background patches during classification. The image patches that are not rejected by the Haar cascade are then fed into a cascade of classifiers using our features. The choice of which cascade level should be used to switch from Haar features to our features is application dependent. Switching in lower levels allows for more accuracy, but switching in higher levels allows for more efficiency. Figure 6 depicts this architecture.

4. MULTI-SCALE HUMAN DETECTION IN SURVEILLANCE VIDEOS

In the previous section, we presented a learning framework to design object detectors based on adaptive local features. This framework can be applied to design people detectors in near-field, mid-field, and far-field surveillance scenarios, which deal with images with different levels of detail. In order to account for these differences, for each scenario we designed a person detector in a scale specifically tailored to the available resolution. We now describe in detail our implementation of the framework for near-field person detection and discuss its advantages. The same concepts could be similarly applied to improve our detectors in the other scenarios (mid-field and far-field), as these detectors are based on local image features as well.

4.1 Near-Field Person Detection

In near-field surveillance videos, resolution is sufficient to make facial features of people clearly visible. We developed a face detector and a tracking system using the learning method described above to detect people in near-field scenes. To design the face detector, we used a frontal face dataset containing 4000 face images for training

Figure 7. The first three general features selected while designing the face detector

Figure 8. Face detection results in one of the CMU+MIT dataset images, and four video frames taken from our surveillance system

purposes. Each training image was cropped and rescaled to a 24x24 patch size. A pool of adaptive features was generated by running the optimization process described in Section 3.2.1, with different wavelet settings (wavelet type, frequency, etc.) for each sample. As a result, a pool of 80000 adaptive features was generated, containing a large variety of wavelet filters. It takes less than a second to create hundreds of adaptive features for a particular 24x24 sample in a conventional 3GHz desktop computer.

For the second step of the algorithm (learning general features), we used an additional database of about 1000 background (non-face) images from

Figure 9. (a) ROC Curve comparing classifiers learned from adaptive (optimized) and non-adaptive (non-optimized) features in the CMU+MIT dataset. (b) Number of classifiers for each level of the cascade in both methods. Our approach offers advantages in terms of detection accuracy and reduced computational costs over traditional methods that use local features uniformly sampled from the parameter space.

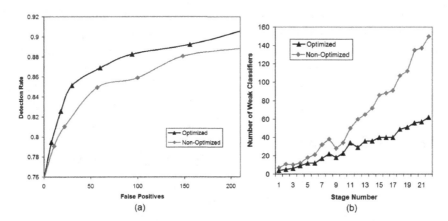

which 24x24 patches are sampled. A cascade classifier was trained by considering 4000 faces and 4000 non-faces at each level, where the non-face samples were obtained through bootstrap [Rowley *et al.* 1998]. Each level in the cascade was trained to reject about half of the negative patterns, while correctly accepting 99.9% of the face patterns. A fully trained cascade consisted of 24 levels. A Haar filter corresponding to the first 18 levels of the cascade was used in our experiments, in order to achieve real-time performance.

Figure 7 shows the first three general features selected by Adaboost. The first selected feature gives more importance to the eyes region. The second selected feature is a local coarse-scale Gabor wavelet with three oscillations, which align with the eyes, nose, and mouth regions. The third feature is a global feature that encodes the rounded face shape.

The CMU+MIT frontal face test set, containing 130 gray-scale images with 511 faces, was used for evaluation. A face is considered to be correctly detected if the Euclidean distance between the center of the detected box and the ground-truth is less than 50% of the width of the ground-truth box, and the width (*i.e.*, size) of the detected face

box is within ±70% of the width of the ground-truth box. Figure 8 shows the detected faces in one of the images from the CMU+MIT dataset, and four video frames taken from our surveillance system.

In order to show the effectiveness of feature adaptation prior to learning, we compared our face detector to a classifier learned from a similar feature pool, containing the same number and type of features (Haar, Gabor, etc.) sampled uniformly from the parameter space (at discrete positions, orientations, and scales), rather than adapted to the local structure of the training samples. Figure 9(a) shows a plot of the Receiver Operating Characteristic (ROC) curves for this comparison, demonstrating the superior performance of our method. In addition to achieving improved detection accuracy, the number of weak classifiers needed for each strong classifier is significantly smaller in our method (see Figure 9(b)). This has a direct impact in both training and testing computational costs. We observed a reduction of about 50%.

Figure 10 shows the comparison between our approach and traditional Haar-like/rectangle features. The cascade detector based on Haar features also consisted of 24 levels, and was learned using the same training set. The feature pool, however, was twice as large as the one used by our approach, containing about 160000 features. With half of the features in the pool, we achieve superior accuracy and a faster learning time. Table 1 confirms this. Although our optimized features can cause over-fitting when a small number of training samples are considered, this issue does not arise when thousands of faces are used for learning.

4.2 Mid-Field Person Detection

In mid-field scenes, facial features may not be visible due to poor resolution. However, the lines that delimit the head and shoulders of an individual are still informative cues to find people in images. For these scenes, we developed a system for tracking and detection which locates people by scanning a window through the image and applying a head and shoulders detector at every position and scale. This detector is designed according to the same learning framework from [Viola & Jones 2001] (as we implemented this classifier prior to our research on feature optimization), *i.e.*, it is a cascade classifier based on Adaboost learning

and Haar features. Similarly to the face detector, a training set of 4000 images containing the head and shoulders region was used for training. As this classifier is based on feature selection from a pool of local features, it is part of our current work to apply the learning framework from Section 3 to first create a pool of adaptive local features and then select the most discriminative features using Adaboost. Figure 11 illustrates the detection results from the head and shoulders detector in our system for mid-field scenes.

4.3 Far-Field Person Detection

In far-field imagery, pedestrians may appear as small as 30-pixels tall. In our scenario, the camera is known to be in a fixed position, making it feasible to use background modeling techniques to segment moving objects. In [Chen *et al.* 2008], we described how our far-field surveillance system classifies blobs obtained from background subtraction into one of three classes: cars, people and groups of people. In [Viola *et al.* 2003], a system for pedestrian detection in videos which extends the technique from [Viola & Jones 2001] was proposed. It augments the feature space by

Figure 10. ROC Curves for our approach and traditional Haar features in the CMU+MIT dataset; We used only half of the number of features in the feature pool compared to Haar features and still get superior performance

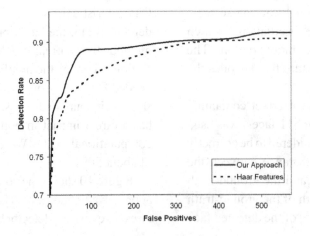

Table 1. By learning adaptive and general features, we can use a smaller feature pool, which results in a reduction in training time, while still maintaining superior performance in detection rate, when compared to a traditional pool of Haar features

Feature Pool	Number of Features	Learning Time
Haar Features	160000	About 5 days
Our Approach	80000	About 3 days

Figure 11. Sample detections in mid-field scenes, using a head and shoulders detector based on Haar features

including Haar features computed from differences between pairs of subsequent frames. Our locally adaptive feature learning framework could also be applied in this case, in order to pre-select the features that best adapt to pedestrians in individual frames or to differences in subsequent frames due to movement. Then, the resulting detector could be combined with our classifier based on foreground measurements in order to confirm that the blobs classified as people in fact do correspond to people.

5. HUMAN TRACKING AND MOTION ANALYSIS

Human tracking and motion analysis are key components of video surveillance systems, and very active research areas. Recently, researchers focused on combining detection and tracking into unified frameworks. Andriluka *et al.* [Andriluka

et al. 2008] proposed a unified framework that combines both pedestrian detection and tracking techniques. Detection results of human articulations using a hierarchical Gaussian process latent variable model are further applied in a Hidden Markov Model to perform pedestrian tracking. Okuma *et al.* [Okuma *et al.* 2004] proposed a target detection and tracking framework by combining two very popular techniques: mixture particle filters for multi-target tracking and Adaboost for object detection. Another Adaboost-based method is presented in [Avidan 2005] by Avidan. In his work, weak classifiers are combined to distinguish foreground objects from the background. The mean-shift algorithm is applied to track the objects using the confidence map generated by the Adaboost method. Leibe *et al.* [Leibe *et al.* 2005, 2007] used a top-down segmentation approach to localize pedestrians in the image using both local and global cues. An implicit human shape model is built to detect pedestrian candidates that are further refined by the segmentation process, using Chamfer matching on the silhouettes. Ramanan *et al.* [Ramanan *et al.* 2007] proposed a "tracking by model-building and detection" framework for tracking people in videos. Predefined human models are combined with candidates detected in the video to form actual human clusters (models). These models are then used to detect the person in subsequent images and perform tracking. Other co-training based approaches are [Javed *et al.* 2005, Grabner *et al.* 2006]. They proposed detecting objects and further using them for online updating of the object classifiers. Object appearance features derived from PCA are iteratively updated using the samples with high detection confidence.

For motion analysis, Stauffer *et al.* [Stauffer *et al.* 2000] proposed a motion tracking framework. Each pixel in the image is modeled by a mixture of Gaussian distributions that represents its color statistics. Object tracks are formed by correlating motion segments across frames using a co-occurrence matrix. Buzan *et al.* [Buzan *et al.* 2004] proposed a clustering technique to group three-dimensional trajectories of tracked objects in videos. A novel measure called the Longest Common Subsequence is employed to match trajectory projections on the coordinate axes. Junejo and Foroosh [Junejo & Foroosh 2008] proposed a trajectory grouping method based on normalized cuts. The matching criteria include spatial proximity, motion characteristics, curvature, and absolute world velocity, which are based on automated camera calibration.

The IBM SSS provides functions for tracking people and detecting trajectory anomalies. The system tracks faces and people, analyzes the paths of tracked people, learns a set of repeated patterns that occur frequently, and detects when a person moves in a way inconsistent with these normal patterns.

5.1 Face Tracking

Once a face is detected in a particular video frame, it is necessary to track it in order to analyze the trajectory of the person and identify a single key frame of the face, to be stored in a database. Our face tracking method is based on applying the face detector to every frame of the video sequence. In order to maintain the track of the face even when the face detector fails, we also use a simple correlation-based tracker. More specifically, when a face is detected, the correlation-based tracker is triggered. For the subsequent frame, if the face detection fails, the track is updated with the window given by the correlation tracker. Otherwise, if the face detector reports a window result with a close position and size to the current tracking window, then this result is used to update the track. This mechanism is important to avoid drifting.

In order to improve the efficiency of our detector and enable real-time face tracking (25/30Hz) on conventional desktop computers, we use the following techniques:

- We only apply the detector at specific scales provided by the user and at motion regions detected by background subtraction;
- An interleaving technique (explained below) combines view-based detectors and tracking.

In most surveillance scenarios, human faces appear in images in a certain range of scales. In our system, the user can specify the minimum and maximum possible face sizes for a particular camera, so that face detection is applied only for sub-windows within this range of scales. We also apply background subtraction, using statistical mixture modeling [Tian *et al.* 2005], to prune sub-windows that do not lie in motion regions. A skin color detector could also be used to speed up the processing.

Figure 12. Our surveillance system interleaves view-based detectors to save frame rate for tracking

Figure 12. Our surveillance system interleaves view-based detectors to save frame rate for tracking

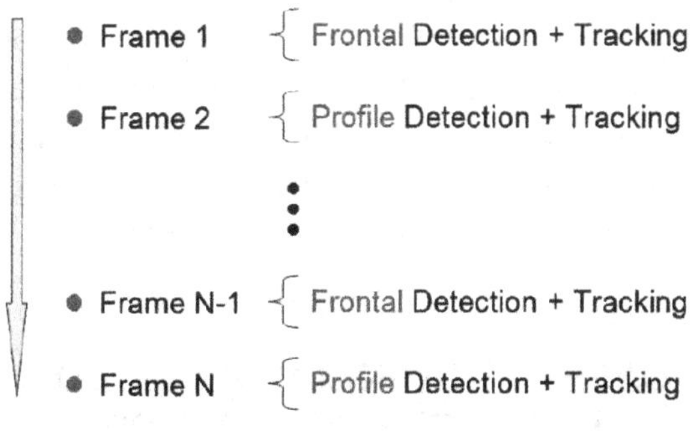

A problem faced by most existing systems is the computational time required to run a set of view-based detectors in each frame. This causes large inter-frame image variation, posing a problem for tracking. We handled this issue by using an interleaving technique that alternates view based detectors in each frame. This idea is illustrated for frontal and profile face detection in Figure 12. In each frame, rather than running both frontal and profile detectors, we run just one detector for a specific view (*e.g.*, frontal view). The detector for the other view (profile view) is applied in the subsequent frame and so forth. This allows us to improve the frame rate by 50%, while facilitating tracking due to less inter-frame variation.

Tracking is terminated when there are no foreground regions (obtained from the background subtraction module) near the current tracking window or when the face detector fails consecutively for a given time or number of frames specified by the user.

5.2 Human Tracking and Motion Analysis

5.2.1 Human Tracking

Tracking can be seen as a problem of assigning consistent identities to visible objects. We obtain a number of observations of objects (detections by the background subtraction algorithm) over time, and we need to label these so that all observations of a given person are given the same label. When one object passes in front of another, partial or total occlusion takes place, and the background subtraction algorithm detects a single moving region. By handling occlusions, we hope to be able to segment this region, appropriately labeling each part and still maintaining the correct labels when the objects separate. In more complex scenes, occlusions between many objects must be handled [Senior *et al.* 2001].

When objects are widely separated, a simple bounding box tracker is sufficient to associate a track identity with each foreground region. Bounding box tracking works by measuring the distance between each foreground region in the current frame and each object that was tracked in the previous frame. If the object overlaps with the region or lies very close to it, then a match is declared.

If the foreground regions and tracks form a one-to-one mapping, then tracking is complete and the tracks are extended to include the regions in the new frame using this association. If a foreground region is not matched by any track, then a new track is created. If a track does not match any foreground regions, then it continues at a constant velocity, but it is considered to have left the scene once it fails to match any regions for a few frames.

Occasionally, a single track may be associated with two regions. For a few frames, this is assumed to be a failure of background subtraction and both regions are associated with the track. If there are consistently two or more foreground regions, then the track is split into two, to model cases as when a group of people separate, a person leaves a vehicle, or an object is deposited by a person. Figure 13 shows some people tracking results.

5.2.2 Motion Analysis

In order to perform motion analysis, as shown in Figure 14, the system begins by detecting the locations where objects enter and exit the scene. The start and end points of tracks are clustered to find regions where tracks often begin or end. These points tend to be where paths or roads reach the edge of the camera's field of view. Having clustered these locations, we classify the trajectories by labeling a track with its start and end location (or as an anomaly when it starts or ends in an unusual location, such as a person walking through the bushes). For example, when we cluster trajectories for the camera placed at the entrance to our building, trajectories are classified into one of 5 classes – entering/exiting to the left side (from the road on the left or from the center), entering/exiting to the right side (from the road on the right or from the center), or moving horizontally across the road. We then apply a secondary clustering scheme to further detect anomalous behavior. This scheme operates as follows: the trajectories of all tracks with a given start/end location labeling are resampled and clustered together. This gives an average or "prototypical" track together with standard deviations. Most tracks going from a given entry location to a given exit will lie close to the prototypical track, with typical normal

variation indicated by the length of the crossbars. Tracks that wander outside this normal area can be labeled as anomalous and may warrant further investigation. The principal components of the cluster indicate typical modes of variation or "eigentracks", providing a more accurate model of normal vs. abnormal. Figure 15 shows some examples of abnormal activities (people loitering) in front of the IBM Hawthorne building.

6. CASE STUDY FOR REAL VIDEO SURVEILLANCE APPLICATIONS

There are many applications for people detection, tracking, and motion analysis in video surveillance. In this section, we present several case studies including people search, retail loss prevention, people counting, and display effectiveness.

6.1 People Search by Clothing Color

An important aspect of human identification for finding and/or matching a person to another person or description, in the short term (*e.g.*, the same day), is based on clothing. Color is one of the most prominent cues for describing clothing. Here, we present our methodology for categoriz-

Figure 13. Examples of people tracking results. (a) People tracking in a shopping mall; (b) tracking of hockey players

(a)   (b)

Figure 14. (a) Summary view showing the retrieval of the trajectories of all events that occurred in the parking lot over a 24 hour period. The trajectory colors are coded: starting points are shown in white and ending points are displayed in red. (b) Activity distribution over an extended time period, where the time is shown on the x-axis and the number of people in the area is shown on the y-axis. Each line represents a different day of the week. (c) Unsupervised behavior analysis. Object entrance/departure zones (green ellipses) and prototypical tracks (brown curves) with typical variation (crossbars) are displayed.

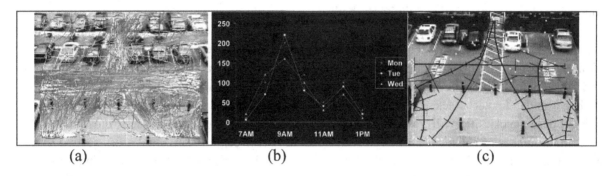

(a)   (b)   (c)

Figure 15. Abnormal activity analysis (people loitering in front of the IBM Hawthorne building)

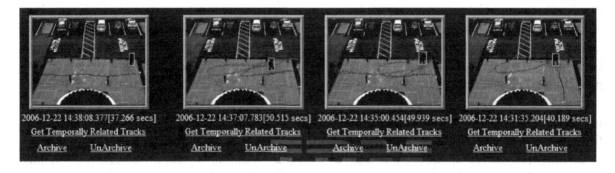

ing the color of people's clothes for the purposes of people search.

We perform clothing color classification based on two body parts segmented from the human silhouette: the torso and the legs. These are determined using the normative spatial relationship to the face location, as detected in Section 4.1. The torso or upper body region represents what is primarily the shirt or jacket, while the legs or lower body region represents the pants or skirt of the tracked human extracted from the camera.

Three issues are critical for successful color classification. The first is the issue of color constancy. People perceive an object to be of the same color across a wide range of illumination conditions. However, the actual pixels of an object, which are perceived by a human to be of the same color, may have values (when sensed by a camera) which range across the color spectrum depending on the lighting conditions. Secondly, moving objects extracted from video are not perfectly segmented from the background. Shadows are often part of the object and errors exist in the segmentation due to the similarity of the object and the background model. Lastly, complex objects (torsos and legs, in this case) may have more than one color.

The method described here is based on acquiring a normalized cumulative color histogram for each tracked object in the bi-conic HSL (hue, saturation, luminance) space. The method is designed with mechanisms to divide this space via parameters that can be set by a user or by active color measurements of the scene. The key idea is to intelligently quantize the color space based on the relationships between hue, saturation and luminance. As color information is limited by both lack of saturation and intensity, it is necessary to separate the chromatic from the achromatic space along surfaces defined by a function of saturation and intensity in the bi-conic space.

In particular, for each tracked body part (torso or legs), the color classifier will create a histogram of a small number of colors. We usually use six colors: black, white, red, blue, green and yellow. However, for clothing from people detected by the cameras used in this study (our facility), we use the following colors based on the empirical distribution and our ability to discern: red, green, blue, yellow, orange, purple, black, grey, brown, and beige. The histogram is created as follows. Each frame of the tracked object that is used for histogram accumulation (every frame the body parts detector finds) is first converted from RGB to HSL color space. Next, the HSL space is quantized into a small number of colors.

In order to quantize this space into a small number of colors, we determine the angular cutoffs between colors. When we use six colors (black, white, yellow, green, blue, red), we need only four cutoffs between the hues: yellow/green, green/

blue, blue/red and red/yellow. However, variations due to lighting conditions, object textures and object-to-camera viewpoint lead to differences in brightness and color saturation. Therefore, we also need to specify lightness and saturation cutoffs. Here, it is interesting to note that saturation and intensity are related. Both properties can make the hue of a pixel indiscernible. For intensity, this occurs when the light is too bright or too dark. For saturation, it happens when there is insufficient saturation. However, as the brightness gets too low or too high, the necessary saturation increases. In general, as intensity increases from 0 up to halfway (the central horizontal cross-section of the bi-conic) or decreases from the maximum (white) down to halfway, the range of pixels with visible or discernable hue increases.

In summary, we first quantize the HSL space based on hue. We subsequently re-label pixels as either white or black depending on whether they lie outside the lightness/saturation curve above or below the horizontal mid-plane. This is related to earlier work in color segmentation performed by Tseng and Chang [Tseng & Chang 1994].

Using this color classification scheme, the system records the colors of torso and legs for each person for whom the detection of the face and the body parts is successful. This information is sent to the database for retrieval. Users may search for people with specific colors of torso and legs. Figure 16 shows the results of a search for

Figure 16. Results of search for people with red torso (shirts)

Figure 17. Results of search for people with white torso (shirt) and red legs (pants/skirt)

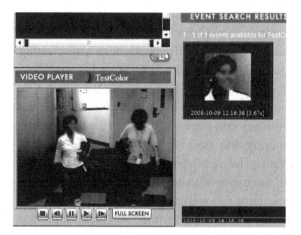

people with red torsos (shirts). Figure 17 shows the results of a search for people with white torso and red legs. The final figure (Figure 18) in this section shows the results of a search for people with yellow torso and black legs. In each picture, the key frames for each event (person) are shown on the right. The user may select any key frame to watch the associated video clip of the person as they walk through the scene. A single frame of this video is shown at the left of each figure.

6.2 Retail Loss Prevention

There are many practical applications for the people search capabilities described in this chap-

ter. Many of these applications involve matching people across cameras, with identification information, or with queries. Matching people across cameras is useful to "track" a person across cameras, thereby linking a person in one camera to their movements and actions in another. In this way, a person can be tracked across non-overlapping cameras. Many important security tasks involve this capability. For example, a person who breaks through a security checkpoint in an airport could be tracked to a different part of the building.

A person can also be "matched" against identification information. This information may be associated with a badge or other type of ID, and may be used to corroborate the legitimacy of their access to a building or a cash register. Lastly, a person can be matched against a query to locate them across several cameras and time periods. We have built an application to match people to improve the detection of returns fraud. In this application, a user is looking to match a person at the returns counter in a department store with people entering the store.

Returns fraud can take one of a number of forms. Our retail customer was particularly interested in the case of returning items that were just picked up in the store, but were never bought. The return could be done either without a receipt (in stores that have liberal return policies), or using a receipt from a previously purchased (and kept) item.

Figure 18. Results of search for people with yellow torso (shirts) and black legs (pants/skirt)

Our approach, described in more detail in a previous paper [Senior, 2007], allows loss prevention staff to quickly determine whether a person returning an item entered the store carrying that item. The system works by detecting and tracking customers at entrances and customer service desks and associating the two events. This solution only requires cameras at the store entrances and the return counters, being simpler than approaches that rely on tracking customers throughout the store (requiring many cameras and very reliable camera hand-off algorithms) and must be continuously monitored to determine whether items are picked up.

Two cameras at the customer service desk record activity there, including the appearance of customers returning items. A separate set of cameras points at the doors and captures all activity of people entering and leaving the store. Figure 19 shows the fields of view of two such cameras. Our approach automatically segments events in each of these cameras, filters them and then provides a user interface which allows the association of each returns event with the door entrance event that corresponds to when the person came into the store. At the customer service desk, the face tracking algorithm tracks customers' faces, generating a single event per customer. Customers at the doors are tracked with our appearance-based tracker [Senior 2001].

The returns fraud interface provides intuitive selection and browsing of the events, summarized by presentation of key frames (at both scales), timestamps and original video clips (from DVR or media server). Search typically begins by selecting a return event from the TLOG (see Figure 20). In response to this, the interface displays the people found at the customer service counter near that time. Selecting one of these then displays people entering the store shortly before the selected event. The user can then browse through the entrance events, using full-frame and zoomed-in key frames as well as original video, and, when a match is found, determine whether a fraud has taken place.

The fundamental indexing attribute of the database is time. All devices are synchronized and events are time-stamped. Temporal constraints from real world conditions are exploited to limit the events displayed. In our implementation, a user may also use color information (Section 6.1) to assist in finding likely matches between the people entering and the person at the returns counter.

6.3 People Counting

As a direct application of person detection and search, people counting has significant importance in various scenarios. In the retail sector, accurate people counts provide a reliable base for high-level store operation analysis and improvements, such

Figure 19. Views from the customer service desk (left) and a door (right). The "region of uninterest" in which detections are ignored to reduce false positives is outlined in blue. Alert tripwires (enter and leave) are drawn on the door view.

Figure 20. Interface for browsing and searching the TLOG (transaction log), showing a table of return transactions

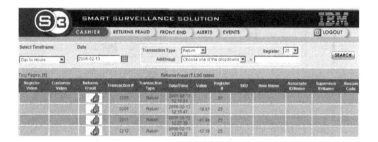

as traffic load monitoring, staffing assignment, conversion rate estimation, etc.

In our solution, we incorporate a people counting framework which effectively detects and tracks moving people in bi-directional traffic flows, denoted as "entries" and "exits." Counting results are indexed into the logical relational database for generating future statistical reports. An example of a report is shown in Figure 21. We demonstrate the people counting application in the cafeteria traffic scenario at our institution. In addition to the statistical reports, individual counting events are also available for investigation by exhibiting corresponding key frames. Disjoint search intervals enable the system's capability of performing cross-time traffic comparison. For instance, in Figure 22, the average traffic counts

between three time intervals on five days of a week are compared. For morning times (8:00AM-11:00AM), Monday has the fewest count. This is due to the fact that employees tend to have a busier morning after the weekend, and thus do not visit the cafeteria as often as on other weekdays. For lunch time (11:00AM-2:00PM) and afternoon tea time (2:00PM-5:00PM), Friday has the least traffic volume. This is due to the fact that some employees leave work earlier, and thus do not have lunch or afternoon tea/coffee at the company.

People counting can also be associated with non-visual sensor data. One application is badge use enforcement, where security wants to ensure that employees always carry identification badges. In certain working environments, employees need to swipe their badges to access critical areas. In

Figure 21. People counting statistical report

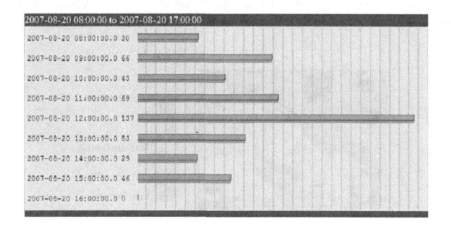

Figure 22. Weekly comparison of the average people counts for three time intervals at the IBM Hawthorne cafeteria

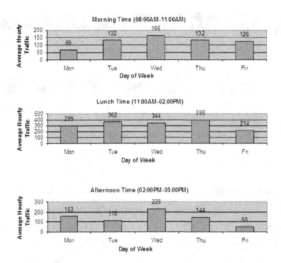

order to detect people entering the critical areas without using their badges (*e.g.*, by tailgating other people who properly swiped their badges), the number of entering people is estimated by applying a person detector (Section 4.1). The people count is then matched with the input signals obtained from the badge reader. If the number obtained from the people counting algorithm is greater than the one indicated by the badge read signals, then an alert is generated.

6.4 Display Effectiveness

In retail stores, a critical problem is to effectively display merchandise at certain places to achieve maximum customer attention and optimal revenue. For instance, the store management is very interested in the average number of people who have stopped in front of a particular item each hour. If the number of people looking at this item is consistently far less than the number of people who have stopped by its neighboring items, then the store management could conclude that this

Figure 23. A heat map of the store's traffic density, where warmer values represent a larger number of people passing through and stopping by the corresponding location, and colder values represent lower traffic

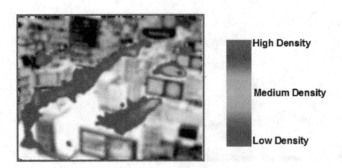

particular item does not attract enough customers. Thus, it brings less value to the store revenue, and may be removed from the display or relocated to a less valued region. This analysis can be accomplished by constructing a "heat map" of the store plan, which represents the traffic density in the store. One such "heat map" is demonstrated in Figure 23, where warmer values represent higher number of people passing through and stopping by the corresponding location, and colder values represent lower traffic. Based on this analysis, the duration of the stay can also be derived. The management can obtain a better understanding on whether the customers are actually looking at a certain item, or are just passing by.

7. DISCUSSION AND CONCLUSION

Effective, efficient, and robust people detection and tracking are core components of video surveillance. In this chapter, we have presented reliable techniques for people detection, tracking, and motion analysis in the IBM Smart Surveillance System (SSS), a commercial video surveillance system. The people detection component is based on local feature adaptation prior to Adaboost learning. This technique offers better detection rates and faster training than traditional methods based on Haar features. It also allows the integration of a large dictionary of features in a principled way. We have described techniques for people detection at different scales. In order to meet the different requirements of video surveillance, we have also implemented two types (detector-based and appearance-based) of human tracking methods. Finally, the applicability and effectiveness of the proposed people detection and motion analysis techniques have been demonstrated in a variety of real surveillance applications, including people search based on clothing color, retail loss prevention, people counting, and display effectiveness.

While technologies like networked video surveillance, smart surveillance, IP cameras, and high density storage continue to improve the tools for surveillance, there are a number of processes, privacy and policy issues that are required for the success of operational security systems. Currently, most of our security agencies are largely geared toward responding to events and using video surveillance in a "reactive monitoring process." Technologies such as smart surveillance begin to enable a proactive monitoring process. We expect to develop more robust people detection algorithms that require a smaller number of examples and work across different environments without need for re-training. This is extremely important for scenarios where it is difficult to collect training examples. Tracking and recognizing people in more complex environments across multiple cameras will be continually investigated.

The adoption of a smart surveillance system introduces a new stream of video based alarms into the command center. To ensure successful deployment, customers and technology providers should jointly address key issues such as the training of operators to use sophisticated technologies, evaluate alarm conditions, and determine appropriate responses to these events. The system must be designed, configured and tuned to minimize the impact of false alarms.

As the technology to monitor areas for purposes of law enforcement and homeland security evolves, such technologies typically raise the issues of citizen privacy in public spaces. These challenges can be addressed both at the technology and policy levels. Citizen privacy can be protected by enabling privacy preserving technologies in the surveillance systems [Senior *et al.* 2005]. The technical enablers of privacy then have to be put into practice by formulating, implementing and enforcing appropriate policies that govern the use of such systems.

REFERENCES

Andriluka, M., Roth, S., & Schiele, B. (2008). People-Tracking-by-Detection and People-Detection-by-Tracking. In *IEEE Conference on Computer Vision and Pattern Recognition (CVPR'08).*

Avidan, S. (2005). Ensemble Tracking. In *IEEE Conference on Computer Vision and Pattern Recognition (CVPR'05).*

Beymer, D., & Konolige, K. (1999). Real-Time Tracking of Multiple People Using Continuous Detection. In *IEEE International Conference on Computer Vision (ICCV'99).*

Brown, L. (2008). Color Retrieval in Video Surveillance. In *Fifth IEEE Int'l Conf. on Advanced Video and Signal Based Surveillance (AVSS)*, Santa Fe, NM.

Buzan, D., Sclaroff, S., & Kollios, G. (2004). Extraction and Clustering of Motion Trajectories in Videos. In *International Conference on Pattern Recognition (ICPR'04).*

Chen, L., Feris, R. S., Zhai, Y., Brown, L., & Hampapur, A. (2008). An integrated system for moving object classification in surveillance videos. In *IEEE International Conference on Advanced Video and Signal-Based Surveillance*, Santa Fe, New Mexico.

Dalal, N., & Triggs, B. (2005). Histograms of Oriented Gradients for Human Detection. In *IEEE Conference on Computer Vision and Pattern Recognition (CVPR'05)* (Vol. 1, pp. 886-893).

Feris, R., Tian, Y., Zhai, Y., & Hampapur, A. (2008). Facial image analysis using local feature adaptation prior to learning. In *IEEE International Conference on Automatic Face and Gesture Recognition*. Amsterdam, Netherlands.

Friedman, J., Hastie, T., & Tibshirani, R. (2000). Additive logistic regression: a statistical view of boosting. *Annals of Statistics, 38*(2), 337–374. doi:10.1214/aos/1016218223

Gavrila, D. (2000). Pedestrian Detection from a Moving Vehicle. In *Europe Conference on Computer Vision (ECCV'00).*

Grabner, H., & Bischof, H. (2006). Online Boosting and Vision. In *IEEE Conference on Computer Vision and Pattern Recognition (CVPR'06)*

Green, M. (1999). *The appropriate and effective use of security in schools.* US Department of Justice, Report NJC178265.

Hampapur, A., Brown, L., Connell, J., Ekin, A., Haas, N., & Lu, M. (2005). Smart video surveillance: exploring the concept of multiscale spatiotemporal tracking. *IEEE Signal Processing Magazine, 22*(2), 38–51. doi:10.1109/MSP.2005.1406476

Han, F., Shan, Y., Cekander, R., Sawhney, H., & Kumar, R. (2006). A Two-Stage Approach to People and Vehicle Detection With HOG-Based SVM. In *Performance Metrics for Intelligent Systems Workshop*, National Institute of Standards and Technology.

Huang, C., Ai, H., Li, Y., & Lao, S. (2005). Vector boosting for rotation invariant multi-view face detection. In *IEEE International Conference on Computer Vision (ICCV'05)*, Beijing, China.

Javed, O., Ali, S., & Shah, M. (2005). Online Detection and Classification of Moving objects Using Progressively Improving Detectors. In *IEEE Conference on Computer Vision and Pattern Recognition (CVPR'05).*

Junejo, I., & Foroosh, H. (2008). Euclidean path modeling for video surveillance. *IVC, 26*(4), 512–528.

Krueger, V. (2001). *Gabor wavelet networks for object representation.* PhD thesis, Christian-Albrecht University, Kiel, Germany.

Leibe, B., Schindler, K., & Van Gool, L. (2007). Coupled Detection and Trajectory Estimation for Multi-Object Tracking. In *International Conference on Computer Vision (ICCV'07).*

Leibe, B., Seemann, E., & Schiele, B. (2005). Pedestrian Detection in Crowded Scenes. In *IEEE Conference on Computer Vision and Pattern Recognition (CVPR'05).*

Liu, C., & Shum, H. (2003). Kullback-leibler boosting. In *IEEE Conference on Computer Vision and Pattern Recognition (CVPR'03)*, Madison, Wisconsin.

Miezianko, R., & Pokrajac, D. (2008). People detection in low resolution infrared videos. In *IEEE International Workshop on Object Tracking and Classification in and Beyond the Visible Spectrum (OTCBVS'08).*

Munder, S., & Gavrila, D. (2006). An experimental study on pedestrian classification. *IEEE Transactions on Pattern Analysis and Machine Intelligence, 28*(11), 1863–1868. doi:10.1109/TPAMI.2006.217

Okuma, K., Taleghani, A., & Freitas, N. (2004). Little J., & Lowe, D. A boosted particle filter: multi-target detection and tracking. In *European Conference on Computer Vision (ECCV'04).*

Patil, R., Rybski, P., Veloso, M., & Kanade, T. (2004). People Detection and Tracking in High Resolution Panoramic Video Mosaic. In *Proceedings of the 2004 IN IEEE/RSJ International Conference on Intelligent Robots and Systems* (pp. 1323-1328).

Pham, M., & Cham, T. (2007). Fast training and selection of Haar features using statistics in boosting-based face detection. In *IEEE International Conference on Computer Vision (ICCV'07)*, Rio de Janeiro, Brazil.

Ramanan, D., Forsyth, D. A., & Zisserman, A. (2007). Tracking people by learning their appearance. *IEEE Transactions on Pattern Analysis and Machine Intelligence, 29*, 65–81. doi:10.1109/TPAMI.2007.250600

Rowley, H., Baluja, S., & Kanade, T. (1998). Neural network-based face detection. *IEEE Transactions on Pattern Analysis and Machine Intelligence, 20*(1), 23–38. doi:10.1109/34.655647

Sabzmeydani, P., & Mori, G. (2007). Detecting Pedestrians by Learning Shapelet Features. In *IEEE Conference on Computer Vision and Pattern Recognition (CVPR'07).*

Schapire, R., & Singer, Y. (1999). Improved boosting algorithms using confidence-rated predictions. *Machine Learning, 37*, 297–336. doi:10.1023/A:1007614523901

Senior, A., Brown, L., Shu, C., Tian, Y., Lu, M., Zhai, Y., & Hampapur, A. (2007). Visual person searches for retail loss detection. *International Conference on Vision Systems.*

Senior, A., Hampapur, A., Tian, Y., Brown, L., Pankanti, S., & Bolle, R. (2001). Appearance models for occlusion handling. *International Workshop on Performance Evaluation of Tracking and Surveillance.*

Senior, A., Pankanti, S., Hampapur, A., Brown, L., Tian, Y., & Ekin, A. (2005). Enabling video privacy through computer vision. *IEEE Security & Privacy, 3*(3), 50–57. doi:10.1109/MSP.2005.65

Stauffer, C., Eric, W., & Grimson, L. (2000). Learning patterns of activity using real-time tracking. *PAMI 2000.*

Tian, Y., Feris, R., & Hampapur, A. (2008). Real-time Detection of Abandoned and Removed Objects in Complex Environments. In *The 8th Int'l Workshop on Visual Surveillance (VS)*.

Tian, Y., Lu, M., & Hampapur, A. (2005). Robust and Efficient Foreground Analysis for Real-time Video Surveillance. In *IEEE Conference on Computer Vision and Pattern Recognition (CVPR'05)*, San Diego.

Tseng, D., & Chang, C. (1994). Color segmentation using UCS perceptual attributes. In *Proc. Natl. Sci. Counc. ROC(A)*, 18(3), 305-314.

Viola, P., & Jones, M. (2001). Rapid object detection using a boosted cascade of simple features. In *IEEE Conference on Computer Vision and Pattern Recognition (CVPR'01)*, Kauai, Hawaii.

Viola, P., Jones, M., & Snow, D. (2003). Detecting Pedestrians Using Patterns of Motion and Appearance. In *IEEE International Conference on Computer Vision (ICCV'03)* (Vol. 2, pp. 734-741).

Wang, P., & Ji, Q. (2005). Learning discriminant features for multiview face and eye detection. In *IEEE Conference on Computer Vision and Pattern Recognition (CVPR'05)*.

Wu, B., & Nevatia, R. (2005). Detection of Multiple, Partially Occluded Humans in a Single Image by Bayesian Combination of Edgelet Part Detectors. In *IEEE International Conference on Computer Vision (ICCV'05)* (Vol. 1, pp. 90-97).

Wu, B., & Nevatia, R. (2006). Tracking of Multiple, Partially Occluded Humans based Static Body Part Detection. In *IEEE Conference on Computer Vision and Pattern Recognition (CVPR'06)*.

Yang, P., Shan, S., Gao, W., Li, S., & Zhang, D. (2004). Face recognition using ada-boosted gabor features. In *International Conference on Automatic Face and Gesture Recognition*, Seoul, Korea.

Zhai, Y., Tian, Y., & Hampapur, A. (2008). Composite Spatio-Temporal Event Detection in Multi-Camera Surveillance Networks. In *Workshop on Multi-camera and Multi-modal Sensor Fusion Algorithms and Applications (M²SFA²)*.

Zhang, D., Li, S., & Gatica-Perez, D. (2004). Real-time face detection using boosting in hierarchical feature spaces. In *International Conference on Pattern Recognition (ICPR'04)*.

Zhang, Q. (1997). Using wavelet network in nonparametric estimation. *IEEE Transactions on Neural Networks*, 8(2), 227–236. doi:10.1109/72.557660

Chapter 7
A Generic Framework for 2D and 3D Upper Body Tracking

Lei Zhang
Rensselaer Polytechnic Institute, USA

Jixu Chen
Rensselaer Polytechnic Institute, USA

Zhi Zeng
Rensselaer Polytechnic Institute, USA

Qiang Ji
Rensselaer Polytechnic Institute, USA

ABSTRACT

Upper body tracking is a problem to track the pose of human body from video sequences. It is difficult due to such problems as the high dimensionality of the state space, the self-occlusion, the appearance changes, etc. In this paper, we propose a generic framework that can be used for both 2D and 3D upper body tracking and can be easily parameterized without heavily depending on supervised training. We first construct a Bayesian Network (BN) to represent the human upper body structure and then incorporate into the BN various generic physical and anatomical constraints on the parts of the upper body. Unlike the existing upper body models, we aim at handling physically feasible body motions rather than only some typical motions. We also explicitly model the body part occlusion in the model, which allows to automatically detect the occurrence of self-occlusion and to minimize the effect of measurement errors on the tracking accuracy due to occlusion. Using the proposed model, upper body tracking can be performed through probabilistic inference over time. A series of experiments were performed on both monocular and stereo video sequences to demonstrate the effectiveness and capability of the model in improving upper body tracking accuracy and robustness.

DOI: 10.4018/978-1-60566-900-7.ch007

1 INTRODUCTION

Human body tracking from 2D images is a challenging problem in computer vision. Assuming human body is composed of N rigid body parts, the whole body pose can be represented as a long vector $\Theta = (\phi_1,...,\phi_N)$, where $\phi_i = \{T_i, R_i\}$ represents the pose (i.e. translation and rotation) of each body part. The whole body pose is usually in a high dimensional continuous space (25-50 dimensions is not uncommon (Deutscher, Blake, & Reid, 2000)). If one simply estimates the whole pose, the high dimensionality of the state space will lead to the problem of intractable computational complexity.

In order to efficiently and robustly search in the high-dimensional body pose space, people use either sampling-based methods or learning-based methods. Sidenbladh et al. (Sidenbladh, Black, & Fleet, 2000), Deutscher et al (Deutscher, et al., 2000) and MacCormick et al. (MacCormick & Isard, 2000) attempt to handle this problem by importance sampling, annealed sampling and partitioned sampling, respectively. In the sampling based method, the posteriori probability distribution of the human pose is represented by a certain number of particles (pose hypothesis). During tracking, these particles are propagated using the dynamical model and weighted by the image likelihood. However, in this kind of basic sequential importance sampling (Sidenbladh, et al., 2000), the required number of particles grows exponentially with the dimension of the pose space (MacCormick & Isard, 2000), which makes it inefficient. To reduce the required samples, Deutscher et al (Deutscher, et al., 2000) use the annealed sampling, which generate the samples through several "annealing" steps, and show that the required number of particles can be reduced by over a factor of 10. MacCormick et al. (MacCormick & Isard, 2000) use partitioned sampling to "partition" the pose space into sub-spaces and then generate samples in these sub-spaces

sequentially, so the number of required samples will not significantly grow with the dimensionality. Although these methods can reduce the samples to around 200-700, they add much more computation load to the sample generation step, which makes them still computationally inefficient.

The learning-based methods attempt to learn a direct mapping from the image feature space to the pose space, and this mapping is learned from the training data. Currently, the most popular learning-based methods in body tracking are the regression learning techniques, such as the regression method in (Agarwal & Triggs, 2006) and the Gaussian process latent variable model (GPLVM) in (Tian, Li, & Sclaroff, 2005). However, the learning-based methods usually can only give good results for specific persons and specific motions that are similar to the training data.

So far, many robust and efficient head and limb detectors have been proposed (Ramanan & Forsyth, 2003). Since the whole body pose Θ is difficult to be recovered directly, more and more body tracking techniques are proposed to track the pose of each body part independently. This independent tracking reduces the problem of high dimensionality, but it can still be difficult due to part occlusion as well as significant changes in part appearances.

On the other hand, two adjacent human body parts are anatomically connected with joints and muscles, and the feasible poses of an upper body must satisfy some anatomical constraints. Researchers have exploited the relationships among human body parts for constraining the body tracking problem. The problem is how to efficiently and effectively capture these relationships in a systematic way.

Probabilistic graphical model (PGM) is a natural way to represent the relationships among the body parts. If the only relationships captured by the PGM are those between the adjacent body parts, the model can be represented as a tree-structured PGM. The simple tree structure allows efficient inference of the body poses, but it fails to capture other important constraints such as the symmetry on human body parts, as also pointed out by Lan et al. (Lan & Huttenlocher, 2005). They also show that there may be relationships between the limbs on the left side and the limbs on the right side when the human undergoes a routine action (e.g. the natural walking and running). However, these action-related constraints are mainly learned from the training data and can only be applied to specific actions.

Besides these action-related constraints, some generic constraints among the body parts should also be exploited for improving human body tracking. Some major generic constraints are listed as follows:

1. **"Kinematics constraint"**. Kinematics constraint is a widely used constraint that is imposed on the relationships among body parts. It means the two adjacent body parts should be connected via a joint. In PGM, this connectivity can be "elastic", i.e. if the distance between the joint points of two adjacent parts is small, the pose has a high probability (P. F. Felzenszwalb & Huttenlocher, 2005; Wu, Hua, & Yu, 2003).

2. **"Physical constraint"**. Physical constraint is imposed to exclude the physically infeasible pose among non-adjacent parts. For example, some 3D body parts cannot intersect with each other (Sminchisescu & Triggs, 2001; Sudderth, Mandel, Freeman, & Willsky, 2004).

3. **"Biomechanics constraint"**. Biomechanics constraint is another type of relationships among body parts. Besides the kinematics constraints, it further restricts the motion of the body parts. For example, each joint angle usually has its feasible range and the body part has its maximum speed (Brubaker, Fleet, & Hertzmann, 2007; NASA, 2000).

4. **"Anthropometrics/anatomical constraint"**. Anthropometrics constraint

provides statistical data about the distribution of body part dimensions. For example, the average width/length ratio for each body part and the relative length ratio between adjacent body parts tend to be constant. The body parts on the left side have similar physical parameters as their counterparts on the right side (NCSH, 1988-1994), etc.

5. **"Appearance constraint"**. All the above relationships are imposed on the pose space of body parts. Besides, there are also some relationships among the appearances of different parts. For example, the appearances of the left and right limbs should be similar to each other (Ren, Berg, & Malik, 2005).

In addition to the aforementioned part relationships and constraints, the self-occlusion is another factor that should be taken into account for upper body tracking. When occlusion happens, the image measurements of the parts (e.g. the position, the length, etc) become less accurate. We believe that if occlusion occurs, we shall depend more on the image measurements of the non-occluded parts and the relationships among body parts to correctly infer the poses of the occluded parts. This requires to detect the occurrence of self-occlusion, and to automatically reduce the confidence in the measurements of the occluded parts.

In this paper, we propose a generic framework for 2D and 3D upper body tracking based on the Dynamic Bayesian Network (DBN) (Murphy, 2002). The model captures both the spatial and the temporal relationships among different body parts. Specifically, we encode various constraints on the body parts into the Conditional Probability Distributions (CPDs) of the model. We also explicitly model the self-occlusion of body parts in the model. We parameterize the model based on the anthropometrical statistics and the statistical performance of the part's measurement detector. It minimizes the requirement of training data and can be generalized to different motions. For tracking, we further use the DBN to incorporate the temporal relationships of the state variables. Robust and accurate tracking results are achieved through a DBN inference process.

2 RELATED WORK

There is much work related to human body pose estimation and tracking based on various graphical models (L. Sigal, Bhatia, Roth, Black, & Isard, 2004; Leonid Sigal, Zhu, Comaniciu, & Black, 2004; Wu, et al., 2003), such as Factor Graph (Noriega & Bernier, 2007), Conditional Random Field (CRF) (Tayche, Shakhnarovich, Demirdjian, & Darrell, 2006), Bayesian network (BN) (Taycher & Darrell, 2003), and DBN (Pavlovic, Rehg, Cham, & Murphy, 1999). Some bottom-up approaches address the dimensionality of the state space by representing each part independently. Each part is searched independently to find its pose, and all the parts are combined together subject to some generic constraints. These approaches normally represent the body parts using a tree-structured undirected graphical model (P. Felzenszwalb & Huttenlocher, 2003; Ramanan & Forsyth, 2003; Ramanan, Forsyth, & Zisserman, 2005; Ronfard, Schmid, & Triggs, 2002; Wu, et al., 2003), because the simple tree structure allows efficient inference.

The potential functions associated with the connected body parts encode the compatibility between pairs of part configurations that penalizes the loose connection at their common joint. These potential functions are typically learned through a supervised training process. Since they strongly depend on the training process to get the model parameters, these models capture only the typical relationships among body parts that exist in the training data, and thus the learned model may not be able to generalize well to unexpected or unusual poses, as also pointed out by (Leonid Sigal & Black, 2006).

Besides modeling the relationships among the connected body parts, some works also use the directed graphical model to capture the dynamics of the body pose (Sidenbladh, et al., 2000; L. Sigal, et al., 2004; Wu, et al., 2003). However, like the modeling of connected parts, the learnt model only reflects the typical pose dynamics (e.g. walking, jogging) in the training data.

Little work tries to capture other types of relationships besides the simple kinematics constraint of joints. Lan et al. (Lan & Huttenlocher, 2005) take into account the coordination relationships between limbs, i.e., the limbs should coordinate with each other to keep the body balanced during a motion. However these coordination constraints are action-related. Although they are important for walking or running, they may not be very useful for other motions.

Sminchisescu et al. (Sminchisescu & Triggs, 2001) incorporate 3D joint limits, non-self intersection constraints and various model priors such as joint angle limits to define their model-image matching cost. They solve the body tracking problem as constrained optimization using Covariance Scaled Sampling followed by local refinements. D. Demirdjian et al. (Demirdjian, 2003; Demirdjian, Ko, & Darrell, 2003) propose similar biomechanics constraints, and solve the pose estimations as constrained optimization. Brubaker et al.(Brubaker, et al., 2007) try to reduce the ambiguity of human low-body tracking by using a physics-based model that captures some important physical properties of bipedal locomotion such as the balance and ground contact. Since they actually use a walking model, the generalization of this approach to other types of motions is a problem.

Self-occlusion is also a significant problem for body tracking. We notice that the works (Deva Ramanan & Zisserman, 2007; Moon & Pavlovic, 2005; Rehg & Kanade, 1995; Leonid Sigal & Black, 2006; Sudderth, et al., 2004) have addressed this issue. Rehg et al. (Rehg & Kanade, 1995) build a deterministic occlusion graph to find the visibility order. Moon et al. (Moon & Pavlovic, 2005) use a layered representation to model the occlusion, but the layered model cannot handle the occlusion in different poses. Ramanan et al. (Deva Ramanan & Zisserman, 2007) handle the occlusion by building an occluded appearance model. Their method is restricted to typical arm and leg occlusions. Sudderth et al. (Sudderth, et al., 2004) model occlusions in 3D cases. Their approach deals with the issue of over-counting image evidence when occlusions happened. Sigal et al. (Leonid Sigal & Black, 2006) try to address the occlusion problem by considering a global likelihood of the image data and incorporating the occlusion states to influence the likelihood of each pixel. Since they define two hidden occlusion variables for each pixel, they need sum out all the hidden occlusion variables for all pixels, which makes their algorithm computationally inefficient. It requires an average of 6.5 minutes to perform pose estimation for each frame.

In summary, the existing works in upper body tracking focus on modeling the connective relationships between adjacent parts. Their models heavily depend on the training data for parameterization and tend to reflect the typical pose configurations existing in the training data. They tend to ignore the different types of constraints on body parts even though these constraints are readily available and they can significantly help regularize the problem, and reduce the dependence on the training data. Therefore, the existing data-driven methods may not generalize well. In addition, the current modeling of part occlusion is computationally very inefficient.

In contrast to the existing works, our model can generalize well. It is based on the generic physical and anatomical constraints, and can be applied to upper body motions that are physically and anatomically possible, independent of any specific training data. Our modeling of occlusion is based on parts instead of pixels. It is simple and effective, allowing us to automatically detect the occlusion and to reduce the effect of inaccurate measurements of the occluded parts. Another important property of our system is that it can handle both 2D and 3D body tracking under the same framework, while current approaches are limited to either 2D or 3D body tracking.

3 UPPER BODY MODEL

Human upper body consists of several parts. There are both spatial correlations and anatomical relationships between these body parts. We use a Bayesian Network (BN) to explicitly model the upper-body structure due to three reasons. First, human upper body structure can be naturally viewed as a directed tree structure, where the limbs and the head are stretching out from the torso. Given the position of a torso, one can infer the positions of the head and the arms. Similarly, given the position of an arm, one can infer the positions of the forearm. Second, due to human body's anatomy, the torso controls the global movements of the head and the arms. The movement of an arm, in turn, controls the global movement of the forearm and the hand. These natural physical relationships are causal in nature. Therefore, we can conveniently use a BN to capture the upper body structure and the relationships among various parts. Third, it makes the parameterization and inference simpler and more efficient.

Our upper body model consists of 6 parts: the head (HE), the torso (TO), the left arm (LA), the left forearm including the hand (LF), the right arm (RA), and the right forearm including the hand (RF). For each part, its reference point is defined as its proximal joint to the torso (Figure 1(a)). Figure 1(b) shows the basic BN structure for our upper body model. Each part corresponds to a hidden state node in the model. It has a directed link to its measurement that is resulted from the independent tracker of each part.

For simplicity, we first explain our model in 2D pose tracking. Our model is later extended for 3D pose tracking (Section 3.4). For the 2D tracking problem, we assume a planar motion of the upper body. The state of each part is a vector

Figure 1. The articulated human upper body (a) and the basic BN upper body model (b). The black dot in (a) indicates the reference point of each part. The empty circles in (b) represent the state variables of body parts. The shaded circles in (b) represent the parts' measurements.

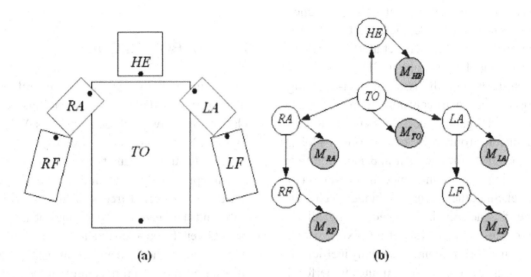

(a)   (b)

(x, y, l, θ), as shown in Figure 2. x and y represent the horizontal and vertical image coordinates of the reference point. l is the length of the part and θ is the orientation of the part. We note that the movement of the upper body part usually has a large degree of freedom in the orientation. For example, one can almost arbitrarily rotate his forearm even if he fixes his arm. Therefore, there is no strong relationship between the orientations of adjacent parts. In our BN, we actually model the physical relationship between the (x, y, l) states of adjacent parts.

The directed links in the BN represent various types of relationships among different parts that will be elaborated in the following sections. Each part also has the measurement of its states, which is obtained from an independent tracker for each part. The conditional probability for the link between a hidden state node and its measurement encodes the uncertainty of the measurement.

3.1 Physical and Anatomical Relationships

The different parts of a human upper body are physically connected. The directed links between the hidden nodes (e.g. RA and RF) in Figure 1(b) represent their connective relationships. Given the states of a parent node (e.g. RA), the state distribution of the child node (e.g. RF) can be inferred. This physically connective relationship is encoded by the conditional probability distribution (CPD) P(child|parent) (e.g. P(RF|RA)).

We analytically derive the physical relationships between adjacent parts. Figure 2 illustrates the physical relationship between the right arm and the right forearm. Given the state vector $(x_{RA}, y_{RA}, l_{RA}, \theta_{RA})$ of the right arm, the estimated position $(\hat{x}_{RF}, \hat{y}_{RF})$ of the right forearm is derived as follows:

$$\hat{x}_{RF} = x_{RA} - l_{RA} \cdot \sin(\theta_{RA})$$
$$\hat{y}_{RF} = y_{RA} - l_{RA} \cdot \cos(\theta_{RA})$$

$$(1)$$

Figure 2. Illustration of the physical relationship between adjacent parts in 2D; Given the states of the parent node (e.g. RA), the estimated position $(\hat{x}, \hat{y})$ of the child node (e.g. RF) can be derived

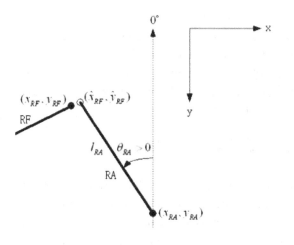

Since the right arm and the right forearm are physically connected via their common joint, the position of the right forearm reference point should be close to the estimated position derived by Eq.(1). The CPD of the right forearm is therefore modeled as a Gaussian distribution, which will be detailed in Section 3.2. The mean position of this Gaussian

is the estimated position in Eq.(1). The variance of this Gaussian is empirically determined. It captures the variability among different people. The conditional probabilities of other hidden state nodes are derived similarly.

3.2 Length Constraints

Human body is anatomically symmetric. The length of each part on the left side and its counterpart on the right side shall be the same. This symmetric relationship is modeled as a constraint into the upper body model. This constraint holds true for 3D body pose tracking. It also holds true for 2D body pose tracking when images are taken from a nearly frontal viewpoint. In order to enforce this constraint, we introduce additional constraint nodes C_1 and C_2 represented as the elliptical nodes in Figure 3. These nodes are continuous nodes. Their CPDs are defined to encode the symmetric relationships between the part on the left side and its counterpart on the right side.

The CPD of a constraint node C_i is defined as Gaussian distributions. The mean of this distribution is the difference of the parent states. The covariance matrix is a diagonal matrix. Its diagonal entries are specifically designed to enforce

Figure 3. The Bayesian Network upper body model with length constraints. The empty circles represent the state variables. The shaded circles represent the state measurements. The elliptical nodes are the constraint nodes.

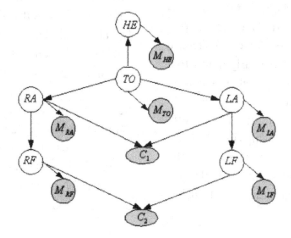

the strong constraint on the part lengths and no constraints on the part positions. For example, the CPD of C_1 is defined as

$$P(C_1 \mid RA, LA) \sim N(\mu_{C_1}, \Sigma_{C_1}), \quad \mu_{C_1} = RA - LA$$

$$(2)$$

where Σ_{C_1} is a 3×3 diagonal matrix. By adjusting the mean and variance, we can impose the length constraint to different levels. For example, to impose the equal-length constraint, we can set the state of C_1 to zero and adjust the variances. When the variances for the x and y positions are set as very large numbers, the constraint is not strictly enforced. However, when the variance of the length l is set as a small constant (e.g. 0.01), the lengths l_{RA} and l_{LA} are strongly restrained by the symmetric relationship. The CPD of $P(C_2 \mid RF, LF)$ is similarly defined.

In order to enforce the symmetry constraint on the lengths, we set the constraint node C_i as an evidence node. Its state is set as zero to enforce this symmetry constraint. Since the variance of the length l is very small, the evidence node C_i requires that the lengths of its parent nodes to be the same. In this way, we encode the symmetry constraint on the lengths. On the other hand, there is no relationship between x_{RA} and x_{LA} (or y_{RA} and y_{LA}) since their variances are very large.

Besides the symmetry constraint, we also incorporate another important anatomical constraint. Anatomically, the parts of a human body have proportional lengths, i.e., the relative length ratio of adjacent body parts is nearly a constant (NCSH, 1988-1994). Such relationships can be exploited to ensure that the tracked upper body parts will have compatible lengths. We directly model such length ratio relationships into the CPD of each body part. For example, the CPD of the right forearm encodes both the physical relationships in Eq.(1) and the anatomical relationship with the right arm, i.e.

$$P(RF^t \mid RA^t) \sim N(\mu_{RF}^t, \Sigma_0), \quad \mu_{RF}^t = \begin{pmatrix} x_{RA^t} - l_{RA^t} \cdot \sin(\theta_{RA^t}) \\ y_{RA^t} - l_{RA^t} \cdot \cos(\theta_{RA^t}) \\ k_{RF} \cdot l_{RA^t} \end{pmatrix}$$

$$(3)$$

Σ_0 is a fixed covariance matrix, which is empirically set in our experiments. The superscript t denotes the frame index. k_{RF} is the relative ratio of the right forearm length to the right arm length, which can be obtained from anthropometrics data (Deutscher, et al., 2000).

3.3 Occlusion Modeling

Occlusion is a typical problem in the upper body tracking. When occlusion happens, the uncertainties of image measurements of the occluded parts increase and hence, their contribution to tracking should be reduced accordingly. Based on this idea, we explicitly model occlusion in the upper body model. For simplicity, we currently model the occlusion of the head by the forearm because both of them have skin color and the occlusion will confuse the tracking of both parts. Other occlusion can be similarly modeled into the BN model. We will demonstrate how to model the head occlusion caused by the left/right forearm (including the hand) in detail.

Figure 4 shows the upper body model with occlusion modeling. Two additional binary nodes O_1 and O_2 are added into the BN for modeling the occlusion of the head. $O_1 = 1$ means that the right forearm occludes the head. $O_2 = 1$ means the left forearm occludes the head.

The occlusion nodes O_1 and O_2 have their measurements M_{O_1} and M_{O_2}. These measurements are obtained from the independent trackers of the head, the right forearm and the left forearm. For example, when the distance between the detected head and the right forearm is smaller than the half size of the head, the head is occluded by the right forearm ($M_{O_1} = 1$). The directed links between the occlusion nodes O_1, O_2 and their measurements

Figure 4. The complete Bayesian Network upper body model with the occlusion modeling

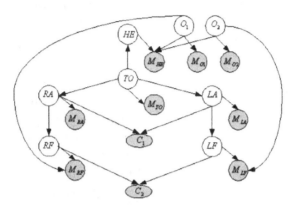

encode the uncertainties of the measurements. The conditional probabilities of $P(M_{O_i} = 1 \mid O_i = 1)$ and $P(M_{O_i} = 1 \mid O_i = 0)$ represent the uncertainty of these measurements and are empirically set as 0.7 and 0.3, respectively.

The occlusion states of O_1 and O_2 influence the uncertainties of the image measurements of the head, the right forearm and the left forearm. If the head is occluded by either part, its image data does not match the template well. As a result, the head measurement becomes less accurate and less reliable. The uncertainty of the head measurement should therefore be increased. The CPD of the head measurement is modeled as conditional Gaussians (Murphy, 1998). Based on the states of O_1 and O_2, the variances of the Gaussians are changed, which modifies the uncertainty of the head measurement. We increase the variances of the Gaussians when occlusion happens. The CPD of the head measurement is defined as

$$P(M_{HE} \mid HE, O_1, O_2) \sim N(\mu_{HE}, \Sigma_{HE})$$
$$\mu_{HE} = HE, \quad \Sigma_{HE} = \begin{cases} k_0 \cdot \Sigma_0, & \text{if } O_1 \text{ or } O_2 \text{ is } 1; \\ \Sigma_0, & \text{otherwise.} \end{cases}$$

$$(4)$$

Σ_0 is the 3×3 diagonal covariance matrix, which is empirically set in our experiments. k_0 is a coefficient greater than 1.0.

Similarly, we also consider the influence of occlusion on the measurements of the forearms. We model the CPDs of the forearm measurements as conditional Gaussians, too. Given the state of O_1 and O_2, the variances of the Gaussians are changed. In this way, we modify the uncertainties of the forearm measurements. The variances of the CPDs are adjusted similarly as in Eq.(4).

3.4 Extension to 3D Pose Tracking

We have extended our approach to 3D upper body tracking from stereo sequences. For 3D pose tracking, the state of each body part is increased to six parameters, i.e., $(x, y, z, l, \alpha, \beta)$, as shown in Figure 5. (x, y, z) are the 3D position of the reference point. l is the length of the body part. α and β represent the 3D orientation of the body part.

The structure of the upper body model remains the same as before (Figure 4). We only need to change some of the CPDs because the state parameters of a body part increase. Our model does not regulate the orientation of the body part because there are no strong relationships between the angles of adjacent body parts due to the freedom of their motions. Each node in the BN model therefore has states (x, y, z, l). Given the states of a parent

Figure 5. Calculate the estimated position of a child node (e.g. RF), given the states of its parent node (e.g. RA) in 3D pose tracking

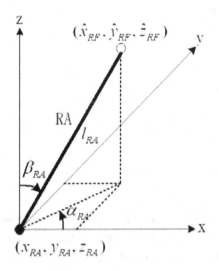

node (e.g. RA), the distribution of the child node state (e.g. RF) is derived as in Figure 5, i.e.,

$$P(RF^t \mid RA^t) \sim N(\mu_{RF}^t, \Sigma_0), \quad \mu_{RF}^t = \begin{pmatrix} x_{RA^t} + l_{RA^t} \cdot \sin(\beta_{RA^t})\cos(\alpha_{RA^t}) \\ y_{RA^t} + l_{RA^t} \cdot \sin(\beta_{RA^t})\sin(\alpha_{RA^t}) \\ z_{RA^t} + l_{RA^t} \cdot \cos(\beta_{RA^t}) \\ k_{RF} \cdot l_{RA^t} \end{pmatrix}$$

(5)

where the covariance matrix Σ_0 is a 4×4 matrix now. Other formulations are similarly defined as before, with the covariance matrix being changed to a 4×4 matrix.

4 TRACKING WITH DYNAMIC BAYESIAN NETWORK

4.1 Extension to Dynamic Bayesian Network

For tracking problem, we need to consider the temporal smoothness of the motion. We assume that the temporal relationship can be modeled as

a first order stationary Markov chain. The tracking problem is solved as an inference problem in a DBN (Murphy, 2002). Figure 6 illustrates our DBN model for upper body tracking. The directed link from $t - 1$ frame to t frame represents the temporal evolution of each state variable.

In the DBN model, the parent nodes of each upper body part consist of its state at the previous frame and its parent nodes in the BN upper body model (Figure 4). The state of each part shall be compatible with both its state at $t - 1$ frame and other part states at t frame. The CPD of the state variable is modeled as a linear Gaussian. For example, the CPD of the right forearm is defined as:

$$P(RF_t \mid RF_{t-1}, RA_t) \sim N(\mu_{RF_t}, \Sigma_0), \quad \mu_{RF_t} = \eta \cdot RF_{t-1} + (1-\eta) \cdot \mu_{RF}^t$$

(6)

It includes two parts. The first part RF_{t-1} represents the estimated mean values by the temporal dynamics. The second part μ_{RF}^t represents the estimated mean values by the relationships among body parts, which are calculated by Eq.(3) or Eq.(5). η is a constant to balance the influence of the temporal dynamics and the constraints among body parts. It is preset as 0.3 and fixed in our experiments. This selection means that the constraints among the upper body parts are more important for tracking.

Let X_t denote all the hidden state variables in the t frame. Z_t denotes all the measurements in the t frame. Given all the measurements $Z_{1..t}$ up to the time frame t, the tracking problem is modeled as an inference problem, i.e.,

$$X_t^* = \arg\max_{X_t} P(X_t \mid Z_{1..t})$$

(7)

where $P(X_t \mid Z_{1..t})$ can be decomposed based on the DBN tracking model and the likelihood of the measurements.

Figure 6. The DBN model for upper body tracking. The dotted links represent the temporal dynamics between the hidden state variables. There are dotted links between each pair of state variables. For clarity, only a few of them are drawn for illustration.

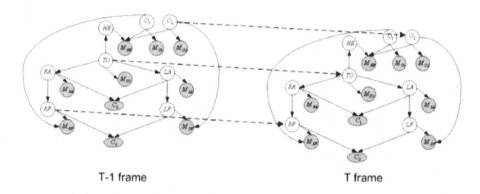

T-1 frame   T frame

$$P(X_t \mid Z_{1..t})$$
$$= \lambda P(Z_t \mid X_t) \int P(X_t \mid X_{t-1}) P(X_{t-1} \mid Z_{1..t-1}) dX_{t-1}$$
$$= \lambda \prod_{i=1}^{N} P(Z_{t,i} \mid pa^t(Z_{t,i})) \times \int \prod_{i=1}^{N} P(X_{t,i} \mid X_{t-1,i}, pa^t(X_{t,i})) P(X_{t-1} \mid Z_{1..t-1}) dX_{t-1}$$

$$(8)$$

where λ is a normalization constant. N is the number of hidden nodes in the BN upper body model. $pa^t(X_{t,i})$ is the parent of the ith hidden node $X_{t,i}$ at the t frame. $pa^t(Z_{t,i})$ is the parent of the ith measurement node $Z_{t,i}$. The likelihood $P(Z_{t,i} \mid pa^t(Z_{t,i}))$ and the conditional probability $P(X_{t,i} \mid X_{t-1,i}, pa^t(X_{t,i}))$ are already defined in the DBN tracking model. $P(X_{t-1} \mid Z_{1..t-1})$ is the joint probability of all hidden variables in the t-1 frame given the observations up to t-1 frame, which is available from previous tracking results.

Given the DBN model, we follow a similar process as (Murphy, 2002) to perform inference in the DBN to solve the tracking problem. Before that, we have to first detect all the measurements $\{Z_{t,i}\}_{i=1}^{N}$ in the current frame (t frame) as described in Section 4.2.

4.2 Measurement Extraction

In order to extract the part measurements, we perform one-step DBN prediction based on the previous estimation:

$$P(\hat{X}_t \mid Z_{1..t-1}) = \int \prod_{i=1}^{N} P(X_{t,i} \mid X_{t-1,i}, pa^t(X_{t,i})) P(X_{t-1} \mid Z_{1..t-1}) dX_{t-1}$$

$$(9)$$

This prediction step is actually an inference process on part of the DBN in Figure 6, i.e. the network which is basically same as Figure 6, but without the measurement nodes in the t frame.

Then, the measurements $(x_k, y_k, z_k, l_k, \alpha_k, \beta_k)$ for the k-th body part are automatically detected in a small neighborhood of the predicted position. For 3D tracking, each hypothesis of a 3D part is projected to the right and left images. For example, given a right forearm hypothesis $(x_{RF}, y_{RF}, z_{RF}, l_{RF}, \alpha_{RF}, \beta_{RF})$, we can project it to the right and left images and extract the right forearm regions (as shown in Figure 7). The extracted regions are then compared to the offline templates using sum-of-squared-distance (SSD) criterion. Based on the SSD of the right and left images, the final SSD score is defined as:

$$f(x, y, z, l, \alpha, \beta, I_r, I_l) = \exp\left(-\frac{SSD(I_r)}{\lambda_r}\right) \exp\left(-\frac{SSD(I_l)}{\lambda_l}\right)$$

$$(10)$$

where $SSD(I_r)$ and $SSD(I_l)$ are the SSD scores of the right and left images respectively. I_r and I_l are the projected right and left images. λ_r and λ_l are the parameters which are manually set to adjust the weights of the left and right image observations. Finally, the hypothesis with the highest SSD score (Eq.(10)) is detected as the part's measurement.

It should be noted that we detect each body part independently, i.e. searching in a 6-dimensional space $(x, y, z, l, \alpha, \beta)$ for each body part. So it is much more computationally efficient than searching in the high-dimensional whole body pose space. Although the detected measurement is usually noisy, they can be refined through the DBN inference by considering the relationships among the body parts. This "detection locally, inference globally" framework can make the algorithm efficient and robust.

5 EXPERIMENTS

We have tested the DBN upper body tracking model on several sequences, including 2D motions and 3D motions. We first compare the performance of our approach against the tracker that tracks each body part independently. We then demonstrate the effect of each major relationship that we have modeled into our model. Finally, we quantitatively evaluate the tracking performance in the five monocular sequences and two stereo sequences.

5.1 Performance of the DBN Tracking Model

We first compare our DBN tracker with the independent tracker, which tracks the body parts independently. In the test sequence, the subject is waving his arms and the forearm occludes the head in some frames. Some tracking results for the sequence 1 are shown in Figure 8.

In frames #5, #8 and #14, the clothes color of the right arm is very similar to that of the torso, and the appearance of the right arm changes very

Figure 7. The projection of the 3D body part to the left and right images; The projected regions are shown as black rectangles in the images and the extracted right forearm regions are shown by the side images

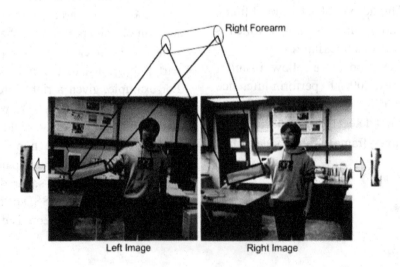

Figure 8. Comparison of the DBN upper body tracker with the independent tracker. The result frames 5,8,14,17,23,25,26 are shown. (a) For the independent tracker, the right arm starts to drift in frames #5, #8 and #14 and the head starts to drift when it is occluded in frames #25 and #26. (b) The DBN upper body tracker will not drift in these frames.

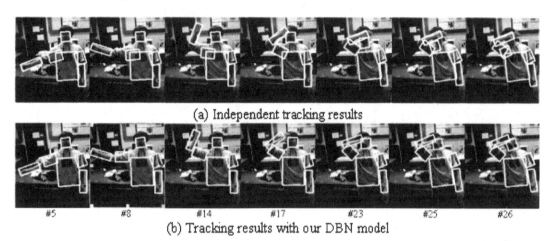

(a) Independent tracking results

    #5   #8   #14   #17   #23   #25   #26

(b) Tracking results with our DBN model

significantly because of the clothes wrinkles. For the independent tracker, the tracking of the right arm will drift quickly to the torso. (In this sequence, the independent tracker can recover the right arm in frame #17, but it is very unstable. The right arm will be lost again in later frames). On the other hand, our DBN tracker tracks the upper body robustly without drift.

In frames #25 and #26, because the forearm occludes the head, the independent tracker drifts quickly and cannot be recovered. Our DBN tracker will not lose the head position with the help of the occlusion nodes. Section 5.2 will discuss more on the effect of the occlusion nodes.

To quantitatively compare the tracking performance, we manually labeled the endpoints of each body part in every frame. The tracking error for each part is computed as the average distance between the tracked ends and the labeled ends. The tracking error for this sequence is shown in Figure 9. Since the independent tracker drifts quickly, we only compare the first 80 frames. The quantitative evaluation for the whole sequence (293 frames) is summarized in Section 5.4.

From Figure 9(a), we can see that the right arm drifts from frame #8 to #15. Although the right arm can be recovered in frame #17, it will drift again from frame #30. We also see that the head drifts from frame #25 when it is occluded, and will never be recovered. On the other hand, from Figure 9(b), we observe that our DBN upper body tracker does not drift at all in these frames.

5.2 Effect of the Occlusion Nodes

To demonstrate the effect of the occlusion nodes, we study the performance of the proposed model with and without using the occlusion nodes. Some tracking results when occlusion happens are shown in Figure 10.

When the right forearm occludes the head, their measurements will become inaccurate. In such a case, the occlusion nodes will reduce the influence of the measurements and estimate the states mostly from the relationships among upper body parts and other more accurate measurements. As a result, the head position will not drift too far, and the tracker can recover the head position as soon as the head appears again. Without using the

Figure 9. Tracking errors over time; For clarity, we only compare the tracking errors for the head, the right arm and the right forearm here

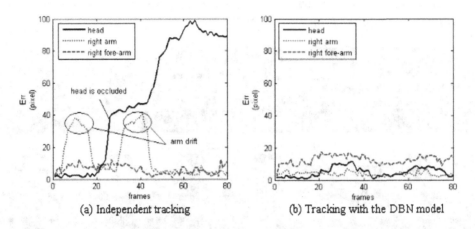

(a) Independent tracking   (b) Tracking with the DBN model

Figure 10. Effect of the occlusion nodes: (a) The tracking results without using occlusion nodes will drift when the head is occluded. (b) However, the tracker with the occlusion nodes estimates the head position mostly from the adjacent body parts, and thus the head will not drift too far and will be recovered when the head appears again.

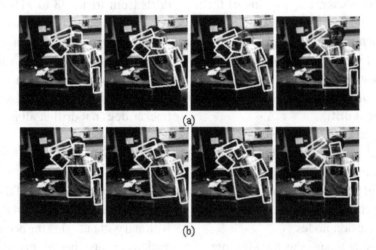

occlusion nodes, the tracking will become incorrect and the head tracking will drift, as shown in Figure 10(a).

5.3 Effect of Length Constraints

In the upper body model, we model the length constraints to keep the relative length relationships among body parts. To show the effect of these length constraints, we tested the DBN tracking model with and without using length constraints. Some results are shown in Figure 11.

We observe that the tracker without length constraints usually tends to gradually shrink the length of each part (e.g. arms or forearms), because the SSD detector tends to detect a smaller region. In contrast, the DBN tracker with length constraints will maintain the reasonable length of

Figure 11. Effect of the length constraints: (a) The tracking results without using the length constraints. The arms and the forearms become shorter in frames #9 and #119, compared to the first frame. (b) The tracker with length constraints maintains the reasonable length of each part.

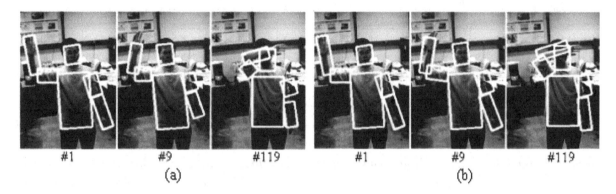

each part, which demonstrates the effectiveness of length constraints.

5.4 Quantitative Evaluation on 2D Pose Tracking

For 2D upper body tracking, the proposed model has been tested on 5 monocular sequences with different subjects in different clothes. The length of the 5 sequences are 293, 1101, 971, 1001, 764

frames, respectively. Example tracking results on the other 4 monocular sequences of different subjects are showed in Figure 12.

For quantitative evaluation of the performance, the average tracking errors (in pixels) for the 5 sequences are calculated and summarized in Table 1. Apparently, the model with occlusion nodes generally has much better performance than the model without using occlusion nodes. These results quantitatively demonstrate the importance

Figure 12. Some example tracking results from several video sequences of different subjects

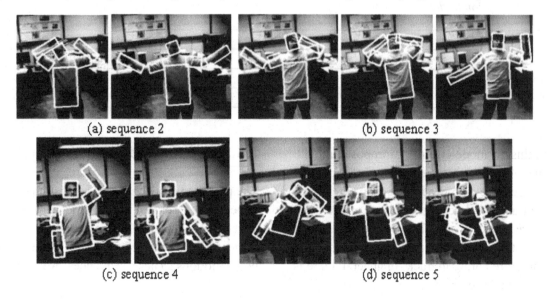

Table 1. Average tracking errors (in pixels) of 2D upper body tracking results (O: with occlusion nodes; N: without occlusion nodes)

Sequence	Head		Torso		Arms		Forearms	
	O	N	O	N	O	N	O	N
sequence 1	4.7	21.5	3.8	5.6	6.4	8.6	9.0	9.4
sequence 2	6.3	7.2	4.6	4.6	6.9	7.1	8.7	9.6
sequence 3	6.7	7.4	6.7	6.8	7.2	7.4	5.6	5.6
sequence 4	4.8	5.4	4.6	3.4	6.7	5.6	6.9	8.1
sequence 5	4.2	6.6	5.8	6.0	5.3	5.3	5.2	6.9

Figure 13. 3D upper body tracking from stereo sequences. In each image, the top-left is the front view of the 3D tracking result. The top-right is the top view of the 3D tracking result. The bottom-left and bottom-right are the projections on the right image and on the left image.

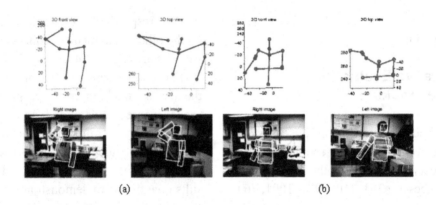

(a)   (b)

Table 2. Average tracking errors (cm) of 3D upper body tracking results (O: with occlusion nodes; N: without occlusion nodes)

Sequence	Head		Torso		Arms		Forearms	
	O	N	O	N	O	N	O	N
stereo sequence 1	5.2	6.6	3.7	3.6	6.4	7.2	5.6	10.3
stereo sequence 2	2.1	1.8	4.6	4.9	6.4	7.4	5.1	10.1

of occlusion modeling in the proposed model. We also observe that the tracking of torso and head is relatively more accurate than other parts. In contrast, the tracking accuracy of the arms and forearms is worse than that of other parts because they move faster and more widely and are therefore harder to track. In general, there is no drift in all sequences.

5.5 3D Upper Body Tracking

The proposed model has also been applied to 3D upper body tracking. We have tested it on two stereo sequences (310 frames and 381 frames respectively), which capture different 3D upper body motions. These sequences are manually labeled to obtain the ground truth for quantitative performance evaluation.

Figure 13 shows some typical 3D pose tracking results. The quantitative evaluation of these results is measured by the average 3D distance (in cm) between the tracked ends and the labeled ends. The quantitative evaluation is summarized in Table 2. The average tracking error is about 5 to 6 cm, which is good enough to recover the true 3D upper body poses. In addition, the model with occlusion nodes generally has lower tracking errors than the model without using occlusion nodes. The performance differences are especially large for the head and the forearms because we explicitly model their inter-occlusions. These results again demonstrate the importance of occlusion modeling in the proposed model.

We implement the tracking approach using a combination of C++ language and Matlab. The SSD detector is implemented using C++ language, while the probabilistic inference in DBN is implemented using Matlab. It usually takes less than 2 seconds to process one frame. A complete implementation using C++ will further improve the efficiency.

6 CONCLUSION

In this paper, we propose a generic framework for 2D and 3D upper body tracking using a Dynamic Bayesian Network model with the physical and anatomical constraints and explicit occlusion modeling. We first construct a Bayesian Network to represent the human upper body structure. We then incorporate into the model several generic physical and anatomical constraints on the upper body parts. The uncertainties of image measurements are also modeled. Furthermore, we explicitly model the part occlusions and the effect of part occlusions on the part measurements. By further incorporating the temporal dynamics using a DBN, we solve the tracking problem as a probabilistic inference problem in the DBN model.

The model is parameterized mainly based on the geometric, physical and anatomical statistics of human body parts and the performance statistics of the SSD tracker for getting the local measurements. It avoids heavy dependence on the training data to fit the model to specific motions. Compared with the existing models for upper body tracking, our model is generic and applicable to different body motions and to different people. In addition, the same framework can be used for both 2D and 3D tracking without much change. The experiments on both 2D and 3D upper body tracking problems demonstrate the capability of our model in improving upper body tracking performance even with a simple body part detector (i.e. SSD detector). In the future, we will further improve the model to handle more complex motions under multiple types of occlusions, and to improve the part's measurement detection with more advanced detectors.

Finally, there are several open issues in object tracking including upper body tracking. First, it might be desirable that the object-tracking model can be adapted online to better fit the new scenario. This requires online target model learning and adaptation. Instead of purely using a pre-trained or parameterized model to handle object tracking in the new video sequences, the adaptive tracking might intelligently adjust to the new videos and therefore improve the object tracking performance. However, how to perform online learning and adaptation is an open issue to be explored. Second, it is still not very clear how to systematically and efficiently model all different kinds of generic constraints on body pose tracking, as summarized in the introduction section of this paper. Third, the occlusion modeling can still be improved. The pixelwise occlusion modeling (Leonid Sigal & Black, 2006) is not efficient and too slow for the practical usage. In contrast, our part-based occlusion modeling is efficient but it does not model pixelwise occlusion. It will be very interesting to study whether it is possible to integrate the advantages of both approaches in the same framework.

REFERENCES

Agarwal, A., & Triggs, B. (2006). Recovering 3D Human Pose from Monocular Images. *IEEE Trans. on Pattern Analysis and Machine Intelligence*.

Brubaker, M. A., Fleet, D. J., & Hertzmann, A. (2007). Physics-Based Person Tracking Using Simplified Lower-Body Dynamics. *Computer Vision and Pattern Recognition*, 1-8.

Demirdjian, D. (2003). Enforcing Constraints for Human Body Tracking. In *Workshop on Multi-object Tracking*.

Demirdjian, D., Ko, T., & Darrell, T. (2003). Constraining Human Body Tracking. In *IEEE International Conference on Computer Vision*.

Deutscher, J., Blake, A., & Reid, I. (2000). Articulated Body Motion Capture by Annealed Particle Filtering. *Computer Vision and Pattern Recognition*, 2, 126–133.

Deva Ramanan, D. A. F., & Zisserman, A. (2007). Tracking People by Learning Their Appearance. *IEEE Trans. Pattern Analysis and Machine Intelligence*.

Felzenszwalb, P., & Huttenlocher, D. (2003). Efficient Matching of Pictorial Structures. *Computer Vision and Pattern Recognition*.

Felzenszwalb, P. F., & Huttenlocher, D. P. (2005). Pictorial Structures for object recognition. *International Journal of Computer Vision*.

Lan, X., & Huttenlocher, D. P. (2005). Beyond Trees: Common Factor Models for 2D human Pose Recovery. *IEEE International Conference on Computer Vision*.

MacCormick, J., & Isard, M. (2000). Partitioned sampling, articulated objects, and interface-quality hand tracking. *European Conference on Computer Vision*.

Moon, K., & Pavlovic, V. (2005). Estimation of Human Figure Motion Using Robust Tracking of Articulated Layers. *CVPR*.

Murphy, K. (1998). Fitting a constrained conditional linear Gaussian distribution. *Technical report*.

Murphy, K. (2002). *Dynamic Bayesian Networks: Representation, Inference and Learning*. PhD Thesis, UC Berkeley, Computer Science Division.

NASA. (2000). *NASA-STD-3000: Man-systems integration standards*. Retrieved from http://msis.jsc.nasa.gov/sections/section03.htm

NCSH. (1994). *Anthropometric Reference Data, United States, 1988-1994*. Retrieved from http://www.cdc.gov/nchs/

Noriega, P., & Bernier, O. (2007). Multicues 3D Monocular Upper Body Tracking Using Constrained Belief Propagation. *British Machine Vision Conference*.

Pavlovic, V., Rehg, J. M., Cham, T.-J., & Murphy, K. P. (1999). A Dynamic Bayesian Network Approach to Figure Tracking Using Learned Dynamic Models. In *IEEE International Conference on Computer Vision*.

Ramanan, D., & Forsyth, D. A. (2003). Finding and Tracking People from the Bottom Up. *Computer Vision and Pattern Recognition*.

Ramanan, D., Forsyth, D. A., & Zisserman, A. (2005). Strike a Pose: Tracking People by Finding Stylized Poses. *Computer Vision and Pattern Recognition*.

Rehg, J. M., & Kanade, T. (1995). Model-Based Tracking of Self-Occluding Articulated Objects. *ICCV*.

Ren, X., Berg, A. C., & Malik, J. (2005). Recovering Human Body Configurations using Pairwise Constraints between Parts. In *IEEE International Conference on Computer Vision*.

Ronfard, R., Schmid, C., & Triggs, B. (2002). Learning to parse pictures of people. In *ECCV* (pp. 700-714).

Sidenbladh, H., Black, M. J., & Fleet, D. J. (2000). Stochastic Tracking of 3D Human Figures Using 2D Image Motion. In *European Conference on Computer Vision* (pp. 702-718).

Sigal, L., Bhatia, S., Roth, S., Black, M. J., & Isard, M. (2004). Tracking Loose-limbed People. *Computer Vision and Pattern Recognition*.

Sigal, L., & Black, M. J. (2006). Measure Locally, Reason Globally: Occlusion-sensitive Articulated Pose Estimation. *Computer Vision and Pattern Recognition*.

Sigal, L., Zhu, Y., Comaniciu, D., & Black, M. (2004). Tracking Complex Objects using Graphical Object Models. In *1st International Workshop on Complex Motion* (LNCS 3417, pp. 227-238).

Sminchisescu, C., & Triggs, B. (2001). Covariance Scaled Sampling for Monocular 3D Body Tracking. *Computer Vision and Pattern Recognition*.

Sudderth, E. B., Mandel, M. I., Freeman, W. T., & Willsky, A. S. (2004). Distributed Occlusion Reasoning for Tracking with Nonparametric Belief Propagation. *Advances in Neural Information Processing Systems (NIPS)*.

Tayche, L., Shakhnarovich, G., Demirdjian, D., & Darrell, T. (2006). Conditional Random People: Tracking Humans with CRFs and Grid Filters. *Computer Vision and Pattern Recognition*.

Taycher, L., & Darrell, T. (2003). Bayesian Articulated Tracking Using Single Frame Pose Sampling Constraints. In *3rd Int'l Workshop on Statistical and Computational Theories of Vision*.

Tian, T.-P., Li, R., & Sclaroff, S. (2005). Articulated Pose Estimation in a Learned Smooth Space of Feasible Solutions. In *Computer Vision and Pattern Recognition - Workshops* (pp. 50).

Wu, Y., Hua, G., & Yu, T. (2003). Tracking Articulated body by Dynamic Markov Network. *Computer Vision and Pattern Recognition*.

Chapter 8
Real–Time Recognition of Basic Human Actions

Vassilis Syrris
Aristotle University of Thessaloniki, Greece

ABSTRACT

This work describes a simple and computationally efficient, appearance-based approach both for human pose recovery and for real-time recognition of basic human actions. We apply a technique that depicts the differences between two or more successive frames and we use a threshold filter to detect the regions of the video frames where some type of human motion is observed. From each frame difference, the algorithm extracts an incomplete and unformed human body shape and generates a skeleton model which represents it in an abstract way. Eventually, the recognition process is formulated as a time-series problem and handled by a very robust and accurate prediction method (Support Vector Regression). The proposed technique could be employed in applications such as surveillance and security systems.

INTRODUCTION

Human actions modeling, detection and recognition from video sequences (i.e. temporal series of frames/images) can have many applications in robot/computer vision, indoor/outdoor surveillance and monitoring, human-computer interaction, computer graphics, virtual reality and video analysis (summarization; transmission; retrieval; compression etc). A typical automated human action recognition system is usually examined in both constituent components:

hardware (processing units, cameras, networks etc.) and software, that is, algorithms based mainly on computational/statistical techniques.

In this work, we focus on the latter; more specifically the recognition problem confronted herein is the classification of elementary human actions like walking, hands-waving and jumping, captured by a steady monocular camera. There are many parameters that affect the problem complexity:

- **Intra- and inter-class variations:** There are large natural differences in performance for many actions considered to belong in the

DOI: 10.4018/978-1-60566-900-7.ch008

same class (e.g. speed and pace length generate different types of walking). In addition, many times the boundaries between two action classes are hard to define (e.g. drawing and moving one hand).

- **Recording conditions:** Existence of one (single data source, monocular camera) or more cameras (binocular or multiple cameras), movement of the camera (autonomous robot) or not (still surveillance camera), indoor or outdoor camera shooting, image resolution (e.g. high quality reduces noise but raises the storage and processing requirements), distance of the observed object and its position in relation to the camera, and so on.
- **Discrepancies in person localization** (either spatial or temporal).
- **Motion alignment in order to compare two video sequences**

Human motion and event analysis has received much attention in the research communities (some indicative review papers of this subject are Gao et al., 2004; Hu et al., 2004; Kumar et al., 2008; Moeslund & Granum, 2001). Nevertheless, it remains a core unsolved machine vision problem due to several reasons: illumination conditions, depth calculation, complex backgrounds, variations of object appearance and posture, representation of human body or its transformation to a more compact and recognizable structure, description and measurement of activities and high pre-processing requirements are some of the factors obstructing an easy, sound and complete problem resolution.

The objective of this work is to describe a computational approach for tackling a single person action recognition problem. During this course, we analyze the processing stages in order to detect the object of interest, to identify appropriate content features that suitably represent it, to exploit the information underlying within the trajectories of this object and to define suitable decision boundaries capable of classifying new unseen human action videos. At the end of the chapter, the future directions section pinpoints the open research issues and stresses the subtle nuances that someone has to consider when dealing with such a hard, automated application.

VIDEO CONTENT ANALYSIS

In general, video content analysis relates to the following tasks:

a. Detecting objects of interest within the frames: a low-level stage of video processing where visual features such as color, image and pixel regions, texture, contours, corners etc are identified/selected/formulated.

b. Assigning meaning to the temporal development of these elements: a high-level stage (recognition phase) where objects and events are classified to some predefined classes that represent patterns of motion. The major issue herein is how to map the low-level features (pixels, transformed features or statistical measures) as semantic content.

In addition, videos consist of massive amounts of raw information in the form of spatial-temporal pixel intensities/color variations, but most of this information is not directly relevant to the task of understanding and identifying the activity occurring in the video.

Most of the current methods employ a number of the following steps:

1. Frame/image segmentation
2. Object identification
3. Object tracking
4. Features extraction from each frame (these features represent the objects or events of interest)

5. Models training based on extracted descriptors
6. 2D/3D models fitting on detected objects.
7. Recognition of a scene/event/action/activity, that is, classification into classes, consisting of similar scenes/events/actions/activities

Several approaches have been proposed for each of the above subjects and many of them present notable performance in specific applications. However, there still remain unsolved problems in many areas in need of active research. On that line, this work focuses on the particular field of real-time recognition of single-person basic actions.

Human Action Recognition

In this chapter, human action recognition is examined along two dimensions:

a. **Image (frame) characteristics/descriptors:** They result from a process which involves features selection (image points or regions selection) and/or features extraction (pixels transformation or computation of the pixels statistical measures). These features aim to describe suitably the objects of interest in each frame. Recognition systems can be broadly split into two major categories according to the visual content representation criterion:

   ○ *Geometry-based*, where geometrical features such as lines, ridges and vertices are extracted and kinematic model-based where a model of the human body and its locomotion is imposed and represent the articulated human motion. For instance, Curio et al. (2000) draw upon biomechanical research to set up a model of the human gait and use it as their primary detection scheme. Some other indicative references are: learned geometrical models of human body parts (Jiang et al., 2006); motion/optical flow patterns (Efros et al., 2003); global motion models (Little & Boyd, 1998).

   ○ *Appearance-based*, where intensity/color values of the pixels in the image characterize the objects under consideration. Such features encode what the body looks like and some context of motion. Various successful appearance-based approaches have been proposed including: characteristic spatial-temporal volumes (Blank et al., 2005); feature points (Madabhushi & Aggarwal, 1999); hierarchical model of shape and appearance (Niebles & Fei-Fei, 2007); motion history images (Bobick & Davis, 2001); region features (Bregler, 1997; Veit et al., 2004); spatial-temporal interest points (Laptev & Perez, 2007; Laptev et al., 2008); reduced stacks of silhouettes (Wang & Suter, 2007) and silhouette histogram of oriented rectangle features (Ikizler & Duygulu, 2007). Cedras & Shah (1995) present a survey on motion based approaches to recognition as opposed to structure-based approaches. They argue that motion is a more important cue for action recognition than the structure of the human body. When considering sub-image retrieval or object recognition, local image characterization approaches provide better results than global characterization techniques classically based on color, texture and shape. The former allows gaining robustness against occlusions and cluttering since only a local description of the patch of interest is involved. The most dominant works on points of interest detection are the Harris and Stephens detector (Harris & Stephens, 1998) which has been used first for stereo purposes and then for image retrieval, and the DoG detector (Lowe, 1999) where Lowe has proposed the Scale Invariant Feature Transform approach (SIFT) for describing the local neighborhood of such points. The points of interest are often called key points or salient points.

b. **Spatial-temporal modeling:** It can be categorized into three major classes: non-parametric, volumetric and parametric time-series approaches. Non-parametric approaches typically extract a set of features from each frame of the video; the features are then matched to a stored template. Volumetric approaches on the other hand do not extract features on a frame-by-frame basis. Instead, they consider a video as a 3D volume of pixel intensities or frame descriptors and extend standard image features such as scale-space extremes, spatial filter responses etc to the 3D case. Parametric time-series approaches specifically impose a model on the temporal dynamics of the motion. The particular parameters for a class of actions are then estimated from training data. Examples of parametric approaches include Hidden Markov Models (HMMs) and Linear Dynamical Systems (LDSs). Most of the aforementioned works use the Hidden Markov Model to manipulate the temporal relationships (Demonceaux & Kachi-Akkouche, 2004). Other examples assume that a linear (Madabhushi & Aggarwal, 1999), non-linear (Bregler, 1997) or stochastic dynamic model (Veit et al., 2004) is controlling the evolution of features that are represented either in terms of image locations of body joints, or as a series of salient image points. The unknown parameters of the dynamic models are learnt using training data of human actions.

The general lines of this work rely on a traditional approach to human action recognition, expressed by Aggarwal and Cai (1999) who discuss three important sub-problems that together form a complete action recognition system: extraction of human body structure from images, tracking across frames and action recognition. First, the human figure detection is the necessary preprocessing operation. The difference with other silhouette-based methods (for instance: Chen et al., 2007; Hsieh et al., 2008) is that the human figure could be incomplete (body parts may be missing) or imperfect (some boundary lines could be misleading). At a second stage, tracking the figure during a frame series follows in order to extract informative trajectories. Generally, extracting unambiguous object trajectories from video is complicated by several factors such as occlusions, noise and background clutter. Accurate tracking algorithms need to be employed in order to obtain motion trajectories (Yilmaz et al., 2006). The tracking process is out of the scope of this work; hence we don't provide any further material. The benchmark data sets used herein consist of a static background and a single moving person; after the pre-processing stage, we consider that in each frame just one object remains which represents parts of the person who executes the specific actions.

The last processing stage is action recognition, a typically dynamic problem. Initially, a set of features (i.e. quantities that describe the object of interest in each frame, keeping a trade-off between low complexity and high clarity) that represent the human body parts is formulated. Secondly, an appropriate mapping that relates the previous frames to the following frames is defined; the type of the mapping function determines whether the motion modeling is linear, non-linear or stochastic dynamic. Significant factors that prohibit the application of differential calculus are:

- The number of variables
- The uncertainty of information

- The small number of frames available
- The severe aliasing in the image acquisition process
- The extended discontinuity intervals

Statistical approaches are usually preferred for the motion modeling, attempting to cope with the information gaps and enhance the generalization performance.

Object Detection

Due to the fact that the intended application is real-time recognition, the efforts focus on techniques with relatively low computational cost. Accordingly, in order to isolate the object of interest, a simple two-frame difference approach combined with a threshold filter is adopted:

$$Diff(x, y, t) = \begin{cases} 0, & \|I(x, y, t+1) - I(x, y, t)\|_1 \leq threshold \\ 1, & \text{otherwise} \end{cases}$$

$$(1.1)$$

where t denotes the frames index (time instant), norm $\|\cdot\|_1$ is the absolute value of an integer number, *threshold* is an integer value defined by the user, $I(x, y, t)$ is a scalar value expressing gray intensity and $I_F(t) = \{I(x, y, t) \mid 1 \leq x \leq n, 1 \leq y \leq m\}$ is the video frame at t, and n and m are the numbers of its rows and columns respectively. Accordingly, we define the matrix:

$$D_F(t) = \{Diff(x, y, t) \mid 1 \leq x \leq n, 1 \leq y \leq m\}$$

The (1) holds for two consecutive frames (see Figure 1). However, when the object motion is very slow, the (1) can be utilized repeatedly for a greater than two number of consecutive scenes.

Next, a noise clear-up filter is required due to the fact that images derived from two-frame difference are often contaminated with noise and clutter which indicates phony changes emerging from outside the area of interest. This type of filter belongs to fundamental morphological operations, which are filtering masks capable of removing pixel groups uncorrelated to the regions of attention and reshaping the object silhouette; some other very popular morphological image processing operations that could be used here are *dilation* and *erosion*.

The algorithm for object detection is displayed in Listing 1. This technique is very simple and adaptable to changes in dynamic environments, without making any assumptions about the scene. However, it can be problematic that only motion at edges is visible for moving objects. An extension of this method is the region-based subtraction between consecutive frames, that is, the difference between features characterizing groups of pixels.

Listing 1. Clearing Background and Isolating Object of Interest

Define T; *number of frames*
for t = 1 to T-1

$I_F(t) = FrameRGB(t)$; convert the *true color image RGB to the grayscale intensity image I_F*

$I_F(t+1) = FrameRGB(t+1)$;

$D(t) = |I_F(t+1) - I_F(t)|$; calculate the *pixel-by-pixel absolute difference of $I_F(t)$ and $I_F(t+1)$*

$$threshold = \frac{1}{n+m}\left(\sum_m \max_m (D(t)) + \sum_n \max_n (D^T(t))\right)$$

n and m are *the number of rows and columns of D(t) matrix*

$$D_F(t) = \{Diff(x, y, t) \mid 1 \leq x \leq n, 1 \leq y \leq m\},$$

Figure 1. The images in the first two rows correspond to walking and bending actions (© Weizmann Action Dataset - L. Gorelick, M. Blank, E. Shechtman, M. Irani, R. Basri. Used with permission), while in the last two, walking and drawing actions (© 2008 Shi, Q., Li, W., Li, C., and Smola, A. Used with permission) are displayed respectively. The first column contains the original frames, the second column contains the difference between the images in the first column and the respective next frames and the last column contains the images after thresholding.

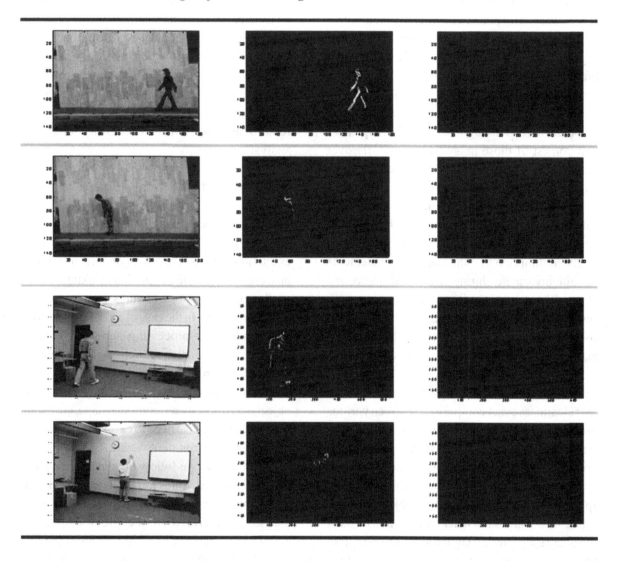

where

$$D_F\left(t\right) = \left\{ Diff\left(x,y,t\right) \mid 1 \le x \le n, 1 \le y \le m \right\}$$

$$Diff\left(x,y,t\right) = \begin{cases} 0, & \forall D(x,y,t) \in D(t) : D(x,y,t) \le threshold \\ 1, & \text{otherwise} \end{cases}$$

where

$$Diff\left(x,y,t\right) = \begin{cases} 0, & \forall D(x,y,t) \in D(t) : D(x,y,t) \le threshold \\ 1, & \text{otherwise} \end{cases}$$

$$BinaryFrame(t) = ClearImage(D_F(t), NoP)$$

remove all con*nected components that have fewer than NoP pixels* next t;

As Figure 1 demonstrates, the objects of interest are not complete human silhouettes. In actions where the person moves his/her legs (like walking and running) more information is captured and the detected region of pixels tends to resemble a human body shape; in other actions like bending, drawing or hands waving, the available information after filtering is decreasing and the object usually results in representing parts of human body such as single hands or head. The challenge herein is whether there is a way to exploit the sequences that consist of those noisy figures and discover patterns of motion, capable of representing basic human actions.

Another approach that could be used is the subtraction of a reference model or background template from the current image. This case is based on the assumption that the background elements remain invariable during the video recording. Depending on the application, for instance, in surveillance/monitoring systems, the background subtraction may exhibit better performance in extracting object information, but in general, it is sensitive to dynamic changes of the environment such as illumination, weather conditions, lens cleanness etc. A comparison between various background modeling algorithms is given (Toyama et al., 1999), as well as a discussion on the general principles of background maintenance systems.

The two aforementioned techniques are only applicable when the foreground (object) is moving against some static background; this ensures sufficient spatial matching and allows background cancellation. A more general approach used for the extraction of moving objects from many types of backgrounds has proved to be the *optic flow analysis* which can be thought of as a vector-field approximation of the retinal projection. Most methods computing optical flow assume that the color/intensity of a pixel is invariant under the displacement from one video frame to the next. Beauchemin & Barron (1995) provide a comprehensive survey and comparison of optical flow computation techniques. Optical flow offers a concise description of both the regions of the image undergoing motion and the velocity of motion. Computation of optical flow is, in practice, susceptible to illumination changes and noise but its time complexity remains high.

Related to the silhouette-based approaches, the detection of distinctive objects from each frame is an essential operation for the later processing stages and the success of the overall application. It reduces redundant information and provides focus of attention which is necessary for activity analysis.

Feature Extraction

The performance of any pattern recognition approach relies heavily on a good and robust feature extraction process. The latter typically follows the process of object detection and tracking so as to get the spatial-temporal features that represent the different actions. In the case of a high-dimensional feature set, a post-processing step such as feature selection or dimension reduction process may be required, in order for the general computation cost to be reduced. The features may include the object's position speed, contour, shape, etc.; some approaches may also need to extract features from the object's environment.

In this work, we follow an appearance-based approach which relies on both statistical and geometrical features. Following the processing steps described in the previous section, every two successive video frames produce an imperfect silhouette, represented in matrix $F = \{v(x,y) \mid 1 \le x \le n, 1 \le y \le m\}$. F is a binary two-dimensional matrix, that is,

$$v(x,y) = \begin{cases} 1, & \text{point of figure} \\ 0, & \text{otherwise} \end{cases},$$

and n, m are the numbers of its rows and columns respectively. The next step is the feature extraction process which attempts to handle the possible failings of the silhouette by describing it in an abstract way: each figure is transformed into a statistical skeleton. The procedure is presented below:

1. Calculate the mean point coordinates of matrix F; actually, this point is the mid-point of the figure under consideration:

$$M\left(x,y\right)=\left(M_x,M_y\right)=\frac{1}{k}\left(\sum_{i=1}^{k}x_i,\sum_{i=1}^{k}y_i\right),$$

where

$$M\left(x,y\right)=\left(M_x,M_y\right)=\frac{1}{k}\left(\sum_{i=1}^{k}x_i,\sum_{i=1}^{k}y_i\right)x_i,y_i,$$

where x_i,y_i are the coordinates of $i=1,...,k$ points of F having value 1.

2. Based on F and $M\left(x,y\right)=\left(M_x,M_y\right)$, generate four 2-column matrices:

$$S_1=\left\{\left(x,y\right)\mid v\left(x,y\right)\in F, x<M_x \text{ and } y<M_y\right\}$$
$$S_2=\left\{\left(x,y\right)\mid v\left(x,y\right)\in F, x<M_x \text{ and } y>M_y\right\}$$
$$S_3=\left\{\left(x,y\right)\mid v\left(x,y\right)\in F, x>M_x \text{ and } y<M_y\right\}$$
$$S_4=\left\{\left(x,y\right)\mid v\left(x,y\right)\in F, x>M_x \text{ and } y>M_y\right\}$$

3. Employ polynomials $p^d(y)$ of degree d to fit the data $x\in S_l$ in a least-squares sense at each matrix $S_{l=1,2,3,4}$, i.e., $\forall\left(x_i,y_i\right)\in S_l:\left(x_i,y_i\right)\approx\left(p_l^d\left(y_i\right),y_i\right)$, where $p_l\left(y_l\right)=a_ly_l+b_l$ in the simple case of linear relation (d=1).

4. Create the 10-dimensional feature vector $feat\left(u_1,u_2,u_3,u_4,v_1,v_2,v_3,v_4,dist_1,dist_2\right)$ in the following way ($l=1,2,3,4$ is the index corresponding to the four matrices S_l):

    ○ $u_l=\left\|\vec{q}_l\right\|_2$: u_l is the *Euclidean* length of vector $\vec{q}_l$, defined by the k=1,2,... points $\left(p_l\left(y_{lk}\right),y_{lk}\right)$ for each $u_l=\left\|\vec{q}_l\right\|_2$ $\vec{q}_l\left(p_l\left(y_{lk}\right),y_{lk}\right)S_{l=1,2,3,4}$: u_l is the *Euclidean* length of vector $\vec{q}_l$, defined by the k=1,2,... points $\left(p_l\left(y_{lk}\right),y_{lk}\right)$ for each $S_{l=1,2,3,4}$. The line length helps to represent the expansion or the shrinkage of figure's sub-parts. In the case of

a perfect figure, these parts can represent approximately the arms and legs of the body. When the pre-processing stage has left much noise or the human figure is partially reformed, these features describe in an abstract way the object under consideration and their contribution depends heavily on the recognition technique used for the action classification.

○ $v_l=\dfrac{p_l\left(y_{l1}\right)-p_l\left(y_{l2}\right)}{y_{l1}-y_{l2}}$: v_l is the slope of the vector $\vec{q}_l$ and $v_l=\dfrac{p_l\left(y_{l1}\right)-p_l\left(y_{l2}\right)}{y_{l1}-y_{l2}}$ $\vec{q}_l\left(p_l\left(y_{l1}\right),y_{l1}\right),\left(p_l\left(y_{l2}\right),y_{l2}\right)$: v_l is the slope of the vector $\vec{q}_l$ and $\left(p_l\left(y_{l1}\right),y_{l1}\right),\left(p_l\left(y_{l2}\right),y_{l2}\right)$ are its two respective end-points. The line slope is chosen because it indicates the direction of motion of the object's sub-parts.

○ $dist_1=\sqrt{\left(\dfrac{p_1\left(y_{12}\right)+p_1\left(y_{21}\right)}{2}\right)^2+\left(\dfrac{y_{12}+y_{21}}{2}\right)^2}$

$dist_2=\sqrt{\left(\dfrac{p_3\left(y_{32}\right)+p_4\left(y_{41}\right)}{2}\right)^2+\left(\dfrac{y_{32}+y_{41}}{2}\right)^2}$

where the notation $\left(p_l\left(y_{lk}\right),y_{lk}\right)$ signifies the one of the two end-points (k=1,2) of vector $\vec{q}_l$ in respect to matrix

$dist_1=\sqrt{\left(\dfrac{p_1\left(y_{12}\right)+p_1\left(y_{21}\right)}{2}\right)^2+\left(\dfrac{y_{12}+y_{21}}{2}\right)^2}$

$dist_2=\sqrt{\left(\dfrac{p_3\left(y_{32}\right)+p_4\left(y_{41}\right)}{2}\right)^2+\left(\dfrac{y_{32}+y_{41}}{2}\right)^2}$

$\left(p_l\left(y_{lk}\right),y_{lk}\right)$ $\qquad$ $\vec{q}_l$ $\qquad$ S_l ,

$dist_2=\sqrt{\left(\dfrac{p_3\left(y_{32}\right)+p_4\left(y_{41}\right)}{2}\right)^2+\left(\dfrac{y_{32}+y_{41}}{2}\right)^2}$

where the notation $\left(p_l\left(y_{lk}\right),y_{lk}\right)$

signifies the one of the two end-points ($k=1,2$) of vector $\vec{q}_i$ in respect to matrix S_i. These two distances provide information about the relative height of the object and they contribute to the distinction between still and moving objects by attempting to capture implicitly the object's velocity. The distances are measured from the left-down corner of the frame.

It is worth mentioning that the feature set is chosen to have small size in order to keep the computational cost low in both the training and the recognition phase. In other instances, the feature set can be enriched with more informative traits and represent in more detail the object under consideration. The described feature extraction procedure is displayed in Figure 2.

Motion Modeling

After feature extraction, the action recognition becomes a multi-dimensional time-series classification problem. Each two-frame difference is represented by a 10-dimensional feature vector; consequently, each video is transformed to a $t \times 10$ matrix, $t = T - 1$ and T denotes the initial number of video frames. Human actions are repetitive and complex patterns, making motion details difficult to capture in a one-by-one feature frame approach. In addition, there are three issues related to timing that affect the comparison of two videos and inhibits the frame-by-frame matching:

a. The action duration is not necessarily fixed for the same action.
b. The scenes may not follow a temporal alignment.
c. The object size (scaling) may vary.

To surpass these critical factors, the model learns to predict the features related to a frame, based on information provided by some previous frames. The problem is formulated as follows:

Given a set of videos corresponding to a finite set of human motion categories, we build the following:

1. For each video, a prediction model that estimates the possible human posture to follow, based on a short posture history.
2. A gradual correspondence function of each model's predictions for the suitable motion category.
   ◦ The prediction scheme is presented in its three operations: Training phase: a model learns the mapping exemplified in the following chain:
   ◦ **Off-line recognition:** A new unseen video recording is transformed according to the previous format. See Figure 3. Next:
   ◦ **Real-time recognition phase:** The frames enter the *SVR* models as they are captured and the error function is applied at a frame level. For instance, if the variable h is set to 5, then the model begins to operate after the sixth frame has been captured. The error function computes the similarity between the *SVR* predictions and the sixth frame. Classification of the first 5 frames takes place according to the minimum value given by the error function. It continues with capturing the seventh frame and now the input of the *SVR* models is the second to the sixth frame, and so on. See Figure 4.

The temporal modeling scheme we employ is based on Support Vector Regression (*SVR*), a very powerful and robust time-series technique. The output of such a regressor is a single real value; hence, for each vector element (feature) we build a different prediction model:

Figure 2. (1) the original frame, (2) the image derived after the subtraction of the two successive frames and the application of thresholding, (3) the object is divided into four regions and (4) the resulting statistical skeleton. The first two rows correspond to the action of running (© Weizmann Action Dataset - L. Gorelick, M. Blank, E. Shechtman, M. Irani, R. Basri. Used with permission), and the last two correspond to the action of bending (© 2008 Shi, Q., Li, W., Li, C., and Smola, A. Used with permission).

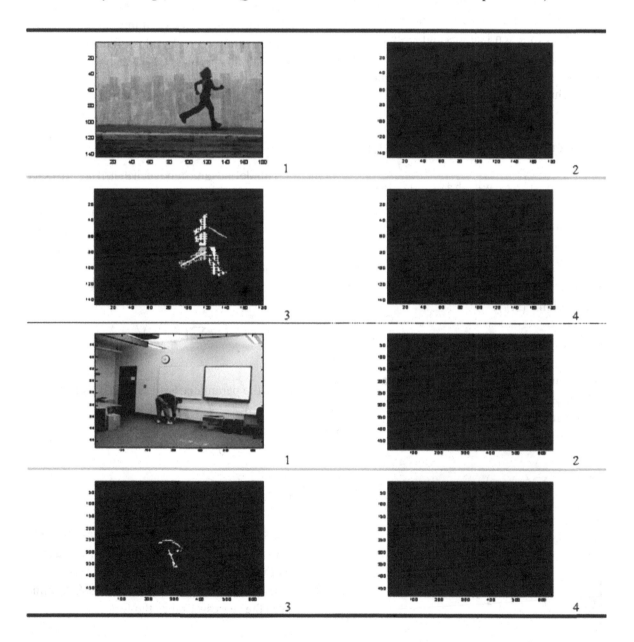

$$\tilde{f}_t = g\left(f_{t-1}, f_{t-2}, \ldots, f_{t-h}\right) \Rightarrow \begin{aligned} \tilde{a}_{t,1} &= g_1\left(f_{t-1}, f_{t-2}, \ldots, f_{t-h}\right) \\ \tilde{a}_{t,2} &= g_2\left(f_{t-1}, f_{t-2}, \ldots, f_{t-h}\right) \\ &\cdots\cdots\cdots\cdots\cdots\cdots\cdots\cdots \\ \tilde{a}_{t,10} &= g_{10}\left(f_{t-1}, f_{t-2}, \ldots, f_{t-h}\right) \end{aligned}$$

To summarize, each video from the training set is transformed to ten Support Vector Regressors (each prediction model corresponds to a specific element of the feature vector). In the recognition phase, a new video enters in all available Support Vector Regressors which return their predictions according to their training. Finally, the error between real values and predictions is calculated. We choose the model which presents the lowest average error for all the sets of frames and for the entire set of the ten features and assign its label to the testing video. The next section makes a concise description of the Support Vector Regression technique.

SUPPORT VECTOR REGRESSION

Suppose that we have a data set $\{(x_i, y_i), i = 1, 2, ..., n\}$ of measurements where $x_i \in X$ are the independent variables (X denotes the space of the input patterns) and $y_i \in R$ are the target variables (real values). We consider that the tuples (x_i, y_i) are taken from an unknown distribution $P(x, y)$.

A. Linear Regression

The formulation of the linear regression task stated by Vapnik (1995; 1997) is the following convex optimization problem:

Minimize

$$\frac{1}{2}\|w\|^2 + C\sum_{i=1}^{n}\left(\xi_i + \xi_i^*\right)$$

subject to

$$\begin{cases} y_i - \langle w, x_i \rangle - b \leq \varepsilon + \xi_i \\ \langle w, x_i \rangle + b - y_i \leq \varepsilon + \xi_i^* \\ \xi_i, \xi_i^* \geq 0 \end{cases} \quad (2.1)$$

where $\langle \cdot, \cdot \rangle$ refers to the inner product in X, $\langle w, x_i \rangle + b$ is a hyperplane that partitions X into two regions, $C>0$ is a pre-specified value that determines the trade-off between the flatness of regressor and the amount up to which deviations larger than ε are tolerated and ξ_i, ξ_i^* are slack variables interpreted as: ξ for exceeding the target value by more than ε and ξ^* for being more than ε below the target value (soft margin regression).

In addition to (2.1) a loss function is minimized. In this problem case we choose the linear ε-insensitive loss function:

$$L_\varepsilon = \begin{cases} 0 & \text{for } \left|y_i - (\langle w, x_i \rangle - b)\right| \leq \varepsilon \\ \left|y_i - (\langle w, x_i \rangle - b)\right| - \varepsilon & \text{otherwise} \end{cases} \quad (2.2)$$

This defines an ε-tube such that, if the predicted value is within the tube then the loss is zero, while if the predicted point is outside the tube, the loss is the magnitude of the difference between the predicted value and the radius ε of the tube.

The problem is transformed to a Lagrangian formulation and leads to the linear relationship:

$$f(x) = wx + b = \sum_{i=1}^{n}\left(a_i - a_i^*\right)\langle x_i, x \rangle + b \quad (2.3)$$

where the parameter b is computed as follows:

$$\begin{aligned} b &= y_i - \langle w, x_i \rangle - \varepsilon & \text{for } a_i \in (0, C) \\ b &= y_i - \langle w, x_i \rangle + \varepsilon & \text{for } a_i^* \in (0, C) \end{aligned} \quad (2.4)$$

B. Nonlinear Regression

In this case the nonlinear function has the form: $f(x) = \langle w, \phi(x) \rangle + b$, where $\phi(x)$ is the image of input vector x in a high dimensional space. Using the trick of kernel functions (Cortes & Vapnik, 1995) the regressor takes the form:

$$f(x) = \sum_{i=1}^{n}\left(a_i - a_i^*\right)K(x_i, x) + b \quad (2.5)$$

where $K\left(x_i, x_j\right) = \left\langle \phi(x_i), \phi(x_j) \right\rangle$ is a kernel function satisfying Mercer's conditions (Cristianini, & Shawe-Taylor, 2000). In that way, we manage to apply linear regression not in the low dimensional input space but in a high dimensional (feature) space via the kernel function which makes the mapping implicitly, i.e. without knowing $\varphi(x)$.

EXPERIMENTAL ANALYSIS

In order to test the model performance on the human action recognition problem and more specifically, in human pose recovery, we applied the method on two well known benchmark data sets. The first can be found in Gorelick et al., (2007) (Weizmann): It consists of 93 uncompressed videos in *avi* format, with low resolution (180x144 pixels, 25 frames/sec), representing 10 different actions (the numbers in parentheses signify the respective number of videos): bending (9), jumping-jack (9), jumping forward on two legs (9), jumping in place on two legs (9), running (10), galloping sideways (9), skipping (10), walking (10), one-hand waving (9), two-hands waving (9). Some supplementary information is: the videos are colorful; the actors are both men and women; the background is homogenous; in each video, a single person executes the action; the average number of frames does not exceed sixty-five frames; videos are shot by one steady, monocular camera. In addition, we test the robustness of our approach on a video dataset built for this specific purpose, provided again by Gorelick et al., (2007), which includes different scenarios of one person's walking such as different shooting views, non uniform backgrounds, occlusions etc (after Table 1 see Table 2). The second set is attributed to Shi et al. (2008) (WBD): A single person in a room performs three actions in a row: walking, bending and drawing. The videos are colorful, with resolution 720x480 pixels, 30 frames/sec (on average each action lasts about 2.5 seconds). We

compressed the videos using DivX codec and the resulting sequences consisted of 640x480 pixels, 29 frames/sec (average number of frames up to 150). The actors are three men, wearing different clothes, walking in an angle, moving towards the same direction and passing from the same spots in the room. The total number of videos is 18 (3 persons x 6 videos).

Table 1 exhibits the performance of several past works that were tested on the same datasets. The list is indicative and the results cannot be compared directly due to the different assumptions, preprocessing steps and testing methods they apply. Most of the references imply a potential real-time application. For instance, Fathi & Mori (2008) argue that their unoptimized implementation in Matlab, exhaustively performs classification with a range of 0.2-4 seconds per frame. In our opinion, the performance of a real-time human action recognition must be measured in terms of accuracy, time complexity in pre-processing, training and on-line mode, and scalability, that is, how easy incorporation and manipulation of new human actions can prove.

In our work, the experiments showed that the performance is affected mainly by the number of training videos, the *SVR* parameters and the

Table 1. Indicative comparison results of other works. The second column displays the accuracy percentage

	Weizmann
Niebles & Fei-Fei (2007)	72.80%
Dollar et al. (2005)	86.70%
Ali et al. (2007)	92.60%
Wang & Suter (2007)	97.80%
Kellokumpu et al. (2008)	97.80%
Jhuang et al. (2008)	98.80%
Fathi & Mori (2008)	100%
Blank et al. (2005)	100%
	WBD
Shi et al. (2008)	85.00%

Table 2. Recognition accuracy on both sets: In Weizmann set we use the leave-one-out testing mode, i.e. 92 training videos and the remaining one as test. In WBD we kept the videos of the two persons for training and the third person's video is used as test; the results are the average percentage of all the different combinations of training and testing videos.

	Off-line	Real-time
Weizmann	91.2%	86.8%
WBD	83.4%	75.1%

history information. As far as the number of training videos is concerned, a careful selection of a representative training set can lead to better classification: a small number of training videos may prove insufficient representation of the whole; on the contrary, a large number of training videos would slow the recognition phase and may lead to false classification due to intense overlapping.

As far as the adjustment of *SVR* parameters is concerned, we experimented with the three basic kernels: $\ker(u,v) = u \cdot v$ (linear), $\ker(u,v) = (u \cdot v + 1)^2$ (polynomial of second degree) and $\ker(u,v) = \dfrac{1}{2\sigma^2} \cdot e^{-\|u-v\|^2}$ (Gaussian radial basis function). The best results were achieved in some cases with the polynomial and in some others with the *rbf* kernel. The width parameter σ of the latter was ranging between 0.5 and 1. Referring to the loss function, the parameter ε is set to 0.01. The modification of parameter C does not affect notably the model's outcome.

Finally, the third factor provides strong empirical evidence in favor of the fact that the amount of past frames controls the representation of the temporal regularities and enhances the model's capability for setting the right boundaries among the candidate categories. In addition, the use of a moderate frames history boosts the regressor's construction since it reduces the time complexity $O(n^2)$ of kernel similarity matrix creation. How-

ever, the selection of past frames h must be done carefully due to the possibility of overfitting. In our experiments, the variable h ranges between 3 and 7 frames without affecting the recognition results significantly.

The model's performance is depicted in Tables 2, 3 and Figures 3, 4. The results are derived without any special parameter tuning or any other pre-processing of the training videos. For instance, if we exclude some very misleading frames or train the prediction models in respect to some negative examples, then the average performance enhances significantly. However, we leave the approach as simple as possible and without any further intervention in order for it to work in a highly automated way and in a noisy environment.

The gaps in Figures 3 and 4 indicate erroneous classifications. In our experiments we employed the *Mean Square Error* (MSE) as error function: $\arg_{t=h+1,\dots}^{\min} MSE\left(\tilde{f}_t, f_t\right)$. While it exhibits acceptable behavior when capturing the switching between the different actions (it needs 4-7 frames in average), it cannot handle satisfactorily faulty predictions during the same action due to the fact that it doesn't consider the recent classifications at all.

FUTURE WORK

The video-based human action recognition remains a difficult and highly challenging pattern recognition problem. There are a few open issues that constitute an active area of research and a field for future work. The following list contains the most significant topics:

- **Complicated image (frame) pre-processing stage.** There is a great need for fully automated algorithms capable of detecting accurately the points/regions of interest or updating the background model. Critical

Table 3. Weizmann robustness dataset; The first and third columns describe the testing videos. The second and fourth column display the respective results

Walking in 0°	Walking	Normal walk	Walking
Walking in 9°	Walking	Walking in a skirt	Walking
Walking in 18°	Walking	Carrying briefcase	Walking
Walking in 27°	Walking	Limping man	Walking
Walking in 36°	Walking	Occluded Legs	Walking
Walking in 45°	Walking	Knees Up	Walking
Walking in 54°	Walking	Walking with a dog	Walking
Walking in 63°	Walking	Sleepwalking	Galloping sideways
Walking in 72°	Walking	Swinging a bag	Walking
Walking in 81°	Skipping	Occluded by a "pole"	Walking

Figure 3. Real-time recognition performance of a compound video consisting of two actions of Weizmann data set: walking, running and walking again. The remaining 91 videos are used for training. The horizontal axis displays the video frames and the vertical axis displays the two action classes (1: walking and 2: running).

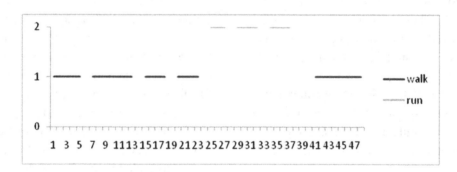

Figure 4. Real-time recognition performance of a video sequence consisting of three actions of WBD data set: one person performing walking, bending and drawing. The videos of the rest two persons are used for training. The horizontal axis displays the video frames and the vertical axis displays the three action classes (1: walking, 2: bending and 3: drawing).

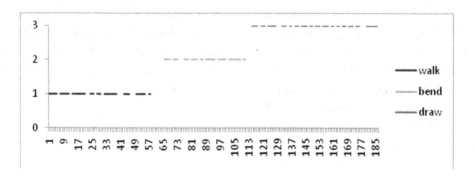

factors are camera motion and view, weather conditions, complex backgrounds, illumination changes, shadows and the individual variations of object appearance and postures. For example, most of the systems presented cannot detect partially occluded pedestrians; this is most often the case for template-based classification (Grubb, 2004), and feature extraction that treats the entire pedestrian as one unit.

- **Robust operation in real world scenarios, characterized by sudden or gradual changes in the input statistics.** We cannot rely on simple methods such as shape templates or color-based extraction.
- **Reduction of problem assumptions and constraints.** For instance, an assumption is often made about the human shape, i.e., proportions are used to filter out candidates that do not comply with this assumption (Zhao & Thorpe, 2000). The assumption results in that only humans complying with the manually specified human ratio can be detected.
- **Need for real-time detection and recognition systems.** This implies algorithms that control the trade-off between complexity/ execution time and accuracy performance.

The presented approach can work either in an off-line or an on-line recognition operation. An interesting future work could be the real-time recognition of different actions as they are captured, consulting in the same time a type of short memory of prior decisions (classifications); in this case, we would also test the algorithm capability in catching the smooth switch between the cascade actions. We plan also to investigate the performance with non-periodical actions, that is, actions that lack regular normality, giving rise to intense non-stationary time-series. Finally, we intend to extend the proposed approach in more complex environments, characterized by non-uniform backgrounds, figure occlusion and

different camera views; in particular, the effect of deviation from front-parallel views during performance needs to be studied.

CONCLUSION

Successful recognition of human actions constitutes a great step forward for the construction of vision-based machines. The issue consists of spatial-temporal patterns that are generated by a complex and non-linear dynamic system. Over the past years, a great number of researchers have proposed several approaches to cope with the representation and modeling of such irregular patterns. In practice, a complete analytic problem description is extremely hard; thus, the types of stochastic and statistical modeling tend to be the standard choices.

This chapter introduces video-based human action recognition handled by machine learning techniques. The problem is formulated as a supervised learning task and more particularly, as a multivariate time-series prediction problem. The feature extraction process relies on statistical and geometrical properties of objects included in video images, whereas the spatial-temporal modeling is achieved through the application of a well-grounded regression method, the Support Vector Regression. Extended experimentation is carried out with two benchmark data sets including ten and three elementary human actions respectively. Both off and on-line recognition results illustrate a satisfactory performance of the proposed approach, comparable to equivalent methods. Frugal pre-processing requirements, easy feature extraction, non-complicated reasoning and application make it an eligible option for the researcher who attempts to mine motion data from human activities.

REFERENCES

Aggarwal, J. K., & Cai, Q. (1999). Human motion analysis: A review. *Computer Vision and Image Understanding*, *73*(3), 428–440. doi:10.1006/cviu.1998.0744

Ali, S., Basharat, A., & Shah, M. (2007). Chaotic invariants for human action recognition. In *IEEE 11th International Conference on Computer Vision* (pp. 1-8).

Beauchemin, S. S., & Barron, J. L. (1995). The computation of optical flow. *ACM Computing Surveys*, *27*(3), 433–466. doi:10.1145/212094.212141

Blank, M., Gorelick, L., Shechtman, E., Irani, M., & Basri, R. (2005). Actions as space-time shapes. In *Proceedings of the Tenth IEEE International Conference on Computer Vision, ICCV 2005* (pp. 1395-1402).

Bobick, A., & Davis, J. (2001). The recognition of human movement using temporal templates. *PAMI*, *23*(3), 257–267.

Bregler, C. (1997). Learning and recognizing human dynamics in video sequences. In *Proceedings IEEE Conf. Computer Vision and Pattern Recognition,* San Juan, Puerto Rico (pp. 568-574).

Cedras, C., & Shah, M. (1995). Motion-based recognition: A survey. *Image and Vision Computing*, *13*(2), 129–155. doi:10.1016/0262-8856(95)93154-K

Chen, D.-Y., Shih, S.-W., & Liao, H.-Y. M. (2007). Human action recognition using 2-D spatio-temporal templates. In *Proceedings of ICME* (pp. 667-670).

Cortes, C., & Vapnik, V. (1995). Support vector networks. *Machine Learning*, *20*, 273–297.

Cristianini, N., & Shawe-Taylor, J. (2000). *An Introduction to Support Vector Machines (and other kernel-based learning methods)*. Cambridge, MA: Cambridge Univ. Press.

Curio, C., Edelbrunner, J., Kalinke, T., Tzomakas, C., & Seelen, W. (2000). Walking pedestrian recognition. *IEEE Transactions on Intelligent Transportation Systems*, *1*, 3. doi:10.1109/6979.892152

Demonceaux, C., & Kachi-Akkouche, D. (2004). Motion detection using wavelet analysis and hierarchical Markov models. In *First International Workshop on Spatial Coherence for Visual Motion Analysis*, Prague.

Dollar, P., Rabaud, V., Cottrell, G., & Belongie, S. (2005). Behavior recognition via sparse spatio-temporal feature. In *2nd Joint IEEE International Workshop on Visual Surveillance and Performance Evaluation of Tracking and Surveillance* (pp. 65-72).

Efros, A. A., Berg, A. C., Mori, G., & Malik, J. (2003). Recognizing action at a distance. In *Proceedings of the Ninth IEEE International Conference on Computer Vision*.

Fathi, A., & Mori, G. (2008). Action recognition by learning mid-level motion features. In *IEEE Computer Society Conference on Computer Vision and Pattern Recognition (CVPR)*.

Gao, J., Hauptmann, A. G., & Wactlar, H. D. (2004). Combining motion segmentation with tracking for activity analysis. In *The Sixth International Conference on Automatic Face and Gesture Recognition (FGR'04)*, Seoul, Korea (pp. 699-704).

Gorelick, L., Blank, M., Shechtman, E., Irani, M., & Basri, R. (2007). Actions as space-time shapes. [from http://www.wisdom.weizmann.ac.il/~vision/SpaceTimeActions.html]. *IEEE Transactions on Pattern Analysis and Machine Intelligence*, *29*(12), 2247–2253. Retrieved June 4, 2008. doi:10.1109/TPAMI.2007.70711

Grubb, G. (2004). *3D vision sensing for improved pedestrian safety*. Master's thesis, Australian National University.

Harris, C., & Stephens, M. (1998). A combined corner and edge detector. In *Proceedings of the 4th Alvey Vision Conference* (pp. 147-151).

Hsieh, J.-W., Hsu, Y.-T., Liao, H.-Y. M., & Chen, C.-C. (2008). Video-based human movement analysis and its application to surveillance systems. *IEEE Transactions on Multimedia*, *10*(3), 372–384. doi:10.1109/TMM.2008.917403

Hu, W., Tan, T., Wang, L., & Maybank, S. (2004). A survey on visual surveillance of object motion and behaviors. *IEEE Transactions on Systems, Man, and Cybernetics*, *34*(3), 334–351. doi:10.1109/TSMCC.2004.829274

Ikizler, N., & Duygulu, P. (2007). Human Action Recognition Using Distribution of Oriented Rectangular Patches. In *ICCV Workshops on Human Motion* (pp. 271-284).

Jhuang, H., Serre, T., Wolf, L., & Poggio, T. (2007). A biologically inspired system for action recognition. In *Proceedings of the Eleventh IEEE International Conference on Computer Vision (ICCV)* (pp. 1-8).

Jiang, H., Drew, M.S., & Ze-Nian Li (2006). Successive convex matching for action detection. In *Proceedings of the 2006 IEEE Computer Society Conference on Computer Vision and Pattern Recognition* (Vol. 2, pp. 1646-1653).

Kellokumpu, V., Zhao, G., & Pietikäinen, M. (2008). Texture based description of movements for activity analysis. In *Proceedings Third International Conference on Computer Vision Theory and Applications* (Vol. 1, pp. 206-213).

Kumar, P., Mittal, A., & Kumar, P. (2008). Study of robust and intelligent surveillance in visible and multimodal framework. In *Informatica*, 32, 63-77.

Laptev, I., Marszalek, M., Schmid, C., & Rozenfeld, B. (2008). learning realistic human actions from movies. In *IEEE Computer Vision and Pattern Recognition, 2008. CVPR 2008* (pp. 1-8).

Laptev, I., & Perez, P. (2007). Retrieving actions in movies. In *IEEE 11th International Conference on Computer Vision, ICCV 2007*.

Little, J. J., & Boyd, J. (1998). Recognizing people by their gait: the shape of motion. *Videre*, *1*(2), 2–32.

Lowe, D. G. (1999). Object recognition from local scale-invariant features. In *International Conference on Computer Vision*, Corfu, Greece (pp. 1150-1157).

Madabhushi, A., & Aggarwal, J. K. (1999). A Bayesian approach to human activity recognition. In *Proceedings Second IEEE Workshop on Visual Surveillance*, Fort Collins (pp. 25-32).

Moeslund, T., & Granum, E. (2001). A survey of computer vision-based human motion capture. *Computer Vision and Image Understanding*, *81*(3), 231–268. doi:10.1006/cviu.2000.0897

Niebles, J. C., & Fei-Fei, L. (2007). A hierarchical model of shape and appearance for human action classification. In *IEEE Conference on Computer Vision and Pattern Recognition, CVPR 2007* (pp. 1-8).

Shi, Q., Li, W., Li, C., & Smola, A. (2008). Discriminative human action segmentation and recognition using semi-Markov model. In *IEEE Conference on Computer Vision and Pattern Recognition, CVPR 2008* (pp. 1-8). Retrieved January 28, 2009, from http://sml.nicta.com.au/~licheng/aSR/

Toyama, K., Krumm, J., Brumitt, B., & Meyers, B. (1999). Wallflower: Principles and practice of background maintenance. In *Proceedings of the Seventh IEEE International Conference on Computer* (Vol. 1, pp. 255-261).

Vapnik, V. (1995). *The nature of statistical learning theory*. New York: Springer.

Vapnik, V., Golowich, S. E., & Smola, A. (1997). Support vector method for function approximation, regression estimation, and signal processing. []. Cambridge, MA: MIT Press.]. *Advances in Neural Information Processing Systems, 9,* 281–287.

Veit, T., Cao, F., & Bouthemy, P. (2004). Probabilistic parameter-free motion detection. In *Proceedings Conf. Computer Vision and Pattern Recognition (CVPR'04),* Washington, DC.

Wang, L., & Suter, D. (2007). Recognizing human activities from silhouettes: Motion subspace and factorial discriminative graphical model. In *IEEE Computer Vision and Pattern Recognition, CVPR '07.*

Yilmaz, A., Javed, O., & Shah, M. (2006). Object tracking: A survey. *ACM Computing Surveys, 38*(4). doi:10.1145/1177352.1177355

Zhao, L., & Thorpe, C. E. (2000). Stereo- and neural network-based pedestrian detection. *IEEE Transactions on Intelligent Transportation Systems, 1*(3), 148–154. doi:10.1109/6979.892151

Chapter 9
Fast Categorisation of Articulated Human Motion

Konrad Schindler
TU Darmstadt, Germany

Luc van Gool
ETH Zürich, Switzerland ESAT/PSI-IBBT, K. U. Leuven, Belgium

ABSTRACT

Visual categorisation of human motion in video clips has been an active field of research in recent years. However, most published methods either analyse an entire video and assign it a single category label, or use relatively large look-ahead to classify each frame. Contrary to these strategies, the human visual system proves that simple categories can be recognised almost instantaneously. Here we present a system for categorisation from very short sequences ("snippets") of 1–10 frames, and systematically evaluate it on several data sets. It turns out that even local shape and optic flow for a single frame are enough to achieve ≈80-90% correct classification, and snippets of 5-7 frames (0.2-0.3 seconds of video) yield results on par with the ones state-of-the-art methods obtain on entire video sequences.

1 INTRODUCTION

Recognising human motion categories in monocular video is an important scene understanding capability, with applications in diverse fields such as surveillance, content-based video search, and human-computer interaction. By *motion categories* we mean a semantic interpretation of the articulated human motion. Most computer vision research in this context has concentrated on human *action* recognition, while we only see actions as one possible

DOI: 10.4018/978-1-60566-900-7.ch009

set of semantic categories, which can be inferred from the visual motion pattern. We will also show a more subtle example, in which emotional states are derived from body language.

Past research in this domain can be roughly classified into two approaches: one that extracts a *global* feature set from a video (Ali et al., 2007; Dollár et al., 2005; Laptev and Lindeberg, 2003; Wang and Suter, 2007), and using these features aims to assign a single label to the *entire video* (typically several seconds in length). This paradigm obviously requires that the observed motion category does not change during the duration of the video.

The other approach extracts a feature set *locally* for a frame (or a small set of frames), and assigns an *individual* label to each frame (Blank et al., 2005; Efros et al., 2003; Jhuang et al., 2007; Niebles and Fei-Fei, 2007). If required, a global label for the sequence is obtained by simple voting mechanisms. Usually these methods are not strictly causal: features are computed by analysing a temporal window centred at the current frame, therefore the classification lags behind the observation—to classify a frame, future information within the temporal window is required.

Both approaches have achieved remarkable results, but human recognition performance suggests that they might be using more information than necessary: we can correctly recognise motion patterns from very short sequences—often even from single frames.

1.1 Aim of This Work

The question we seek to answer is *how many frames are required to categorise motion patterns?* As far as we know, this is an unresolved issue, which has not yet been systematically investigated (in fact, there is a related discussion in the cognitive sciences, see section 4). However, its answer has wide-ranging implications. Therefore, our goal is to establish a baseline, how long we need to observe a basic motion, such as *walking* or *jumping*, before we can categorise it.

We will operate not on entire video sequences, but on very short sub-sequences, which we call *snippets*. In the extreme case a snippet can have length 1 frame, but we will also look at snippets of up to 10 frames. Note that in many cases a single frame is sufficient, as can be easily verified by looking at the images in Figure 1. The main message of our study is that *very short snippets (1-7 frames), are sufficient to distinguish a small set of motion categories, with rapidly diminishing returns, as more frames are added*.

This finding has important implications for practical scenarios, where decisions have to be taken online. Short snippets greatly alleviate the problem of temporal segmentation: if a person switches from one action to another, sequences containing the transition are potentially problematic, because they violate the assumption that a single label can be applied. When using short snippets, only few such sequences exist. Furthermore, short snippets enable fast processing and rapid attention switching, in order to deal with further subjects or additional visual tasks, before they become obsolete.

Figure 1. Examples from databases WEIZMANN (left), KTH (middle), and LPPA (right); Note that even a single frame is often sufficient to recognise an action, respectively emotional state

1.2 Method

To investigate the influence of snippet length on the categorisation performance, we present a *causal* categorisation method, which uses only information from few past frames. The method densely extracts form (local edges) and motion (optic flow) from a snippet, and separately compares them to learnt templates. The similarity scores for both feature sets are concatenated to a single vector and passed on to a classifier. As far as we know, this is also the first practical implementation of a "biologically inspired" system with both a form and a motion pathway. The strategy to process form and motion independently with a similar sequence of operations was inspired by the seminal work of Giese and Poggio (2003). In their paper, they describe the only other simulation of both pathways, however their proof-of-concept implementation is only designed for simple, schematic stimuli.

In detailed experiments we evaluate the effect of changing the snippet length, as well as the influence of form and motion features. We also compare to other methods on two standard data sets, both at the level of snippets and whole sequences, and obtain results on par with or better than the state-of-the-art.

2 PRELIMINARIES

A basic assumption underlying most of the literature on automatic "action recognition" is that perception is (at least to a certain degree) *categorical*, meaning that an observed pattern can be assigned to one out of a relatively small set of categories. This assumption is in line with the prevalent view in the cognitive sciences (e.g. Harnad, 1987). The categorical approach has several advantages: in terms of scene understanding, categories offer a discrete, higher-level abstraction of the continuous space of articulated motions; on the computational side, categorisation is a discriminative task, and

can be solved without a complete generative model of human behaviour.

2.1 Defining Categories

In the previous section, we have used the term *basic* motion to describe the units, into which the articulated motion shall be classified. The reason for this terminology is that there is another unresolved issue looming behind our question, namely the definition of what constitutes a motion category. Obviously, the amount of information which needs to be accumulated, and also the number of relevant classes for a given application, both depend on the complexity (e.g., recognising a high-jump takes longer than separately recognising the three components *running*, *jumping*, and *falling on the back*). This leads to the problem of decomposing motion patterns: can, and should, complex motion patterns be decomposed into sequences of simpler "atomic motions", which again can be recognised quickly?

The decomposition problem appears to be application-dependent, and is *not* the topic of this study. We assume that a relatively small set of basic categories, such as *walking* or *waving*, form the set of possible labels, and that the labels are relatively unambiguous.[1] These assumptions have been made implicitly in most of the published work on action recognition, as can be seen from the standard databases (the ones also used in this work).

2.2 Motion Snippets

The aim of the present work is not only to introduce yet another motion classification method, but also to systematically investigate, how much information needs to be accumulated over time to enable motion classification. In a setup with discrete time steps, this boils down to the question, how many frames are required.

Very short snippets provide less data to base a decision on, hence it becomes important to extract as much information as possible. We will therefore collect both shape information from every frame and optic flow. In real video with discrete time steps, optic flow has to be computed between neighbouring frames. By convention, we will regard the optic flow computed between consecutive frames $(t-1)$ and t as a feature of frame t. Hence, when we refer to a *snippet of length 1*, or a *single frame*, this flow field is included. In the same way, a snippet of length, say, $L=7$ comprises the shape descriptors for 7 frames, and 7 flow fields (not 6).

As will be demonstrated in section 5, using both shape and flow yields a marked improvement in categorisation performance, compared to shape alone, or flow alone.

2.3 The "Right" Snippets

It is obvious that not all parts of a video carry the same amount of category information. Some parts of a motion (or motion cycle) are highly distinctive, while others may be totally ambiguous. This leads to the question which "key-snippets" of a motion sequence are most suitable, respectively unsuitable, to determine a given class. It is trivial, but sometimes overlooked, that the best key-frames or key-snippets are not a fixed property of a category's motion pattern, but depend on the entire set of categories in a given application (the most suitable snippets being the ones which are rarely confused with any of the other categories).

A framework based on discriminative classification provides an easy way to identify particularly distinctive (or ambiguous) snippets, by looking at their classification margins. In the experiments section, we will show some examples of this analysis. Note that, although not investigated further in the present work, one could use this information as a confidence measure in a recognition system with variable snippet length. Such a system would then be able to decide online, whether it can reliably classify a snippet, or needs to accumulate more frames.

3 RELATED WORK

Early attempts at human action recognition used the tracks of a person's body parts as input features (Fanti et al., 2005; Rao et al., 2002; Yacoob and Black, 1999). This representation is an obvious choice, because physically the dynamics of the body parts relative to each other is what defines a motion pattern. However, it depends on correct tracking of either an articulated human model, or many separate regions, both difficult tasks, especially in monocular video.

Carlsson and Sullivan (2001) cast action recognition as a shape matching problem. An action is represented by a single unique pose, and categorisation is performed by comparing poses, described by edge maps. This demonstrated the importance of shape, while later research focused on the dynamic aspect of human actions. In this work we will use both pieces of information.

A drawback of early approaches was that tracking, as well as contour detection, become unreliable under realistic imaging conditions. Following a general trend in computer vision, researchers therefore moved away from the high-level representation of the human body, and replaced it by a collection of low-level features, which are less compact and less intuitive, but can be extracted more reliably. Efros et al. (2003) apply optic flow filters to a window centred at the human, and use the filter responses as input to an exemplar-based classifier. Their method is probably the first one to aim for classification at the frame level from flow alone; however, although they individually label each frame, a large temporal window (up to 25 past and 25 future frames) is employed to estimate its flow.

Jhuang et al. (2007) have extended the static scene categorisation model of Serre et al. (2007), by replacing form features with motion features. Like Efros et al. (2003), they extract dense local motion information with a set of flow filters. The responses are pooled locally, and converted to higher-level responses by comparing to more complex templates learnt from examples. These are pooled again, and fed into a discriminative classifier. This approach is the most similar in spirit to our work.

Niebles and Fei-Fei (2007) also classify at the frame level. They represent a frame by sparse sets of local appearance descriptors extracted at spatial interest points, and a similar set of local motion descriptors extracted from a sub-sequence centred at the current frame, with the method of Dollár et al. (2005). A constellation model for the features is learnt, and used to train a discriminative classifier.

Laptev and Lindeberg (2003) represent an entire video sequence as a sparse set of spatio-temporal interest points, which are found with a 3D version of the Harris corner detector. Different descriptors are proposed for the space-time window around an interest point: histograms of gradients, histograms of optic flow, PCA projection of gradients, or PCA projection of optic flow. Classification is done at sequence level, either by nearest-neighbour matching (Laptev and Lindeberg, 2003), or with a SVM (Schüldt et al., 2004).

Dollár et al. (2005) present a different spatio-temporal interest point detector based on 1D Gabor filters, essentially searching for regions where the intensity changes suddenly or periodically over time. Optic flow is computed as descriptor for each 3D interest region. The set of descriptors is quantised to a fixed set of 3D visual words, and a new sequence is classified by nearest-neighbour matching of its histogram of visual words. The method was extended to unsupervised learning with pLSA by (Niebles et al., 2006).

Blank et al. (2005) extract the human silhouette from each frame, and represent the sequence as a set of "space-time shapes" defined by (overlapping) 10-frame sequences of silhouettes. Local properties of such a 3D shape are extracted from the solution of its Poisson equation, and classified with an exemplar-based nearest-neighbour classifier.

Wang and Suter (2007) also use silhouettes to classify at the sequence level. They extract features from the sequence of silhouettes by non-linear dimensionality reduction with Kernel PCA, and train a Factorial Conditional Random Field to classify new sequences.

Ali et al. (2007) return to an articulated model, but follow only the main joints to make tracking more robust. Skeletonisation is applied to silhouettes to obtain 2D stick figures, and their main joints are connected to trajectories. A video is represented by a set of chaotic invariants of these trajectories, and classified with a kNN-classifier.

4 SYSTEM DETAILS

Our system independently processes dense form (shape) and motion (flow) features, in what is sometimes called a "biologically inspired" manner due to the similarity with the ventral and dorsal pathways of the primate visual cortex (Felleman and van Essen, 1991): two sets of low-level cues are extracted from the data with independent algorithms and are separately converted to sets of high-level features. The idea is to minimise correlations between the two sets and in this way provide a richer description to the actual labelling algorithm (in our case is a discriminative classifier). Figure 2 illustrates the complete processing pipeline.

Using both types of features for motion perception is in line with the predominant view in neuro-science, (e.g. Casile and Giese, 2005), but some researchers are of the opinion, that only form information from a number of consecutive frames is required (e.g. Beintema and Lappe, 2002). The key-frame paradigm has also been explored in machine vision (Carlsson and Sullivan, 2001). Our experiments support the first view: using form and motion consistently improves categorisation, at least with our system architecture.

Figure 2. System overview. From a snippet, features are extracted in two parallel processing streams. The form pathway (top) extracts local shape at multiple scales. The motion pathway (bottom) extracts local optic flow at multiple scales. In both pathways, the filter responses are max-pooled, and compared to a set of learnt templates. The similarity scores are concatenated to a feature vector, and classified with a bank of binary classifiers.

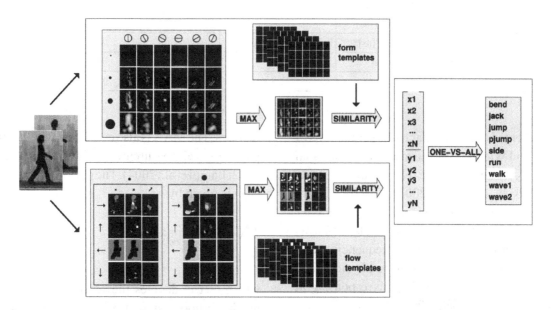

Feature extraction and categorisation are performed independently for every snippet. Similar to other frame-based methods (Jhuang et al., 2007; Niebles and Fei-Fei, 2007), the labels assigned to individual snippets are converted to a sequence label with a simple majority vote, corresponding to a "bag-of-snippets" model.

4.1 Input Data

We use a simple attention model to obtain a person-centred coordinate frame: our input is a sequence of fixed-size image windows, centred at the person of interest. Note that there is a subtle difference to Efros et al. (2003): they assume that the person is seen on a uniform background, so that only the relative articulations are extracted. In contrast, our method, and also the one of Jhuang et al. (2007), can see the inverse flow of the background. This means that they can take into account a person's motion through the image coordinate

frame, if there is enough background structure (for uniform background all three methods will behave the same, because the latter two will not be able to learn any coherent optic flow on the background).

Other than for silhouette-based methods (Ali et al., 2007; Blank et al., 2005; Wang and Suter, 2007), no figure-ground segmentation is required, thus making the method more widely applicable. In particular, reliable silhouette extraction in practice requires a static background. In contrast, human detectors based on sliding windows (e.g. Dalal and Triggs, 2005) and trackers based on rectangular axis-aligned regions (e.g. Comaniciu et al., 2003) naturally provide bounding boxes.

4.2 Form Features

Local shape is extracted from each frame in a snippet separately with a bank of Gabor-like filters. Gabor filtering is a standard way to find

Table 1. Summary of parameter values used in our implementation

step	parameter	form	motion	
low-level	direction [deg]	0, 30, ..., 150	0, 90, 180, 270	
filtering	scale [px]	2, 4, 8, 16	8	16
	velocity [px/frame]	—	0, 2, 4	0, 4, 8
MAX-	sampling step [px]	5	5	
Pooling	window size [px]	9	9	
high-level	# templates	500	500	
features	relative weight	0.3	0.7	

local oriented edges (similar to the simple cells of Hubel and Wiesel (1962) in area V1 of the visual cortex)—for details please refer to standard texts (e.g. Forsyth and Ponce, 2003). Specifically, we use log-Gabor filters, which allow a better coverage of the spectrum than the standard (linear) version with fewer preferred frequencies, and are also consistent with electro-physiological measurements (Field, 1987). The response g at position (x,y) and spatial frequency w is

$$g^{w}(x,y) = \frac{1}{\mu} \left\| e^{-\frac{\log(w(x,y)/\mu)}{2\log\sigma}} \right\| , \qquad (1)$$

with μ the preferred frequency of the filter, and σ a constant, which is set to achieve even coverage of the spectrum. $\|\cdot\|$ denotes the magnitude of the (complex) response. The phase is discarded. The filter gain is adapted to the frequency spectrum of natural images: the gain factor is proportional to the frequency, to give all scales equal importance. We filter with 6 equally spaced orientations and 4 scales (see Table 1 for parameter values of the implementation).

To increase robustness to translations, the response map for each orientation/scale pair is down-sampled with the MAX-operator. Using the MAX, rather than averaging responses, was originally proposed by Fukushima (1980) and has been strongly advocated by Riesenhuber and Poggio (1999), because it does not blur contrast

features. The MAX is also consistent with electro-physiological measurements (Gawne and Martin, 2002; Lampl et al., 2004). The response at location (x,y) is given by

$$h^{F}(x,y) = \max_{(i,j)\in\mathcal{G}(x,y)} [g(i,j)] , \qquad (2)$$

where $G(x,y)$ denotes the receptive field (local neighbourhood) of the pixel (x,y). Our receptive field size of 9×9 pixels (determined experimentally) agrees with the findings of Jhuang et al. (2007); Serre et al. (2005) (see Table 1).

In a last step, the orientation patterns are compared to a set of templates, resulting in a vector $\mathbf{q}^{F}$ of similarity scores. In order to learn an informative set of templates, the pooled orientation maps are rearranged into one vector $\mathbf{h}^{F}$ per snippet, and simple linear PCA is applied. A fixed number N of basis vectors $\{\mathbf{b}_i^F, i=1...N\}$ are retained and are directly viewed as templates for relevant visual features.

The incoming vector $\mathbf{h}^F$ from a new image is scaled to norm 1 (corresponding to a normalisation of signal "energy"), and projected onto the set of templates. The linear projection

$$q_i^F = \left\langle \tilde{\mathbf{h}}^F, \mathbf{b}_i^F \right\rangle = \cos(\angle_{\mathbf{b}_i^F}^{\tilde{\mathbf{h}}^F}) \quad , \quad \tilde{\mathbf{h}}^F = \frac{\mathbf{h}^F}{\left\|\mathbf{h}^F\right\|} \quad (3)$$

Figure 3. Learning complex templates with PCA. Shown are the first 6 templates (basis vectors) of the form pathway for one run of the WEIZMANN dataset. Note how the templates capture complex shapes such as different arm configurations.

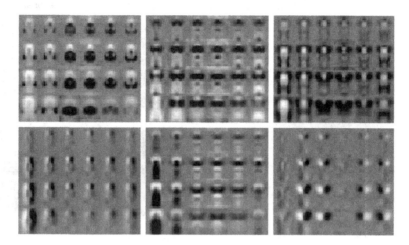

onto template $\mathbf{b}_i^{\mathrm{F}}$ can be directly interpreted as a similarity measure, where 1 means that the two are perfectly equal, and 0 means that they are maximally dissimilar. In our implementation, we use 500 templates (see also Table 1). Note that with PCA we learn a template set which is in some sense optimal (the best linear subspace to represent the training data), whereas Jhuang et al. (2007); Serre et al. (2007) use random features to enable a biologically more plausible learning rule.

4.3 Motion Features

At every frame, dense optic flow is estimated directly, by template matching: at every image location, we take the intensity pattern in a local window (receptive field), and find the most similar location in the previous frame, using the L_1-distance (sum of absolute differences). Although optic flow is notoriously noisy, we do not smooth it in any way, because smoothing blurs the flow field at discontinuities (edges in the spatial domain, direction changes in the time domain), where the information is most important, if no figure-ground segmentation is available.

To obtain a representation analogous to the log-Gabor maps for form, the optic flow is discretised into a set of response maps for different "flow filters", each with different preferred flow direction and speed. A filter's response $r(x,y)$ is maximal, if the direction and speed at location (x,y) exactly match the preferred values, and decreases linearly with changing direction and/or speed. Responses are computed at 2 spatial scales (receptive field sizes), 4 equally spaced directions (half-wave rectified), and 3 scale-dependent speeds (see Table 1 for parameter values of our implementation).

The remaining processing steps of the flow channel are the same as for the form channel. Flow maps are MAX-pooled to coarser maps

$$h^{\mathrm{M}}(x,y) = \max_{(i,j)\in\mathcal{G}(x,y)} \left[r(i,j) \right], \tag{4}$$

and these are converted to a vector $\mathbf{q}^{\mathrm{M}}$ of similarity values by comparing to a set of flow templates learnt with PCA,

$$q_i^{\mathrm{M}} = \left\langle \tilde{\mathbf{h}}^{\mathrm{M}}, \mathbf{b}_i^{\mathrm{M}} \right\rangle. \tag{5}$$

Figure 4. Illustration of feature extraction. Left: image with extracted bounding box. Middle: feature maps after MAX-pooling. Right: feature maps reconstructed from 500 templates per channel.

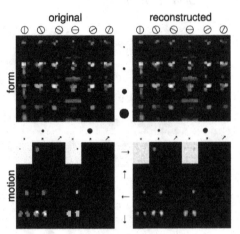

Note that although we compute optic flow without smoothing, the templates are smooth due to the denoising effect of PCA. The same parameters are used in the form and flow pathways (see Table 1). An illustrative example of the feature extraction process is shown in Figure 4.

4.4 Classifier

For classification, the feature vectors for form and motion are simply concatenated, $\mathbf{q} = [(1 - \lambda)\mathbf{q}^F, \lambda\mathbf{q}^M]$. The optimal weight $\lambda \in [0..1]$ has been determined experimentally, and has proved to be stable across different datasets, see Section 5.1.

As a classifier, we use a bank of linear *support vector machines* (SVMs). A description of the SVM algorithm is beyond the scope of this chapter, we refer the interested reader to standard texts (e.g. Shawe-Taylor and Christianini, 2000). To assign a motion to one of K classes, we train a bank of binary *one-vs-all* SVMs, i.e. each binary classifier is trained to separate one class from all others, and the class with the highest cofidence (largest classification margin) is selected. During training of the binary classifiers, in-class samples are assigned weights $W=(K-1)$, and out-of-class samples are assigned weights $W=1$, to account for the uneven number of samples.

We purposely keep the classifier simple. Using non-linear kernels for the SVM yields no significant improvement—presumably due to the high dimensionality of the data. Alternative multi-class extensions, such as the *all-pairs* strategy, give similar results in practice, but require a larger number of binary classifiers. Note also that *one-vs-all* has an obvious interpretation in terms of biological vision, with each binary classifier representing a neural unit, which is activated only by a certain category

4.5 Relation to Existing Methods

Since recent methods for motion categorisation, including the present one, are quite related, this section analyses some important similarities and differences.

In terms of the required preprocessing, our method uses a very crude attention model, namely a fixed-size bounding box centred at the person, like Efros et al. (2003); Jhuang et al. (2007). These three methods are less demanding than Ali et al. (2007); Blank et al. (2005); Wang and Suter (2007), which require a segmented silhouette, but more demanding than interest-point based methods (Laptev and Lindeberg, 2003; Niebles and Fei-Fei, 2007), which at least conceptually operate on the whole image—although in practice the amount of clutter must be limited, to ensure a significant number of interest points on the person. No method has yet been tested in cluttered environments with many distractors.

In terms of features used, Efros et al. (2003); Jhuang et al. (2007) extract only optic flow, Blank et al. (2005); Wang and Suter (2007) only silhouette shape. Dollár et al. (2005); Laptev and Lindeberg (2003) extract feature points in 3D space-time, and use either only flow, or combined space-time gradients as descriptors, while our work, as well as Niebles and Fei-Fei (2007), extract both cues independently.

More generally, our method belongs to a school, which favours densely sampled features over sparse interest points for visual classification problems (e.g. Dalal and Triggs, 2005; Pontil and Verri, 1998). It can also be considered a biologically inspired model, with parallels to the "standard model" of the visual cortex (Riesenhuber and Poggio, 1999): a layer of simple neurons sensitive to local orientation and local flow; a layer of pooling neurons with larger receptive fields to increase invariance and reduce the amount of data; a layer of neurons, each comparing the incoming signal to a learnt complex pattern; and a small layer of category-sensitive neurons, each firing when presented with features of a certain motion category.

The other model, which intentionally follows a biologically inspired architecture (Jhuang et al., 2007), currently only implements the motion pathway. Other than our model, it uses some temporal look-ahead to compute motion features. Furthermore, its complex templates are smaller (ours have the same size as the bounding box), and are found by random sampling, while we apply PCA to find a template set, which is in some sense optimal (albeit with a less biologically plausible learning rule).

5 EXPERIMENTAL EVALUATION

We use three data sets for our evaluation. The first two have become the de-facto standards for human *action* recognition, while the third one has been designed for the study of *emotional body language*, i.e. emotional categories expressed in human motion.

The WEIZMANN database (Blank et al., 2005) consists of 9 subjects (3 female, 6 male) performing a set of 9 different actions: *bending down, jumping jack, jumping, jumping in place, galloping sideways, running, walking, waving one hand, waving both hands*. To avoid evaluation biases due to varying sequence length, we trim all sequences to 28 frames (the length of the shortest sequence). Due to the periodic nature of the actions, this gives sufficient training data, and makes sure all actions have the same influence on overall results. All evaluations on this data set were done with leave-one-out cross-validation: 8 subjects are used for training, the remaining one for testing; the procedure is repeated for all 9 permutations, and the results are averaged.

The KTH database (Laptev and Lindeberg, 2003; Schüldt et al., 2004) consists of 25 subjects (6 female, 19 male) performing 6 different actions: *boxing, hand-clapping, jogging, running, walking, hand-waving*. The complete set of actions was recorded under 4 different conditions: outdoors (s1), outdoors with scale variations (s2), outdoors with different clothes (s3), and indoors (s4). *Jogging, running*, and *walking* are performed multiple times in each video, separated by large numbers of frames, where the subject is outside the field of view. These parts are obviously meaningless in an evaluation at snippet level, so we use only one pass of each action. Again, all sequences are trimmed to the length of the shortest, in this case 18 frames. All evaluations were done with 5-fold cross-validation: the data is split into 5 folds of 5 subjects each, 4 folds are used for training, 1 for testing. The results are averaged over the 5 permutations. In the literature, KTH has been treated either as one large set with strong intra-subject variations, or as four independent scenarios, which are trained and tested separately (i.e., four visually dissimilar databases, which share the same classes). We run both alternatives.

The LPPA database has been collected for research into emotional body language. It consists of 9 trained actors (5 female, 4 male) walking in 5 different emotional styles: *neutral, happy, sad, fearful, angry*. For each subject there are 4 independent trials of each style. All sequences are trimmed to 40 frames, and evaluations are performed with leave-one-out cross-validation. This dataset is considerably harder than the schematic action datasets, because of the more subtle visual differences. As a baseline, the data was also validated in a psychophysical experiment with human observers: the full-length videos were shown to 12 subjects (5 female, 7 male), who had to assign emotion labels to them. The classification by humans was 85% correct (average over all classes).

To account for the symmetry of human body motion w.r.t. the sagittal plane, we also use all sequences mirrored along the vertical axis, for both training and testing (in practice, the extracted feature maps are mirrored to save computations). We always use *all* possible (overlapping) snippets of a certain length as data, both for training and testing (so for example a video of 27 frames yields 23 snippets of length $L=5$). In each run, both the classifier *and* the set of templates are re-trained (although the template sets for different training sets are nearly identical except for occasional changes in the order of the basis vectors). The parameter settings given in the previous section were kept unchanged for all reported experiments.

5.1 Contributions of Form and Motion Features

A main strength of the presented approach, compared to most other methods, is that it exploits dense form *and* motion features. A natural question

therefore is, whether this is necessary, and how to combine the two. We have run experiments with our system, in which we have changed the relative weight λ of the two cues, or turned one of them off completely. The combination of form and motion consistently outperforms both form alone and motion alone, in all experiments we have conducted. Furthermore, the optimal relative weight turned out to be approximately the same across different data sets, and for snippets of different length (for our normalised similarity scores $\lambda=0.7$, but being a scale normalisation between two independently computed feature sets, the value may depend on both the implementation and the parameters of feature extraction). For some datasets, form alone is a better cue than flow, while for others it is the other way round, depending on the set of actions and the recording conditions (see Figure 5). This makes it unlikely that a strong bias towards one or the other pathway is introduced by our implementation, and supports the claim that explicitly extracting both cues increases performance.

5.2 How Many Frames?

Categorisation results of our method are shown in Figure 6 and Figure 7. For WEIZMANN, even $L=1$ achieves 93.5% correct classification, snippets of ≥ 3 frames yield essentially perfect categorisation (<1 wrong snippet per sequence). For LPPA, the result also saturates at $L=3$. Note that for this dataset, the performance using only form *decreases* with growing snippet length— as more frames are added, the less schematic categories produce a larger variety of patterns, which becomes harder to capture with a small number of templates. In the KTH data, outdoor scenarios are more difficult than indoor (s4), because of extreme lighting variations. s2 performs worst, because we have no dedicated mechanism for scale invariance. Snippets of >5 frames bring very little improvement. For the LPPA database, note that the "gold standard" achieved by human observers in the psychophysics experiment was

Figure 5. Influence of form and motion features on categorisation performance. Left: Recognition rates at snippet length L=1 with different relative weights of both pathways, computed on all three databases. Middle: Recognition rates with different relative weights and different snippet lengths, shown for the WEIZMANN database (peaks marked by bold lines). Right: Recognition rates for WEIZMANN and KTH (average of all scenarios) using only form, only motion, and the best combination.

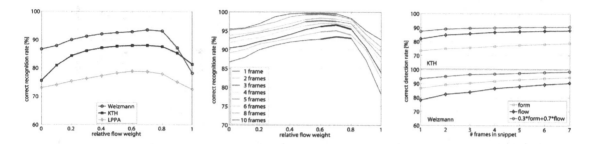

85% correct classification, meaning that the system's performance is 92.5% of the gold standard at $L=1$, and 95% at $L=7$. Longer snippets slightly increase performance, but the required length is not class-specific: the same classes are "easy", respectively "difficult", independent of the snippet length.

Table 2 gives a comparison to other methods operating on single frames or snippets. Note that there are two groups using different paradigms, which cannot be directly compared. Our method, as well as Blank et al. (2005), look at snippets as atomic units, and assign a label to a snippet.

The methods of Jhuang et al. (2007); Niebles and Fei-Fei (2007) use a temporal window to compute features, but label only the central frame of the window. So for example, BLANK assigns a label to each snippet of 10 frames, using features computed on those 10 frames, whereas JHUANG assigns a label to every frame, using features computed in a 9-frame window. The first approach has the advantage that it does not require temporal look-ahead. Note especially the high classification rates even at snippet length $L=1$ frame. The confusions, which do occur, are mainly between visually similar classes, such as *jogging/walking*,

Figure 6. Confusion matrices for L=1 (form and motion at a single frame). Left to right are the true categories, top to bottom the estimated categories. Results are given in percent of the true answer— columns add up to 100.

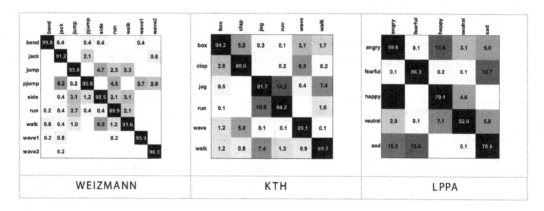

Figure 7. Performance for different snippet lengths. Left: WEIZMANN and LPPA databases. Middle: KTH by scenario. Each scenario is trained and tested separately. Right: Per-category classification rates for increasing snippet length L (average over all KTH scenarios).

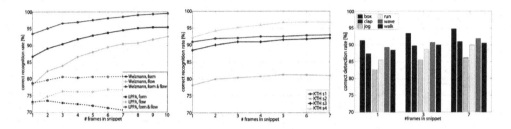

or *hand-clapping/hand-waving*. See confusion matrices in Figure 6.

Furthermore, we compare categorisation with snippets to the available results at *sequence* level, see Table 3. At *L*=7 frames (less than 0.3 seconds of video), our results are comparable to the best ones obtained with full video sequences—in several cases, they are even better. The comparison confirms the message that a handful of frames are almost as informative for categorisation as the entire video.

5.3 Good and Bad Snippets

Clearly, not all parts of a motion sequence are equally suited for recognition. In a categorical (i.e., discriminative) framework this translates to the fact that certain snippets are easily miss-classified, because similar snippets occur in more than one category. Consequently, which snippets are distinctive for a certain category depends not only on the category itself, but on the entire set of "competing" categories as well. Note that the discriminative approach does not create this dependency, but only makes it apparent: with a generative model, one can measure the ability to reconstruct a pattern, independent of other categories. However, this does not change the fact that the model could reconstruct a very similar pattern for a different category.

When using a labelling algorithm made up of binary classifiers (such as our *one-vs-all* SVM), one has direct access to the "good" and "bad" snippets of each category: the most useful ones are those, which have a large margin (distance from the decision boundary), while the most ambiguous ones are those, which come to lie close to, or on the wrong side of, the decision boundary. By analysing the classifier output, one can therefore determine the usefulness of different snippets for the task.

Table 2. Comparison with other results at snippet level (WEIZMANN database). The last column indicates the number of frames in a snippet (the unit for classification), and the number of frames used to compute features.

	correct	frames		correct	frames
BLANK	99.6%	10 / 10	*snippet1*	93.5%	1 / 1
NIEBLES	55.0%	1 / 12	*snippet3*	96.6%	3 / 3
JHUANG	93.8%	1 / 9	*snippet7*	98.5%	7 / 7
			snippet10	99.6%	10 / 10

Table 3. Categorisation results using snippets of different lengths, and comparison with published results for whole sequences. For KTH s2, note that we have no mechanism for scale invariance.

	snippet1	*snippet7*	**entire seq.**
KTH *all-in-one*	88.0%	**90.9%**	81.5% [NIEBLES]
KTH s1	90.9%	93.0%	**96.0%** [JHUANG]
KTH s2	78.1%	81.1%	**86.1%** [JHUANG]
KTH s3	88.5%	**92.1%**	89.8% [JHUANG]
KTH s4	92.2%	**96.7%**	94.8% [JHUANG]
WEIZMANN	93.5%	98.6%	**100.0%** [BLANK]
LPPA	78.7%	**80.7%**	—

Figure 8 shows a few examples for the WEIZMANN dataset, computed at snippet length $L=1$. For each class, we show the output of the binary *class-vs-nonclass* classifier on all frames (in-class samples as light-gray circles, out-of-class samples as dark crosses). Furthermore we show: the frames with the largest positive and negative margins, corresponding to the most confident decisions (top image on left side and bottom image on right side, respectively), the least distinctive in-class frames for four different subjects (remaining images on left side), and the most confusing out-of-class frames for four different subjects (remaining images on right side).[2] One can clearly see that the confusions are indeed caused by ambiguous body poses, such as similar parts of the *walking* and *running* cycle, and similar gestures, such as the arm movement of *jumping jack* and *waving both hands*.

5.4 Comparison at Sequence Level

Most results in the literature are reported at the level of correctly classified sequences. To put our method in context, we therefore also compare it to the state-of-the-art at sequence level. Like other frame-based methods, we simply run our algorithm for all frames (snippets of length $L=1$) of a sequence,

Figure 8. Discriminative power of different frames for example classes jumping jack, walking, and waving both hands. See text for details.

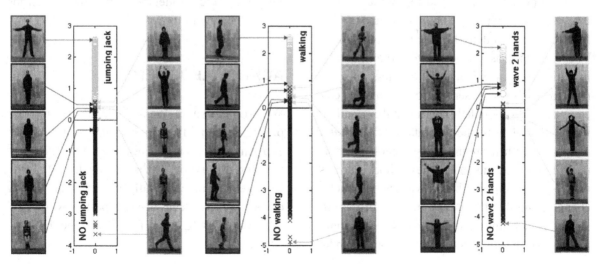

Table 4. Comparison of classification results at sequence level

KTH *all-in-one*		WEIZMANN	
bag-of-*snippet1*	**92.7%**	bag-of-*snippet1*	**100.0%**
NIEBLES	81.5%	BLANK	**100.0%**
DOLLÁR	81.2%	JHUANG	98.8%
SCHÜLDT	71.7%	WANG	97.8%
JHUANG	91.7%	ALI	92.6%
(average of scenarios s1–s4,		DOLLÁR	86.7%
trained and tested separately)		NIEBLES	72.8%

and convert their individual labels to a sequence label through majority voting (a simplistic "bag-of-frames" model). The results are given in Table 4. Although our method was not specifically designed for this application, it achieves top performance on both data sets. This demonstrates the power of using dense form and motion.

The comparison should be taken with a grain of salt: in the action recognition literature, there is no established testing protocol, and different researchers have used varying sizes of training and test sets, different ways of averaging over runs, e.t.c. We always quote the best results someone has achieved. Still, the comparison remains indicative.

6 CONCLUSION

We have presented a method for human motion categorisation, which uses both form and motion features sampled densely over the image plane. The method was employed to experimentally investigate the question, how long video snippets need to be in order to serve as basic units for categorisation. In a detailed experimental evaluation, we have confirmed the advantage of explicitly extracting both form and motion cues. Furthermore, it has been shown that the method performs well on different databases without parameter changes, and that it matches the state-of-the-art, using fewer frames and no look-ahead. A main message of the study is that basic motion can be

recognised well even with very short snippets of 1-7 frames (at frame rate 25 Hertz), as anticipated from biological vision.

A limitation of our current system is that it does not incorporate mechanisms for invariance to scale, rotation, and viewpoint (although it successfully handles scale changes up to a factor of ≈ 2, and viewpoint changes up to ≈ 30, which are present in the KTH database). An open research question, which needs to be addressed before motion categorisation can be applied to realistic problems, is what the right "basic units" of human motion are, and how complex motion patterns—and ultimately unscripted human behaviour—can be represented as sequential or hierarchical combinations of such basic units. Another open issue is how to extend categorisation to scenarios with large numbers of categories, where it is no longer feasible to independently learn a classifier for each category.

ACKNOWLEDGMENT

We would like to thank Hueihan Jhuang for providing unpublished per-frame results of her experiments, and for the accompanying explanation and discussion. Lydia Yahia-Cherif (LPPA, Collège de France) kindly provided the LPPA dataset. This work has been supported by EU FP6 projects COBOL (NEST-043403) and DIRAC (IST-027787).

REFERENCES

Ali, S., Basharat, A., & Shah, M. (2007). Chaotic invariants for human action recognition. In *Proc. 11th International Conference on Computer Vision,* Rio de Janeiro, Brazil.

Beintema, J. A., & Lappe, M. (2002). Perception of biological motion without local image motion. *Proceedings of the National Academy of Sciences of the United States of America, 99,* 5661–5663. doi:10.1073/pnas.082483699

Blank, M., Gorelick, L., Shechtman, E., Irani, M., & Basri, R. (2005). Actions as space-time shapes. In *Proc. 10th International Conference on Computer Vision,* Beijing.

Carlsson, S., & Sullivan, J. (2001). Action recognition by shape matching to key frames. In *Proc. Workshop on Models versus Exemplars in Computer Vision.*

Casile, A., & Giese, M. A. (2005). Critical features for the recognition of biological motion. *Journal of Vision (Charlottesville, Va.), 5,* 348–360. doi:10.1167/5.4.6

Comaniciu, D., Ramesh, V., & Meer, P. (2003). Kernel-based object tracking. *IEEE Transactions on Pattern Analysis and Machine Intelligence, 25*(5), 564–575. doi:10.1109/TPAMI.2003.1195991

Dalal, N., & Triggs, B. (2005). Histograms of oriented gradients for human detection. In *Proc. 10th International Conference on Computer Vision,* China.

Dollár, P., Rabaud, V., Cottrell, G., & Belongie, S. (2005). Behavior recognition via sparse spatio-temporal features. In *Workshop on Performance Evaluation of Tracking and Surveillance (VS-PETS).*

Efros, A. A., Berg, A. C., Mori, G., & Malik, J. (2003). Recognizing action at a distance. In *Proc. 9th International Conference on Computer Vision,* Nice.

Fanti, C., Zelnik-Manor, L., & Perona, P. (2005). Hybrid models for human motion recognition. In *Proc. IEEE Conference on Computer Vision and Pattern Recognition,* San Diego, CA.

Felleman, D. J., & van Essen, D. C. (1991). Distributed hierarchical processing in the primate visual cortex. *Cerebral Cortex (New York, N.Y.), 1,* 1–47. doi:10.1093/cercor/1.1.1-a

Field, D. J. (1987). Relations between the statistics of natural images and the response properties of cortical cells. *Journal of the Optical Society of America. A, Optics and Image Science, 4*(12), 2379–2394. doi:10.1364/JOSAA.4.002379

Forsyth, D. A., & Ponce, J. (2003). *Computer Vision—A Modern Approach.* Upper Saddle River, NJ: Prentice Hall Inc.

Fukushima, K. (1980). Neocognitron: a self-organizing neural network model for mechanisms of pattern recognition unaffected by shift in position. *Biological Cybernetics, 36,* 193–202. doi:10.1007/BF00344251

Gawne, T. J., & Martin, J. (2002). Response of primate visual cortical V4 neurons to two simultaneously presented stimuli. *Journal of Neurophysiology, 88,* 1128–1135. doi:10.1152/jn.00151.200

Giese, M. A., & Poggio, T. (2003). Neural mechanisms for the recognition of biological movements. *Nature Neuroscience, 4,* 179–192. doi:10.1038/nrn1057

Harnad, S. (Ed.). (1987). *Categorical perception: the groundwork of cognition.* Cambridge, MA: Cambridge University Press.

Hubel, D. H., & Wiesel, T. N. (1962). Receptive fields, binocular interaction and functional architecture in the cat's visual cortex. *The Journal of Physiology, 160,* 106–154.

Jhuang, H., Serre, T., Wolf, L., & Poggio, T. (2007). A biologically inspired system for action recognition. In *Proc. 11th International Conference on Computer Vision,* Rio de Janeiro.

Lampl, I., Ferster, D., Poggio, T., & Riesenhuber, M. (2004). Intracellular measurements of spatial integration and the max operation in complex cells of the cat primary visual cortex. *Journal of Neurophysiology, 92,* 2704–2713. doi:10.1152/jn.00060.2004

Laptev, I., & Lindeberg, T. (2003). Local descriptors for spatio-temporal recognition. In *Proc. 9th International Conference on Computer Vision,* Nice.

Niebles, J. C., & Fei-Fei, L. (2007). A hierarchical model of shape and appearance for human action classification. In *Proc. IEEE Conference on Computer Vision and Pattern Recognition,* Minneapolis, MN.

Niebles, J. C., Wang, H., & Fei-Fei, L. (2006). Unsupervised learning of human action categories using spatio-temporal words. In *Proc. 17th British Machine Vision Conference,* Edinburgh.

Pontil, M., & Verri, A. (1998). Support vector machines for 3d object recognition. *IEEE Transactions on Pattern Analysis and Machine Intelligence, 20*(6), 637–646. doi:10.1109/34.683777

Rao, C., Yilmaz, A., & Shah, M. (2002). View-invariant representation and recognition of actions. *International Journal of Computer Vision, 50*(2), 203–226. doi:10.1023/A:1020350100748

Riesenhuber, M., & Poggio, T. (1999). Hierarchical models of object recognition in cortex. *Nature Neuroscience, 2,* 1019–1025. doi:10.1038/14819

Schüldt, C., Laptev, I., & Caputo, B. (2004). Recognizing human actions: a local SVM approach. In *Proc. International Conference on Pattern Recognition,* Cambridge.

Serre, T., Wolf, L., Bileschi, S., Riesenhuber, M., & Poggio, T. (2007). Object recognition with cortex-like mechanisms. *IEEE Transactions on Pattern Analysis and Machine Intelligence, 29*(3), 411–426. doi:10.1109/TPAMI.2007.56

Serre, T., Wolf, L., & Poggio, T. (2005). Object recognition with features inspired by visual cortex. In *Proc. IEEE Conference on Computer Vision and Pattern Recognition,* San Diego, CA.

Shawe-Taylor, J., & Christianini, N. (2000). *Support Vector Machines*. Cambridge, MA: Cambridge University Press.

Wang, L., & Suter, D. (2007). Recognizing human activities from silhouettes: motion subspace and factorial discriminative graphical model. In *Proc. IEEE Conference on Computer Vision and Pattern Recognition,* Minneapolis, MN.

Yacoob, Y., & Black, M. J. (1999). Parameterized modeling and recognition of activities. *Computer Vision and Image Understanding, 72*(2), 232–247. doi:10.1006/cviu.1998.0726

ENDNOTES

[1]   In practice, some categories will by their nature be ambiguous and lack well-defined boundaries, e.g. *jogging* vs. *running*, or *sad walking* vs. *neutral walking* performed by a tired person.

[2]   Gaps between the displayed data points are from nearby, similar frames of the same subjects.

Chapter 10
Human Action Recognition with Expandable Graphical Models

Wanqing Li
University of Wollongong, Australia

Zhengyou Zhang
Microsoft Research, Redmond, USA

Zicheng Liu
Microsoft Research, Redmond, USA

Philip Ogunbona
University of Wollongong, Australia

ABSTRACT

This chapter first presents a brief review of the recent development in human action recognition. In particular, the principle and shortcomings of the conventional Hidden Markov Model (HMM) and its variants are discussed. We then introduce an expandable graphical model that represents the dynamics of human actions using a weighted directed graph, referred to as action graph. Unlike the conventional HMM, the action graph is shared by all actions to be recognized with each action being encoded in one or multiple paths and, thus, can be effectively and efficiently trained from a small number of samples. Furthermore, the action graph is expandable to incorporate new actions without being retrained and compromised. To verify the performance of the proposed expandable graphic model, a system that learns and recognizes human actions from sequences of silhouettes is developed and promising results are obtained.

INTRODUCTION

Human motion analysis has attracted increasing attention in the past decade due to its scientific challenges and social and economic significance in a wide range of applications including video sur-veillance for home, workplace and public environment, human computer interface (HCI), study and diagnosis of movement disorder, tele-monitoring of patients and elderly people and sports training. This problem has been addressed mainly from two aspects: kinetics and kinematics. Kinetics studies the forces and torques that generate the movement.

DOI: 10.4018/978-1-60566-900-7.ch010

Kinematics concerns the geometry of human body, such as position, orientation and deformation, and the changes of the geometry during the motion. Visual analysis is usually concerned with the kinematics and so is this chapter.

Anatomically, human body consists of many parts including head, torso, arms and legs. Motion of the body can be caused by the movement of any parts. Human body parts are usually not rigid. However, they are customarily treated as such in the studies of human motion. Therefore, the human body is often viewed as an articulated system of rigid links or segments connected by joints and its motion can be considered as a continuous evolution of the spatial configuration of the segments or body posture (Zatsiorsky, 1997). Accordingly, effective characterization and modeling of the posture (shape) and its dynamics (kinematics) has been central to the success of human action recognition.

Study of human motion often abstracts the motion hierarchically into *motion primitives*, *actions* and *activities*. While the definitions of these terms vary substantially depending on the applications, we adopt in this chapter the definition of an *activity* as the human's interaction with the environment, whereas an *action* is the motion performed by the individual body parts. We consider actions as the smallest recognizable semantically meaningful motion units. This chapter focuses on the recognition of actions, such as *run*, *walk* and *jump*.

Ideally, an action recognition system is desired to be independent of the subjects who perform the actions, independent of the speed at which the actions are performed, robust against noisy extraction of features used to characterize the actions, scalable to a large number of actions and expandable with new actions. Despite the considerable research in the past few years, such a system is yet to be developed. In this chapter, we describe a recently proposed expandable graphical model of human actions that has the promise to realize such a system (Li, Zhang, & Liu, 2008b, 2008a).

This chapter first presents a brief review of the recent development in human action recognition. To contrast with our approach, we describe the principle of modeling actions based on conventional Hidden Markov Model (HMM) and its variants. Then, the expandable graphical model is presented in detail and a system that learns and recognizes human actions from sequences of silhouettes using the expandable graphical model is developed. Conclusion and discussion on future challenges are made in the last section.

RECENT DEVELOPMENT

A rich palette of diverse ideas has been proposed during the past few years on the problem of recognition of human actions by employing different types of visual information. A good review can be found in (Gavrila, 1999; Hu, Tan, Wang, & Maybank, 2004; Moeslund, Hilton, & Kruger, 2006; Moeslund & Granum, 2001). This section presents a brief review of the recent development in action recognition.

Study of the kinematics of human motion suggests that a human action can be divided into a sequence of postures. The sequence is often repeated by the same subject at different times or different subjects with some variations. Methods proposed so far for action recognition differs in the way that the postures are described and the dynamics of the posture sequence is modeled. In general, they fall into two categories based on how they model the dynamics of the actions: *implicit* and *explicit* models.

In an implicit model, *action descriptors* are extracted from the action sequences such that the action recognition is transformed from a temporal classification problem to a static classification one. The action descriptors are supposed to capture both spatial and temporal characteristics of the actions. For instance, Bobick and Davis (Bobick & Davis, 2001) proposed to stack silhouettes into a Motion Energy Images (MEI) and Motion-

History Images (MHI). Seven Hu moments (M. Hu, 1962) are extracted from both MEI and MHI to serve as action descriptors. Their action recognition is based on the Mahalanobis distance between each moment descriptor of the known actions and the input action. Meng et al. (Meng, Freeman, Pears, & Bailey, 2008) extended the MEI and MHI into a hierarchical form and used a support vector machine (SVM) to recognize the actions. Babua and Ramakrishnan (Babua & Ramakrishnan, 2004) introduced the motion flow history (MFH) and combined with MHI for action recognition. The concept of MHI has also been extended to volumetric MHI (VMHI) to analyze the irregularities in human actions (Albu, Beugeling, Virji-Babul, & Beach, 2007). In the method proposed by Chen et al. (Chen, Liao, & Shih, 2007, 2006), star figure models (Fujiyoshi & Lipton, 1998) are fitted to silhouettes to capture the five extremities of the shape that correspond to the arms, legs and head. Gaussian mixture models (GMMs) are used to capture the spatial distribution of the five extremities over the period of an action, ignoring the temporal order of the silhouettes in the action sequence. Davis and Yyagi (Davis & Tyagi, 2006) also used GMM to capture the distribution of the moments of the silhouettes of an action sequence.

Approaches to describing actions by spatio-temporal volumes have been actively studied recently. Yilmaz and Shah (Yilmaz & Shah, 2005) treated a sequence of silhouettes as a spatiotemporal volume and proposed to extract the differential geometric surface properties, i.e. Gaussian curvature and mean curvature, to form a descriptor for each action, known as an action sketch. Gorelick et al. (Blank, Gorelick, Shechtman, Irani, & Basri, 2005; Gorelick, Blank, Shechtman, Irani, & Basri, 2007) extracted space-time features including space-time saliency, action dynamics, shape structure and orientation by utilizing the properties of the solution to the Poisson equation and Mokhber et al. (Mokhber, Achard, & Milgram, 2008) extracted the 3D geometric moments from

the volumes; both of them employed K-nearest neighbour (KNN) algorithm to classify the actions. Direct 3D volume matching for action recognition has also been studied by Shechtman (Shechtman & Irani, 2005) and Rodriguez (Rodriguez, Ahmed, & Shah, 2008).

Another recent development in the implicit modeling is to characterize an action using a set of spatio-temporal interest points (STIP) (Dollar, Rabaud, Cottrell, & Belongie, 2005; Laptev & Lindeberg, 2003). Features are extracted from the local volume windows centered at the STIPs and action classifiers are built upon the features. For instance, Fathi (Fathi & Mori, 2008) and Laptev (Laptev & Perez, 2007) built the classifiers using Adaboost . The STIPs were also used to form a "Bag of Visual Words" and latent topic models such as the probabilistic latent semantic analysis (pLSA) model and latent Dirichlet allocation (LDA) were used to achieve action recognition (Niebles, Wang, & Li, 2008; Savarese, DelPozo, Niebles, & Li, 2008; Liu & Shah, 2008; Liu, Ali, & Shah, 2008).

The implicit modeling approach has the advantages that the recognition is relatively simple and is able to handle small number of training samples. However, it usually offers weak encoding of the action dynamics and requires good temporal segmentation before the actions can be recognized. In addition, periodic or cyclic actions have to be dealt with differently (Wang & Suter, 2007).

On the other hand, the explicit model follows the concept that an action is composed of a sequence of postures and usually consists of two components: description of the postures and modeling of the dynamics of the postures. Various features have been employed to describe the postures. They include binary masks (Wang, Jiang, Drew, Li, & Mori, 2006), moments (Hu, 1962), Fourier shape descriptors (Kellokumpu, Pietikainen, & Heikkila, 2005), Kendall's shape description (Kendall, Barden, Carne, & Le, 1999), shape-context (Belongie, Malik, & Puzicha, 2002) and joint geometric and motion features (Li et al., 2008b, 2008a; Achard, Qu, Mokhber, & Milgram, 2008). Strategies that have been proposed to model the dynamics include direct sequence matching (DSM) (Colombo, Comanducci, & Del Bimbo, 2007; Wei, Hu, Zhang, & Luo, 2007), dynamic time warping (DTW) (Wang & Suter, 2007), spatiotemporal correlation (Wei et al., 2007; Veeraraghavan, Chowdhury, & Chellappa, 2004), HMM (Rabiner, 1989; Yamato, Ohya, & Ishii, 1992; Green & Guan, 2004; Davis & Tyagi, 2006; Achard et al., 2008; Ahmad & Lee, 2008; Cuntoor, Yegnanarayana, & Chellappa, 2008) and their variants such as parameterized HMMs (Wilson & Bobick, 1998), Entropic-HMMs (Brand & Kettnaker, 2000), Variable-length HMMs (Galata, Johnson, & Hogg, 2001) and Layered-HMMs (Oliver, Garg, & Horvits, 2004; Wu, Chen, Tsai, Lee, & Yu, 2008; Natarajan & Nevatia, 2008). Divis and Tyagi (Davis & Tyagi, 2006) used moments to describe shapes of a silhouette and continuous HMM to model the dynamics. In (Kellokumpu et al., 2005), Kellokumpu et al. chose Fourier shape descriptors and classified the postures into a finite number of clusters. Discrete HMM are then used to model the dynamics of the actions where the posture clusters are considered to be the discrete symbols emitted from the hidden states. A simple comparative study of the use of HMM and its variants in action recognition can be found in (Mendoza & Blanca, 2008). Sminchisescu et al. (Sminchisescu, Kanaujia, Li, & Metaxas, 2005) relaxed the HMM assumption of conditional independence of observations given the actions by adopting the Conditional Random Field (CRF) model and Shi et al. (Shi, Wang, Cheng, & Smola, 2008) proposed a semi-Markov model for joint segmentation and recognition. Carlsson and Sullivan (Carlsson & Sullivan, 2001) took an extreme method to describe and match tennis strokes using single key-frames. Veerarahavan, et al. (Veeraraghavan et al., 2004) proposed to use autoregressive (AR) model and autoregressive moving average (ARMA) model to capture the

kinematics of the actions. They adopted Kendall's representation of shape as shape features.

Recently, Wang and Suter (Wang & Suter, 2007) employed locality preserving projection (LPP) to learn a subspace to describe the postures, and DTW and temporal Hausdorff distance to classify the actions in the subspace. Colombo, et al. (Colombo et al., 2007) proposed to find the subspace for each type of actions through principal component analysis (PCA). Wei et al. (Wei et al., 2007) clustered the postures into a set of clusters, known as symbols, based on the shape-context. Direct sequence matching was applied to the symbolized sequences for recognition. Lv and Nevatia (Lv & Nevatia, 2007) took the approach a step further. They modeled the dynamics using an *unweighted directed graph*, referred to as action net, where nodes in the graph represented key-postures learned from simulated actions based on the data captured from motion capture devices. The direct links indicate the allowed transition between postures. Each action is represented by *one path* in the action net. Given an input sequence of silhouettes, the likelihood of each frame belonging to every posture is computed and the input is recognized as the action which gives the maximum accumulated likelihood along the path of the action.

Similar to the implicit model, most proposed explicit modeling approaches mentioned above also require segmentation of the actions from the input video sequences before an action can be recognized. In addition, the dynamics of the actions are modeled individually and separately (i.e. no connection among actions), such as the conventional HMM based approach. As a result, they often require a large number of training samples, which can be costly and tedious to obtain.

It has to be pointed out that all methods reviewed above are view-dependent. A few attempts have been made to address this issue by including videos from multiple viewpoints or recovering 3D postures from 2D image/image sequences. Lv and Nevatia (Lv & Nevatia, 2007) includes simulated multiple view silhouettes in each node of their action net. Ahmad and Lee (Ahmad & Lee, 2006, 2008) built multiple HMMs for each action, each HMM modeling the action observed from a particular viewpoint. Pierobon et al. (Pierobon, Marcon, Sarti, & Tubaro, 2005) used the 3D postures recovered from multiple cameras. Green and Guan (Green & Guan, 2004) recovered 3D postures from monocular image sequences.

HIDDEN-MARKOV BASED MODELING

In this section, the fundamental theory of Hidden Markov Model (HMM) and the HMM based action modeling are briefly reviewed for the purpose of completeness and contrasting with our proposed expandable graphical model to be introduced later.

Theory of Hidden Markov Model (HMM)

In its basic form an HMM is characterized by a set of N states, $S = \{s_1, s_2, ..., s_N\}$, that obey the first-order Markovian property and represent the temporal dynamics of the system being modeled. The state, Q at time t, denoted by q_t, could be any of the s_i. We capture the transition from one state to another in the transition probability matrix, $A = \{a_{ij}\}$, $i, j = 1, 2, ..., N$, where the entry a_{ij} denotes the probability of the model being in state $q_{t+1} = s_j$ at time $t + 1$ given that it was in state $q_t = s_i$ at time t. At each state the model undergoes an emission process that captures locally stationary part of the system being modeled. The emission in state i is described by the emission probabilities $B = \{b_i(k)\}$ that denote the probability of emitting symbol $k \in K$ in state i. The symbol set K represents the possible values of the observation variable O; the observation at time t is denoted O_t. A sequence of such data will be used to train (or estimate the

parameters of) the model. In essence the HMM consists of two stochastic processes, namely, the first-order Markov process representing the states which are ***hidden***; and the emission process that yields the observed data. The probability distribution of the starting state usually denoted by π is the probability of $q_1 = s_i$. A complete characterization of the model is achieved by specifying A, B and π; compactly, we write the model as $\lambda = (A, B, \pi)$. The description given pertains to a discrete HMM; a continuous HMM will have a probability density function modeling the emission process and the observed output will be continuous random vector variables. An extensive description of the hidden Markov model can be found in (Rabiner, 1989; Bishop, 2006).

Three pertinent questions that HMM answers in relation to modeling problems (Rabiner, 1989),

- **Evaluation:** compute $P(O|\lambda)$ given the observation sequence $O = \{O_1, O_2, ..., Q_T\}$ and a model $\lambda = (A, B, \pi)$.
- **Decoding:** find the most likely state sequence $Q = \{q_1, q_2, ... q_T\}$ given the observation $O = \{O_1, O_2, ... Q_T\}$ and a model $\lambda = (A, B, \pi)$.
- **Training:** given a set of observation sequences, estimate the model parameters $\lambda = (A, B, \pi)$ to maximize $P(O|\lambda)$.

An HMM for which the elements a_{ij} of A is zero if $j < i$ is called a left-to-right HMM.

The joint distribution over the hidden variables and the observation sequence is given by,

$$p(Q, O \mid \lambda) = p(q_1 \mid \pi) \left[\prod_{t=2}^{T} p(q_t \mid q_{t-1}, A) \right] \prod_{t=1}^{T} p(O_t \mid q_t, B)$$

(1)

The likelihood function is easily obtained by marginalizing the joint distribution over the hidden state sequence variables, Q to yield,

$$p(O \mid \lambda) = \sum_Q p(Q, O \mid \lambda) \qquad (2)$$

The *Forward-Backward Algorithm* is often used to evaluate Eq.(2).

For decoding the most likely state sequence, $Q = \{q_1, q_2, \ldots q_T\}$, given the observation, $O = \{O_1, O_2, \ldots Q_T\}$, can be efficiently found by the *Viterbi algorithm* and the state sequence is often called a Viterbi sequence or path.

The parameters of the HMM are determined by maximizing the likelihood function for a set of training observations. This maximization has no closed-form solution and the expectation maximization (EM) algorithm is generally employed as the optimization technique. The EM algorithm is iterative and in the expectation (E) step it uses the current values of the parameters of the Markov model (i.e. the transition probabilities, initial state distribution and the output probability distribution) to estimate the posterior distribution of the hidden variables. These probabilities are then used as weights and new estimates for the transition probability distribution and the emission probability distribution are computed. More specifically, we use initial model parameters, denoted λ^{old}, to estimate the posterior distribution of the hidden variables, $(Q|O, \lambda^{old})$.

The estimated posterior is used to evaluate the expectation of the logarithm of the complete-data likelihood function,

$$D(\lambda, \lambda^{old}) = \sum_Q p(Q \mid O, \lambda^{old}) \ln p(O, Q \mid \lambda)$$

$$(3)$$

The function $D(\lambda, \lambda^{old})$ can be expressed in terms of the marginal posterior distribution of the hidden variable, $\gamma(q_n)$, and the joint posterior distribution of two hidden variables, $\zeta(q_{n-1}, q_n)$. These quantities are defined as,

$$\gamma(q_n) = p(q_n \mid O, \lambda^{old}) \qquad (4)$$

$$\zeta(q_{n-1}, q_n) = p(q_{n-1}, q_n \mid O, \lambda^{old}) \qquad (5)$$

An efficient method of evaluating $\gamma(q_n)$ and $\zeta(q_{n-1}, q_n)$ is the *Baum-Welch algorithm*.

In the maximization (M) step of the EM algorithm, the function $D(\lambda, \lambda^{old})$ is maximized with respect to λ to obtain new estimates for initial state probability distribution, π, and the transition probabilities, A. The emission probability distribution obtained depends on the assumption made about the emission densities.

Action Modeling Using HMM

The temporal characteristics of human motion has made the HMM a useful tool for human motion analysis. Modeling actions using HMMs often involves the following steps:

- Define the observations $O = \{O_1, O_2, \ldots, Q_T\}$. Often the observation O_t is the features extracted from the video sequences to describe the configuration and/or motion of the human body at time t
- Choose a suitable HMM structure and topology including the number of states N for characterizing the actions
- Collect the training data and estimate the model parameters

The basic approach is to construct one left-to-right HMM model per action and the number of states for each action is optimized through trials and errors. Let $\lambda_i = (A_i, B_i, \pi_i)$ be the HMM model for the $i\,'th$ action. Assume L HMM models have been trained for L actions. Given an observation sequence $O = \{O_1, O_2, \ldots, Q_T\}$, the recognition of the action that generates O is achieved by

$$\lambda^* = \arg \max_j P(O \mid \lambda_j) \qquad (6)$$

Research in action modeling using HMMs has been mainly focused on the selection of the features (observations). Various features have been studied in the past, including the mesh features (Yamato et al., 1992), moments calculated from silhouettes (Davis & Tyagi, 2006), 3D joint angles (Lv & Nevatia, 2006; Green & Guan, 2004), joint Zernike moments and local-global optical flow (Ahmad & Lee, 2008) and 3D moments calculated from space-time micro-volumes (Achard et al., 2008).

There have also been several extensions of the HMMs to deal with some of the complex system models (Oliver et al., 2004; Nguyen, Phung, Venkatesh, & Bui, 2005; Wu et al., 2008; Mendoza & Blanca, 2008). Three notable extensions are Coupled HMM, Variable length HMM and Layered HMM.

Coupled HMMs are the model of choice when multiple parts are undergoing temporal changes. Examples of studies where coupled HMM have been used include, actions involving body parts, interaction between two persons and applications requiring sensor fusion across modalities. In the case of multiple body parts, states of the HMM represent the motion of different parts of the body and are constrained to make transitions simultaneously. Brand, Oliver and Pentland (Brand, Oliver, & Pentland, 1997) applied coupled HMM to the classification of two handed actions. Their model is based on the assumption of causal coupling between the systems executing the actions. In other words one action from one system (or entity) forces a responsive action from the other system. Two HMMs are coupled by introducing conditional probabilities between their hidden state variables and thus the usual Markovian property of the state sequence distribution no longer holds. They introduced a novel method of training the model that admits an oversized parameter space and embeds within it a subspace manifold representing all possible parameterizations of a much smaller system of coupled HMMs. The usual forward-backward algorithm was used to estimate the posterior state probabilities in the larger space. Finally, through a computation of the closest point on the manifold

the re-estimation was carried to ensure that the posterior probability of the model increases but the parameters stay on the manifold.

One of the drawbacks of the basic HMM is that order of the Markov chain (dependence relation of the state sequence) is fixed during the model design. However, there are applications where variable chain length will allow the modeling of varying dependencies with varying time steps. In (Galata et al., 2001) a novel approach for automatically acquiring stochastic models of the high-level structure of an activity without the assumption of any prior knowledge is presented. The process involves temporal segmentation into plausible atomic behavior components and the use of variable-length Markov models (VLMM) for the efficient representation of behaviors. In their presentation, they employ VLMM to model behavior at different temporal scales. At one scale, a VLMM is used to encode sequences of prototypical configurations of short-term structure and motion (typically spanning on the order of 20 ms). At another scale (larger) another VLMM is used to encode sequences of atomic behaviors representing primitive actions (typically lasting on the order of a second). The VLMM has been used to encode different temporal dependencies that otherwise could not be achieved using a fixed HMM.

Layered HMMs are used to model actions at different levels of temporal granularity. Usually the HMMs assume a parallel structure. A layered structure allows the decoupling of different levels of analysis for training and inference. In fact each level of the hierarchy can be trained independently, with different feature vectors and time granularities. Another important property of the layered HMM is that it is possible to train the lowest level without having to retrain any other level in the hierarchy and once the system is trained, inference can be performed at any level of the hierarchy. In their work, Wu et al. (Wu et al., 2008) proposed a layered HMM framework to decompose the human action recognition problem into two layers. Their work is centred on the problem of understanding upper human body from video sequences. A layer of HMM was devoted to modeling the actions of two arms individually and second layer models the interaction of the two arms. In another extension, Oliver et al. (Oliver et al., 2004) studied the use of layered HMM in representing and inferring office activity from multiple sources. Each layer of HMM was trained on sensory data to model sound, human detection, keyboard activity, etc. The HMMs were then coupled through an expected utility analysis that provides the required classification.

In all, the assumption of Markovian dynamics and the time-invariant nature of the model restrict the applicability of HMMs to relatively simple and stationary temporal patterns. Several shortcomings of the HMMs can be identified. It is well known that the HMM requires a large training sample data to learn the model. So for a large number of actions we require a large data set. The assumption about a start state and an end state is rigid and will necessitate that actions have to be segmented from the video sequence to fit the model. In addition, the concept of one HMM per action has limited its scalability to large number of actions and expandability to the inclusion of new actions into an existing system without a need for retraining the entire system. The expandable graphical model presented in the next section overcomes these shortcomings of the HMMs.

EXPANDABLE GRAPHICAL MODELING

In the expandable graphical modeling, we characterize actions with sequences of finite salient postures and propose to model the dynamics or kinematics of the actions using a weighted directed graph, referred to as *action graph*, and to model the salient postures with Gaussian mixture models (GMM). In the action graph, nodes represent

salient postures that may be *shared* by actions and the weight between two nodes measures the transition probability between the two postures represented by the two nodes. This transition probability is effectively governed by the kinematics of the human body. An action is encoded in *one or multiple paths* in the action graph. The GMM model of the salient postures provides a compact description of the spatial distribution of the poses belonging to the same salient posture and allows robust matching between imperfect or noisy observations of the poses. Furthermore, the GMM together with the graphical model of actions create a mechanism for a trained system to learn a new action with a small number of samples without compromising the existing system. In other words, the model is expandable to incorporate new actions into an existing system without the need for retraining the entire system.

The expandable graphical model is substantially differentiated from and possesses advantages over the previously proposed methods based on postures (or key-frames) (Wei, Hu & Luo, 2007; Lv & Nevatia, 2007; Chen, Liao & Shih, 2007; Kellokumpu, Pietikainen & Heikkila 2005) and the HMM (Yamato, Ohya & Ishii, 1992; Bobick & Davis, 2001; Davis & Tyagi; 2006). Firstly, the model shares postures among different actions and, hence, enables efficient learning from a small number of samples instead of modelling each action with an individual HMM in a traditional way which often requires a large amount of training data. This advantage is particularly evident when an existing model is expanded to incorporate a new action. Secondly, one action may be encoded into multiple paths (i.e., sequences of salient postures) in the action graph to accommodate the variations of the action (e.g., performed by different persons or captured from different viewpoints) as opposed to one single sequence of postures (or key-frames) in most methods proposed so far. Thirdly, there is no specific beginning or ending posture for any action path. This allows continuous recognition of actions without segmentation. Moreover, cyclic and non-cyclic actions can be dealt with in the same way. Fourthly, the model facilitates different action decoding schemes (as described later) that require different computing resources. From this perspective, the expandable graphical model can be considered as a generalization of the previous works which usually employ only one of the decoding schemes. Lastly, the model can be easily scaled up to incorporate a large number of actions without adversely impacting on the decoding speed, or expanded to new actions without compromising the actions that have been previously learned in the model.

Let $X = \{x_1, x_2, \ldots, x_n\}$ be the observations of an action performed by a subject, where x_t is the observation at time t and each observation can be a silhouette, optical flows and/or spatial-temporal feature points. Let $\Omega = \{\omega_1, \omega_2, \ldots, \omega_M\}$ be the set of M salient postures that constitute actions. The corresponding posture sequence derived from X is denoted as $S = \{s_1, s_2, \ldots s_n\}$, where $s_t \in \Omega$, $t = 1, 2, \ldots$. Assume that $\Psi = \{\psi_1, \psi_2, \ldots, \psi_L\}$ denotes a set of L actions and X is generated from one of the actions. The recognition of the most likely action that generates the observation of X can be formulated as

$$
\begin{aligned}
\psi^* &= \arg \max_{\psi \in \Psi, S \subset \Omega} p(X, S, \psi) \\
&\propto \arg \max_{\psi \in \Psi, S \subset \Omega} p(\psi)p(S \mid \psi)p(X \mid S, \psi) \\
&\propto \arg \max_{\psi \in \Psi, S \subset \Omega} p(\psi)p(s_1, \cdots, s_n \mid \psi)p(x_1, \cdots, x_n \mid s_1, \cdots, s_n, \psi)
\end{aligned}
$$

$$(7)$$

where $p(\psi)$ is the prior probability of action ψ, $p(S|\psi)$ is the probability of S given action ψ and $p(X \mid S, \psi)$ is the probability of X given S and ψ.

Assume that i) x_t is statistically independent of ψ given S, ii) x_t statistically depends only on s_t. Then, Eq.(5) can be written as

$$
\psi^* = \arg \max_{\psi \in \Psi, s \subset \Omega} p(\psi)p(s_1, \cdots, s_n \mid \psi)\prod_{t-1}^{n} p(x_t \mid s_t)
$$

$$(8)$$

where $p(x_t \mid s_t)$ is the probability for x_t to be generated from state or salient posture s_t. It is referred to as posture or state model. Contrary to conventional HMM, we assume the set of postures is known or can be computed from training data.

Notice that the second term of Eq.(8), $p(s_1, s_2, \ldots, s_n \mid \psi)$, describes the context of the possible posture sequences for action ψ. The chain rule yields:

$$
p(s_1, \cdots, s_n \mid \psi) = p(s_1 \mid \psi)s(s_2 \mid s_1, \psi) \cdots p(s_n \mid s_{n-1}, \cdots, s_1, \psi)
$$

$$(9)$$

This is actually a Markov Model with known states or Visible Markov Model (VMM) (Manning & Schtze, 1999) and often referred to as the "grammar" of action ψ, In the rest of the chapter, we assume that s_t is independent of the future states and only depends on its previous state s_{t-1}, known as bi-gram. The results can be easily extended to higher order grams, such as tri-gram.

Action Graph

Eq.(8) can be represented or interpreted as a set of weighted directed graphs, G, that are built upon the set of postures.

$$
G = \{\Omega, A_1, A_2, \cdots, A_L\}
$$

$$(10)$$

where each posture serves as a node, $A_k = \{p(\omega_j \mid \omega_i, \psi_k)\}_{i,j=1:M}^{k=1:L}$ is the transitional probability matrix of the $k'th$ action and $A = \{p(\omega_j \mid \omega_i)\}_{i,j=1}^{M}$ is the global transitional probability matrix of all actions. We refer to G as an *Action graph*.

In an action graph, each action is encoded in one or multiple paths. Figure 1 shows an example action graph for three actions: *Run*, *Walk* and Side, where the observations are silhouettes. The three actions share nine states/postures whose representative silhouettes are shown in Figure 1(d). Notice that a particular action may only undergo a subset of the postures. For instance, action *Run* may go through postures: S1, S4 and S3; action *Walk* may go through postures: S6, S4, S0, S7 and S5; and action *Side* may undergo postures: S6, S2, S4, S7 and S8. Clearly, the three actions share postures and each action has multiple paths in the action graph. In addition, action paths in the graph are usually cyclic and, therefore, there are no specific beginning and ending postures/states for the action from the recognition point of view.

With the graphical interpretation, a system that follows the model of Eq.(8) can be described by a quadruplet,

$$\Gamma = (\Omega, \Lambda, G, \Psi) \tag{11}$$

where

$$\Omega = \{\omega_1, \omega_2, \cdots, \omega_M)$$
$$\Lambda = \{p(x \mid \omega_1), p(x \mid \omega_2), \cdots, p(x \mid \omega_M)\}$$
$$G = (\Omega, A_1, A_2, \cdots, A_L)$$
$$\Psi = \{\psi_1, \psi_2, \cdots, \psi_L\} \tag{12}$$

Action Decoding

Given a trained system $\Gamma = (\Omega, \Lambda, G, \Psi)$, The action of a sequence $X = \{x_1, x_2, ..., x_n\}$ is generally decoded in three major steps: i) find the most likely path in the action graph, G, that generates X: ii) compute the likelihood of each action, $\psi \in \Psi$; and, iii) decode the action as the one having the maximum likelihood which is greater than a threshold. If none of the likelihoods is greater than the threshold, the action of X is unknown. Eq.(8) offers a number of ways to find the most likely path and estimate the likelihood.

*Figure 1. An action graph for three actions with nine postures. In each graph, the numerical values next to the highlighted links (in red) are the transitional probabilities. (a) Action **Run**; (b) Action **Walk**; (c) Action **Side**; (d) The representative silhouettes.*

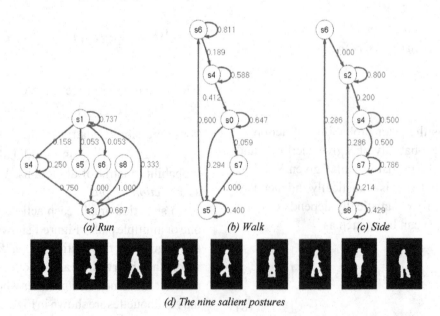

(a) Run　　*(b) Walk*　　*(c) Side*

(d) The nine salient postures

Action Specific Viterbi Decoding

The most obvious one is to search for an Action Specific Viterbi decoding (ASVD) in the action graph and calculate the likelihood as follows,

$$L(\psi_i) = \max_{s \in \Omega} p(\psi_i) \prod_{t=1}^{n} p(s_t \mid s_{t-1}, \psi_i) \prod_{t=1}^{n} p(x_t \mid s_t)$$

(13)

where $L(\psi_i)$, $i = 1, 2, \ldots, L$, is the likelihood of X belonging to action ψ_i and $p(s_1 \mid s_0, \psi_i) = 1$. X is decoded as action ψ_k if the following condition is met

$$\frac{L(\psi_k)}{\sum_{j=1}^{L} L(\psi_i)} \geq TH_1$$

(14)

where TH_1 is a threshold.

Besides the memory requirement for Viterbi search, ASVD decoding method can be computationally expensive when the number of recognizable actions, L, is large since it searches for the optimal path with respect to every action. A sub-optimal, but computationally efficient, decoding scheme is to search for a Viterbi path with respect to the global transitional probability and decode the path with action specific transitional probabilities. We refer to this method as Global Viterbi decoding (GVD).

Global Viterbi Decoding

In GVD, the most likely path is the one, $s^* = \{s_1^*, s_2^*, \cdots, s_n^*\}$, that satisfies

$$s^* = \arg \max_{s_t \in \Omega} \prod_{t=1}^{n} p(s_t \mid s_{t-1}) p(x_t \mid s_t)$$

(15)

The likelihood of an action that generates s* can be computed either using uni-gram or bi-gram model as below:

$$L(\psi_i) = \arg \max_{\psi \in \Psi} p(\psi) \prod_{t=1}^{n} p(s_t^* \mid \psi_i) \, \text{uni-gram}$$

(16)

$$L(\psi_i) = \arg \max_{\psi \in \Psi} p(\psi) \prod_{t=1}^{n} p(s_t^* \mid s_{t-1}^*, \psi_i) \, \text{bi-gram}$$

(17)

GVD decoding only requires about $1/L$ computational resources of what is required by ASVD.

Maximum Likelihood Decoding

Both ASVD and GVD require memory to buffer previous frames for Viterbi search. A decoding method that does not require buffering can be devised by searching for the sequence of most likely states/postures rather than the most likely sequence of states (Viterbi path), i.e.

$$s^* = \arg \max_{s_t \in \Omega} \prod_{t=1}^{n} p(x_t \mid s_t)$$

(18)

The likelihood of an action to generate the path s* can be calculated using either Eq.(16) or Eq.(17).

In all, there are five different decoding schemes: 1) Action Specific Viterbi Decoding (ASVD); 2) Uni-gram with Global Viterbi Decoding (UGVD); 3) Bi-gram with Global Viterbi Decoding (BGVD); 4) Uni-gram with Maximum Likelihood Decoding (UMLD); and 5) Bi-gram with Maximum Likelihood Decoding (BMLD)

Construction of the Action Graph

Construction of the action graph from training samples involves the establishment of the posture models Λ and all transitional matrices for G. The set of postures Ω should be ideally derived from the kinematics and kinetics of human motion, however, such a set of postures are yet to be researched, In this chapter, we propose to automatically learn Ω from the training samples. A simple approach is to group the samples into M clusters.

Posture Models p(x|s)

Let $_J$ be the total number of observations (poses) in the training samples for all L actions, $d(x_i, x_j)$ be a function measuring the dissimilarity between the observations x_i and x_j, where $d(x_i, x_j) = d(x_j, x_i)$. A posture represents a set of similar poses. Considering the temporal nature of the human motion, we measure the similarity between two poses in terms of joint shape and motion, rather than shape or motion alone as used in most extant work (Lv & Nevatia, 2007; Wei et al., 2007). Let f_i^{sp} and f_i^{mt} be respectively the shape and motion features extracted from the observation x_i and possibly its neighboring observations. $d_{sp}(f_i^{sp}, f_j^{sp})$ measures the shape dissimilarity of observation x_i and x_j and $d_{mt}(f_i^{mt}, f_j^{mt})$ measures the motion dissimilarity. The overall dissimilarity of two observations is defined as the product of their motion and shape dissimilarity, i.e.

$$d = d_{sp} * d_{mt} \qquad (19)$$

The choices of the dissimilarity measurements, $d_{sp}(\cdot)$ and $d_{mt}(\cdot)$, depend on the selection of the features, f_i^{sp} and f_i^{mt}. In later this chapter, we will present specific forms of f_i^{sp}, f_i^{mt} and the two dissimilarity functions when the observations are silhouettes.

Let $D = [d_{ij}]_{i,j=1}^{J}$ be the dissimilarity matrix of all pairs of the $_J$ observations, where D is a $J \times J$ similarity matrix. The J observations are then clustered into M clusters by employing a pair-wise clustering algorithm which takes the dissimilarity matrix of every pair of samples to be clustered. Choices of such a clustering algorithm include Normalized Cuts (NCuts) (J. Shi & Malik, 2000) and Dominant Sets (DS) (Pavan & Pelillo, 2007). In this chapter, we adopt the traditional Non-Euclidean Relational Fuzzy (NERF) C-Means (Hathaway & Bezdek, 1994). The NERF C-means is derived from conventional Fuzzy C-means specifically for the pair-wise clustering where

the dissimilarity measurement does not follow Euclidean properties. It finds the M clusters by minimizing the following objective function.

$$J_{NERF} = \sum_{i=1}^{M} \frac{\sum_{j=1}^{J} \sum_{k=1}^{J} u_{ij}^m u_{ik}^m d_{jk}^2}{\sum_{j=1}^{J} u_{ij}^m} \qquad (20)$$

where $u_{ij} \in [0, 1]$ is the membership value of the j'th observation belonging to i'th cluster and $\sum_{i=1}^{M} u_{ij} = 1$; $m > 1$ is a fuzzifier.

After the clustering, $p(x \mid s)$, $\forall s \in \Psi$ has to be estimated from the clustered observations. Gaussian mixture models (GMMs) are fitted using the expectation and maximization (EM) algorithm to represent the statistical distributions of the shape and motion features of the observations belonging to the same posture cluster to obtain a compact representation of the posture models.

Let

$$p_{sp}(f^{sp} \mid s) = \sum_{k=1}^{C^{sp}} \pi_{k,s}^{sp} g(f^{sp}; \mu_{k,s}^{sp}; \Sigma_{k,s}^{sp}) \qquad (21)$$

$$p_{mt}(f^{mt} \mid s) = \sum_{k=1}^{C^{mt}} \pi_{k,s}^{mt} g(f^{mt}; \mu_{k,s}^{mt}; \Sigma_{k,s}^{mt}) \qquad (22)$$

denote, respectively, the GMM with C^{sp} components for shape and C^{mt} components for motion, where s represents salient posture/state s or cluster of the silhouettes, $g(\cdot)$ is a Gaussian function; f^{mt} represents the motion feature vector; $\mu_{k,s}^{mt}$ is the mean motion vector of the k'th Gaussian for salient posture s; $\Sigma_{k,s}^{mt}$ is the covariance of the motion features; f^{sp} represents the shape features; $\mu_{k,s}^{sp}$ is the center of the k'th Gaussian for state s; $\Sigma_{k,s}^{sp}$ is a covariance matrix; $\pi_{k,s}^{sp}$ and $\pi_{k,s}^{mt}$ are the mixture proportion, $\sum_{k=1}^{C^{sp}} \pi_{k,s}^{sp} = 1$ and $\sum_{k=1}^{C^{mt}} \pi_{k,s}^{mt} = 1$

The posture model can then be defined as

$$p(x \mid s) = p_{mt}(f^{mt} \mid s)p_{sp}(f^{sp} \mid s) \qquad (23)$$

where x is an observation, f^{mt} and f^{sp} represent respectively the motion and shape features extracted from x.

Estimation of Transitional Probabilities

With the posture models, the action graph is built by linking the postures with their transitional probabilities. Given the statistical independence assumptions introduced previously and the posture models, we estimate the action specific and global transitional probability matrices, $\{A_i\}_{i=1}^{L}$ and A, from the training samples as follows:

$$p(\omega_i \mid \omega_j) = \frac{\sum_{t=1}^{J} p(\omega_i \mid x_t)p(\omega_j \mid x_{t-1})}{\sum_{t=1}^{J} p(\omega_i \mid x_t)} \qquad (24)$$

$$p(\omega_i \mid \omega_j, \psi_l) = \frac{\sum_{t=1}^{J_l} p(\omega_i \mid x_t, \psi_l)p(\omega_j \mid x_{t-1}, \psi_l)}{\sum_{t=1}^{J_l} p(\omega_i \mid x_{t-1}, \psi_l)} \qquad (25)$$

where J is the total number of training silhouettes for all the actions and J_l is the number of silhouettes contained in the training samples for action ψ_l. The marginalization of $p(\omega_i|\omega_j)$ and $p(\omega_i|\omega_j, \psi_l)$ gives the estimation of $p(\omega_i)$ and $p(\omega_i|\psi_l)$ respectively.

Expansion of the Action Graph

Obtaining training data of human actions can be costly and tedious (Zheng, Li, Ogunbona, Dong, & Kharitonenko, 2006, 2007). On the other hand, to retain all the training data for retraining in the future would be impractical. It is desirable that a trained system, whenever needed, be expanded with new actions without a need for retraining the entire system. Our representation of the action graph and GMM postures enables this expan-

sion. In this section, we present an algorithm to add a new action to an existing system without compromising the recognition of the previous learned actions.

Let $\Gamma = (\Omega, \Lambda, G, \Psi)$ be the system that has been trained for L actions. Assume that a new action ψ_{L+1} is required to be added to Γ. The new action ψ_{L+1} has K training sequences of observations, $\{y_t^k\}, k = 1, \cdots, K; t = 1, \cdots, T_k$, where T_k is the number of observations in the k'th training sequence. When the new action is included into the system, it is in general expected that both the action graph and postures need to be updated. In order to minimize the impact to the existing system and also considering that K is usually small in practice, it is reasonable and probably necessary to limit the update to the following three operations: insertion of new postures required to describe ψ_{L+1}, modification of A, and insertion of A_{L+1}. Let's consider the following two cases:

- *Ω has all the postures that are required to describe action ψ_{L+1}. In this case, postures should be shared and only new paths are required to be inserted into the action graph by updating A and A_{L+1}.*
- *Ω does not have all postures that are needed to describe action ψ_{L+1}. Therefore, new postures have to be created for ψ_{L+1} and the action graph needs to be expanded by updating A and A_{L+1}.*

As seen, the key issue is how to judge whether new postures are required and how to create them if required. A simple approach is to find the salient postures for the new action first and, then, decide whether these postures have already been learned in the system by comparing the new postures to those residing in the existing system. Following this idea, we propose an algorithm for adding the new action ψ_{L+1} to Γ.

1. *Clustering the samples of the new action into* m *postures,* $\Omega' = \{\omega_1', \omega_2', \cdots, \omega_m'\}$ whose prototypes are $\Lambda' = \{p'(x \mid \omega_1'), p'(x \mid \omega_2'), \cdots, p'(x \mid \omega_m')\}$ using the same method as the one used in the system construction.

2. *For each new posture,* $\omega_i', i = 1, 2, \cdots, m$, Compare it with each posture in Ω. If ω_i' is similar *to any one of the posture in Ω, then discard* ω_i'. Otherwise, keep it in Ω'.

3. Set Ω^{new} as the union of Ω and Ω', and let Λ^{new} be the posture models of Ω^{new}.

4. *Estimate the transitional probabilities,* A_{L+1} *and* A' *from the K training samples for* ψ_{L+1} based on Λ^{new}. Update A *as follows:*

$$A^{new} = (1 - \beta) * A + \beta * A', \qquad (26)$$

where $\beta \in (0, 1)$ is a weighting factor controlling the contribution of the new action samples to the global transition. Since the number of training samples, K, for the new action would be small compared to the number of samples used to train A, A' is often much less reliable than A, therefore, we limit the contribution of A' to the final global transitional probabilities by the factor of β, which should reflect the ratio of size of the new training samples to the size of the samples used to estimate A.

Similarity Between Postures

Since postures are modeled by GMMs for both motion and shape, the similarity between two postures can be measured by Kullback–Leibler divergence. We adopt the variational estimation of KL-divergence recently proposed by Hershey and Olsen (Hershey & Olsen, 2007).

The KL-divergence between two GMMs, p and p', can be calculated as follows.

$$KL(p \| p') = \sum_a \pi_a \log \frac{\sum_{a'} \pi_{a'} e^{-D(g_a \| g_{a'})}}{\sum_b \pi_b e^{-D(g_a \| g_b)}} \qquad (27)$$

where $D(g \mid g')$ is the KL-divergence between two Gaussians of dimension d, g *and* g',

$$D(g(f; \mu; \Sigma) \| g(f'; \mu'; \Sigma'))$$
$$= [\log \frac{\det(\Sigma')}{\det(\Sigma)} + tr(\Sigma^{-1}\Sigma) - d + (\mu - \mu')\Sigma'^{-1}(\mu - \mu')]$$

$$(28)$$

s' *will be discarded if the following condition is met*

$$(KL_{mt} - \overline{KL}_{mt}) < \alpha_{mt} * \sigma_{KL_{mt}}$$

or

$$(KL_{mt} - \overline{KL}_{mt}) < \alpha_{mt} * \sigma_{KL_{mt}}$$
$$(KL_{sp} - \overline{KL}_{sp}) < \alpha_{sp} * \sigma_{KL_{sp}}$$

or

$$(KL_{sp} - \overline{KL}_{sp}) < \alpha_{sp} * \sigma_{KL_{sp}} \qquad (29)$$

where KL_{mt} and KL_{sp} are the KL-divergences for motion and shape. $\overline{KL}_{mt}$, $\sigma_{KL_{mt}}$, $\overline{KL}_{sp}$ and $\sigma_{KL_{sp}}$ are the means and standard deviations of the KL divergences of all pairs of postures in the system before updating; $\alpha_{mt} \in (0, 1]$ *and* $\alpha_{sp} \in (0, 1]$ are constants.

Estimation of A_{L+1}

Estimation of A_{L+1} is critical to the recognition of the new action ψ_{L+1}. When the number *of training samples is small, it's likely that the training samples only capture a small proportion of possible posture transition that are associated with the new action. This phenomenon is called "rare events" in learning grammars in speech recognition. Often,* A_{L+1} will not be a reliable estimation of the true transition. Research in speech (Beccehetti & Ricotti, 2002; Huang, Acero, & Hon, 2001) has suggested many strategies, known as smoothing, to compensate the small number of samples. Here, we adopt a simple and linear model to smooth A_{L+1}.

$$p(s_i \mid s_j, \psi_{L+1}) = (1 - e^{-p(s_j, s_i, \psi_{L+1})}) \frac{p(s_j, s_i, \psi_{L+1})}{p(s_j, \psi_{L+1})} + e^{-p(s_j, s_i, \psi_{L+1})} p(s_i, \psi_{L+1})$$

(30)

where s_i, $s_j \in \Omega^{new}$ and $p(s_i, s_j, \psi_{L+1})$ is the joint probability of being in posture s_i when the previous posture is s_j. Eq.(30) is actually an interpolation of bi-gram and uni-gram transitional probabilities. For unseen events, the transitional probability is set to be the uni-gram probability of the second posture of the bi-gram. Giving too much weight to uni-gram probability may result in faulty estimation if s_i is very frequent. Therefore, the value of the weight decreases exponentially with the number of bi-gram observations.

A SILHOUETTE-BASED ACTION RECOGNITION SYSTEM

In this section, we present a silhouette based action recognition system using the proposed graphical model and some experimental results. To construct a system $\Gamma = (\Omega, \Lambda, G, \Psi)$ from a set of training silhouette sequences requires the extraction of shape and motion descriptors (features) from the silhouettes and definition of the shape and motion dissimilarities between two silhouettes so as to the silhouettes can be clustered.

Shape Features and Dissimilarity

There are many shape descriptors available as mentioned previously. For the sake of scale invariance and noise tolerance, we choose a set of points on the silhouette contour after scale normalization as the shape descriptor. As shown in Figure 2(b), the contour of a silhouette is first normalized and then resampled to a small number of points with two purposes: noise and computation reduction.

Let $f_i^{sp} = \{y_1^i, y_2^i, \cdots, y_b^i\}$ and $f_j^{sp} = \{y_1^j, y_2^j, \cdots, y_b^j\}$ be the shapes described by a set of b points on the contours of silhouettes x_i and x_j respectively, their dissimilarity is defined as

$$d_{sp} = \frac{1}{1 + e^{-a(d_h(f_i^{sp}, f_j^{sp}) - c)}}$$

(31)

where $d_h(X, Y)$ is the Hausdorff distance between two sets X and Y; a and c are two constants.

Figure 2. Feature extraction. (a) A typical silhouette; (b) Normalized and resampled points of the contour; (c) The ellipse fitted to the contour and gravity center.

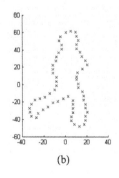
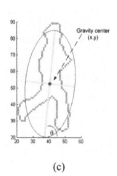

(a)   (b)   (c)

Motion Features and Dissimilarity

Motion features include the change of the orientation of the entire body and the local motion of its gravity center. The orientation of the body is estimated by fitting an ellipse into the silhouette shape and measured as the angle (anticlockwise) between the horizontal axis and the major axis of the fitted ellipse as shown in Figure 2(c).

Let $f_i^{mt} = \{\delta x_i, \delta y_i, \delta\theta_i\}$ and $f_j^{mt} = \{\delta x_j, \delta y_j, \delta\theta_j\}$ be the motion feature vectors of silhouettes x_i and x_j respectively, where $(\delta x, \delta y)$ is the locomotion of the gravity center and $\delta\theta$ is the change of the orientation. The dissimilarity of the x_i and x_j in terms of motion is measured as follows.

$$d_{mt} = \frac{1}{1 + e^{-a(corr(f_i^{mt}, f_j^{mt}) - c)}} \tag{32}$$

where $corr(\cdot, \cdot)$ represents correlation.

Posture Model $p(x \mid s)$

To estimate the posture model $p(x \mid s)$, a Gaussian mixture model (GMM) is fitted to the shape component to represent the spatial distribution of the contours of the silhouettes belonging to the same posture cluster, as shown in Figure 3, and one Gaussian is fitted to its motion component.

Let

$$p_{sp}(y \mid s) = \sum_{k=1}^{C} \pi_{k,s} N(y; \mu_{k,s}; \Sigma_{k,s}) \tag{33}$$

$$p_{mt}(f^{mt} \mid s) = N(f^{mt}; \mu_{mt,s}; \Sigma_{mt,s}) \tag{34}$$

be respectively the GMM with C components for shape and the Gaussian for motion, where s represents salient posture/state s or cluster of the silhouettes, $N(\cdot)$ is a Gaussian function; f^{mt} represents the motion feature vector; $\mu_{mt,s}$ is the mean motion vector for salient posture s; $\Sigma_{mt,s}$ is a 3×3 matrix denoting the covariance of the motion features; y represents the 2D coordinates of a point on the contours of silhouettes; $\mu_{k,s}$ is the center of the kth Gaussian for state s; $\Sigma_{k,s}$ is a 2×2 covariance matrix; $\pi_{k,s}$ is the mixture proportion, $\sum_{k=1}^{C} \pi_{k,s} = 1$.

The posture model can then be defined as

$$p(x \mid s) = p_{mt}(f^{mt} \mid s) \prod_{i=1}^{b} p_{sp}(y_i \mid s) \tag{35}$$

Figure 3. GMM representation of a salient posture (a) The contours of a silhouette cluster; (b) The GMM fitted to the contours in (a)(each ellipse represents one Gaussian component).

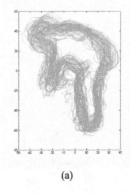

(a)

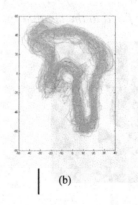

(b)

where x is a silhouette, f^{mt} and y_i represent respectively the motion feature and the $i'th$ point on the resampled contour of x.

Experimental Results

Datasets

We evaluated our model on the most widely used Weizmann dataset created (Blank et al., 2005). The dataset contains 93 low resolution video (188×144, 25 fps) sequences for ten actions. These ten actions are *run, walk, wave with one hand, wave with two hands, galloping sideway, jumping-in-place, jumping, jumping jack, bend and skip*. Nine subjects played each action once (with an exception that one subject played three actions twice). Silhouettes were obtained using simple background subtraction in color space. Global motion was removed by fitting quadratic function to the trajectory of the gravity centers. This dataset is currently the most realistic and challenging one publicly available compared to those employed in other papers (e.g. (Veeraraghavan, Chellappa, & Roy-Chowdhuryh, 2006)). Some silhouettes are noisy as shown in Figure 4. Action *walk* and *jumping-in-place* appears very similar to action *galloping sideway* and *jumping* respectively when the global motion is removed from the silhouettes.

Experimental Setup

As adopted in most previous works (Blank et al., 2005; Gorelick et al., 2007; L. Wang & Suter, 2007; Ali, Basharat, & Shah, 2007) using the same dataset, we conducted leave-one-sample-out test to verify the overall performance of the proposed model. To evaluate its robustness against various factors including the dependence on subjects, viewpoints, action speed and styles and video capturing environment, we also conducted the following experiments:

- **Leave-one-subject-out test**;
- **Robust test** against viewpoints and action styles for action *walk* using the sequences designed by Blank et al. (Blank et al., 2005; Gorelick et al., 2007); and,
- **Cross-dataset test.** In this test, we trained an action graph using Weizmann dataset and employed the action graph to recognize 68 sequences of actions *walk* and *run* extracted from the video sequences included in the KTH dataset (Laptev & Lindeberg, 2003).

To test the algorithm for learning new actions, we intentionally left one action out when training the system and, then, added this action into the system using the proposed method. Recognition of the new actions and the impact on the performance of the system with respect to recognizing previously trained actions were evaluated.

Figure 4. Examples of nosy silhouettes

203

In all experiments, silhouette contours were sampled to 64 points after normalization and GMMs with 32 spherical Gaussians were fitted to the shape of the contours. In the learning of new actions, both α_{sp} and α_{mt} were set to 0.3 and β was set to the ratio of the number of frames in the training samples for the new action to the number of frames in the sequences used to train the existing system. The following summarizes the experimental results.

Results

Leave-One-Sample-Out Test

In the leave-one-sample-out test, each sample was taken as the test sample and the residual samples were used as training samples to train the action graph. Recognition rate was calculated over all the actions in the dataset. Figure 5(a) shows the recognition rates of the five decoding schemes vs. number of postures, M. As expected, the two bi-gram decoding schemes (BMLD & BGVD) outperformed the two uni-gram schemes (UMLD

& UGVD). The ASVD consistently outperformed both uni-gram and bi-gram decoding schemes for all M. Notice that the recognition rates of all decoding methods increase as the number of of postures increases. When M $\geq$ 20, the recognition rates are all above 90%. When $M = 45$, the recognition rates of BMLD, BGVD and ASVD have reached 97.8%, which are comparable to the best rates (96.5%~100%) obtained in (Blank et al., 2005; Gorelick et al., 2007; L. Wang & Suter, 2007) and better than the rate (92.6%) achieved in (Ali et al., 2007). It has to be pointed that in (Blank et al., 2005; Gorelick et al., 2007; L. Wang & Suter, 2007) all training samples were kept and K-NN was employed to classify the actions.

Leave-One-Subject-Out Test

In the leave-one-sample-out test, the training dataset contained the samples of other actions performed by the same subject. This certainly helps the action graph to capture the styles of the postures performed by the subject and therefore benefits recognition. In the leave-one-subject-out test, we purposely took all samples performed

Figure 5. Recognition rates vs. number of postures. (a) Leave-one-sample-out test; (b) Leave-one-subject-out test

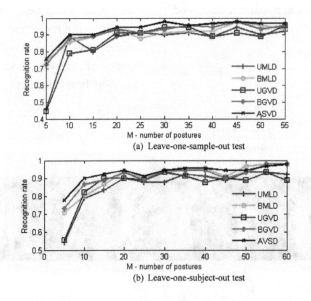

by the same subject as the test samples and the samples performed by other subjects as the training samples. In other words, the trained action graph did not have any knowledge about the test subject. In addition, there was less number of training samples compared to the leave-one-sample-out test. Figure 5(b) shows the recognition rates of the five decoding schemes vs. number of postures, *M*. The curves demonstrate similar patterns to those of the leave-one-sample-out test. BMLD, BGVD and ASVD achieved recognition accuracies of 97.8% at *M* = 60.

Table 1 shows the number of correct decoding (out of 9) for each action. As seen, *Jumping* and *Jumping-in-place* are the most challenging actions to recognize. Both uni-gram decoding schemes had some difficulties to recognize them and the BGVD and ASVD misclassified once the actions *Jumping* and *Jumping-in-place* to actions *skip* and *side* respectively.

Since both leave-one-sample-out test and leave-one-subject-out test have shown that bi-gram and action specific Viterbi decoding schemes are preferred to the uni-gram decoding schemes,

we excluded the uni-gram decoding schemes from the following experiments.

Robustness Test

Together with the action Weizmann dataset, Blank et al. (Blank et al., 2005) also supplied additional 20 samples of the action *walk* captured from ten different viewpoints (0 degrees to 81 degrees relative to the image plan with steps of 9 degrees) and ten different styles from zero degree viewpoint (normal, walking in a skirt, carrying briefcase, limping man, occluded Legs, knees Up, walking with a dog, sleepwalking, swinging a bag and occluded by a "pole"). We trained an action graph with 30 postures using the 93 samples (from about zero degree viewpoint) for the ten actions (none of the 20 *walk* samples were included in the training data), BMLD, BGVD and ASVD all recognized most samples and only failed to recognize the actions in the cases of 72 and 81 degree viewpoints. For different walking styles, "Occluded by a pole" was excluded in the test since the silhouettes in this case consist of disconnected regions and our method assumes

Table 1. The number of correct decoding (out of 9) for each type of actions in leave-one-subject-Out test when the number of postures is 60.

	UMLD	BMLD	UGVD	BGVD	ASVD
Run	9	9	8	9	9
Walk	9	9	9	9	9
One-hand-wave	8	9	8	9	9
Two-hands-wave	9	9	9	9	9
Galloping-sideway	8	9	8	9	9
Jumping-in-place	8	8	6	8	8
Jumping	5	8	5	8	8
Jumping-jack	9	9	9	9	9
Bending	9	9	9	9	9
Skip	9	9	9	9	9
Overall Accuracy (%)	92.22	97.8	91%	97.8	97.8

the silhouette is a connected region. Among the rest 9 different styles, BMLD, BGVD and ASVD only failed to recognize the "*moonwalk*" (walking with arms being raised to the horizontal position). It is probably not unreasonable to consider the "*moonwalk*" as another type of action.

Cross-Dataset Test

We further evaluated the robustness of the proposed model by conducting a cross-dataset test. In this test, we trained an action graph using Weizmann dataset and employed it to recognize the action samples from a different dataset. We chose the KTH dataset (video sequences) (Laptev & Linde-berg, 2003). The dataset comes as uncompressed video sequences with spatial resolution of 160 × 120 pixels and comprises six actions (*walking, jogging, running, boxing, hand waving* and *hand clapping*) performed by 25 subjects. Each subject performed each action in four different scenarios: 0 degree viewpoint, scale variations (from different viewpoints with the subject gradually approaching to or departing from the camera), different clothes

(e.g. big pullovers or trench coats) and lighting variations. Two of the six actions, *walking* and *running*, overlap with the actions of Weizmann dataset. We implemented a simple median filtering based background modeling to extract the silhouettes. Since many sequences have severe jitter, the median filter failed to extract the silhouettes. Nevertheless, we managed to extract 36 samples of action *walk* and 32 samples of action *run*. These samples were performed by six different subjects. Figure 6 are a few examples of the extracted silhouettes. It can be seen that the silhouettes are noisy and, in Figure 6(d), the subject wore a trench coat that distorted the silhouette shape. Table 2 is the number of recognition errors (out of 68) vs. number of postures and Table 3 shows the confusion matrices. As seen, the recognition rates are over 95% for BMLD, BGVD and ASVD when the number of postures is *60* and most misclassifications happened between action *run* and action *skip*. Notice that BMLD and BGVD performed better than ASVD. This is probably because ASVD is less generalized than BMLD and BGVD.

Table 2. Cross-dataset Test: recognition errors (out of 68) vs. number of postures for BMLD, BGVD and ASVD

# of Postures/Decoding method	20	30	45	60
BMLD	11	5	1	0
BGVD	11	8	2	2
ASVD	14	7	5	3

Table 3. Confusion matrices for BMLD, BGVD and ASVD when the number of postures is 60. A1 though A10 represent actions Run, Walk, One-hand-wave, Two-hand-wave, Galloping-sideway, Jumping-in-place, Jumping, Jumping-jack, Bending and Skip.

		A1	A2	A3	A4	A5	A6	A7	A8	A9	A10
BMLD	A1	32	0	0	0	0	0	0	0	0	0
	A2	0	36	0	0	0	0	0	0	0	0
BGVD	A1	31	0	0	0	0	0	0	0	0	1
	A2	0	35	0	0	1	0	0	0	0	0
ASVD	A1	29	0	0	0	0	0	0	0	0	3
	A2	0	36	0	0	0	0	0	0	0	0

Figure 6. Sample silhouette sequences from KTH dataset. (a) and (b) "walk"; (c) and (d) " run"

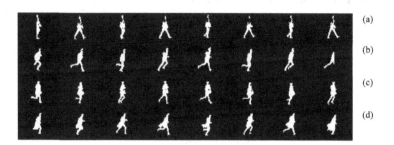

Learning New Actions

With respect to learning new actions, we first evaluated the significance of *smoothing*. Table 4 shows the recognition error rates of the new action for the cases of sharing postures vs. not sharing postures and smoothing vs. not smoothing when the number of training samples for the new action is only **one**. In sharing, we forced the algorithm not to create any new postures. In the case of not sharing, the algorithm was forced to create three new postures specifically for the new action. In each test, one sample of the action was used as training sample and the rest samples of the same action were used as test samples. The errors showed in the figure were averaged over all actions and all samples in each action. It is apparent that sharing and smoothing significantly reduced the recognition errors and are essential to learning a new action. Notice that, in the case of not sharing, the ASVD scheme is equivalent to the conventional methods where the model for each action is trained independently. It is obvious that our method outperforms the conventional ones.

Figure 7(a) is the recognition errors of the added new action against the number of training samples. Surprisingly, the BMLD constantly outperformed BGVD and ASVD. On average, we achieved over 85% recognition rate for the new action even there were only 3~4 training samples. When the number of training samples reached 8, the recognition rate was improved to over 95%

We also evaluated the impact on the recognition of previously learned actions when a new action was added. We trained a system by leaving one action out and tested the trained system against the training samples at $M = 30$. In all cases, the training samples were recognized without any error. We then added the left-out action to the system using the proposed method. The new system was evaluated against the samples used for training the previous system. Errors were recorded. Figure 7(b) shows the averaged errors over all actions when the number of training samples for the new action was 3 and 4. The error rates are around 0.1% for all of the bi-gram decoding schemes. In other

*Table 4. Study on the importance of sharing postures and smoothing transitional probabilities. The percentages shown in the table are the recognition error rates of the new action. The rates were averaged over all cases when **one of the actions** is considered as a new action and added to the system with 20 salient postures. Only **one training sample** was used for the new action.*

	BMLD	BGVD	ASVD
Smoothing, not sharing	50%	57%	53%
Sharing, not smoothing	47%	49%	40%
Sharing and smoothing	27%	32%	33%

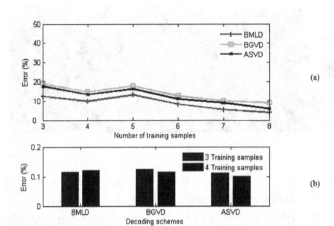

Figure 7. Learning new actions (a) Overall recognition rates of new actions vs. number of postures; (b) Impact on the existing system when a new action is added

words, the system was only degraded on average by 0.1% for the previously trained actions after it was updated with a new action.

DISCUSSION AND CONCLUSION

Recognition of human actions is still in its infancy compared to other extensively studied topics like human detection and tracking. This paper has presented a graphical model of human actions and GMM modeling of postures. Experiments have verified that the proposed model is robust against the subjects who perform the actions, tolerant to noisy silhouettes and, to certain degree, viewpoints and action styles. Most importantly, it is scalable and expandable through adaptive sharing of postures. The scalability and expandability are desirable features for any action recognition systems, but these have rarely been studied before.

Our experiments have demonstrated that on average about 3 to 5 postures per action were required to model the actions in the dataset. The average number of postures per action indicates the average length of the action paths in the graph. It is also noticed that an action graph of 30 postures that encodes the ten actions has sparse global and action-specific transitional probability matrices.

In other words, many paths in the graph have not been utilized. This leaves much room for the action graph to be expanded with new actions. For an action graph with M postures that encodes L actions, there are on average $M^{M/L}$ paths with M/L postures. For instance, there are about $30^3 = 27000$ paths with 3 postures in an action graph of $M=30$ and $L=10$, offering a large capacity to encode a large number of actions and their variations. In addition, the proposed graphical model is easy to train with a small number of samples thanks to the sharing of the postures amongst the actions.

Several decoding schemes have been studied. It is found that there is no significant difference in performance between the decoding scheme Bi-gram with Maximum Likelihood Decoding (BMLD) and Bi-gram with Global Viterbi Decoding (BGVD). Action Specific Viterbi Decoding (ASVD) can outperform BMLD and BGVD when there are sufficient training samples, but the gain in the performance is at the expense of more computational complexity with less flexibility for continuous decoding of actions.

Furthermore, the proposed model of actions opens a number of theoretical and practical questions to be researched. For instance, what is the optimal number of postures for a given set of actions and desired expandability, and how can the postures be learned from the samples such that the recognition errors can be minimized?

REFERENCES

Achard, C., Qu, X., Mokhber, A., & Milgram, M. (2008). A novel approach for recognition of human actions with semi-global features. *Machine Vision and Applications*, *19*(1), 27–34. doi:10.1007/s00138-007-0074-2

Ahmad, M., & Lee, S.-W. (2006). Human action recognition using multi-view image sequences features. In *Proc 7'th conf. on AFGR* (pp. 523-528).

Ahmad, M., & Lee, S.-W. (2008). Human action recognition using shape and CLG-motion flow from multi-view image sequences. *Pattern Recognition*, *41*(7), 2237–2252. doi:10.1016/j.patcog.2007.12.008

Albu, A., Beugeling, T., Virji-Babul, N., & Beach, C. (2007). Analysis of irregularities in human actions with volumetric motion history images. In *IEEE workshop on motion and video computing (WMVC)* (pp. 16-16).

Ali, S., Basharat, A., & Shah, M. (2007). Chaotic invariants for human action recognition. In *Proc. Intl. Conf. on Computer Vision (ICCV 2007)* (pp. 1-8).

Babua, R. V., & Ramakrishnan, K. (2004). Recognition of human actions using motion history information extracted from the compressed video. *Image and Vision Computing*, *22*, 597–607. doi:10.1016/j.imavis.2003.11.004

Beccehetti, C., & Ricotti, L. P. P. (2002). *Speech recognition: Theory and C++ implementation.* Hoboken, NJ: John Wiley & Sons.

Belongie, S., Malik, J., & Puzicha, J. (2002). Shape matching and object recognition using shape contexts. *IEEE Trans. PAMI*, *24*(4), 509–522.

Bishop, C. M. (2006). *Pattern recognition and machine learning.* New York: Springer.

Blank, M., Gorelick, L., Shechtman, E., Irani, M., & Basri, R. (2005). Actions as space-time shapes. In *Proc. Intl. Conf. on Computer Vision (ICCV 2005)* (pp. 1395-1402).

Bobick, A., & Davis, J. (2001). The recognition of human movement using temporal templates. *IEEE Trans. PAMI*, *23*(3), 257–267.

Brand, M., & Kettnaker, V. (2000). Discovery and segmentation of activities in video. *IEEE Trans. PAMI*, *22*(8), 844–851.

Brand, M., Oliver, N., & Pentland, A. (1997). Coupled hidden Markov models for complex action recognition. In *Proc. Intl. Conf. on Computer Vision (CVPR 1997)* (pp. 994-999).

Carlsson, S., & Sullivan, J. (2001). Action recognition by Shape Matching to Key Frames. In *Workshop on Models versus Exemplars in Computer Vision.*

Chen, D.-Y., Liao, H.-Y. M., & Shih, S.-W. (2006). Continuous human action segmentation and recognition using a spatio-temporal probabilistic framework. In *Proc. of the eighth IEEE Intl. Symposium on Multimedia* (pp. 1-8).

Chen, D.-Y., Liao, H.-Y. M., & Shih, S.-W. (2007). Humnn action reocgnition using 2-D spatio-temporal templates. In *Proc. IEEE Intl. Conf. on Multimedia and Expo (ICME 2007)* (pp. 667-670).

Colombo, C., Comanducci, D., & Del Bimbo, A. (2007). Compact representation and probabilistic classification of human actions in videos. In *Proc IEEE conf. advanced video and signal based surveillance (AVSS 2007)* (pp. 342-346).

Cuntoor, N., Yegnanarayana, B., & Chellappa, R. (2008). Activity modeling using event probability sequences. *IEEE Transactions on Image Processing*, *17*(4), 594–607. doi:10.1109/TIP.2008.916991

Davis, J. W., & Tyagi, A. (2006). Minimal-latency human action recognition using reliable-inference. *Image and Vision Computing*, *24*(5), 455–472. doi:10.1016/j.imavis.2006.01.012

Dollar, P., Rabaud, V., Cottrell, G., & Belongie, S. (2005). Behavior recognition via sparse spatio-temporal features. In *2nd joint IEEE international workshop on visual surveillance and performance evaluation of tracking and surveillance* (pp. 65-72).

Fathi, A., & Mori, G. (2008). Action recognition by learning mid-level motion features. In *IEEE conf. on Computer Vision and Pattern Recognition (CVPR 2008)* (pp. 1-8).

Fujiyoshi, H., & Lipton, A. (1998). Real-time human motion analysis by image skeletonization. In *Proc. fourth IEEE workshop on applications of computer vision* (pp. 15-21).

Galata, A., Johnson, N., & Hogg, D. (2001). Learning variable-length Markov models of behaviour. *Computer Vision and Image Understanding*, *81*, 398–413. doi:10.1006/cviu.2000.0894

Gavrila, D. M. (1999). The visual analysis of human movement: A survey. *Computer Vision and Image Understanding*, *73*(1), 82–98. doi:10.1006/cviu.1998.0716

Gorelick, L., Blank, M., Shechtman, E., Irani, M., & Basri, R. (2007). Actions as space-time shapes. *IEEE Trans. PAMI*, *29*(12), 2247–2253.

Green, R. D., & Guan, L. (2004). Quantifying and recognizing human movement patterns from monocular video images part i: A new framework for modeling human motion. *IEEE Transactions on Circuits and Systems for Video Technology*, *14*(2), 179–190. doi:10.1109/TCSVT.2003.821976

Hathaway, R., & Bezdek, J. (1994). NERF C-means: non-Euclidean relational fuzzy clustering. *Pattern Recognition*, *27*, 429–437. doi:10.1016/0031-3203(94)90119-8

Hershey, J. R., & Olsen, P. P. A. (2007). Approximating the Kullback Leibler divergence between Gaussian mixture models. In *Proc ICASSP 2007* (Vol. 4, pp. 317-320).

Hu, M. (1962). Visual pattern recognition by moment invariants. *I.R.E. Transactions on Information Theory*, *8*(2), 179–187. doi:10.1109/TIT.1962.1057692

Hu, W., Tan, T., Wang, L., & Maybank, S. (2004). A survey on visual surveillance of object motion and behaviors. *IEEE Trans. SMC-C*, *34*(3), 334–351.

Huang, X., Acero, A., & Hon, A.-W. (2001). *Spoken language processing: A guide to theory, algorithm and system development*. Prentice Hall.

Kellokumpu, V., Pietikainen, M., & Heikkila, J. (2005). Human activity recognition using sequences of postures. In *Proc IAPR conf. machine vision applications* (pp. 570-573).

Kendall, D., Barden, D., Carne, T., & Le, H. (1999). *Shape and shape theory*. New York: Wiley.

Laptev, I., & Lindeberg, T. (2003). Space-time interest points. In *Proc. Intl. Conf. on Computer Vision (ICCV 2003)* (pp. 432-439).

Laptev, I., & Perez, P. P. (2007). Retrieving actions in movies. In *Proc. Intl. Conf. on Computer Vision (ICCV 2007)* (pp. 1-8).

Li, W., Zhang, Z., & Liu, Z. (2008a). Expandable data-driven graphical modeling of human actions based on salient postures. *IEEE Transactions on Circuits and Systems for Video Technology*, *18*(11), 1499–1510. doi:10.1109/TCSVT.2008.2005597

Li, W., Zhang, Z., & Liu, Z. (2008b). Graphical modeling and decoding of human actions. In *Proc. IEEE 10th international workshop on multimedia signal processing (MMSP '08)*.

Liu, J., Ali, S., & Shah, M. (2008). Recognizing human actions using multiple features. In *IEEE conf. on Computer Vision and Pattern Recognition (CVPR 2008)* (pp. 1-8).

Liu, J., & Shah, M. (2008). Learning human actions via information maximization. In *IEEE conf. on Computer Vision and Pattern Recognition (CVPR 2008)* (pp. 1-8).

Lv, F., & Nevatia, R. (2007). Single view human action recognition using key pose matching and viterbi path searching. In *IEEE conf. on Computer Vision and Pattern Recognition (CVPR 2007)*.

Manning, C. D., & Schtze, H. (1999). *Foundations of statistical natural language processing*. Cambridge, MA: MIT Press.

Mendoza, M. A., & de la Blanca, N. P. (2008). Applying space state models in human action recognition: A comparative study. In *Articulated motion and deformable objects* (LNCS 5098, pp. 53-62).

Meng, H., Freeman, M., Pears, N., & Bailey, C. (2008). Real-time human action recognition on an embedded, reconfigurable video processing architecture. *Journal of Real-Time Image Processing, 3*(3), 163–176. doi:10.1007/s11554-008-0073-1

Moeslund, T. B., & Granum, E. (2001). A survey of computer vision-based human motion capture. *Computer Vision and Image Understanding, 81*, 231–268. doi:10.1006/cviu.2000.0897

Moeslund, T. B., Hilton, A., & Kruger, V. (2006). A survey of advances in vision-based human motion capture and analysis. *Computer Vision and Image Understanding, 104*(2-3), 90–126. doi:10.1016/j.cviu.2006.08.002

Mokhber, A., Achard, C., & Milgram, M. (2008). Recognition of human behavior by space-time silhouette characterization. *Pattern Recognition, 29*(1), 81–89. doi:10.1016/j.patrec.2007.08.016

Natarajan, P., & Nevatia, R. (2008). Online, real-time tracking and recognition of human actions. In *IEEE workshop on motion and video computing (WMVC)* (pp. 1-8).

Niebles, J. C., Wang, H., & Fei-Fei, L. (2008). Unsupervised learning of human action categories using spatial-temporal words. *International Journal of Computer Vision, 79*(3), 299–318. doi:10.1007/s11263-007-0122-4

Oliver, N., Garg, A., & Horvits, E. (2004). Layered representations for learning and inferring office activity from multiple sensory channels. *Computer Vision and Image Understanding, 96*, 163–180. doi:10.1016/j.cviu.2004.02.004

Pavan, M., & Pelillo, M. (2007). Dominant sets and pairwise clustering. *IEEE Trans. PAMI, 29*(1), 167–172.

Pierobon, M., Marcon, M., Sarti, A., & Tubaro, S. (2005). Clustering of human actions using invariant body shape descriptor and dynamic time warping. In *Proc. IEEE AVSS 2005* (pp. 22-27).

Rabiner, L. R. (1989). A tutorial on hidden Markov models and selected applications in speech recognition. *Proceedings of the IEEE, 77*(2), 257–286. doi:10.1109/5.18626

Rodriguez, M., Ahmed, J., & Shah, M. (2008). Action mach a spatio-temporal maximum average correlation height filter for action recognition. In *IEEE conf. on Computer Vision and Pattern Recognition (CVPR)* (pp. 1-8).

Savarese, S., DelPozo, A., Niebles, J., & Fei-Fei, L. (2008). Spatial-temporal correlations for unsupervised action classification. In *IEEE workshop on motion and video computing (WMVC)* (pp. 1-8).

Shechtman, E., & Irani, M. (2005). Space-time behavior based correlation. In *IEEE conf. on Computer Vision and Pattern Recognition (CVPR 2005)* (Vol. 1, pp. 405-412).

Shi, J., & Malik, J. (2000). Normalised cuts and image segmentation. *IEEE Trans. PAMI, 22*(8), 888–905.

Shi, Q., Wang, L., Cheng, L., & Smola, A. (2008). Discriminative human action segmentation and recognition using semi-markov model. In *IEEE conf. on Computer Vision and Pattern Recognition (CVPR 2008)* (pp. 1-8).

Sminchisescu, C., Kanaujia, A., Li, Z., & Metaxas, D. (2005). Conditional models for contextual human motion recognition. In *Proc. Intl. Conf. on Computer Vision (ICCV 2005)* (Vol. 2, pp. 808-815).

Veeraraghavan, A., Chowdhury, A. R., & Chellappa, R. (2004). Role of shape and kinematics in human movement analysis. In *IEEE conf. on Computer Vision and Pattern Recognition (CVPR 2004)* (Vol. 1, pp. 730-737).

Veeraraghavan, A., Chellappa, R., & Roy-Chowdhuryh. (2006). The function space of an activity. In *IEEE conf. on Computer Vision and Pattern Recognition (CVPR 2006)*.

Wang, L., & Suter, D. (2007). Learning and matching of dynamic shape manifolds for human action recognition. *IEEE Transactions on Image Processing, 16*, 1646–1661. doi:10.1109/TIP.2007.896661

Wang, Y., Jiang, H., Drew, M. S., Li, Z.-N., & Mori, G. (2006). Unsupervised discovery of action classes. In *IEEE conf. on Computer Vision and Pattern Recognition (CVPR 2006)* (pp. 1-8).

Wei, Q., Hu, M., Zhang, X., & Luo, G. (2007). Dominant sets-based action recognition using image sequence matching. In *Proc. Intl. Conf. on Image Processing (ICIP 2007)* (Vol. 6, pp. 133-136).

Wilson, A., & Bobick, A. (1998). Recognition and interpretation of parametric gesture. In *Proc. Intl. Conf. on Computer Vision (ICCV 1998)* (pp. 329-336).

Wu, Y.-C., Chen, H.-S., Tsai, W.-J., Lee, S.-Y., & Yu, J.-Y. (2008). Human action recognition based on layered-hmm. In *Proc. IEEE Intl. Conf. on Multimedia and Expo (ICME 2008)* (pp. 1453-1456).

Yamato, J., Ohya, J., & Ishii, K. (1992). Recognizing human action in time-sequential images using hidden Markov model. In *IEEE conf. on Computer Vision and Pattern Recognition (CVPR 1992)* (pp. 379-385).

Yilmaz, A., & Shah, M. (2005). Actions sketch: a novel action representation. In *IEEE conf. on Computer Vision and Pattern Recognition (CVPR 2005)* (Vol. 1, pp. 984-989).

Zatsiorsky, V. M. (1997). *Kinematics of human motion.* Champaign, IL: Human Kinetics Publishers.

Zheng, G., Li, W., Ogunbona, P., Dong, L., & Kharitonenko, I. (2006). Simulation of human motion for learning and recognition. In A. Sattar & B. Kang (Eds.), *LNAI 4304* (pp. 1168-1172). New York: Springer.

Zheng, G., Li, W., Ogunbona, P., Dong, L., & Kharitonenko, I. (2007). Human motion simulation and action corpus. In V. Duffy (Ed.), *Digital human modeling,* (LNCS 4561, pp. 314-322). New York: Springer.

Chapter 11
Detection and Classification of Interacting Persons

Scott Blunsden
European Commission Joint Research Centre, Italy

Robert Fisher
University of Edinburgh, UK

ABSTRACT

This chapter presents a way to classify interactions between people. Examples of the interactions we investigate are: people meeting one another, walking together, and fighting. A new feature set is proposed along with a corresponding classification method. Results are presented which show the new method performing significantly better than the previous state of the art method as proposed by Oliver et al. (2000).

INTRODUCTION

This chapter presents an investigation into classification of multiple person interactions. There has been much previous work identifying what activity individual people are engaged in. (Davis and Bobick, 2001) used a moment based representation based on extracted silhouettes and (Efros et al., 2003) modeled human activity by generating optical flow descriptions of a person's action. Descriptions were generated by first hand-tracking an individual, re-scaling to a standard size and then taking the optical flow of person's actions over several frames. A database of these descriptions

was created and matched to novel situations. This method was extended by (Robertson, 2006) who also included location information to help give contextual information to a scene. Location information is of assistance when trying to determine if someone is loitering or merely waiting at a road crossing. Following on from flow based features (Dollar et al., 2005) extracted spatial-temporal features to identify sequences of actions.

Ribeiro and Santos-Victor (2005) took a different approach to classify an individual's actions in that they used multiple features calculated from tracking (such as speed, eigenvectors of flow) and selected those features which best classified the person's actions using a classification tree with each branch using at most 3 features to classify the example.

DOI: 10.4018/978-1-60566-900-7.ch011

The classification of interacting individuals was studied by Oliver et al. (2000) who used tracking to extract the speed, alignment and derivative of the distance between two individuals. This information was then used to classify sequences using a coupled hidden Markov model (CHMM). Liu and Chua (2006) expanded the two person classification to three person sequences using a hidden Markov model (HMM) with an explicit role attribute. Information derived from tracking was used to provide features such as the relative angle between two persons to classify complete sequences. Xiang and Gong (2003) again used a CHMM to model interactions between vehicles on an aircraft runway. These features are calculated by detecting significantly changed pixels over several frames. The correct model for representing the sequence is determined by the connections between the separate models. Goodness of fit is calculated by the Bayesian information criterion. Using this method a model representing the sequence's actions is determined.

Multi-person interactions within a rigid formation was also the goal of (Khan and Shah, 2005) who used a geometric model to detect rigid formations between people, such an example would be a marching band. Intille and Bobick (2001) used a pre-defined Bayesian network to describe planned motions during American football games. Others such as Perse et al. (2007) also use a pre-specified template to evaluate the current action being performed by many individuals. Pre-specified templates have been used by Van Vu et al. (2003) and Hongeng and Nevatia (2001) within the context of surveillance applications.

SPECIFICALLY WHAT ARE WE TRYING TO DO?

Given an input video sequence the goal is to automatically determine if any interactions are taking place between two people. If any are taking place then we want to identify the class of the interaction. Here we limit ourselves to pre-defined classes of interaction. To make the situation more realistic there is also a 'no interaction' class. We seek to give each frame this label from this predefined set. For example a label may be that person 1 and person 2 are walking together in frame 56.

The ability to automatically classify such interactions would be useful in cases which are typical of many surveillance situations. Such an ability to automatically recognize interactions would also be useful in video summarization where it could be possible to focus only on specific interactions.

FEATURES AND VARIABLES

Video data is rich in information with the resolution of modern surveillance cameras capable of delivering megapixel resolution at a sustained frame rate of greater than 10fps. Such data is overwhelming and mostly unnecessary for classification of interactions. As a first step, tracking of the individuals is employed. There is a rich body of work on tracking of people and objects within the literature. See the review by Yilmaz et al. for a good survey of current tracking technology (Yilmaz, A et al. 2006). For all experiments performed in this chapter the bounding box method of tracking a person was used. The positional information was calculated based upon the centre of this box. This process is illustrated in Figure 1. Such tracking information is typical of the output of many tracking procedures and it will be assumed that such a tracker is available throughout all experiments carried out in this chapter.

Here three types of features are used as input to a classifier. We make use of movement, alignment and distance based features. More details are given in the following sections.

Figure 1. Bounding box tracking- Colored lines show the previous position of the centre of the tracked object; Images adapted from the CAVIAR dataset (EC Funded CAVIAR.. (2004))

Movement Based features

Movement plays an important role in recognizing interactions. The speed s_i^t of an individual is calculated as shown in equation (1.1). The double vertical bar ($\|..\|$) represents a vector L2 norm.

$$s_i^t = \frac{\left\| \mathbf{p}_i^t - \mathbf{p}_i^{t-w} \right\|}{w} \qquad (1.1)$$

Here $\mathbf{p}_i^t$ refers to the position of the tracked object at time t for object i. Within this work only the two dimensional ($\mathbf{p}_i^t = \left[x_i^t, y_i^t \right]$) case is considered due to tracking information only being available in two dimensions. The temporal offset w is introduced due to the high rates which typify many modern video cameras. With frame rates of around 25 frames per second this can mean that differences between the current and last frame (w=1) are very small and may be dominated by noise. The difference in speed $\hat{s}_i^t$ is given by the difference between the speed at time t and time t-w.

The absolute difference in speed ($\varepsilon_{i,j}^t$) between two tracks is also calculated ($\left| s_i^t - s_j^t \right|$). The vorticity ($v_t^i$) is measured as a deviation from a line. This line is calculated by fitting a line to a set of previous positions of the trajectory $\mathbf{P}_i^t = \left[\mathbf{p}_i^{t-w}, .., \mathbf{p}_i^t \right]$. The window size w is the same as that used in equation

(1.1). At each point the orthogonal distance to the line is found. The total distance of all points are then summed and normalized by window length and so give a measure of the vorticity.

Alignment Based Features

The alignment of two tracks can give valuable information as to how they are interacting. The degree of alignment is common to Gigerenzer et al. (1999), Oliver et al. (2000) and Liu and Chua (2006) who all make use of such information when classifying trajectory information. To calculate the dot product the heading ($\mathbf{h}$) of the object is taken as in equation (1.2) and the dot product (1.3) is calculated from the directions of tracks i and j.

$$\hat{\mathbf{h}}_i^t = \frac{\mathbf{p}_i^t - \mathbf{p}_i^{t-w}}{\left\| \mathbf{p}_i^t - \mathbf{p}_i^{t-w} \right\|} \qquad (1.2)$$

$$a_{i,j}^t = \hat{\mathbf{h}}_i^t \cdot \hat{\mathbf{h}}_j^t \qquad (1.3)$$

In addition to the alignment between two people the potential intersection ($\gamma_t^{i,j}$) of two trajectories is also calculated. Such features are suggested in (Gigerenzer et al., 1999) and (Liu and Chua, 2006). We first test for an intersection of the headings. To achieve this, a line intersection test is performed (the lines are determined by fitting a line to prior positions as done in the previous section). If the lines intersect then we check that the people are both heading towards the point of intersection (as the lines are undirected). The feature $\gamma_{i,j}^{t}$ has a value of 1 if an intersection is possible or a 0 value if it is not.

Distance Based Features

Distance is a good measure for many types of interaction, for example meeting is not possible without being in close physical proximity. First the Euclidean distance is taken and is used as given in equation (1.4) below.

$$d_{i,j}^{t} = \left\| \mathbf{p}_i^t - \mathbf{p}_j^t \right\| \qquad (1.4)$$

The derivative of the distance was also calculated. This is the difference in distance at contiguous time steps. It is calculated as shown in equation (1.5) below.

$$\hat{d}_{i,j}^{t} = \frac{\sum_{t-w}^{t} d_{i,j}^{t}}{w} \qquad (1.5)$$

An instantaneous measure such as the distance and the derivative of the distance can both be prone to short term tracking errors. In an effort to remove this effect a window size containing w points was averaged (as in $\mathbf{P}_i^t$ in the previous section). The distance was calculated for every point (as in equation (1.4)) in this window.

Final Feature Vector

The final feature vector for each pair of people is given in equation (1.6) below:

$$\mathbf{r}_{i,j}^{t} = \left[s_i^t, s_j^t, \hat{s}_i^t, \hat{s}_j^t, \varepsilon_{i,j}^t, a_{i,j}^t, d_{i,j}^t, \hat{d}_{i,j}^t, v_i^t, v_j^t, \gamma_{i,j}^t \right]$$

$$(1.6)$$

The vector between persons i and j at time t is made up of the speed of each person (s_i^t, s_j^t) and the change in speed $\hat{s}_i^t, \hat{s}_j^t$ along with the difference in speed $\varepsilon_{i,j}^t$. The alignment, distance and change in distance at a particular point in time is given by $a_{i,j}^t, d_{i,j}^t$ and $\hat{d}_{i,j}^t$. The vorticity at a particular point in time for each person is given by v_i^t, v_j^t whilst the possibility of an intersection between two trajectories is given by $\gamma_{i,j}^t$. This gives a final feature vector containing 11 elements. A further processing step of normalizing the training data to have zero mean and unit variance was also taken.

Observation Window Size

Throughout these experiments we investigated the impact of varying the number of video frames used before making a decision as to what is happening within the frame. Figure 2 (below) shows how this is achieved. Throughout this work we used information from before and after the current frame in order to classify it. Typically the frames relate to a small quantity of time (1-2 seconds) and help with the lag problem when the decision is biased by the large amount of previous information used in the classification. The window size variation throughout this work is equivalent to a few seconds delay. This was not foreseen as a problem if such an approach was taken in a real surveillance application. The fact that there would be a lag in classification if making use of only previous information seems an appropriate trade-off for an increase in accuracy.

CLASSIFICATION

This section introduces the classifiers which are used throughout subsequent experiments. We make use of a simple linear discriminate classifier (LDA) which is non-probabilistic and provides a baseline for performance. This is introduced in

Figure 2. The frame to classify (t) uses information from w frames around the current frame in order to classify the frame

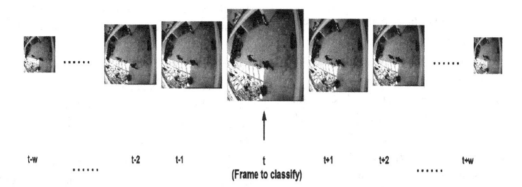

the next section. We then briefly introduce the hidden Markov model (HMM) which is widely used throughout the literature. We then introduce a newer model, the conditional random field (CRF). Finally the previous best method as suggested by Oliver (2000) is briefly reviewed.

Linear Discriminant Classifier

Linear discriminant analysis (LDA) seeks to maximize the objective function given in equation (1.7) below. Here S_W is the within class scatter matrix with S_B being the between class scatter matrix.

$$J(\mathbf{w}) = \frac{\mathbf{w}^T \mathbf{S}_B \mathbf{w}}{\mathbf{w}^T \mathbf{S}_W \mathbf{w}} \quad (1.7)$$

The objective function (equation (1.7)) is often referred to as the signal to noise ratio. What we are trying to achieve is a projection ($\mathbf{w}$) which maximizes the distance of the class means relative to the (sum of) variances of a particular class. To generate a solution it is noted that equation (1.7) has a property whereby it is invariant with respect to scaling of the $\mathbf{w}$ vectors (eg $\mathbf{w} \rightarrow \alpha\mathbf{w}$ where α is some arbitrary scaling). Therefore $\mathbf{w}$ can be chosen such that $\mathbf{w}^T \mathbf{S}_W \mathbf{w} = 1$. It is also common (and indeed the case here) to perform a whitening step (zero mean and unit variance) on the data prior to input into this method.

This maximization can be turned into a regular eigenvalue problem. Projections are found for each class (ie one class vs all others) and the mean and variance ($\mathbf{C}$) of the class projection are found. In order to classify a novel point the new point is projected with S_W^{-1}. The class label is determined by taking the smallest Mahalonobis distance between the calculated class model's mean and variance and the new test point.

Hidden Markov Model

Hidden Markov model's (HMM's) have been introduced by (among others) Rabiner (1990). The model is parameterized by the prior distribution $\prod$ with each element π_i representing $\pi_i = p(x = i)$ across all hidden states $i \in [1, .., N]$. The stationary state transition matrix $\mathbf{A}$ is used to represent the probability of a transition from one state (i) to another (j) through time. An entry within the stochastic matrix $\mathbf{A}$ is referenced by $a_{i,j} = p(x_t = i \mid x_{t-1} = j)$. Within this work we are concerned with continuous real valued inputs ($\mathbf{r}_t$) which can be accommodated within the model by using a Gaussian mixture model to represent the input distribution.

217

$$p(\mathbf{r}_t \mid x_t = j) = \sum_{m=1}^{M} c_{j,m} \mathbf{N}(\mathbf{r}_t, \mu_{j,m}, \mathbf{C}_{j,m}) \quad (1.8)$$

Here the observed data $\mathbf{r}_t$ is the vector being modeled, $c_{j,m}$ is the mixture coefficient for the mth mixture in state j. $\mathbf{N}$ is a Gaussian distribution with mean vector $\mu_{j,m}$ and covariance $\mathbf{C}_{j,m}$ for the mth mixture component in state j. The mixture coefficients c_j, m must sum over all m to 1. The hidden Markov model's parameters can thus be represented as $\lambda = (\Pi, \mathbf{A}, \Theta)$ where Θ represent the parameters of the mixture model.

Conditional Random Field

In this section the workings of a conditional random field (CRF) are explained and then the specific formulation as applied in this chapter is given. The structure of the CRF we use is shown in Figure 3. The CRF can be configured to resemble HMM-like models. However they can be more expressive in that arbitrary dependencies on the observations are allowed. Using the feature functions of the CRF allow any part of the input sequence to be used at any time during the inference stage. It is also possible that different states (classes) can have differing feature functions (though we do not make use of this here). The feature functions describe the structure of the model. The CRF is also a discriminative model whereas the HMM

is a generative one. A potential advantage of the discriminative CRF over generative models is that they have been shown to be more robust to violations of independence assumptions (Lafferty et al., 2001).

The discrete temporal state at a particular timestep t is given by x_t which takes a value from the set of all possible class labels $x \in X = \{1, 2, .., C\}$. Here C is the maximum number of class labels whilst t represents the time with T being the maximum length of the sequence. Observations at time t are denoted as r_t with the joint observations given as $\mathbf{R}_t = (\mathbf{r}_1, .., \mathbf{r}_t)$. Likewise the joint state is given by $\mathbf{X}_t = (x_1, .., x_t)$. For notational compactness we shall refer to $\mathbf{X}_t$ as $\mathbf{X}$ and $\mathbf{R}_t$ as $\mathbf{R}$ in accordance with other author's (Sminchisescu et al.,2005, and Wallach, 2004).

The distribution over joint labels $\mathbf{X}$ given observations $\mathbf{R}$ and parameters θ are given by:

$$p_\theta(\mathbf{X} \mid \mathbf{R}) = \frac{1}{Z_\theta(\mathbf{R})} \prod_{c \in C(\mathbf{X},\mathbf{R})} \phi_\theta^c(\mathbf{X}_c, \mathbf{R}_c) \quad (1.9)$$

Within this equation ϕ_θ^c is a real valued potential function of the clique c and $Z_\theta(\mathbf{R})$ is the observation dependent normalization (sometimes referred to as a partition function). C(**X**,**R**) is the set of maximal cliques.

Here a first order linear chain is used (as shown in Figure 3). The cliques are pairs of neighboring

Figure 3. CRF model-The observations (r) are shown for each timestep; The class label x is also shown

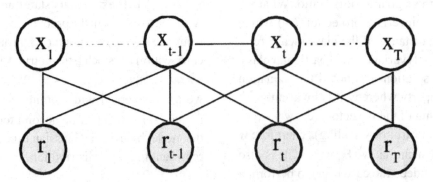

states ($x_t, x_t + 1$), whilst the connectivity among observations is restricted to that shown in the graph (Figure 3- CRF model. The observations (r) are shown for each timestep. The class label x is also shown.). A CRF model with T timesteps, as used here, can be re-written in terms of exponential feature functions F_θ computed in terms of weighted sums over the features of the cliques. This exponential feature formulation is given below in equation (1.10)

$$p_\theta(\mathbf{X} \mid \mathbf{R}) = \frac{1}{Z_\theta(\mathbf{R})} \exp(\sum_{t=1}^{T} F_\theta(x_t, x_{t-1}, \mathbf{R}))$$

(1.10)

The conditional log likelihood of the CRF is given below. Assuming that the training data is fully labeled $\{\mathbf{X}^d, \mathbf{R}^d\}_{d-1,\ldots,D}$ the parameters of the model are obtained by optimization of the following function:

$$L_\theta = \sum_{d=1}^{D} \log p_\theta(\mathbf{X}^d \mid \mathbf{R}^d) = \sum_{d=1}^{D} (\sum_{i=t}^{T} F_\theta(x_t^d, x_{t-1}^d, \mathbf{R}^d) - \log Z_\theta(\mathbf{R}^d))$$

(1.11)

In order to make parameter optimization more stable the problem often makes use of a regularized term (R_θ). The problem then becomes one of optimizing the penalized likelihood ($L_\theta + R_\theta$). The regularizing term used here was chosen to be $R_\theta = -\|\theta\|^2$.

Once trained novel input is given to a CRF model and a probability distribution is given throughout all timesteps for all classes. In this case we choose the highest probability as being the classification label of the new example. A Gaussian prior over the input data was used throughout all experiments.

Oliver's Coupled Hidden Markov Model

Here we briefly cover Oliver's method (Oliver et al., 2000) of classifying interacting individuals. This work is reviewed as it provides a state of the art method to compare our results with. Oliver used coupled hidden Markov models to model five different interactive behaviors.

Oliver's work is used for comparison with the work presented here. Oliver et al. (2000) use two feature vectors (one for each chain, each of which represents one person's behavior). These feature vectors are made up of the velocity of the person, the change in distance between the two people and the alignment between the two people. This gives two feature vectors, one for each chain.

For each class the parameters of a two chain coupled hidden Markov model are trained. When classifying, the model which produces the highest likelihood for a test sequence is taken as the class label.

RESULTS

This section presents the results obtained by using the methods described in the preceding sections. Results using a conditional random field (CRF), hidden Markov model (HMM) and its coupled variation (CHMM) are presented. Results using a linear discriminant model (LDA) are also presented and used as a baseline non-probabilistic method to which results are compared. We present the result of classification over many training and testing subsets to give an indication of the standard deviation and the expected performance when using a method. Results are presented over many different window sizes. The graphs show the averaged performance of the classifier over 50 runs. The standard deviation is given by the shaded regions.

Figure 4. Two people approaching one another

Experimental Setup

The CAVIAR dataset has been previously used in (Dee and Hogg, 2004a, Wu and Nevatia, 2007) however there is not a universally agreed training and testing set. Therefore it was deemed that in order to characterize an algorithm's true performance upon a dataset it should be tested with different subsets of the entire data. This will give an indication of the expected performance of the algorithm rather than finding a particularly good (in terms of classification accuracy) subset.

We are interested in comparing the four methods as described in the previous section. Furthermore the role of time is investigated. We seek to investigate what is the optimal length of time a sequence should be watched before a decision is made. Results comparing each method and the effects of time are given in the following sections.

Throughout the training procedure the testing set was kept separate from the training data and was unseen by the learning algorithm until testing time. Therefore only the training set was used when determining the parameters of the learning model. Training and testing sets were split 50/50 on a per class basis. Partitioning was done per-class rather than over the whole dataset due to the uneven distribution of classes. Such a step means that in the training stage the learning algorithm will have examples of every type of class. We would not

expect a correct classification on unseen classes and so this measure can stop misleading results. In order to show the average performance this procedure was repeated over 50 different partitions of the training and test data.

The dataset contains examples of complete sequences. For example, a sequence consisting of two people walking together may be hundreds of frames long. Our goal is to classify each frame correctly. If we were to take this sequence and split it up as training and testing frames then the classification task would be much simpler as training and testing points would be simply a matter of interpolation between highly similar points. It is for this reason that when deciding on the training and testing data we partition based on the complete sequences. This means that an entire walking together sequence will be assigned to the training set whilst another complete walking together sequence will be assigned to the testing set. This should avoid the pitfall of having training and testing data which is essentially the same. This is especially true as the data has a very strong temporal coupling.

What we are aiming to do is try to give a class label to two interacting individuals. This is shown in Figure 4. The two people are approaching one another. Between the first and second frame the distance between them decreases. The classifier would assign one label for this interaction (covering both people) to indicate 'approaching'.

Classification Results

CAVIAR Dataset

The CAVIAR dataset (EC Funded project CAVI-AR (2004)) contains 11,415 frames with labeled examples of interactions. Within this set there are 5 distinct classes which we seek to identify and classify. The 5 classes consist of examples of people: walking together (2,543), approaching (942), ignoring (4,916), meeting one another (1,801), splitting up (879) and fighting (334). The numbers in brackets indicates how many frames contain this behavior.

Overall results for the dataset are shown in Figure 5. These results are then further broken down and shown for each class in Figure 6, Figure 7 and Figure 8. Graphs are presented showing the averaged performance over 50 runs. These runs consisted of a random partitioning of training and testing data. The shaded areas show the variance of the classification performance. The window size which denotes the amount of information which was used in the classifier is increased along the x axis.

For the smallest window sizes (up until window size 10) the CRF method offers the best overall performance although the HMM method give similar performance. However in this dataset the

Figure 5. Overall results on the CAVIAR dataset for each method; Lines show averaged results (over 50 runs) whilst the shaded regions show one standard deviation

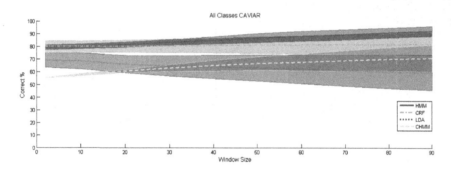

Figure 6. Results on the 'approaching' and 'fighting' class, for the CAVIAR data

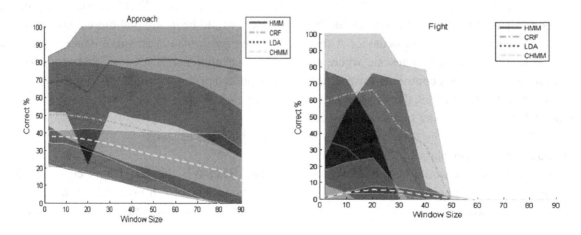

Figure 7. Results on the 'ignore' and 'meet' class, for the CAVIAR data

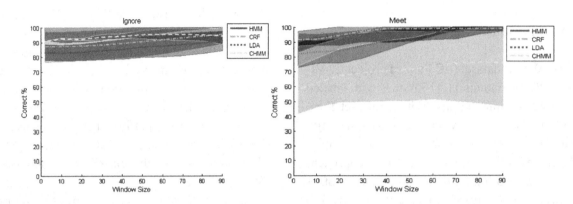

Figure 8. Results on the 'split' and 'walk together' class, for the CAVIAR data

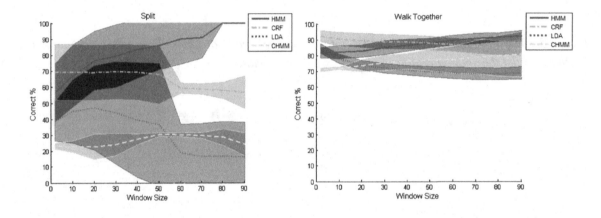

HMM model gives the best possible average performance for window sizes greater than 10. Both the HMM and the CRF using the new proposed features show superior performance to Oliver's method. A particular problem for all methods is in the classification of fighting behavior. A small sample size and the short timescale where any fighting actually occurs contribute towards this. We see that for some cases the window can be too small (such as walking together in the case of the HMM) or too large (such as fighting for all classifiers). A per class time window or an enhanced feature set would help this problem. Table 1 displays the best performing classifier for several window sizes.

One of the other features of this dataset is that for "approaching", "splitting" and "fighting" there were perhaps not enough examples to build a sufficiently generalisable model. A simple answer would be to say that more data is required. However in many real surveillance applications such an approach is not possible so showing how a method performs using only limited data is still of value.

BEHAVE Dataset

The BEHAVE dataset (Blunsden et al. 2007) contains 134,457 frames which have labeled examples of interactions. Within this set there

Table 1. Best performing classifier for 3 different window sizes for the CAVIAR dataset. In some cases there is little difference in performance and so more than one classifier is listed. In the case of fighting larger window sizes give equally poor performance across all classifiers.

Class	w=5	w=50	w=90
All	CRF	HMM	HMM
Approach	HMM	HMM	HMM
Fight	CRF	CRF	Same
Ignore	LDA	LDA	LDA
Meet	HMM/CRF	CRF	HMM/CRF
Split	CRF	HMM	HMM
Walk To-gether	CRF	HMM/CRF	HMM

are 5 distinct classes which we seek to identify and classify. The 8 classes consist of examples of people: "in group" (91,421), "approaching" (8,991), "walking together" (14,261), "splitting" (11,046), "ignoring" (1,557), "fighting" (4,772). The numbers in brackets indicates how many frames contain this behavior.

The overall averaged classification is shown in Figure 9. The CRF clearly performs better than all other methods on this dataset for all window sizes. There is a slight increase in performance when the window size is increased when using a CRF. However the effect is more dramatic for both the CHMM, HMM and the LDA method. All three of these methods (HMM, CHMM, LDA) increase in performance as the window size is increased. Significant performance increases are observed between window sizes of 1 and 20.

Per class results (figures Figure 10, Figure 11 and Figure 12) display a similar story where increasing the window size has little effect upon CRF classification. When classifying splitting, approaching (Figure 10) and fighting (Figure 11) increasing the window size improves the performance of the HMM, CHMM and the LDA classifiers. The HMM classifier gives the best performance of all methods when classifying fighting (Figure 6). Increasing window size also gives a similar increase in performance for both the "in group" classification and the "walking together" class (Figure 12). However when classifying people "in a group" the LDA method decreases in performance. The best performing classifier at window size 5, 50 and 90 is given in Table 2.

Figure 9. Overall performance on the BEHAVE dataset for each method. Lines show averaged results (over 50 runs) whilst the shaded regions show one standard deviation

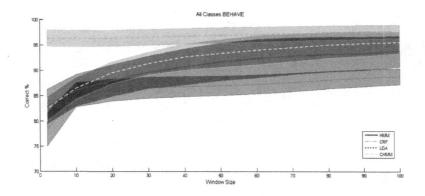

Figure 10. Results on the 'split and 'approach' classes for the BEHAVE dataset

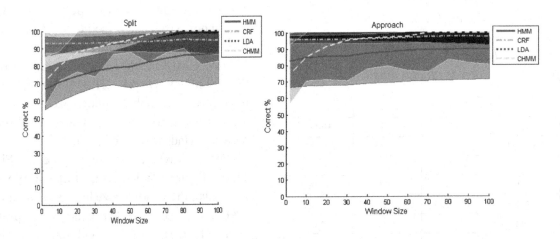

Figure 11. Results on the 'fight' and 'ignore' classes for the BEHAVE dataset

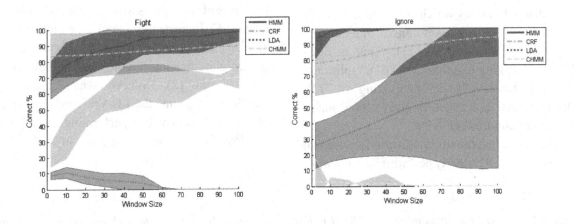

Figure 12. Results on the 'walk together' and 'in group' classes for the BEHAVE dataset

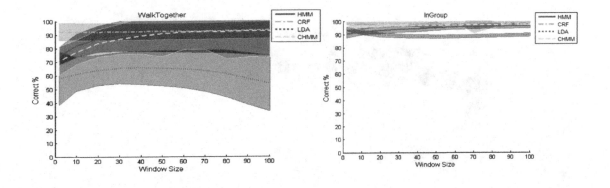

Table 2. Best performing classifier for 3 different window sizes for the BEHAVE dataset. In some cases there is little difference in performance and so more than one classifier is listed.

Class	w=5	w=50	w=90
All	CRF	CRF	CRF
Split	CRF	LDA/CHMM	LDA/CHMM
Approach	LDA	LDA	CHMM
Fight	CRF	HMM	HMM
Ignore	HMM	HMM	HMM
Walk Together	CRF	CRF/HMM/CHMM	CRF/CHMM
In Group	CRF	CRF	CRF

CONCLUSION

Over all datasets the CRF classifier performs well (80-95%) when using limited information. The previous best method suggested by Oliver et al. (2000) is improved upon using the CRF classifier in conjunction with the new proposed feature set. The new proposed feature set also outperforms Oliver's method when using a HMM model for a great many cases.

The CRF classifier displays an ability to better classify data in the short term compared to the HMM. In contrast the HMM model improves more rapidly when the observation window size is increased suggesting it is better at smoothing the signal over longer sequences. The forward algorithm used to determine the likelihood seems to smooth the signal much better than the CRF. In the case of the CHMM the more gradual improvement could be attributable to the larger number of parameters which requires more data in order to represent the data adequately. A suggestion for future work would be therefore to improve the long term temporal model of the CRF that we are using. It should be noted that these comments about the CRF model apply for the single chain structure which is used here. There are many configurations which can be used within the CRF framework. A higher order CRF may produce a better temporal model and so we would expect to see larger improvements when the observa-

tion window size is increased. However a CRF model will always be discriminative compared to the HMM and CHMM's generative ability. The ability to generate samples may be important in certain cases (such as estimating a model's complexity (Gong and Xiang, 2003) however this ability is not required for the classification tasks as presented here.

Throughout all experiments on all of the datasets it is visible that there seems to be an optimal window size for classification of a particular class. For some activities such as fighting in the CAVIAR dataset (Figure 6) the window size is quite short (due to the speed of a fight) whereas for other classes such as the ignore behavior (Figure 7) a longer window size improves performance.

FUTURE WORK

The significance of the role of time within this work has been demonstrated. Future work should seek to exploit this in a principled way. It would also be fruitful to investigate in a principled way automatic feature selection. It would be envisaged that such a procedure could incorporate lots of features and chose them automatically rather than the case here, where it is only possible to use a limited number of features. By having a comparative study of the classifiers on the dataset is also possible to know how much you should rely on them, if, for instance, you were using some classification criteria in feature selection or to establish an optimal time window.

REFERENCES

Blunsden, S., Andrade, E., Laghaee, A., & Fisher, R. (2007). *Behave interactions test case scenarios, EPSRC project gr/s98146*. Retrieved September 6, 2007, from http://groups.inf.ed.ac.uk/vision/BEHAVEDATA/INTERACTIONS/index

Davis, J. W., & Bobick, A. F. (2001). The representation and recognition of action using temporal templates. *IEEE Transactions on Pattern Analysis and Machine Intelligence, 23*(3), 257–267. doi:10.1109/34.910878

Dee, H. M., & Hogg, D. C. (2004, September). Detecting inexplicable behaviour. In *British Machine Vision Conference* (pp. 477–486).

Dollar, P., Rabaud, V., Cottrell, G., & Belongie, S. (2005). Behavior recognition via sparse spatio-temporal features. In *Performance Evaluation of Tracking and Surveillance*, China (pp. 65–72).

ECFunded CAVIAR project/IST. (2004). Retrieved from http://homepages.inf.ed.ac.uk/rbf/CAVIAR/

Efros, A. Berg, A. Mori, G., & Malik, J. (2003). Recognising action at a distance. *Proc. 9th International Conference on Computer Vision, 9*(2), 726–733.

Gigerenzer, G., Todd, P. M., & ABC Research Group. (1999). *Simple Heuristics That Make Us Smart*. Oxford, UK: Oxford University Press.

Intille, S. S., & Bobick, A. F. (2001, March). Recognizing planned, multiperson action. [CVIU]. *Computer Vision and Image Understanding, 81*(3), 414–445. doi:10.1006/cviu.2000.0896

Liu, X., & Chua, C. S. (2006, January). Multi-agent activity recognition using observation decomposed hidden Markov models. *Image and Vision Computing, 2626*(1), 247–256.

Oliver, N. M., Rosario, B., & Pentland, A. P. (2000). A Bayesian computer vision system for modeling human interactions. *IEEE Transactions on Pattern Analysis and Machine Intelligence, 22*(8), 831–843. doi:10.1109/34.868684

Perse, M., Kristan, M., Pers, J., & Kovacic, S. (2006, May). A template-based multi-player action recognition of the basketball game. In J. Pers & D. R. Magee (Eds.), *ECCV Workshop on Computer Vision Based Analysis in Sport Environments*, Graz, Austria (pp. 71–82).

Rabiner, L. R. (1990). A tutorial on hidden Markov models and selected applications in speech recognition. In *Readings in speech recognition* (pp. 267–296). San Francisco, CA: Morgan Kaufmann.

Ribeiro, P., & Santos-Victor, J. (2005, September). Human activities recognition from video: modeling, feature selection and classification architecture. In *Workshop on Human Activity Recognition and Modelling (HAREM 2005 - in conjunction with BMVC 2005)*, Oxford (pp. 61–70).

Robertson, N. M. (2006, June). *Automatic Causal Reasoning for Video Surveillance*. PhD thesis, Hertford College, University of Oxford.

Sminchisescu, C. Kanaujia, A. Li, Z. & Metaxas, D. (2005). Conditional models for contextual human motion recognition. In *International Conference on Computer Vision* (Vol. 2, pp. 1808-1815).

Van Vu, T., Bremond, F., & Thonnat, M. (2003). Automatic video interpretation: A recognition algorithm for temporal scenarios based on precompiled scenario models. In *International Conference on Computer Vision Systems* (Vol. 1, pp. 523-533).

Wallach, H. M. (2004). *Conditional random fields: An introduction*. Technical report, University of Pennsylvania, CIS Technical Report MS-CIS-04-21.

Wu, B., & Nevatia, R. (2007). Detection and tracking of multiple, partially occluded humans by Bayesian combination of edgelet based part detectors. *International Journal of Computer Vision*, *75*(2), 247–266. doi:10.1007/s11263-006-0027-7

Xiang, T., & Gong, S. (2003, October). Recognition of group activities using a dynamic probabilistic network. In *IEEE International Conference on Computer Vision* (Vol. 2, pp. 742–749).

Yilmaz, A., Javed, O., & Shah, M. (2006, December). Object tracking: A survey. *ACM Computing Surveys*, *38*(4), 13. doi:10.1145/1177352.1177355

Chapter 12
Action Recognition

Qingdi Wei
National Laboratory of Pattern Recognition, Institute of Automation, CAS, Beijing, China

Xiaoqin Zhang
National Laboratory of Pattern Recognition, Institute of Automation, CAS, Beijing, China

Weiming Hu
National Laboratory of Pattern Recognition, Institute of Automation, CAS, Beijing, China

ABSTRACT

Action recognition is one of the most active research fields in computer vision. This chapter first reviews the **action recognition** *methods in literature from two aspects: action representation and recognition strategy. Then, a novel method for classifying human actions from image sequences is investigated. In this method, each human action is represented by a sequence of* **shape context** *features of human silhouette during the action, and a* **dominant set**-*based approach is employed to classify the action to the predefined classes. The* **dominant set**-*based approach to classification is compared with K-means, mean shift, and Fuzzy-Cmean approaches.*

1. INTRODUCTION

Action recognition has been extensively studied in the computer vision and pattern recognition community due to its crucial value in numerous applications including video surveillance and monitoring, human-computer interaction, video indexing and browsing. Despite the increasing amount of work done in this field in recent years, human **action recognition** remains a challenging task for several

reasons: (i) it is hard to find a general descriptor for human action, because human body is non-rigid with many degrees of freedom, (ii) the time taken for an action is variable, which poses the problem of action segmentation, (iii) nuisance factors, such as environment, self-occlusion, low quality video and irregularity of camera parameters often cause more difficulties to the problem.

In this chapter, a novel **action recognition** approach is introduced. Unlike traditional methods, it does not require the segmentation of actions. In more detail, first, a set of **shape context** (Serge,

DOI: 10.4018/978-1-60566-900-7.ch012

Jitendra, & Jan, 2002; Wang, Jiang, Drew, Li, & Mori, 2006; de Campos, & Murray, 2006; Ling, & Jacobs, 2007) features are extracted to represent the human action, and then a special clustering approach- **Dominant Set** (Pavan, & Pelillo, 2003; Hu, & Hu, 2006) is employed to cluster action features into an action database. Finally, the testing video sequence is classified by comparing them to the action database.

The rest of the paper is organized as follows. Related work is discussed in Section 2. Section 3 will deal with the major problem, in which action feature and **action recognition** method are respectively presented in Section 3.1 and Section 3.2. Experimental results are shown in Section 4, and Section 5 is devoted to conclusion.

2. RELATED WORK

Generally, there are two main parts in a human **action recognition** system: human action representation and recognition strategy.

Human action representation model is a basic issue in an **action recognition** system. Human contours, shapes (Elgammal, Shet, Yacoob, & Davis, 2003), and silhouettes (Weinland, Boyer, 2008; Cheung, Baker, & Kanade, 2003) of the human body contain rich information about human action. Liu & Ahuja (2004) used shape Fourier descriptors (SFD) to describe each silhouette. Gorelick, Meirav, Sharon, Basri, & Brandt (2006) suggested using Poisson equation to represent each contour. Kale, Sundaresan, Rajagopalan, Cuntoor, Roy-Chowdhury, Kruger, Chellappa, (2004) utilized a vector of widths to reach the same objective. Carlsson, & Sullivan, (2001) extracted shape information from individual frames to construct prototypes representing key frames of the action. Goldenberg, Kimmel, Rivlin, & Rudzsky (2005) adopted principal component analysis (PCA) to extract eigenshapes from silhouette images for behavior classification. Ikizler, & Duygulu (2007) extracted the rectangular regions from a human

silhouette and formed a spatial oriented histogram of these rectangles.

The silhouette-based representations lack time information. To provide time information, Bobick, & Davis (2001) extracted a motion energy image (MEI) and a motion history image (MHI) from image sequences. Later, Zhang, Hu, Chan & Chia (2008) proposed motion context (MC) based on the MHI. Irani and her colleagues (Gorelick, Blank, Shechtman, Irani, & Basri, 2007; Ukrainitz, & Irani, 2006; Caspi, Simakov, & Irani, 2006; Shechtman, & Irani, 2005) analyzed actions by treating a video sequence as a space-time intensity volume. Yilmaz & Shah (2005) used the differential geometric surfaces describing the spatio-temporal action volumes to identify action. Li & Greenspan (2005) represented actions by a 3D spatio-temporal surface, as in (Peixoto, Goncalves, & Araujo, 2002; Wang, Tan, Ning, & Hu, 2003). Another important feature is the space time (ST) interest points and their trajectories for action and activity analysis (Gilbert, Illingworth, & Bowden 2008; Niebles, & Li, 2007; Laptev, & Lindeberg, 2003; Schuldt, Laptev, & Caputo, 2004; Niebles, Wang, &. Li, 2006; Dollar, Rabaud, Cottrell, & Belongie, 2005; Jhuang, Serre, Wolf, & Poggio, 2007). The ST feature does not require any segmentation or tracking of the individual performing the action. Wang & Suter (2007) embedded space-time silhouettes into a low-dimensional kernel-derived space. Jia & Yeung (2008) proposed a local spatio-temporal discriminant embedding (LSTDE) descriptor, to represent the silhouettes. Optical flow (Wang, Tan, et al.; Zhang, Huang, & Tan, 2008) and shape flow (Natarajan, & Nevatia, 2008; Jiang, & Martin, 2008) have similar advantages to the ST feature. The idea is to directly use the optical flow as a basis feature describing action that can be used for recognition.

Action representation based on a single feature is sometimes not enough to capture the action attributes. More reliable results can be obtained from the combination of multiple features based action representation. Schindler, & van Gool,

Figure 1. Examples of video sequences and extracted silhouettes (Adapted from 2007 weizmann action dataset)

(i) *Original Images*

(ii) *Background Subtraction*

(iv) *Contour*

(2008) merged the responses of orientation filters computed densely at each pixel and the optic flow, by simple concatenation. Ke, Sukthankar, & Hebert (2007) used a combination of shape and flow features for event detection in several cluttered scenes. In (Filipovych, & Ribeiro, 2008), Filipovych extracted low-level features: ST and optical flow, and then proposed a method that learned spatio-temporal relationships between descriptive motion parts and the appearance of individual poses. Shi, Wang, Cheng, & Smola, (2008) combined SIFT (Lowe, 2004) and **shape context** (Serge, et al. 2002) to describe foreground object after background subtraction. Chen & Fan, (2008) proposed a hybrid body representation, containing both template-like view information and part-based structural information. Liu, Ali, & Shah,

(2008) fused local spatio-temporal (ST) volumes (or cuboids) and spin-images for improved **action recognition** in videos. Mikolajczyk & Uemura, (2008) used a large number of low dimensional local features such as MSER (Matas, Chum Urban, & Pajdla, 2002) edge segments inspired by pairs of adjacent segments from (Ferrari, Jurie, & Schmid, 2007), Harris- Laplace and Hessian-Laplace (Mikolajczyk, & Schmid, 2003). Laptev & Perez (2007) extracted histograms of spatial gradient and optical flow (Dalal, Triggs & Schmid, 2006; Lucas, & Kanade, 1981) in four discrete motion directions. In (Farhadi, & Tabrizi, 2008; Tran, & Sorokin, 2008), each frame is described by the vertical optical flow, horizontal optical flow, silhouette. Then 5-frame block is projected via PCA to form middle-level action features, and each of the two adjacent neighborhoods is added into the feature.

There are many published papers on recognition strategies, see for example (Lu, & Little, 2006; Veeraraghavan, Roy-Chowdhury, & Chellappa, 2005; Shi, at el. 2008; Mikolajczyk, & Uemura, 2008). Many impressive results have been obtained over the past several years. Recognition strategies can be generally divided into the following three categories.

- **Exemplar based methods:** Labeled exemplars of actions are matched to a test image sequence. The action class is assumed to be the same as the most similar exemplar (Schuldt, at el. 2004; Lu, & Little, 2006; Bobick, & Davis, 2001; Rodriguez, Ahmed, & Shah, 2008). In (Mori, & Malik, 2002), a test shape is matched to each stored exemplar 2D view, using the technique of **shape context** matching in conjunction with a kinematic chain-based deformation model. Weinland, & Boyer, (2008) extracted silhouettes of human body, and selected the key-pose as exemplars.
- **Direct sequence matching:** Among this category, the most typically methods are Dynamic Time Warping (DTW) (Veeraraghavan, at el. 2005), Hausdorff distance (Masoud, & Papanikolopoulos, 2003), and spatiotemporal correlation (Efros, Berg, Mori, & Malik, 2003) on time-varying features without further feature extraction;
- **State space methods:** Classical state space models include Hidden Markov Models (HMMs), Autogressive Moving Average (ARMA) (Veeraraghavan, at el. 2005), Conditional Random Fields (CRFs) (Sminchisescu, Kanaujia, Li, & Metaxas, 2005; Crivelli, Piriou, Bouthemy, Cernuschi-Frías, & Yao, 2008), Finite State Machine(FSM)(Natarajan, & Nevatia, 2008; Zhao, & Nevatia, 2002) and their

variations (Nguyen, Phung, Venkatesh, & Bui, 2005; Sminchisescu, Kanaujia, Li, & Metaxas, 2005), semi-Markov model (Shi, at el. 2008), switching hidden semi-Markov model (S-HSMM) (Duong, Bui, Phung, & Venkatesh, 2005), 1-Nearest Neighbor with Metric Learning (Tran, & Sorokin, 2008), ActionNets (Lv, & Nevatia, 2007), and LDCRF (Morency, Quattoni, & Darrell, 2007). Wang, & Suter, (2007) presented the use of FCRF in the vision community, and demonstrated its superiority to both HMM and general CRF. Ning, Xu, Gong, & Huang, (2008) improved the standard CRF model for continuous **action recognition**, by replacing the random field with a latent pose estimator. Boiman, & Irani, (2005) proposed a graphical Bayesian model which describes the motion data using hidden variables that correspond to hidden ensembles in a database of spatio-temporal patches. Vitaladevuni, Kellokumpu, & Davis, (2008) presented a Bayesian framework for **action recognition** through ballistic dynamics.

3. A NOVEL ACTION RECOGNITION METHOD

The symbols used in this chapter are defined. Denote $S = \{s_t\}_{t=1}^{T}$ as the input sequence, where each s_t is an image at time t. The purpose of **action recognition** is to find a function $f: f(S) = c$ that classifies a given sequence into a certain action $c \in C = \{1, ..., n_c\}$, where C is a set of actions in which we are interested.

To give a clear view, the flow chart of the **dominant set** based recognition method is shown in Figure 2. The method is composed of a training phase and a testing phase. The main parts of training phase and testing phase are list as follows. A more detailed description is given in the following sections.

Training Phase:

- **Step 1:** Preprocess the video sequences to obtain contours of the moving region.
- **Step 2:** Extract **shape context** features from each contour.
- **Step 3:** Cluster features in each sequence to get image classes, which form a sample database.
- **Step 4:** Count the frequency of each image class in each action class to obtain the priori probability.

Testing Phase:

- **Step 1:** Preprocess test video sequences to obtain contours of the moving region.
- **Step 2:** Extract **shape context** features from each contour.
- **Step 3:** Classify features according to the frequency map of image class to the action class.

3.1. Action Feature

The contour of the moving region is obtained by preprocessing. This objective could be realized by many methods, e.g. background subtraction (Stauffer, & Grimson, 1999), border following (Suzuki, & Abe, 1985) and optical flow (Lucas, & Kanade, 1981). Here, a background subtraction algorithm is used to obtain foreground region (See Figure 2).

After obtaining the contour of the foreground region, a **shape context** descriptor is adopted to describe the human contour. **Shape context** on point l is a matrix sc_l, which describes local distribution around the point, as shown in Figure 3. For human contour at each moment, its length varies with the distance to camera, camera parameters and different postures. Thus, we sample $L=50$ points from the contour to normalize the length of contour. For the same reason, when calculating SC, the distances between landmark points are also normalized by Equation(1),

$$\hat{d}_{i,j} = \frac{d_{i,j} \times L(L+1)}{\sum_{i=1}^{L}\sum_{j=1}^{L} d_{i,j}} \qquad (1)$$

Figure 2. Flow chart of our action recognition method

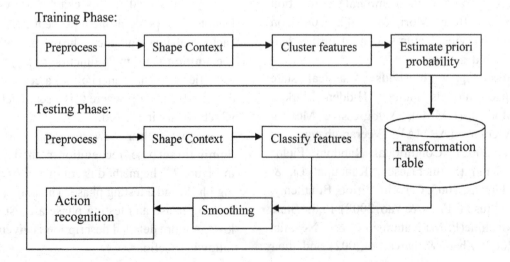

232

where $d_{i,j}$ is the Euclidean distance between point i to point j. When calculating **shape context** on one point, the 0 degree direction is the tangent direction, as a result, the shape context is robust to rotation. But in the **action recognition**, the same pose with different angles from the ground conveys different information. Hence, we need **shape context** to be sensitive to rotation when it is used in **action recognition**. For each point, its coordinate axes are based on image instead of tangent direction (Figure 3). So the contour is represented by a discrete set $SC = \{sc_l\}_{l=1}^{L}$, of L points sampled from the external contours, and the image sequence is represented by $ims = \{SC_i\}_{i=1}^{n}$.

In addition, the robustness of **shape context** to rotation is also guaranteed by its matching technique (Jitendra, & Jan, (2001). The core of this matching technique is to find the 'best' matching point on the second shape for each point on the first shape. In this chapter, a similar but simple and effective method is chosen for **action recognition**. The lowest left point on the contour is taken as the starting point of SC sequence for matching.

3.2. Clustering

In the training phase, the feature samples are clustered by a spectral clustering technique- **Dominant set**, because of its high purity results.

Dominant set, proposed by Pavan and Pelillo (Pavan, & Pelillo, 2003), is a new graph-theoretic approach for clustering and segmentation which performs well in practice. A set of data points $\{p_1, \ldots, p_n\}$ to be clustered can be represented as an undirected edge-weighted graph without self-loop $G = (V, E)$, where $V = \{v_1, \ldots, v_n\}$ is the vertex set and $E \subseteq V \times V$ is the weighted edge set with edge-weight w_{ij}. Vertices in G correspond to data points, edges represent neighborhood relationships, and edge-weight w_{ij} reflects the similarity between point i and point j: $w_{ij} = \exp(-dis(x_i, x_j)/(2\sigma^2))$, $dis(\cdot,\cdot)$ is the distance metric and the Euclidean distance is used in our approach. Then we represent the graph G by an $n \times n$ symmetric affinity matrix $A = (a_{ij})$, which is defined as:

$$a_{ij} = \begin{cases} w_{ij} & \text{if } (i, j) \in E \\ 0 & \text{otherwise} \end{cases}$$

Figure 3. (a) original image (b) background subtraction (c) contour (d) shape context of a point of the contour (e) each shape context is a log-polar histogram of the coordinates of the rest of the point set measured using the reference point as the origin(Dark=large value).

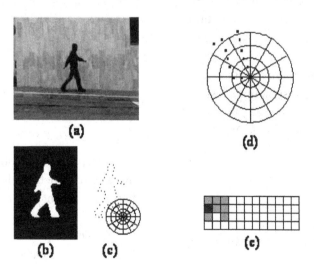

The "**dominant set**" is defined as follows: provided that $W(S) > 0$ for any non-empty $S \subseteq D$, and that D is a non-empty subset of vertices, $D \subseteq V$, D would be dominant if:

1. $w_D(i) > 0$, for all $i \in D$
2. $w_{D \cup \{i\}}(i) < 0$, for all $i \notin D$

$$(2)$$

where $W(D)$ denotes the total weight of D:

$$W(D) = \sum_{i \in D} w_D(i) \tag{3}$$

and $w_D(i)$ is a function of the weights on the edges of the subgraph induced by D.

Pavan, & Pelillo, (2003) proved that finding a "**dominant set**" is equivalent to solve a quadratic program:

$$\begin{aligned} \text{maximize} \quad & f(u) = \frac{1}{2} u^T A u \\ \text{subject to} \quad & u \in \Delta \end{aligned} \tag{4}$$

where

$$\Delta = \{u \in \mathbb{R}^n : u_i \geq 0 \text{ and } \sum_{i=1}^n u_i = 1\}$$

and A is the symmetric affinity matrix. If there exists u^*, a strict local solution of the optimization problem in Equation(4), C_{u^*} is equivalent to a **dominant set** of the graph, where $C_u = \{i : u_i > 0\}$. In addition, the local maximum $f(u)$ indicates the "cohesiveness" of the corresponding cluster.

Replicator equation can be used to solve the optimization problem in Equation(4):

$$u_i(t+1) = u_i(t) \frac{(Au(t))_i}{u(t)^T A u(t)} \tag{5}$$

The **dominant set** clustering algorithm is shown in Table 3, which shows the kth iteration

of clustering process. A **dominant set** is split out from the current graph in each iteration, until the rest of graph can not generate any **dominant set**. The number of clusters K is therefore automatically determined.

To group any new samples after the clustering process has taken place, Pavan and Pelillo proposed an out-of-sample extension for **dominant set** clustering (Pavan, & Pelillo, 2004). We adopt the idea to classify a new sample p^{new}. Given a new sample p^{new} and $\bigcup_{k=1}^K \{S^k, u^k, f(u^k)\}$ of a trained database, which is the output of Algorithm 3, we first construct an affinity vector a which represents the distance between p^{new} and n existing samples. And the assignment algorithm is shown in Table 1. k^* is the cluster to which p^{new} belongs.

3.3. Recognition

In this chapter, the recognition task is conducted as follows. A set of image classes are obtained by the step 3 in training phase. Since an image class is rarely comprised of images belonging to the same action class, it is reasonable to count the frequencies of an image class appearing in each action class, and then estimate the probability transformation T:

$$image\ class\ i \rightarrow \begin{cases} action\ class\ 1 & p_{i1} \\ \vdots & \vdots \\ action\ class\ n & p_{in} \end{cases} \tag{6}$$

where

$$\sum_{j=1}^n p_{ij} = 1$$

In step 3 of the testing phase, each image in the test sequence is classified by Dominant-Set Fast Assignment Algorithm to get an image class sequence. Then the transformation is applied to the image class sequence: *action class sequence = T (image class sequence)*. Action class sequence is

Table 1. Dominant-set fast assignment algorithm

Algorithm 1: Dominant-Set Fast Assignment Algorithm
Input: Affinity vector $a \in \mathbb{R}^{n \times 1}, \bigcup_{k=1}^{K} \{S^k, u^k, f(u^k)\}$
1. $\dfrac{w_{S^k \cup \{p^{new}\}}(p^{new})}{W(S^k \cup \{p^{new}\})} = \dfrac{\left\|S^k\right\| - 1}{\left\|S^k\right\| + 1}\left(\dfrac{a^T u^k}{f(u^k)} - 1\right)$ for all $k \in \{1, ..., K\}$
2. if $w_{S^{k^*} \cup \{p^{new}\}}(p^{new}) > 0$, then assign p^{new} to cluster S^{k^*}
3. Return: (k*)
Output: k*

Table 2. Smooth algorithm

Algorithm 2: Smooth Algorithm
Input: action class sequence
1, Calculate local action class probability LAP, from i to i+7,by equation (7)
2, default = max (LAP)
3, Compare action class$_{i+1}$ to default, if equal then SIGN increase 1, else SIGN decrease 1.
4, real action$_i$= default, SIGN 5.
5,repeat 3,4, Until SIGN<0 repeat 1.
Output: real action sequence

not an $n \times 1$ vector, but an $n \times n$ matrix. Each frame in test video sequence corresponds to a $1 \times n$ vector in action class sequence. The primary **action recognition** is done by max action class sequence on each frame.

For a better recognition, we prefer the smoothing algorithm to the max process, because the former can reduce noise. In the smooth algorithm, sum up probabilities of action class sequences in a time section T by equation(7), and then take the max(LAP) as the default class in this time section.

$$LAP(p_1, ..., p_n) = \sum_{i=1}^{T} (p_{1i}, ..., p_{ni}) \qquad (7)$$

Verify images one by one, until that the default class could not fit the broken image. Then repeat the process around broken image. Through the

smooth algorithm, we can label the local sequence by the most frequent action class. The smooth algorithm is shown in Table 2.

4. EXPERIMENTS

4.1. Simulated Videos

In the first experiment, the method is tested on the CMU database[1]. This database contains thousands of videos for actions, such as "walking", "running", "boxing", "jumping", "waiting" and "wiping" etc. Each action is captured by a professional equipment to store the 3D information, and represented in several formats.

We selected 45 video sequences in 5 action classes with an image size of 320×240 and a frame

Table 3. Dominant-set clustering algorithm

Algorithm 3: Dominant-Set Clustering
Input: Affinity matrix for kth iteration A^k
1. If A^k is empty, return NULL
2. Calculate the local solution of (4)by(5): u^k and $f(u^k)$
3. Get the dominant set: $S^k = C_{u^k}$
4. Split out S^k from the present graph and get a smaller graph with new affinity matrix A^{k+1}
Output: A^{k+1}, S^k, u^k, $f(u^k)$

rate of 15 frames/sec. 30 video sequences are used for training and 15 for testing. The 5 action classes are 'walk', 'run', 'wipe', 'jump', 'box'. In this experiment, the corresponding simulated videos using AMC tool on 3D information are selected since they do not need preprocessing. The normalized length L of the contour is 50. The **shape context** is a 4×12 matrix.

The results are evaluated by the *recognition rate*, which is defined as the percentage of correctly classified images.

Moreover, three classical clustering techniques are tested for comparison: K-means, meanshift, and Fuzzy-Cmean. **Dominant set** clusters the training data into 42clusters, and for other three techniques, we obtained respectively 20 (K-means), 21(meanshift), and 40 (Fuzzy-Cmean) clusters. Besides, in these experiments, the test data is classified by looking for the nearest cluster centers in Euclidean distance. Table 4 shows the recognition rates with and without the smoothing algorithm. For most of the actions, the **Dominant**

Set-based approach outperforms the other three techniques, except for "wiping", for which the Kmeans-based method and the meanshift-based method achieve similar results to **Dominant set**, and "boxing", for which FCM demonstrates better recognition rate. The results show that the three classical techniques can not distinguish the five actions in the experiments. It means the three classical techniques can not work well in Euclidean space to distinguish human action. On the contrary, the **dominant set**-based approach can classify most video sequence correctly, and the score becomes higher after smoothing which demonstrates its effectiveness in clustering.

The reasons for the experimental results are investigated. As we mentioned in Section 3.1, each contour is represented by a discrete set $SC = \{sc_l\}_{l=1}^L$, so the SC can be considered as a curve. Hence, to match SC is equal to match curve. The unsatisfying results of the three techniques may be due to the poor performance of Euclidean distance for matching curves. In contrast, **Domi-**

Table 4. Recognition rates on CMU database

	KMEANS	MEANSHIFT	FCM	DOMINANT SET	Dom-Sets with smooth
walk	1.92	21.15	7.69	78.85	100.00
Run	1.65	0	0	74.38	100.00
Wipe	96.35	95.62	0	97.08	100.00
Jump	0	0	0	50.00	67.50
Box	6.41	0	99.36	57.05	78.85

nant set has quite a good overall performance because this clustering method simultaneously emphasizes on *internal homogeneity* and *external inhomogeneity*. However, we observe that all the four approaches perform less well for the 'jumping' action. This can be explained by the fact that we have not yet taken sequential information of contour in the sequence into consideration. Therefore, "jumping" is misclassified as "standing" category, which is the common area of "boxing" and "wiping". When the recognition rate is over a certain threshold, smoothing algorithm can improve the recognition rate by reducing noise; conversely, when ordinary recognition rate is quite low, the smoothing algorithm may worsen the performance.

4.2. Real Videos

The data set used in Section 3.1 is simulated videos of skeleton generated by AMC tool. To demonstrate the effectiveness of our work, we also conducted experiments on real videos from 2007 weizmann action dataset (Gorelick, at el. 2007). The database, collected by Michal Irani, has 81 low-resolution video sequences showing nine different people, each performing nine natural actions such as "running", "walking", "jumping", "jumping-forward-on-two-legs", "jumping-in-place-on-two-legs", "galloping-sideways", "waving-two-hands", "waving-one-hand", "bending". In the database, 5 people's actions are used for training and 4 people's actions are testing data. The video sequences have 180×144 pixel resolution and 25 frames per second.

Figure 4. Some noisy foreground maps. (Adapted from 2007 weizmann action dataset)

(1)	*(2)*	*(3)*	*(4)*	*(5)*	*(6)*	*(7)*

Walking with bag

(1)	*(2)*	*(3)*	*(4)*	*(5)*	*(6)*	*(7)*

Walking with dog

(1)	*(2)*	*(3)*	*(4)*	*(5)*	*(6)*	*(7)*

Walking with feet occlusion

(1)	*(2)*	*(3)*	*(4)*	*(5)*	*(6)*	*(7)*

Walking with raising arm and some shadow

Gorelick, at el. (2007) extracts space-time features, and classifies them using the nearest neighbor procedure. This method misclassified 1 out of 549 space-time cubes, which meant 0.36% error rate. Note, Irani's experimental data is single action, while our method deals with action sequence containing multi-actions. Experimental results show that the image recognition rate is 74.18%, and the **action recognition** rate attains 86.84%, with only one person's actions not totally recognized. The misclassification is mainly due to the deformity of contours issued from simple technique of background subtraction. Although our recognition rate was not as high as Irani's rate, the advantage of our method resides in the fact that we can avoid considering the length of action period. Thus, **Dominant Set** based approach is demonstrated to be able to work in real videos composed of multi-actions.

4.3. Robustness

In this experiment, we also demonstrate that **Dominant Set**-based approach is robust on non-rigid deformities, partial occlusions and other defects in video sequences. In 2007 weizmann action dataset (Gorelick, at el. 2007), there are ten videos of walking persons in different backgrounds, which are difficult to segment (see Figure 4). Our method only failed in only one video (the person walking with bag) out of 10. Since the person swings his hands with bag dramatically, this sequence is misclassified into "jacking" category.

5. CONCLUSION

In this chapter, we have presented a novel method for **action recognition**, and experimental results have demonstrated that the method is very effective. **Dominant set** have such a good performance in clustering and classification, even in noisy data, that it can be used in both simulated videos and real videos.

Our approach has several advantages. First, it is robust to the variation of action duration. In (Li, & Greenspan, 2005; Gorelick, at el. 2007), it is necessary to estimate the length of action periods, while we don't have to consider this factor because our approach focuses on per-frame image. Second, our approach has the potential to be applied in videos comprising various kinds of actions. Because in our approach, known action parts can compose a new action, our sample database has limits in size while database in other methods increases linearly without limit. Finally, this approach can also be used without great change on general 3D shapes.

At present, our approach does not consider the displacement of contour in the sequence. So we can not distinguish directed actions. In other words, we can only recognize "waving hands", but we can not discern "waving up" and "waving down" yet. Therefore, in future, we will try to introduce displacement features into our approach, in order to recognize directed actions.

REFERENCES

Bobick, A. F., & Davis, J. W. (2001). The recognition of human movement using temporal templates. *IEEE Transactions on Pattern Analysis and Machine Intelligence*, *23*(3), 257–267. doi:10.1109/34.910878

Boiman, O., & Irani, M. (2005). Detecting irregularities in images and in video. In *Tenth IEEE International Conference on Computer Vision, (ICCV 2005)* (Vol. 1, pp. 462-469).

Carlsson, S., & Sullivan, J. (2001). Action recognition by shape matching to key frames. In *Workshop on Models versus Exemplars in Computer Vision*.

Caspi, Y., Simakov, D., & Irani, M. (2006). Feature-Based Sequence-to-Sequence Matching. [IJCV]. *International Journal of Computer Vision*, *68*(1), 53–64. doi:10.1007/s11263-005-4842-z

Chen, C., & Fan, G. (2008). Hybrid body representation for integrated pose recognition, localization and segmentation. *IEEE Conference on Computer Vision and Pattern Recognition (CVPR 2008)* (pp. 1-8, 23-28).

Cheung, K. M. G., Baker, S., & Kanade, T. (2003). Shape-from-silhouette of articulated objects and its use for human body kinematics estimation and motion capture. In *Proceedings. IEEE Computer Society Conference on Computer Vision and Pattern Recognition, 2003* (vol. 1, pp. 77-84).

Crivelli, T., Piriou, G., Bouthemy, P., Cernuschi-Frías, B., & Yao, J. (2008). Simultaneous Motion Detection and Background Reconstruction with a Mixed-State Conditional Markov Random Field. *ECCV 2008.*

Dalal, N., Triggs, B., & Schmid, C. (2006). Human detection using oriented histograms of flow and appearance. In *Proc. ECCV* (pp. 428–441).

de Campos, T. E., & Murray, D. W. (2006). Regression-based Hand Pose Estimation from Multiple Cameras. In *IEEE Computer Society Conference on Computer Vision and Pattern Recognition, 2006* (vol.1, pp. 782-789).

Dollar, P., Rabaud, V., Cottrell, G., & Belongie, S. (2005). Behavior recognition via sparse spatio-temporal features. In *2nd Joint IEEE International Workshop on Visual Surveillance and Performance Evaluation of Tracking and Surveillance, 2005* (pp. 65-72).

Duong, T. V., Bui, H. H., Phung, D. Q., & Venkatesh, S. (2005). Activity recognition and abnormality detection with the switching hidden semi-Markov model. In *CVPR 2005. IEEE Computer Society Conference on Computer Vision and Pattern Recognition, 2005* (vol.1, pp. 838-845).

Efros, A. A., Berg, A. C., Mori, G., & Malik, J. (2003. Recognizing action at a distance. In *Proceedings. Ninth IEEE International Conference on Computer Vision, 2003* (pp.726-733).

Elgammal, A., Shet, V., Yacoob, Y., & Davis, L. S. (2003). Learning dynamics for exemplar-based gesture recognition. In *IEEE Computer Society Conference on Computer Vision and Pattern Recognition, 2003* (vol. 1, pp. 571-578).

Farhadi, A., & Tabrizi, M.K. (2008). Learning to Recognize Activities from the Wrong View Point. *ECCV 2008.*

Ferrari, V., Jurie, F., & Schmid, C. (2007). Accurate Object Detection with Deformable Shape Models Learnt from Images. In *CVPR '07. IEEE Conference on Computer Vision and Pattern Recognition, 2007.*

Filipovych, R., & Ribeiro, E. (2008). Learning human motion models from unsegmented videos. In *IEEE Conference on Computer Vision and Pattern Recognition (CVPR 2008)* (pp.1-7, 23-28).

Gilbert, A., Illingworth, J., & Bowden, R. (2008). Scale Invariant Action Recognition Using Compound Features Mined from Dense Spatio-temporal Corners. *ECCV 2008.*

Goldenberg, R., Kimmel, R., Rivlin, E., & Rudzsky, M. (2005). Behavior classification by eigendecomposition of periodic motions. *Pattern Recognition, 38*, 1033–1043. doi:10.1016/j.patcog.2004.11.024

Gorelick, L., Blank, M., Shechtman, E., Irani, M., & Basri, R. (2007). Actions as Space-Time Shapes. *Transactions on Pattern Analysis and Machine Intelligence, 29*(12), 2247–2253. doi:10.1109/TPAMI.2007.70711

Gorelick, L., Meirav, G., Sharon, E., Basri, R., & Brandt, A. (2006). Shape representation and classification using the Poisson equation. *Transactions on Pattern Analysis and Machine Intelligence, 28*(12), 1991–2005. doi:10.1109/TPAMI.2006.253

Hu, W., & Hu, W. (2006). HIGCALS: a hierarchical graph-theoretic clustering active learning system. *IEEE International Conference on Systems, Man and Cybernetics (SMC '06)* (vol. 5, pp.3895-3900).

Ikizler, N., & Duygulu, P. (2007) Human Action Recognition Using Distribution of Oriented Rectangular Patches. In *Human Motion ICCV'07*.

Jhuang, H., Serre, T., Wolf, L., & Poggio, T. (2007). A Biologically Inspired System for Action Recognition. In *IEEE 11th International Conference on Computer Vision (ICCV 2007)* (pp.1-8, 14-21).

Jia, K., & Yeung, D. (2008). Human action recognition using Local Spatio-Temporal Discriminant Embedding. In *IEEE Conference on Computer Vision and Pattern Recognition (CVPR 2008)* (pp.1-8, 23-28).

Jiang, H., & Martin, D. R. (2008). Finding Actions Using Shape Flows. *ECCV*.

Jitendra, M., & Jan, P. (2001). Matching shapes. *Proceedings. Eighth IEEE International Conference on Computer Vision (ICCV 2001)* (vol.1, pp.454-461).

Kale, A., Sundaresan, A., Rajagopalan, A. N., Cuntoor, N. P., Roy-Chowdhury, A. K., Kruger, V., & Chellappa, R. (2004). Identification of humans using gait. *IEEE Transactions on Image Processing, 13*(9), 1163–1173. doi:10.1109/TIP.2004.832865

Ke, Y., Sukthankar, R., & Hebert, M. (2007). Event Detection in Crowded Videos. In *IEEE 11th International Conference on Computer Vision. ICCV 2007* (pp.1-8, 14-21).

Laptev, I., & Lindeberg, T. (2003). Space-time interest points. In *Proceedings. Ninth IEEE International Conference on Computer Vision, 2003* (pp. 432-439).

Laptev, I., & Perez, P. (2007). Retrieving actions in movies. *ICCV 2007. IEEE 11th International Conference on Computer Vision* (pp.1-8, 14-21).

Li, H., & Greenspan, M. (2005). Multi-scale gesture recognition from time-varying contours. *Tenth IEEE International Conference on Computer Vision, 2005 (ICCV 2005), 1*, 236-243.

Ling, H., & Jacobs, D. W. (2007). Shape Classification Using the Inner-Distance. *IEEE Transactions on Pattern Analysis and Machine Intelligence, 29*(2), 286–299. doi:10.1109/TPAMI.2007.41

Liu, C., & Ahuja, N. (2004). A model for dynamic shape and its applications. In *Proceedings of the 2004 IEEE Computer Society Conference on Computer Vision and Pattern Recognition (CVPR 2004)* (Vol. 2, pp. 129-134).

Liu, J., Ali, S., & Shah, M. (2008). Recognizing human actions using multiple features. In *CVPR 2008. IEEE Conference on Computer Vision and Pattern Recognition, 2008* (pp.1-8, 23-28).

Lowe, D. (2004). Distinctive image features from scale-invariant keypoints. *International Journal of Computer Vision, 60*(2), 91–110. doi:10.1023/B:VISI.0000029664.99615.94

Lu, W., & Little, J. J. (2006). Simultaneous Tracking and Action Recognition using the PCA-HOG Descriptor. In *The 3rd Canadian Conference on Computer and Robot Vision, 2006* (pp. 6-6).

Lucas, B. D., & Kanade, T. (1981). An iterative image registration technique with an application to stereo vision. In *DARPA Image Understanding Workshop*.

Lv, F., & Nevatia, R. (2007). Single View Human Action Recognition using Key Pose Matching and Viterbi Path Searching. In *IEEE Conference on Computer Vision and Pattern Recognition (CVPR '07)* (pp.1-8, 17-22).

Masoud, O., & Papanikolopoulos, N. (2003). A method for human action recognition. *Image and Vision Computing, 21*, 729–743. doi:10.1016/S0262-8856(03)00068-4

Matas, J., Chum, O., Urban, M., & Pajdla, T. (2002). Robust Wide Baseline Stereo from Maximally Stable Extremal Regions. In *Proc. 13th British Machine Vision Conf.* (pp. 384-393).

Mikolajczyk, K., & Schmid, C. (2003). A performance evaluation of local descriptors. In *Proceedings. 2003 IEEE Computer Society Conference on Computer Vision and Pattern Recognition* (vol. 2, pp. 257-263).

Mikolajczyk, K., & Uemura, H. (2008). Action recognition with motion-appearance vocabulary forest. In *CVPR 2008. IEEE Conference on Computer Vision and Pattern Recognition, 2008* (pp. 1-8, 23-28).

Morency, L.-P., Quattoni, A., & Darrell, T. (2007). Latent-Dynamic Discriminative Models for Continuous Gesture Recognition. In *CVPR '07. IEEE Conference on Computer Vision and Pattern Recognition, 2007* (pp.1-8, 17-22).

Mori, G., & Malik, J. (2002). Estimating human body configurations using shape context matching. In *European Conference on Computer Vision*.

Natarajan, P., & Nevatia, R. (2008). View and scale invariant action recognition using multiview shape-flow models. In *CVPR 2008. IEEE Conference on Computer Vision and Pattern Recognition, 2008* (pp.1-8, 23-28).

Nguyen, N.T., Phung, D.Q., Venkatesh, S., & Bui, H. (2005). Learning and detecting activities from movement trajectories using the hierarchical hidden Markov model. *Computer Vision and Pattern Recognition, 2005* (vol. 2, pp. 955-960).

Niebles, J. C., & Li, F. (2007). A Hierarchical Model of Shape and Appearance for Human Action Classification. In *CVPR '07. IEEE Conference on Computer Vision and Pattern Recognition* (pp.1-8, 17-22).

Niebles, J. C., Wang, H., & Li, F. (2006). Unsupervised learning of human action categories using spatial-temporal words. In *British Machine Vision Conference*.

Ning, H., Xu, W., Gong, Y., & Huang, T. (2008). Latent Pose Estimator for Continuous Action Recognition. *ECCV*.

Pavan, M., & Pelillo, M. (2003). A new graph-theoretic approach to clustering and segmentation. In *Proceedings. 2003 IEEE Computer Society Conference on Computer Vision and Pattern Recognition, 2003* (vol.1, pp. 18-20).

Pavan, M., & Pelillo, M. (2004). Efficient out-of-sample extension of dominant-set clusters. In *Proceedings of Neural Information Processing Systems*.

Peixoto, P., Goncalves, J., & Araujo, H. (2002). Real-time gesture recognition system based on contour signatures. In *Proceedings. 16th International Conference on Pattern Recognition, 2002* (vol.1, 447-450).

Rodriguez, M. D., Ahmed, J., & Shah, M. (2008). Action MACH a spatio-temporal Maximum Average Correlation Height filter for action recognition. In *IEEE Conference on Computer Vision and Pattern Recognition (CVPR 2008)* (pp.1-8, 23-28).

Schindler, K., & van Gool, L. (2008). Action snippets: How many frames does human action recognition require? In *IEEE Conference on Computer Vision and Pattern Recognition (CVPR 2008)* (pp.1-8, 23-28).

Schuldt, C., Laptev, I., & Caputo, B. (2004). Recognizing human actions: a local SVM approach. In *ICPR 2004. Proceedings of the 17th International Conference on Pattern Recognition, 2004* (vol. 3, pp. 32-36).

Serge, B., Jitendra, M., & Jan, P. (2002). Shape matching and object recognition using shape contexts. *IEEE Transactions on Pattern Analysis and Machine Intelligence, 24*(4), 509–522. doi:10.1109/34.993558

Shechtman, E., & Irani, M. (2005). Space-time behavior based correlation. In *CVPR 2005. IEEE Computer Society Conference on Computer Vision and Pattern Recognition, 2005* (Vol. 1, pp. 405-412).

Shi, Q., Wang, L., Cheng, C., & Smola, A. (2008). Discriminative human action segmentation and recognition using semi-Markov model. *CVPR 2008. IEEE Conference on Computer Vision and Pattern Recognition* (pp.1-8, 23-28).

Sminchisescu, C., Kanaujia, A., Li, Z., & Metaxas, D. (2005). Conditional models for contextual human motion recognition. In *Tenth IEEE International Conference on Computer Vision, 2005* (vol. 2, pp.1808-1815).

Sminchisescu, C., Kanaujia, A., Li, Z., & Metaxas, D. (2005). Conditional models for contextual human motion recognition. In *Tenth IEEE International Conference on Computer Vision, 2005* (vol. 2, pp.1808-1815).

Stauffer, C., & Grimson, W. E. L. (1999). Adaptive background mixture models for real-time tracking. *IEEE Computer Society Conference on Computer Vision and Pattern Recognition* (vol.2, pp. 252).

Suzuki, S., & Abe, K. (1985). Topological structural analysis of digitized binary images by border following. *Computer Vision Graphics and Image Processing, 30*, 32–46. doi:10.1016/0734-189X(85)90016-7

Tran, D., & Sorokin, A. (2008). Human Activity Recognition with Metric Learning. *ECCV 2008.*

Ukrainitz, Y., & Irani, M. (2006). Aligning Sequences and Actions by Maximizing Space-Time Correlations. *European Conference on Computer Vision (ECCV).*

Veeraraghavan, A., Roy-Chowdhury, A. K., & Chellappa, R. (2005). Matching shape sequences in video with applications in human movement analysis. *Pattern Analysis and Machine Intelligence, 27*(12), 1896–1909. doi:10.1109/TPAMI.2005.246

Vitaladevuni, S. N., Kellokumpu, V., & Davis, L. S. (2008). Action recognition using ballistic dynamics. In *IEEE Conference on Computer Vision and Pattern Recognition, 2008 (CVPR 2008)* (pp.1-8, 23-28).

Wang, L., & Suter, D. (2007). Recognizing Human Activities from Silhouettes: Motion Subspace and Factorial Discriminative Graphical Model. In *CVPR '07. IEEE Conference on Computer Vision and Pattern Recognition* (pp.1-8, 17-22).

Wang, L., Tan, T., Ning, H., & Hu, W. (2003). Silhouette analysis-based gait recognition for human identification. *IEEE Transactions on Pattern Analysis and Machine Intelligence, 25*(12), 1505–1518. doi:10.1109/TPAMI.2003.1251144

Wang, Y., Jiang, H., Drew, M. S., Li, Z. N., & Mori, G. (2006). Unsupervised Discovery of Action Classes. In *IEEE Computer Society Conference on Computer Vision and Pattern Recognition, 2006* (vol.2, pp. 1654-1661).

Weinland, D., & Boyer, E. (2008). Action recognition using exemplar-based embedding. In *IEEE Conference on Computer Vision and Pattern Recognition (CVPR 2008)* (pp.1-7, 23-28).

Yilmaz, A., & Shah, M. (2005). Actions sketch: a novel action representation. In *IEEE Computer Society Conference on Computer Vision and Pattern Recognition, 2005* (vol. 1, pp. 984-989).

Zhang, Z., Hu, Y., Chan, S., & Chia, L. (2008). Motion Context: A New Representation for Human Action Recognition. *ECCV 2008.*

Zhang, Z., Huang, K., & Tan, T. (2008). Multi-thread Parsing for Recognizing Complex Events in Videos. *ECCV 2008.*

Zhao, T., & Nevatia, R. (2002). 3D tracking of human locomotion: a tracking as recognition approach. In *Proceedings. 16th International Conference on Pattern Recognition* (vol. 1, pp. 546-551).

ENDNOTE

[1]   *The data used in this project was obtained from mocap.cs.cmu.edu.*

Chapter 13
Distillation:
A Super-Resolution Approach for the Selective Analysis of Noisy and Unconstrained Video Sequences

Dong Seon Cheng
University of Verona, Italy

Marco Cristani
University of Verona, Italy

Vittorio Murino
University of Verona, Italy

ABSTRACT

Image super-resolution is one of the most appealing applications of image processing, capable of retrieving a high resolution image by fusing several registered low resolution images depicting an object of interest. However, employing super-resolution in video data is challenging: a video sequence generally contains a lot of scattered information regarding several objects of interest in cluttered scenes. Especially with hand-held cameras, the overall quality may be poor due to low resolution or unsteadiness. The objective of this chapter is to demonstrate why standard image super-resolution fails in video data, which are the problems that arise, and how we can overcome these problems. In our first contribution, we propose a novel Bayesian framework for super-resolution of persistent objects of interest in video sequences. We call this process Distillation. In the traditional formulation of the image super-resolution problem, the observed target is (1) always the same, (2) acquired using a camera making small movements, and (3) found in a number of low resolution images sufficient to recover high-frequency information. These assumptions are usually unsatisfied in real world video acquisitions and often beyond the control of the video operator. With Distillation, we aim to extend and to generalize the image super-resolution task, embedding it in a structured framework that accurately distills all the informative bits of an object of interest. In practice, the Distillation process: i) individuates, in a semi supervised way, a set of objects of interest, clustering the related video frames and registering them with respect to global rigid trans-formations; ii) for each one, produces a high resolution image, by weighting each pixel according to the

DOI: 10.4018/978-1-60566-900-7.ch013

information retrieved about the object of interest. As a second contribution, we extend the Distillation process to deal with objects of interest whose transformations in the appearance are not (only) rigid. Such process, built on top of the Distillation, is hierarchical, in the sense that a process of clustering is applied recursively, beginning with the analysis of whole frames, and selectively focusing on smaller sub-regions whose isolated motion can be reasonably assumed as rigid. The ultimate product of the overall process is a strip of images that describe at high resolution the dynamics of the video, switching between alternative local descriptions in response to visual changes. Our approach is first tested on synthetic data, obtaining encouraging comparative results with respect to known super-resolution techniques, and a good robustness against noise. Second, real data coming from different videos are considered, trying to solve the major details of the objects in motion.

1. INTRODUCTION

In the emerging fields within video analysis, such as video indexing, video retrieval, video summarization and video surveillance, the quality of the video frames represents the essential source of information for the identification, classification or recognition of targets of interest, like objects or people. The widespread use of low-cost hand-held cameras, web-cams, and mobile phones with cameras has multiplied the sources of video production, but at the cost of a lower quality. The reasons are several: starting from careless acquisitions of inexperienced operators to low resolution cameras with low gains. The analysis of this data is problematic at best, and useless in many cases, because the noise and the resolution may not allow any meaningful processing, even if the object of interest is present in quite a few frames.

The problem of obtaining a highly informative image starting from noisy and coarsely resolved input images is known in literature as (image) super-resolution. When the input consists in only one low resolution image, we refer to the problem as "single-frame super-resolution" (Kursun & Favorov, 2002), when several frames are considered, the problem is called "multi-frame super-resolution" or simply super-resolution (Baker & Kanade, 2002; Schultz & Stevenson, 1994). There are other kinds of super-resolution currently under study, for example, the super-resolution enhancement of video (Bishop, Blake,

& Marthi, 2003; Shechtman, Caspi, & Irani, 2002) whose goal consists in improving the quality of each single frame through the addition of high frequency information.

Recently, the attention devoted to the development of super-resolution algorithms is sensibly grown, in both the single image (Kim, Franz, & Scholkopf, 2004), and the multi-frame cases (Baker & Kanade, 2002; Ben-Ezra, Zhouchen, & Wilburn, 2007; Freeman, Jones, & Pasztor, 2002; Freeman, Pasztor, & Carmichael, 2000; Lin & Shum, 2004; Pickup, Capel, Roberts, & Zisserman, 2006; Pickup, Roberts, & Zisserman, 2006; Tipping & Bishop, 2002). Clearly, in the latter case, the information encoded in the resulting image is considerably larger, giving a more accurate representation (for an overview, see Sec. 2).

In video analysis, several tasks of recognition and detection are in fact based on visual data (Kanade, Collins, & Lipton, 2000). For example, in a video surveillance context, a common task consists in detecting the identity of a person captured with a camera, and therefore highly detailed images are desirable. In another context, video summarization considers the problem of generating a concise and expressive summary of a video sequence by extracting and abstracting the most relevant features in the scene. The higher the quality of this summary, the higher the capability of building an effective indexing capable of distinguishing among similar sequences. For these reasons, the application of super-resolution techniques in these fields is highly relevant.

In general, all super-resolution algorithms are based on three basic hypotheses:

1. All the images must portray the same scene, meaning that they can be compared without being deceived
2. Small movements of the scene should be present across images, such that each provides a slightly different "point of view" that can be integrated; in case of known large movements, this constraint may be relaxed by pre-registering the images
3. The number of available images should be sufficient for recovering high frequency information

These constraints are quite hard and penalizing, in particular for a video sequence, making the super-resolution image estimation possible only in supervised and controlled conditions, strongly reducing its applicability in wider contexts. For the sake of clarity, in the following we will specify the term super-resolution as the process of combining several low resolution (LR) images in order to produce a higher resolution (HR) one only when all the above constraints are satisfied. Under these circumstances, the super-resolution process inverts the generative process model in which the LR frames are generated from the HR one, when correctly warped, sub-sampled and blurred by the Point Spread Function (PSF) of the camera device (Baker & Kanade, 2002).

When one of the three constraints is missing, the efficacy of any of the super-resolution methods fails seriously, as we see in the following sections.

After a short foreword, aimed at explaining the Bayesian super-resolution (Sec. 3), over which our contributions are built upon, the first part of the chapter is related to the *Distillation* process (Sec. 4). Especially, we show how it is possible to recover the super-resolution constraints listed above in

arbitrary video sequences, by using a fully Bayesian framework, in order to acquire highly detailed information about the target of interest. Basically, with the term Object Of Interest (OOI) we name an object, person or, generally, an entity, present in most of the frames of the sequence. The idea is that the more frequently an object appears in the scene, the more presumably such target represents the OOI, whose information should be increased.

Distillation is composed of two phases: in the first one, the *image clustering* phase, we exploit the transformed-invariant component analysis, as presented in Kannan, Jojic, & Frey (2008). In such clustering framework, each cluster represents a particular object, through a mean that subsumes its main visual appearance, a subspace representation that spans its appearance variability, *i.e.*, due to local variations, and the covariance matrix that mirrors the uncertainty due to discrepancy between the image formation process and the model. Note that the Distillation process assumes that the OOI is subjected *only* to rigid transformations, modeled by using a discrete approximation formed by invertible rigid translation and rotations. This assumption will be relaxed in the second part of the chapter.

After the image clustering step the following information becomes available:

1. A partition of the LR frames in which each cluster carries information about each different OOI in the sequence
2. A "mean" low resolution image of each OOI; such image is representative of each cluster, normalized with respect to invertible rigid transformations
3. A coarse alignment of each frame with respect to the related OOI, owing to a normalization process
4. An accuracy measure that exploits the goodness with which the OOIs are represented in the related frames, encoded in the covariance of the cluster, which will drive the process of super-resolution

This image clustering phase permits us to recover the three fundamental hypotheses required to place our data in a super-resolution framework, plus an accuracy measure between frames and the mean representation, dependent on the covariance term. In the second step of Distillation, the *image fusion* phase, the super-resolution task is carried out considering the frames of each cluster (for all the clusters), and actively exploiting the covariance term in order to build higher resolved images for each cluster, taking differently into account the value of each pixel of the LR frames involved in the process. The intuitive idea is that the more present a pixel value in the normalized versions of the grouped LR frames, the more probably this pixel holds an important role in the HR image reconstruction step.

The most related super-resolution structure used as a basis for the proposed method is presented in Tipping & Bishop (2002). In this work, a video of a static scene is considered as affected by translation/rotation variations, even if arbitrary transformations can be dealt too. The problem is managed in a fully Bayesian approach, by marginalizing over the HR image to determine the LR images' registration parameters, and, possibly, the PSF parameters. Our method actively develops further this structure, introducing a novel likelihood term in the Bayesian structure that weights differently each pixel in the estimation of the HR image, proportionally to its accuracy measure. Unlike the previous approaches and owing to the generative process applied to the input video sequence, the proposed probabilistic framework is able to recover super-resolution images of well defined targets in a fully automatic, efficient, and flexible manner.

The second part of the chapter extends the Distillation process, proposing an iterative framework yielding to a super resolved hierarchical summarization of a video sequence, called *Super-resolved Digests* (Sec. 5). Basically, we show how it is possible to apply *locally* the Distillation process, in order to deal with complex motion phenomena

(*i.e.*, non rigid). In other words, the identification of OOIs with persistent appearances might not be sufficient to guarantee correct sub-pixel registrations on the *whole* area covered by the OOIs. In fact, it is a common feature of many interesting objects (e.g., human beings) that they present moving parts or regions that abruptly change appearance; moreover, OOIs may appear at the same time in the same set of LR images, exhibiting different dynamics. It makes sense, then, to cut those regions that present high variability and treat them hierarchically as a new sequence of (sub)-images to be analyzed locally. In this way, the complete hierarchy composed by alternating clusters and regions maintains a consistent set of global/local registrations among frames, allowing Distillation to be effective in integrating the remaining uncertainties. At the end, the resulting process represents a novel kind of video summarization in which all the generated high resolution images can be registered against a common coordinate system by applying the several inverse transformations that affected local patches.

In the remaining of the chapter, we report an experimental session (Sec. 6) where we carefully test the Distillation process and the Super-resolved Digest formation on real data, commenting the results and identifying a qualitative range of applications for the two contributions. Finally, in Sec. 7, conclusions are drawn and future perspectives for a more general application of super-resolution techniques to video data are envisaged.

2. STATE OF THE ART

The literature concerning the classical SR (in the sense that all the three constraints listed in Sec. 1 are met, also named here signal-based SR or reconstruction-based SR (Lin & Shum, 2004)) is large and multifaceted, although two subgroups can be devised. In the first one, the alignment of LR images is separated from the fusion step, which estimates the PSF parameters (Cheeseman, Kanefsky, Kraft, Stutz, & Hanson, 1996); in the second group, all the parameters are jointly estimated (Hardie, Barnard, & Armstrong, 1997; Pickup, Capel, Roberts, & Zisserman, 2006; Tipping & Bishop, 2002). Here the HR estimation is either performed by a maximum-likelihood (ML) approach, or in a Maximum A-Posteriori (MAP) fashion, regularizing the ill-conditioning of the ML framework using some priors (Pickup, Capel, Roberts, & Zisserman, 2006; Tipping & Bishop, 2002).

In Lin & Shum (2004), the limits of the reconstruction-based SR algorithms are reported, as a function of the registration error, de-noising accuracy, and high frequency details in the HR image. Moreover, it gives also the sufficient number of LR images to estimate an HR image with magnification factor M, resulting in $4M^2$ for a fractional M, and M^2 for an integer M.

In Ben-Ezra, Zhouchen, & Wilburn (2007), an innovative approach is presented, that is based on an irregular displacement of pictorial details of the LR images, called Penrose tiling. This approach outperforms several existing reconstruction-based algorithms for regular pixel arrays, and has performances which are not described by the constraints expressed in Lin & Shum (2004). In Pickup, Roberts, & Zisserman (2006), the handled registration model is fully projective, incorporating also a photometric component to handle brightness changes potentially present in the frames of a temporal sequence. Additionally, the algorithm learns parameters for the regularizing high-resolution image prior.

An additional group of approaches of SR can also be considered, i.e. the learning-based approaches (Baker & Kanade, 2002; Freeman, Pasztor, & Carmichael, 2000). Learning-based SR algorithms are techniques that do not process images at the signal level; instead, they use case-dependent priors to infer missing details in low resolution images. The seminal papers of this class of approaches are the methods proposed in Freeman, Pasztor, & Carmichael (2000) and the

"Hallucination" algorithm (Baker & Kanade, 2002). In practice, the basic idea is to discover similarity (usually, per-patch) among the input LR image and LR training images, which are in turn collected together their correspondent high resolution versions. Once the similarities have been computed, the HR images related to the similar training LR images are employed to statistically infer the high frequency details of the super resolved version of the input images. The inference is usually cast as a *maximum a posteriori* (MAP) estimation.

In general, the pros of the learning-based SR approaches are that they work on fewer LR images but can still achieve a higher magnification factor as traditional algorithms can. Most of them can even work on a single image. Cons are that, usually, the magnification factor is usually fixed and the performances depend on the matching with the training low resolution samples. Because of their characteristic, learning-based SR algorithms have become very popular.

In Lin, He, Tang, & Tang (2007), the limits of the learning-based super-resolution approaches for natural images are estimated, exploiting the statistics of the natural images, and ignoring the effects of the image noise. Such limits are modeled as an upper bound of the magnification factor, such that the expected risk (RMSE between the HR input image and the HR ground truth) is below a relatively large threshold. Moreover, a formula that gives the sufficient number of HRIs to be sampled in order to ensure the accuracy of the estimate is provided.

3. THE BAYESIAN SUPER-RESOLUTION FRAMEWORK

Let the observed data consists in K low-resolution images $\{x_k\}_{k=1}^{K}$, stored as one-dimensional column vectors obtained by raster-scanning. We assume these images have the same size $O_x \times O_y$, and hence the same number of pixels $O_n = O_x \cdot O_y$.

The classical super-resolution formulation describes how these observed data are generated from the unknown high-resolution image $\mathbf{z}$, with $H_n = H_x \cdot H_y$ pixels, where $H_x = qO_x$ and $H_y = qO_y$, depending on the linear magnification factor $q > 1$.

The likelihood of observing each image $\mathbf{x}_k$ is modeled by the following Gaussian probability density:

$$p(\mathbf{x}_k \mid \mathbf{z}, \mathbf{s}_k, \theta_k, \gamma) \sim \mathcal{N}(\mathbf{x}_k; \mathbf{W}_k \mathbf{z}, \Upsilon), \qquad (1)$$

where $\mathbf{s}_k$ is the global sub-pixel shift, θ_k is the orientation displacement and γ regulates the width of the PSF.

The image formation process is neatly rendered by the projection matrix $\mathbf{W}_k$, which takes the high-resolution image $\mathbf{z}$ and warps it according to $\mathbf{s}_k$ and θ_k, blurring and down-sampling according to the PSF and the magnification factor. Finally, $\Upsilon = \epsilon^2 \mathbf{I}$ represents the residual post-transformation noise variance.

In particular, $\mathbf{W}_k$ is an $O_n \times H_n$ matrix with elements $w_{i,j}^{(k)}$ given by

$$w_{i,j}^{(k)} \propto \exp\left\{\frac{\| \mathbf{v}_j - \mathbf{u}_i^{(k)} \|^2}{\gamma^2}\right\}, \qquad (2)$$

where the vector $\mathbf{v}_j$ represents the spatial position of the jth HR pixel.

The vector $\mathbf{u}_i^{(k)}$ is the center of the PSF and is located according to the following transformation:

$$\mathbf{u}_i^{(k)} = \mathbf{R}_k(\mathbf{u}_i - \bar{\mathbf{u}}) + \bar{\mathbf{u}} + \mathbf{s}_k \qquad (3)$$

where the position $\mathbf{u}_i$ of the ith LR pixel is rotated around the center $\bar{\mathbf{u}}$ of the image space by the

standard rotation matrix $\mathbf{R}_k$, expressing the orientation displacement θ_k, and then shifted by $\mathbf{s}_k$.

To complete the Bayesian formulation of the super-resolution model, the following Gaussian regularization prior $p(\mathbf{z})$ over the HR image constrains the values of nearby pixels:

$$p(\mathbf{z}) = \mathcal{N}(\mathbf{z}; \mathbf{0}, \mathbf{C}), \qquad (4)$$

where the covariance matrix $\mathbf{C}$ has the following $c_{i,j}$ elements:

$$c_{i,j} = \frac{1}{A} \exp\left\{-\frac{\| \mathbf{v}_i - \mathbf{v}_j \|^2}{r^2}\right\}. \qquad (5)$$

This prior enforces some smoothness on the high-resolution image by linking every i^{th} and j^{th} pixel values according to their relative locations in the image space and the parameters A and r, which represent the strength and range of the correlation, respectively.

Assuming flat priors on the model parameters $\{\mathbf{s}_k, \theta_k\}_{k=1}^K$ and γ, the posterior over the high-resolution image is proportional to the product of the prior and the joint likelihood terms:

$$p(\mathbf{z} \mid \{\mathbf{x}_k, \mathbf{s}_k, \theta_k\}_{k=1}^K, \gamma) \propto p(\mathbf{z})\prod_{k=1}^K p(\mathbf{x}_k \mid \mathbf{z}, \mathbf{s}_k, \theta_k, \gamma) \qquad (6)$$

After some matrix manipulations (see Tipping, 2001), observing that we have a conjugate prior, it is possible to rewrite this posterior in the following Gaussian form:

$$p(\mathbf{z} \mid \{\mathbf{x}_k, \mathbf{s}_k, \theta_k\}_{k=1}^K, \gamma) = \mathcal{N}(\mathbf{z}; \boldsymbol{\mu}, \Sigma), \qquad (7)$$

where

$$\Sigma = \left(\mathbf{C}^{-1} + \epsilon^{-2}\sum_{k=1}^K \mathbf{W}_k^T \mathbf{W}_k\right)^{-1} \qquad (8)$$

$$\boldsymbol{\mu} = \epsilon^{-2}\Sigma\left(\sum_{k=1}^{K}\mathbf{W}_k^T\mathbf{x}_k\right) \qquad (9)$$

This posterior is basically a prior-compensated pseudo inverse matrix. The covariance in Eq. (1.8) encodes the uncertainty over each HR image pixel: this uncertainty is mainly driven by the smallest value between the prior covariance and the covariance of the likelihood term, weighted by noise variance δ^2.

Given this Bayesian formulation of the super-resolution problem, learning is achieved through the EM algorithm (Dempster, Laird, & Rubin, 1977), treating the low-resolution images $\{\mathbf{x}_k\}_{k=1}^K$ as the observed variables and the high-resolution image $\mathbf{z}$ as a hidden variable.

The EM algorithm iterates between two steps: in the E-step, given the current estimates of the model parameters $\{\mathbf{s}_k, \theta_k\}_{k=1}^K$ and γ, it computes new optimal estimates for Σ and μ; in the M-step, it updates the estimates for the model parameters.

4. SUPER-RESOLUTION OVER PERSISTENT OBJECTS: DISTILLATION

The process of Distillation performs super-resolution starting from a video sequence, by first recovering the fundamental conditions under which the image super-resolution problem becomes well-behaved and then integrating the low resolution data into a high resolution image. These two steps can be identified as: 1) image clustering and 2) image fusion.

4.1. Image Clustering

Let $\{\mathbf{x}_k\}_{k=1}^K$, be the K frames of a given video sequence, treated as a set of images. Our first goal is to isolate the interesting visual objects, which we call *objects of interest* (OOIs): intuitively, OOIs are those objects which appear more times in the sequence. Distillation assumes that, at each frame, only one object of interest is present. For example, let us consider the handmade video shown in Figure 4. Here, a person walks through an indoor environment, alternating randomly different poses and expressions. In this case, the object of interest of each frame is the head of the person, and the rest of the scene, being highly variable, is disregarded as clutter.

Another assumption of Distillation is that, in general, an OOI can be described by a single rigid appearance, possibly affected by global translations and rotations. Due to these restrictions (relaxed in the creation of the Super-resolved Digests) we employ the mixture of transformation-invariant component analyzers (MTCA) (Kannan, Jojic, & Frey, 2008) to perform transformation-invariant clustering of the frames $\{\mathbf{x}_k\}_{k=1}^K$ (each frame having O_n pixels) and learn a subspace representation within each cluster. From a generative point of view, given C clusters with parameters $\{\boldsymbol{\mu}_c, \boldsymbol{\Phi}_c, \boldsymbol{\Lambda}_c\}_{c=1}^C$, where μ_c is the mean cluster image, Φ_c is a diagonal covariance, and Λ_c is an $O_n{'}$ F factor loading matrix, we first generate a latent image $\mathbf{z}_k$ with the following distribution:

$$p(\mathbf{z}_k \mid \mathbf{y}_k, c_k) = \mathcal{N}(\mathbf{z}_k; \boldsymbol{\mu}_c + \rangle_c\mathbf{y}_k, |_c), \qquad (10)$$

where $\mathbf{y}_k$ is an F-dimensional Gaussian $N(\mathbf{0}, \mathbf{I})$ random variable representing the subspace coefficients.

The observed image $\mathbf{x}_k$ is then obtained by applying a transformation $\mathbf{T}_k \in T$ on the latent image $\mathbf{z}_k$ and adding independent Gaussian noise Ψ:

$$p(\mathbf{x}_k \mid \mathbf{z}_k, \mathbf{T}_k) = \mathcal{N}(\mathbf{x}_k; \mathbf{T}_k\mathbf{z}, ") \qquad (11)$$

where the set of transformations T for which the model is invariant to must be specified a priori.

Model learning in MTCA is performed using the EM algorithm (Kannan, Jojic, & Frey,

2008) starting from the joint distribution over all variables:

$$p(\{\mathbf{x}_k, \mathbf{z}_k, \mathbf{y}_k, \mathbf{T}_k, c_k\}_{k=1}^K) = \prod_{k=1}^K p(\mathbf{x}_k, \mathbf{z}_k, \mathbf{y}_k, \mathbf{T}_k, c_k) = \tag{12}$$

$$= \prod_{k=1}^K p(\mathbf{x}_k \mid \mathbf{z}_k, \mathbf{T}_k) p(\mathbf{z}_k \mid \mathbf{y}_k, c_k) p(\mathbf{y}_k) P(\mathbf{T}_k) P(c_k) = \tag{13}$$

$$= \prod_{k=1}^K \mathcal{N}(x_k; T_k z, \Psi) \mathcal{N}(z_k; \mu_c + \Lambda_c y_k, \Phi_c) \mathcal{N}(y_k; 0, I) \pi_{T_k} \pi_{c_k} \tag{14}$$

After MTCA is performed, and interpreting each cluster as representing an OOI, we can split the observed K frames based on the MAP values for c_k and invert the MAP transformations $\mathbf{T}_k$, to effectively obtain C new data sets with image frames registered on the visual objects whose mean appearances are represented by μ_c. Each OOI image also comes with a subspace representation $\Lambda_c \mathbf{y}_k$, whose coefficients $\mathbf{y}_k \mathbf{y}_k$ allow us to study the dynamics of the structural changes in the appearance of the visual object.

In practice, considering the LR frames as points living in a multidimensional manifold, MTCA isolates frames with strongly different appearance into separate multidimensional Gaussian clusters, normalizing with respect to global rigid transformations that afflict images belonging to the same cluster. Under the hypothesis of a perfect registration, component analysis learns a linearized manifold which considers images with similar appearance as linear composition of eigenvectors (eigen-images). LR images with very similar $\mathbf{y}_k$ indicate frames that share structural similarities, *i.e.*, portraying the same object only affected by a very small transformations, that could be considered as consequence of small camera movements, leading to intra-pixel discrepancies.

In this sense, we derive a rough measure of similarity between the frames in a given cluster, useful to select the most useful images for super-resolution. Let $\mathbf{Y} = [\mathbf{y}_1 \mathbf{y}_2 \ldots \mathbf{y}_L]$ be the $F \times L$ matrix obtained by assembling the subspace coefficients of all L images in a given cluster c, then the square $L \times L$ matrix $\mathbf{Y}^T\mathbf{Y}$ represents a similarity matrix defined on the inner product in the subspace Λ_c.

Reasoning on $\mathbf{Y}^T\mathbf{Y}$ allows us to compare frames within a cluster, identifying blocks of similar frames. Frames that form the larger block in such matrix are forwarded to the image fusion step as representatives of their cluster.

The diagonal covariance matrix Φ_c contains the residual variance not explained by the subspace representation. These imperfections exist in the first place only if the number F of hidden factors is limited by design to a small fixed number. It is the same design decision as choosing to keep only F principal components, accounting for only a fraction of the total variance. At this point, we prune the cluster set, by maintaining only those clusters whose Φ_c have all the values under a certain threshold λ_{VAR}.

This operation potentially eliminates those clusters where the OOI appearance dynamics cannot be explained by the learned subspace representation.

4.2. Image Fusion

For the sake of simplicity, let $\{\mathbf{x}_l\}_{l=1}^L$, be the L transformation corrected images, of size $O_x \times O_y$, belonging to cluster c. We propose to modify Eq. (1.1) to take into account the residual cluster variance Φ_c in the following way:

$$p(x_l \mid z, s_l, \theta_l, \gamma) \sim \mathcal{N}(x_l; W_l z, \Phi_c + \mathbf{i}) \tag{15}$$

where the new covariance term $\Phi_c + \mathbf{i}$ in the LR image formation process expresses sensor noise contributions and contributions from the OOI detection process, specifically indicating sites that may need more "slack", or, in other words, should be trusted less to derive a correct sub-pixel registration.

After some matrix manipulations, and denoting $\Delta = \Phi_c + \gamma$, we can update Eqs. (1.7), (1.8) and (1.9) in the following way:

$$p(z \mid \{x_l, s_l, \theta_l\}_{l=1}^{L}, \gamma) = \mathcal{N}(z; \mu', \Sigma') \qquad (16)$$

where

$$\Sigma' = \left(C^{-1} + \sum_{l=1}^{L} W_l^{T} \Delta^{-1} W_l \right)^{-1} \qquad (17)$$

$$\mu' = \Sigma' \left(\sum_{l=1}^{L} W_l^{T} \Delta^{-1} x_l \right). \qquad (18)$$

The model learning is performed through EM, similarly to what explained in Sec. 3 for the classical Bayesian model.

5. SUPER-RESOLVED DIGESTS

Super-resolved Digests solve the weaknesses induced by the two most important constraints underlying the Distillation process: 1) each LR frame portrays at most one OOI and 2) each OOI is subject to rigid transformations only. Here, we assume, in general, that an OOI cannot be described by a single rigid appearance, but can be explained adequately by breaking it down hierarchically into parts, in turn broken down into sub-parts if needed, which we call secondary and tertiary OOIs, respectively. We informally describe each OOI as a set of alternative visual appearances and dynamics.

Our proposed procedure for the Super-resolved Digests creation iteratively applies two phases: *DetectOOI* and *SplitOOI*, aimed at isolating OOIs and to break down an OOI into parts, respectively.

In the *DetectOOI* phase, MTCA image clustering is performed, in the same way explained in Sec. 4.1, obtaining C clusters of parameters $\{\mu_c, \Phi_c\}_{c=1}^{C}$, where each Φ_c contains the residual variance not explained by the subspace representation. In this case we latch onto this "imperfections" in the *SplitOOI* operation to decide if the OOI is well characterized as it stands or needs to be subdivided again.

More in detail, in the *SplitOOI*, we isolate image regions where the residual variance is higher than a given threshold, which can be decided a priori (*i.e.*, the λ_{VAR} of the Distillation process) or computed from the distribution of the actual values. This operation potentially determines multiple sites where the OOI appearance dynamics cannot be explained by the learned subspace representation. As an example, it might occur that an OOI representing a face may contain *eyes* and *mouth* regions that are badly modeled. We determine compact and connected regions by using simple small-valued morphological operators (closing, dilation) and proceed to identify the image frames of the given OOI in correspondence of the bounding box of each separated part. This gives rise to new data sets, each representing a secondary OOI, with reduced size and number of images.

At this point, *DetectOOI* and *SplitOOI* are performed again to detect, if they exist, tertiary OOIs. After each *SplitOOI*, the procedure might be halted when some conditions are met, for example if there are no sizable residual variance regions or there is no reduction in size, meaning MTCA has failed to identify and characterize consistent clusters.

The result of this iterative procedure is a multi-level video clustering: OOIs and portions (secondary, tertiary) of OOIs are represented by clusters whose mean and covariance parameters refer to sets of frames and portions of frames. We apply the image fusion phase of the Distillation process to each cluster, obtaining thus high resolved versions of whole OOIs and parts of them.

Finally, all the gathered information after the image fusion phase can be used to synthesize a highly informative summary of the given video sequence. First, we take each cluster and perform image super-resolution through the image fusion step of Distillation, with the goal of representing all the frames of such clusters with single images at a higher resolution.

Second, we build the timeline of switches between the different clusters at the different hierarchical levels, so as to know which super-resolved images must be combined to rebuild a complete-frame reconstruction starting from the broken down representation built in the analysis phase.

6. EXPERIMENTAL SESSION

This session is organized in two parts: in the first one, we show how Distillation operates on synthetic and real data, performing also comparative tests. In the second part, we apply the Super-resolved Digests creation process on two real sequences, showing how different visual objects with complex motions can be locally super-resolved.

Distillation

On the one hand, Distillation can be viewed as an instance of image super-resolution, since the clustering step recovers the three basic constraints under which super-resolution is well defined. On the other hand, while this step is usually considered as a nuisance-removing pre-processing, it is an integral part of our framework, intended to cope with video data, where the constraints are only roughly satisfied, since the aligned frames do not exactly show the same scene, but rather they depict a local prominent object immersed in different background scenes. In this sense, our method compensates this uncertainty by introducing a structured covariance term in the generative process of the LR images.

Thus, to effectively compare our method to previous super-resolution algorithms, we apply them directly to the same aligned LR frames after clustering. In this way, each set of frames can be thought of as an ordinary input for an image super-resolution process, with the only crucial difference being that these frames also contain uncorrelated pixels of the background scene, which are irrelevant with respect to the object of interest. This condition is dealt effectively by Distillation, while it degrades the performance of the other methods. In particular, we compare with standard bi-cubic image interpolation and Bayesian image super-resolution (Tipping & Bishop, 2002).

In the clustering step, the number of clusters C can be determined heuristically, in accord to Kannan, Jojic, & Frey (2008). Otherwise, a model selection procedure may be embedded in the framework. *Invalid* clusters are those clusters whose covariance matrix exhibits values higher than λ_{VAR}; such clusters are not further considered in the analysis.

Synthetic Data

In this session, we consider two synthetic sequences. In the following, we analyze the image clustering step separately for each sequence, resorting later to a joint review of the image fusion results. The first synthetic sequence can be seen summarized in Figure 1a: we create a sixteen-image dataset created from a lowercase black letter 'r' on a white background of size 32 ´ 32 pixels. Data is generated at a zoom factor of 4, using a 2D translation-only model and a Gaussian PSF with $\gamma = 2$. The sub-pixel shifts are evenly spaced over a 4 ´ 4 high-resolution grid spanning a corresponding low-resolution pixel.

The goal of this experiment is to reproduce as best as possible the original image, comparing the results of our method and the other algorithms. We perform the image clustering step, setting intuitively the number of clusters $C = 1$, and the number of loading factors $F = 2$. Figure 1b shows

Figure 1. Clustering results over "clean" synthetic data: a) example of an original 32 ´ 32 frame (top) and sub-sampled 8 ´ 8 image (bottom); b) results of the image clustering step; in the covariance matrix, the darker the pixel value, the lowest the corresponding variance.

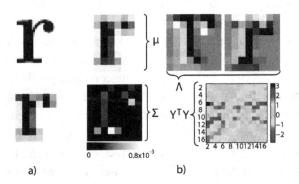

a)   b)

the mean and diagonal covariance of the cluster: note how the least variance is expressed by the leg of the letter and the background. The loading factors are not of particular interest, while the matrix expressing $\mathbf{Y}^T\mathbf{Y}$ indicates that the images are quite similar.

In the second sequence, we keep the same sixteen shifts but replace the white background with a sequence of images coming from a movie of moving terrains, generating a dataset of 100 frames. The intent is to mimic the presence of structured background behind our "shaking" object. Figure 2a shows one HR frame (top) and its corresponding LR image (bottom).

After clustering with the same parameters as in the previous test (Figure 2), it is clear that the background has filled the covariance matrix with high values, resulting in comparatively lower values for the OOI. Figure 3 compares the root mean square (RMS) errors against the true image obtained by interpolating a single LR image, applying Tipping & Bishop's algorithm, and the present approach.

The top row proves that our method performs slightly better than Tipping & Bishop's provided with perfect data. The results on the noise-corrupted images are more interesting (bottom row). Even if Tipping & Bishop's algorithm does a

very good job, sometimes it is deceived by the structured noise and provides a less-than-perfect result. Clear failures are the shrinking of the leg width and the smaller serifs, whereas our approach consistently reproduces all the details, showing that it is not mislead.

Real Data

In this test, we capture a video sequence (the "indoor" sequence) using a Sony TRV120E hand held camera, at 20 Hz acquisition rate. The video sequence consists in a person walking quickly through an indoor environment, alternating randomly different poses and expressions, as shown in Figure 4.

Video data are acquired at 320 ´ 240 pixels, and the subject captured is about 10 meters away from the camera. Such data represent a sort of ground truth for the test. Then, 100 frames of the sequence are sub-sampled by a linear magnification factor $q = 4$, with a PSF width $\gamma = 2$. We perform the image clustering step with $C = 4$ clusters and $F = 5$, obtaining 4 groups of images aligned at LR pixel level. We eliminate two of these clusters, considering them invalid with respect to a covariance threshold of $\lambda_{VAR} = 0.1$ (Figure 5).

Figure 2. Clustering results over "noisy" synthetic data: a) example of an original 32 ´ 32 frame (top) and sub-sampled 8 ´ 8 image (bottom); b) results of the image clustering step; in the covariance matrix, the darker the pixel value, the lowest the corresponding variance.

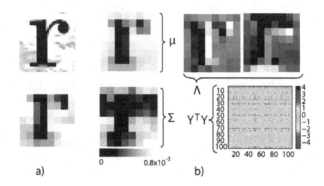

Figure 3. Super-resolved images and RMS values obtained in the "clean" (top row) and in the "noisy" (bottom row) synthetic sequences, respectively. From the left: one frame of the original sequence; single-image interpolation; Tipping & Bishop's method; our approach.

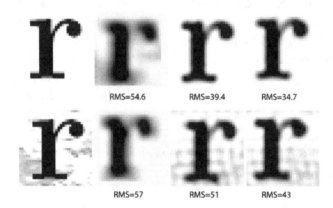

Figure 4. Twelve original images from the "indoor" sequence

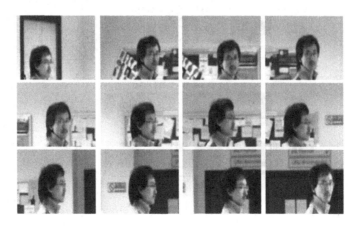

The covariance matrices of the valid clusters show that the highest uncertainty is found on the background pixels, while the remaining pixels portraying the face exhibit higher confidence. Concerning the loading factors, we note how they mostly model small changes in the appearance, such as those caused by the changing pose of the face, albeit capturing also spurious correlations with concurrent background features (*e.g.*, leaflets, billboard).

The $\mathbf{Y}^T\mathbf{Y}$ matrices highlight those LR frames that exhibit similar structure, concerning the OOI appearance. In the red-dotted box we highlighted the frames we chose for the image fusion step in order to narrow further down the noise for this particular test. Such manual selection of the frames gives, in general, a slightly better result than taking all the frames of a valid cluster, which is still a good default choice. An alternative solution is to let the user pick a particular frame in the cluster and automatically select the most similar frames with any given similarity-based algorithm.

In Figure 6, we show some LR frames of the valid clusters where the OOI, *i.e.*, the person's head, is aligned in a fixed position.

The results of the image fusion step are shown in Figure 7: in correspondence of low cluster covariance, our method actively uses the pixel information contained in the LR images, correctly estimating the sub-pixel shift parameters and the face, in both poses. Conversely, the classical Bayesian framework erroneously takes equally into account all the LR pixel values and produces worse results (some over-fitting is evident in the checkered pattern).

While the significance of these particular comparative results are limited to only one well-known image super-resolution technique, on one hand we may presume to claim that even recent techniques (like Lin & Shum, 2004; Pickup, Capel, Roberts, & Zisserman, 2006) would likewise perform badly, since they are based on the same basic assumptions that are here unsatisfied.

On the other hand, this test is still a simplified setting with respect to the range of variability in video data: singular objects of interest with rigid

Figure 5. Clustering results on the "indoor" sequence; in the covariance matrix, the darker the pixel value, the lowest the corresponding variance

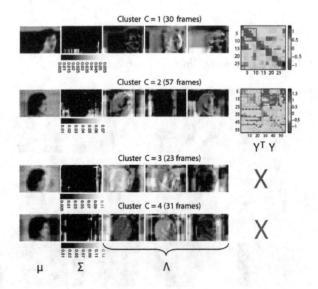

Figure 6. Clustered and aligned LR images of the "indoor" sequence: on the top row, from the first cluster; on the bottom, from the second cluster; note the alignment

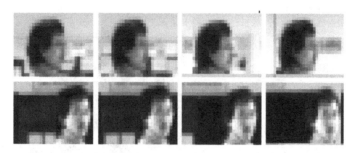

Figure 7. High resolution image estimation results: on the top are the results for the first cluster (see the text), on the bottom for the second cluster; from the left: bi-cubic interpolation, Bayesian super-resolution, our approach, and a high resolution image which could be referred as ground truth, presenting the most similar face portion.

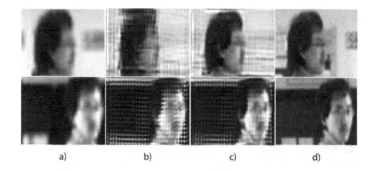

a)   b)   c)   d)

appearance and motion. More complex situations would definitely break any image super-resolution technique.

As a final experiment, we perform Distillation on the originally acquired images. In this case, the linear magnification factor applied is $q = 2$. Here, we find only one valid cluster, shown in Figure 8.

Such cluster is formed by 7 consecutive images, aligned with respect to the head of the person. In this sense, they represent a setting which is quite similar to the usual one for the super-resolution (one OOI, with LR aligned images portraying the same scene); actually, Figure 9 shows that both Tipping & Bishop's approach and the image fusion step give similar results.

Super-Resolved Digests

In this section, we show two real data experiments that demonstrate the effectiveness of the Distillation process in super resolving portions of video sequences, providing highly informative patches, *i.e.*, the Super-resolved Digests. The first test takes the "Claire" test video sequence, in its short version of about 30 frames sized 176 ´ 144 (see Figure 10 for a few frames).

This sequence exhibits a clear example of OOI with non-rigid local motions that cannot be normalized by considering the whole frames. In Figure 11, we report a detailed scheme that summarizes the most important steps of the Super-resolved Digests creation. In particular, after a *SplitOOI* phase, only the biggest OOIs are considered, for

Figure 8. Clustering results for the "indoor" sequence, taken at the original 320 ´ 240 resolution: the mean and covariance images of the only valid cluster; the darker the pixel value in the covariance, the lowest the corresponding variance.

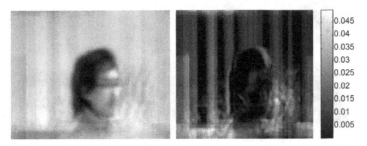

Figure 9. High resolution image estimation results: on the top row, the super-resolution results; on the bottom row, some enlargements; from the left: a LR image, bi-cubic interpolation, classical Bayesian super-resolution, our approach.

Figure 10. Six frames from the "Claire" video sequence, a publicly available benchmark.

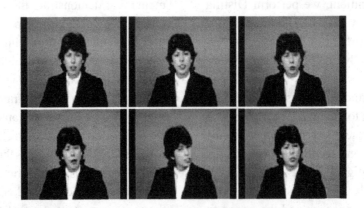

the sake of clarity. Also, for this experiment we considered only translational motions to ease the computations, but we reserve to model rotations, scaling and other warpings in future improvements. This analysis is mostly focused on the detection of the different poses and expressions of the given person.

By looking at the similarity matrix in the first *DetectOOI* phase (second to last diagram in the first row of Figure 11), it looks like there are four main blocks of similar frames plus a small transitioning phase before the last block. This fact becomes evident while perusing the timeline of the Super-resolved Digest in Figure 13, where the transition cluster is actually pretty garbage. In this digest, no frames were eliminated prior to the image fusion process, leading to high-resolution images that are slightly imperfect. To avoid this problem, we can examine the Y^TY similarity matrix, in order to choose either the biggest group of similar frames, or to use all the available frames. We opt for the second choice, after considering that the process of image fusion is generally well behaved.

In Figure 12, we show the analysis of the "Claire" sequence along with the Distillation results. The tree structure is determined by the hierarchical detection and splitting procedure, where the nodes in the diagram are determined by split maps and the arrows represent clustering results, with the edges labels showing the number of frames being partitioned. Each node in the figure shows the Distillation super-resolved image alongside either the mean cluster image or a low-resolution frame.

An alternative and more meaningful way to look at the Super-resolved Digest is shown in Figure 13, where the super-resolved pieces are put back together according to the reconstructed timeline of "events". Basically, each original time instant in the sequence corresponds to a collage of super-resolved images, and we can follow the "compressed" events sequence unfolding.

However, this representation is only feasible with relatively simple sequences.

The second test is focused on a widely circulating "Police chase" sequence, available on YouTube (© 2009, YouTube LLC) and other video sharing sites, showing a Mustang followed and hit several times from different police cars. We set here a magnification factor of $M = 2.6$. For the sake of clarity, we report the results obtained on two subsequences relative to frames 1826-1880 (Figure 14, top row) and 1969-2023 (bottom row).

In the first case, the police car rams the fugitive's Mustang from behind, making it spin. In the second case the fugitive car outruns the police car. In both cases, we have two objects of interest, i.e., the police car and the Mustang. In both cases, the motion of the two OOIs is different, and approximately rigid. In Figure 15 and Figure 16, we show the Super-resolved Digests results of the respective cases. In the first subsequence, the two cars are identified as different OOIs by the *DetectOOI* phase. The fugitive's car is modeled as a single OOI and super-resolved by the image fusion step. The police car is considered as two OOIs, capturing its front and rear separately. As shown in Figure 15, the super-resolved OOIs are informative, capturing the structure of the car. Note that the original sequence is affected by heavy compression artifacts, limiting the high frequency components, thus bounding the amount of informative content that the Super-resolved Digest can distill from the sequence.

In the second subsequence (Figure 16), after two *SplitOOI* steps, we isolate two OOIs, i.e., the Mustang and the police car. We show here only the results regarding the police car, being more interesting.

In particular, we portray the two OOIs regarding the roof portion of the car, presenting a number (372), which is scarcely visible. After the application of the image fusion step the visual quality increases, permitting a better visualization of the structure of the digits "7" and "2", especially in one of the two OOI, while the "3" digit remains

Figure 11. Detailed view of the analysis performed on the "Claire" video. In the first row, from left to right, a sample image followed by the single cluster mean, covariance, loading factors, similarity matrix and split targets. The following rows present the mean, variance and similarity matrices of the hierarchical decomposition of the video. Split target maps are given for those OOI that have been split, with the results in the row immediately below.

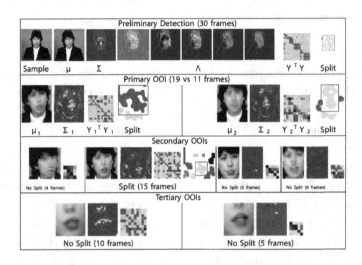

Figure 12. Side by side comparisons of Distillation results for each cluster in the analysis of the "Claire" sequence. Non-terminal nodes in this split tree (indicated by the split maps and the clustering arrows) show triplets of: split map over-imposed on mean image, clean mean image and super-resolved image. Terminal nodes, except the bad one in the center, show doublets of: super-resolved image and comparable low-resolution frame.

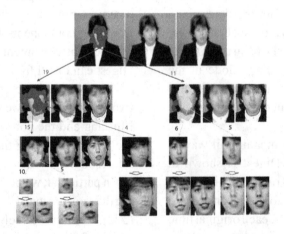

Figure 13. Super-resolved Digest of the "Claire" video. At the bottom, the reconstructed timeline of "events" that trigger the cluster switches. Linked to the main events are the super-resolved frame reconstructions on the top.

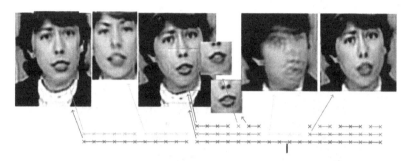

Figure 14. Eight frames from the "Police chase" video sequence, one of the widely circulating news pieces on popular websites like YouTube (© 2009, YouTube LLC)

Figure 15. Graphical representation of the Super-resolved Digest for the "Police chase" sequence. Empty arrows point to Distillation results. Red solid arrows show zoomed details of the super-resolution images, side by side with the corresponding LR detail.

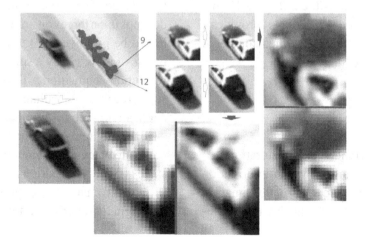

Figure 16. Super-resolved Digest for the second subsequence in the "Police chase" sequence: emphasis on the roof of the police car.

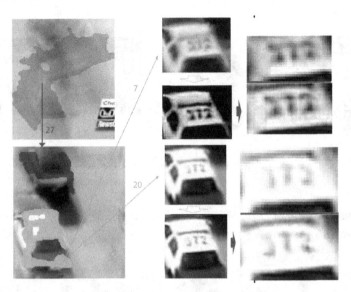

Figure 17. Roof details of the police car: a) original LR frame, b) bicubic interpolation, c) Distillation.

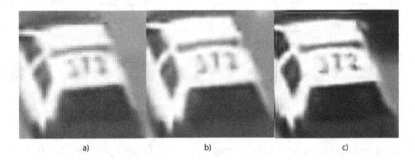

shadowed. Anyway, as visible in Figure 17, the Super-resolved Digest of the roof part provides a richer informative content, also when compared to an interpolated LR frame.

7. CONCLUSION

Super-resolution is a fundamental restoration process that permits to integrate visual information coming from numerous low resolution images, synthesizing a single, coherent, higher resolu-

tion image. The proper outcome of this process depends upon three constraints: (1) the same scene has to be portrayed, (2) under slightly different points of view, (3) by a sufficient number of low resolution acquisitions. These restrictions make super-resolution unsuitable for a wide spectra of applications such as surveillance, or video analysis in general (summarization, restoration), wherever the inadequacy of the cameraman or the circumstances of the acquisitions strongly intervene.

In this chapter, we presented a Bayesian paradigm for super-resolution, called Distillation, which processes video data in order to recover those optimal conditions, *distilling* from the low resolution images only the information which is functional to the creation of high resolution representations. This process can be applied to whole video frames, assuming that the objects of interest are subjected to rigid motion only or selectively on image patches, decomposing complex motions into a hierarchical chain of local rigid dynamics. This second strategy gives rise to the Super-resolved Digests, which can be employed to summarize a video sequence as a collection of high resolved collages.

Far from being perfect, Distillation and Super-resolved Digests can be improved in several ways, from better algorithms for the identification, labeling and rating of visual information, to more refined image fusion techniques. Moreover, some information has not been yet exploited to the fullest, such as the relative pixel-wise registrations, which collectively determine the objects trajectories, and which have been "neutralized" to focus on the objects appearances. This temporal aspect of the analysis has been briefly used only within the timeline collage representation, but could be used to trace objects behaviors.

However, we believe our approach is an important step towards achieving practical super-resolution in a wide range of settings, thus providing a new valuable tool for potential applications. A small list of these applications is: video summarization, easily the most immediate usage of a compressed, information-rich representation of a video sequence; video restoration, by enhancing or recovering the noisy, corrupted or missing low resolution data; activity analysis, by tracing objects behaviors in the form of trajectories, interactions and switches.

REFERENCES

Baker, S., & Kanade, T. (2002). Limits on Super-Resolution and How to Break Them. *IEEE Transactions on Pattern Analysis and Machine Intelligence, 24*(9), 1167–1183. doi:10.1109/TPAMI.2002.1033210

Ben-Ezra, M., Zhouchen, L., & Wilburn, B. (2007, October). Penrose Pixels Super-Resolution in the Detector Layout Domain. In *IEEE International Conference on Computer Vision*, Rio de Janeiro, Brazil.

Bishop, C. M., Blake, A., & Marthi, B. (2003). Super-resolution enhancement of video. In C. M. Bishop, & B. Frey (Eds.), *Proceedings Artificial Intelligence and Statistics.*

Cheeseman, P., Kanefsky, B., Kraft, R., Stutz, J., & Hanson, R. (1996). *Super-Resolved Surface Reconstruction from Multiple Images.* (G. R. Heidbreder, Ed.) Dordrecht, the Netherlands: Kluwer Academic Publishers.

Dempster, A. P., Laird, N. M., & Rubin, D. B. (1977). Maximum Likelihood from incomplete data via the EM algorithm. In . *Proceedings of the Royal Statistical Society, 39*, 1–38.

Freeman, W. T., Jones, T. R., & Pasztor, E. C. (2002). Example-Based Super-Resolution. *IEEE Computer Graphics and Applications, 22*(2), 56–65. doi:10.1109/38.988747

Freeman, W. T., Pasztor, E. C., & Carmichael, O. T. (2000). Learning Low-Level Vision. *International Journal of Computer Vision, 40*(1), 25–47. doi:10.1023/A:1026501619075

Hardie, R. C., Barnard, K. J., & Armstrong, E. E. (1997). Joint MAP registration and high-resolution image estimation using a sequence of undersampled images. *IEEE Transactions on Image Processing, 6*, 1621–1633. doi:10.1109/83.650116

Kanade, T., Collins, R., & Lipton, A. (2000). Special Issue on Video Surveillance. *IEEE Transactions on Pattern Analysis and Machine Intelligence, 22*(8).

Kannan, A., Jojic, N., & Frey, B. J. (2008). Fast Transformation-Invariant Component Analysis. *International Journal of Computer Vision, 77*(1-3), 87–101. doi:10.1007/s11263-007-0094-4

Kim, K. I., Franz, M. O., & Scholkopf, B. (2004). Kernel Hebbian Algorithm for single-frame super-resolution. In A. Leonardis & H. Bischof (Eds.), *Statistical Learning in Computer Vision* (pp. 135-149).

Kursun, O., & Favorov, O. (2002). Single-frame super-resolution by a cortex based mechanism using high level visual features in natural images. In *Workshop on Application of Computer Vision* (pp. 112-117).

Lin, Z., & Shum, H. Y. (2004). Fundamental Limits of Reconstruction-Based Superresolution Algorithms under Local Translation. *IEEE Transactions on Pattern Analysis and Machine Intelligence, 26*(1), 83–97. doi:10.1109/TPAMI.2004.1261081

Lin, Z. C., He, J. F., Tang, X., & Tang, C. K. (2007). Limits of Learning-Based Superresolution Algorithms. In *IEEE International Conference on Computer Vision,* Rio de Janeiro, Brazil (pp. 1-8).

Pickup, L. C., Capel, D. P., Roberts, S. J., & Zisserman, A. (2006). Bayesian Image Super-Resolution, Continued. In *Advances in Neural Information Processing Systems*, Vancouver, Canada.

Pickup, L. C., Roberts, S. J., & Zisserman, A. (2006). Optimizing and Learning for Super-resolution. In *Proceedings of the British Machine Vision Conference.*

Schultz, R. R., & Stevenson, R. L. (1994). A Bayesian approach to image expansion for improved definition. *IEEE Transactions on Image Processing, 3*(3), 233–242. doi:10.1109/83.287017

Shechtman, E., Caspi, Y., & Irani, M. (2002). Increasing Space-Time Resolution in Video. In [Berlin: Springer-Verlag.]. *Proceedings of the European Conference on Computer Vision-Part, I,* 753–768.

Tipping, M. E. (2001). Sparse Bayesian Learning and the Relevance Vector Machine. *Journal of Machine Learning Research, 1,* 211–244. doi:10.1162/15324430152748236

Tipping, M. E., & Bishop, C. M. (2002). Bayesian Image Super-resolution. In *Advances in Neural Information Processing Systems,* Vancouver, Canada.

Compilation of References

Achard, C., Qu, X., Mokhber, A., & Milgram, M. (2008). A novel approach for recognition of human actions with semi-global features. *Machine Vision and Applications*, *19*(1), 27–34. doi:10.1007/s00138-007-0074-2

Agarwal, A., & Triggs, B. (2004). Learning to track 3D human motion from silhouettes. *International Conference on Machine Learning* (pp. 9-16).

Agarwal, A., & Triggs, B. (2006). Recovering 3D Human Pose from Monocular Images. *IEEE Transactions on Pattern Analysis and Machine Intelligence*, *28*(1). doi:10.1109/TPAMI.2006.21

Aggarwal, J. K., & Cai, Q. (1999). Human motion analysis: A review. *Computer Vision and Image Understanding*, *73*(3), 428–440. doi:10.1006/cviu.1998.0744

Ahmad, M., & Lee, S.-W. (2008). Human action recognition using shape and CLG-motion flow from multi-view image sequences. *Pattern Recognition*, *41*(7), 2237–2252. doi:10.1016/j.patcog.2007.12.008

Albu, A., Beugeling, T., Virji-Babul, N., & Beach, C. (2007). Analysis of irregularities in human actions with volumetric motion history images. In *IEEE workshop on motion and video computing (WMVC)* (pp. 16-16).

Alexa, M. (2002). Linear combination of transformations. *SIGGRAPH* (pp. 380-387).

Ali, S., Basharat, A., & Shah, M. (2007). Chaotic invariants for human action recognition. In *Proc. Intl. Conf. on Computer Vision (ICCV 2007)* (pp. 1-8).

Allwein, E. L., Schapire, R. E., & Singer, Y. (2000). Reducing multiclass to binary: a unifying approach for margin clas-sifiers. *Journal of Machine Learning Research*, *1*, 113–141. doi:10.1162/15324430152733133

Amit, Y., & Geman, D. (1997). Shape quantization and recognition with randomized trees. *Neural Computation*, *9*(7), 1545–1588. doi:10.1162/neco.1997.9.7.1545

Andriluka, M., Roth, S., & Schiele, B. (2008). People-Tracking-by-Detection and People-Detection-by-Tracking. In *IEEE Conference on Computer Vision and Pattern Recognition (CVPR'08)*.

Avidan, S. (2005). Ensemble Tracking. In *IEEE Conference on Computer Vision and Pattern Recognition (CVPR'05)*.

Babua, R. V., & Ramakrishnan, K. (2004). Recognition of human actions using motion history information extracted from the compressed video. *Image and Vision Computing*, *22*, 597–607. doi:10.1016/j.imavis.2003.11.004

Baker, S., & Kanade, T. (2002). Limits on Super-Resolution and How to Break Them. *IEEE Transactions on Pattern Analysis and Machine Intelligence*, *24*(9), 1167–1183. doi:10.1109/TPAMI.2002.1033210

Batra, D., Chen, T., & Sukthankar, R. (2008). Space-time shapelets for action recognition. In *Proceedings of the Workshop on Motion and Video Computing (WMVC'08)*, Copper Mountain, CO (pp. 1–6).

Beauchemin, S. S., & Barron, J. L. (1995). The computation of optical flow. *ACM Computing Surveys*, *27*(3), 433–466. doi:10.1145/212094.212141

Beccehetti, C., & Ricotti, L. P. P. (2002). *Speech recognition: Theory and C++ implementation*. Hoboken, NJ: John Wiley & Sons.

Beintema, J. A., & Lappe, M. (2002). Perception of biological motion without local image motion. *Proceedings of the National Academy of Sciences of the United States of America, 99*, 5661–5663. doi:10.1073/pnas.082483699

Belongie, S., Malik, J., & Puzicha, J. (2002). Shape matching and object recognition using shape contexts. *IEEE Trans. PAMI, 24*(4), 509–522.

Ben-Ezra, M., Zhouchen, L., & Wilburn, B. (2007, October). Penrose Pixels Super-Resolution in the Detector Layout Domain. In *IEEE International Conference on Computer Vision*, Rio de Janeiro, Brazil.

Beymer, D., & Konolige, K. (1999). Real-Time Tracking of Multiple People Using Continuous Detection. In *IEEE International Conference on Computer Vision (ICCV'99)*.

Bishop, C. M. (2006). *Pattern recognition and machine learning*. New York: Springer.

Bishop, C. M., Blake, A., & Marthi, B. (2003). Super-resolution enhancement of video. In C. M. Bishop, & B. Frey (Eds.), *Proceedings Artificial Intelligence and Statistics*.

Black, M., & Jepson, A. (1998). Eigentracking: Robust matching and tracking of articulated objects using a view-based representation. *International Journal of Computer Vision, 26*, 63–84. doi:10.1023/A:1007939232436

Blank, M., Gorelick, L., Shechtman, E., Irani, M., & Basri, R. (2005). Actions as space-time shapes. In *Proc. Intl. Conf. on Computer Vision (ICCV 2005)* (pp. 1395-1402).

Blum, A. L., & Langley, P. (1997). Selection of relevant features and examples in machine learning. *Artificial Intelligence, 97*(1), 245–271. doi:10.1016/S0004-3702(97)00063-5

Blunsden, S., Andrade, E., Laghaee, A., & Fisher, R. (2007). *Behave interactions test case scenarios, EPSRC project gr/s98146*. Retrieved September 6, 2007, from http://groups.inf.ed.ac.uk/vision/BEHAVEDATA/INTERACTIONS/index

Bobick, A. F., & Davis, J. W. (2001). The recognition of human movement using temporal templates. *IEEE Transactions on Pattern Analysis and Machine Intelligence, 23*(3), 257–267. doi:10.1109/34.910878

Boiman, O., & Irani, M. (2005). Detecting irregularities in images and in video. In *Tenth IEEE International Conference on Computer Vision, (ICCV 2005)* (Vol. 1, pp. 462-469).

Bowden, R. (2000). Learning statistical models of human motion. *IEEE Workshop on Human Modeling, Analysis and Synthesis, Internation Conference on Computer Vision & Pattern Recognition*.

Bradski, G. (1998). Computer vision face tracking as a component of a perceptual user interface. In *Workshop on Applications of Computer Vision* (pp. 214–219).

Brand, M. (1996). *Coupled hidden Markov models for modeling interacting processes* (Tech. Rep. 405). MIT Media Lab Vision and Modeling.

Brand, M., & Kettnaker, V. (2000). Discovery and segmentation of activities in video. *IEEE Trans. PAMI, 22*(8), 844–851.

Brand, M., Oliver, N., & Pentland, A. (1997). Coupled hidden markov models for complex action recognition. In *Proceedings of the CVPR* (pp. 994-999).

Bregler, C. (1997). Learning and recognizing human dynamics in video sequences. In *Proceedings IEEE Conf. Computer Vision and Pattern Recognition*, San Juan, Puerto Rico (pp. 568-574).

Bregler, C., & Malik, J. (1998). Tracking People with Twists and Exponential Maps. *International Conference on Computer Vision & Pattern Recognition* (pp. 8-15).

Brown, L. (2008). Color Retrieval in Video Surveillance. In *Fifth IEEE Int'l Conf. on Advanced Video and Signal Based Surveillance (AVSS)*, Santa Fe, NM.

Brubaker, M. A., Fleet, D. J., & Hertzmann, A. (2007). Physics-Based Person Tracking Using Simplified Lower-Body Dynamics. *Computer Vision and Pattern Recognition*, 1-8.

Bui, H., Phung, D., & Venkatesh, S. (2004). Hierarchical hidden markov models with general state hierarchy. In *Proceedings of the National Conference in Artificial Intelligence* (pp. 324-329).

Bui, H., Venkatesh, S., & West, G. (2002). Policy recognition in the abstract hidden markov model. *Journal of Artificial Intelligence Research, 17*, 451–499.

Buzan, D., Sclaroff, S., & Kollios, G. (2004). Extraction and Clustering of Motion Trajectories in Videos. In *International Conference on Pattern Recognition (ICPR'04).*

Caillette, F., Galata, A., & Howard, T. (2008). Real-time 3-d human body tracking using learnt models of behavior. *Computer Vision and Image Understanding, 109*(2), 112–125. doi:10.1016/j.cviu.2007.05.005

Carlsson, S., & Sullivan, J. (2001). Action recognition by Shape Matching to Key Frames. In *Workshop on Models versus Exemplars in Computer Vision.*

Carr, J. C., Beatson, R. K., McCallum, B. C., Fright, W. R., McLennan, T. J., & Mitchell, T. J. (2003). Smooth Surface Reconstruction from Noisy Range Data. *Applied Research Associates NZ Ltd.*

Carr, J.C., Beatson, R.K., Cherrie, J.B., Mitchell, T.J., Fright, W.R., McCallum, B.C., & Evans, T.R. (2001). Reconstruction and Representation of 3D Objects with Radial Basis Functions. *SIGGRAPH*, 67-76.

Casile, A., & Giese, M. A. (2005). Critical features for the recognition of biological motion. *Journal of Vision (Charlottesville, Va.), 5*, 348–360. doi:10.1167/5.4.6

Caspi, Y., Simakov, D., & Irani, M. (2006). Feature-Based Sequence-to-Sequence Matching. [IJCV]. *International Journal of Computer Vision, 68*(1), 53–64. doi:10.1007/s11263-005-4842-z

Cedras, C., & Shah, M. (1995). Motion-based recognition: A survey. *Image and Vision Computing, 13*(2), 129–155. doi:10.1016/0262-8856(95)93154-K

Chai, J., & Hodgins, J. K. (2005). Performance animation from low-dimensional control signals. *ACM Transactions on Graphics, 24*(3), 686–696. doi:10.1145/1073204.1073248

Chan, M., Hoogs, A., Bhotika, R., Perera, A., Schmiederer, J., & Doretto, G. (2006). Joint recognition of complex events and track matching. In *Proceedings of the 2006 IEEE Computer Society Conference on Computer Vision and Pattern Recognition - Volume 2 (CVPR'06)* (pp. 1615-1622).

Cheeseman, P., Kanefsky, B., Kraft, R., Stutz, J., & Hanson, R. (1996). *Super-Resolved Surface Reconstruction from Multiple Images.* (G. R. Heidbreder, Ed.) Dordrecht, the Netherlands: Kluwer Academic Publishers.

Chen, C., & Fan, G. (2008). Hybrid body representation for integrated pose recognition, localization and segmentation. *IEEE Conference on Computer Vision and Pattern Recognition (CVPR 2008)* (pp. 1-8, 23-28).

Chen, D.-Y., Liao, H.-Y. M., & Shih, S.-W. (2006). Continuous human action segmentation and recognition using a spatio-temporal probabilistic framework. In *Proc. of the eighth IEEE Intl. Symposium on Multimedia* (pp. 1-8).

Chen, D.-Y., Shih, S.-W., & Liao, H.-Y. M. (2007). Human action recognition using 2-D spatio-temporal templates. In *Proceedings of ICME* (pp. 667-670).

Chen, L., Feris, R. S., Zhai, Y., Brown, L., & Hampapur, A. (2008). An integrated system for moving object classification in surveillance videos. In *IEEE International Conference on Advanced Video and Signal-Based Surveillance*, Santa Fe, New Mexico.

Chen, Y., Lee, J., Parent, R., & Machiraju, R. (2005). Markerless monocular motion capture using image features and physical constraints. *Computer Graphincs International*, 36-43. Carnegie Mellon University Graphics Lab Motion Capture Database. (n.d.). Retrieved from http://mocaps.cs.cmu.edu

Cheung, K. M. G., Baker, S., & Kanade, T. (2003). Shape-from-silhouette of articulated objects and its use for human body kinematics estimation and motion capture. In *Proceedings. IEEE Computer Society Conference on Computer Vision and Pattern Recognition, 2003* (vol. 1, pp. 77-84).

Collins, R. T., Liu, Y., & Leordeanu, M. (2005). Online selection of discriminative tracking features. *IEEE Transactions on Pattern Analysis and Machine Intelligence, 27*(10), 1631–1643. doi:10.1109/TPAMI.2005.205

Colombo, C., Comanducci, D., & Del Bimbo, A. (2007). Compact representation and probabilistic classification of human actions in videos. In *Proc IEEE conf. advanced video and signal based surveillance (AVSS 2007)* (pp. 342-346).

Comaniciu, D., Ramesh, V., & Meeh, P. (2000). Real-time tracking of non-rigid objects using mean shift. *IEEE Conference on Computer Vision and Pattern Recognition, 2,* 142–149.

Comaniciu, D., Ramesh, V., & Meer, P. (2003). Kernel-based object tracking. *IEEE Transactions on Pattern Analysis and Machine Intelligence, 25*(5), 564–575. doi:10.1109/TPAMI.2003.1195991

Cortes, C., & Vapnik, V. (1995). Support vector networks. *Machine Learning, 20,* 273–297.

Cristianini, N., & Shawe-Taylor, J. (2000). *An Introduction to Support Vector Machines (and other kernel-based learning methods).* Cambridge, MA: Cambridge Univ. Press.

Crivelli, T., Piriou, G., Bouthemy, P., Cernuschi-Frías, B., & Yao, J. (2008). Simultaneous Motion Detection and Background Reconstruction with a Mixed-State Conditional Markov Random Field. *ECCV 2008.*

Csurka, G., Dance, C., Fan, L., Willamowski, J., & Bray, C. (2004). Visual categorization with bags of keypoints. In *Proceedings ECCV Intl. Workshop on Statistical Learning in Computer Vision* (pp. 1–22).

Cuntoor, N., Yegnanarayana, B., & Chellappa, R. (2008). Activity modeling using event probability sequences. *IEEE Transactions on Image Processing, 17*(4), 594–607. doi:10.1109/TIP.2008.916991

Curio, C., Edelbrunner, J., Kalinke, T., Tzomakas, C., & Seelen, W. (2000). Walking pedestrian recognition. *IEEE Transactions on Intelligent Transportation Systems, 1,* 3. doi:10.1109/6979.892152

Dalal, N., & Triggs, B. (2005). Histograms of oriented gradients for human detection. In *Proc. 10th International Conference on Computer Vision,* China.

Dalal, N., Triggs, B., & Schmid, C. (2006). Human detection using oriented histograms of flow and appearance. In *Proc. ECCV* (pp. 428–441).

Davis, J. W., & Bobick, A. F. (2001). The representation and recognition of action using temporal templates. *IEEE Transactions on Pattern Analysis and Machine Intelligence, 23*(3), 257–267. doi:10.1109/34.910878

Davis, J. W., & Tyagi, A. (2006). Minimal-latency human action recognition using reliable-inference. *Image and Vision Computing, 24*(5), 455–472. doi:10.1016/j.imavis.2006.01.012

de Campos, T. E., & Murray, D. W. (2006). Regression-based Hand Pose Estimation from Multiple Cameras. In *IEEE Computer Society Conference on Computer Vision and Pattern Recognition, 2006* (vol.1, pp. 782-789).

Dee, H. M., & Hogg, D. C. (2004, September). Detecting inexplicable behaviour. In *British Machine Vision Conference* (pp. 477–486).

Demirdjian, D. (2003). Enforcing Constraints for Human Body Tracking. In *Workshop on Multi-object Tracking.*

Demirdjian, D., Ko, T., & Darrell, T. (2003). Constraining Human Body Tracking. In *IEEE International Conference on Computer Vision.*

Demonceaux, C., & Kachi-Akkouche, D. (2004). Motion detection using wavelet analysis and hierarchical Markov models. In *First International Workshop on Spatial Coherence for Visual Motion Analysis,* Prague.

Dempster, A. P., Laird, N. M., & Rubin, D. B. (1977). Maximum Likelihood from incomplete data via the EM algorithm. In . *Proceedings of the Royal Statistical Society, 39,* 1–38.

Deutscher, J., Blake, A., & Reid, I. (2000). Articulated Body Motion Capture by Annealed Particle Filtering. *Computer Vision and Pattern Recognition, 2,* 126–133.

Deva Ramanan, D. A. F., & Zisserman, A. (2007). Tracking People by Learning Their Appearance. *IEEE Trans. Pattern Analysis and Machine Intelligence.*

Dietterich, T. G., & Bakiri, G. (1995). Solving multiclass learning problems via error correcting output codes. *Journal of Artificial Intelligence Research, 2,* 263–286.

Dollar, P., Rabaud, V., Cottrell, G., & Belongie, S. (2005). Behavior recognition via sparse spatio-temporal features. In *2nd Joint IEEE International Workshop on Visual Surveillance and Performance Evaluation of Tracking and Surveillance, 2005* (pp. 65-72).

Dornaika, F., & Davoine, F. (2005). Simultaneous facial action tracking and expression recognition using a particle filter. *IEEE International Conference on Computer Vision,* 1733-1738.

Doucet, A., Godsill, S., & Andrieu, C. (2000). On sequential Monte Carlo sampling methods for bayesian filtering. *Statistics and Computing, 10*(3), 197–208. doi:10.1023/A:1008935410038

Duong, T. V., Bui, H. H., Phung, D. Q., & Venkatesh, S. (2005). Activity recognition and abnormality detection with the switching hidden semi-Markov model. In *CVPR 2005. IEEE Computer Society Conference on Computer Vision and Pattern Recognition, 2005* (vol.1, pp. 838-845).

ECFunded CAVIAR project/IST. (2004). Retrieved from http://homepages.inf.ed.ac.uk/rbf/CAVIAR/

Efros, A. A., Berg, A. C., Mori, G., & Malik, J. (2003). Recognizing action at a distance. In *Proc. 9th International Conference on Computer Vision,* Nice.

Elgammal, A., & Lee, C.-S. (2004). Inferring 3D Body Pose from Silhouettes using Activity Manifold Learning. *International Conference on Computer Vision & Pattern Recognition* (pp. 681-688).

Elgammal, A., Shet, V., Yacoob, Y., & Davis, L. (2003). Learning dynamics for exemplar-based gesture recognition. In *Proceedings of the CVPR* (pp. 571-578).

Fanti, C., Zelnik-Manor, L., & Perona, P. (2005). Hybrid models for human motion recognition. In *Proc. IEEE Conference on Computer Vision and Pattern Recognition,* San Diego, CA.

Farhadi, A., & Tabrizi, M.K. (2008). Learning to Recognize Activities from the Wrong View Point. *ECCV 2008.*

Fathi, A., & Mori, G. (2008). Action recognition by learning mid-level motion features. In *IEEE Computer Society Conference on Computer Vision and Pattern Recognition (CVPR).*

Felleman, D. J., & van Essen, D. C. (1991). Distributed hierarchical processing in the primate visual cortex. *Cerebral Cortex (New York, N.Y.), 1,* 1–47. doi:10.1093/cercor/1.1.1-a

Felzenszwalb, P. F., & Huttenlocher, D. P. (2005). Pictorial Structures for object recognition. *International Journal of Computer Vision.*

Felzenszwalb, P., & Huttenlocher, D. (2003). Efficient Matching of Pictorial Structures. *Computer Vision and Pattern Recognition.*

Feris, R., Tian, Y., Zhai, Y., & Hampapur, A. (2008). Facial image analysis using local feature adaptation prior to learning. In *IEEE International Conference on Automatic Face and Gesture Recognition.* Amsterdam, Netherlands.

Ferrari, V., Jurie, F., & Schmid, C. (2007). Accurate Object Detection with Deformable Shape Models Learnt from Images. In *CVPR '07. IEEE Conference on Computer Vision and Pattern Recognition, 2007.*

Field, D. J. (1987). Relations between the statistics of natural images and the response properties of cortical cells. *Journal of the Optical Society of America. A, Optics and Image Science, 4*(12), 2379–2394. doi:10.1364/JOSAA.4.002379

Filipovych, R., & Ribeiro, E. (2008). Learning human motion models from unsegmented videos. In *IEEE Conference on Computer Vision and Pattern Recognition (CVPR 2008)* (pp.1-7, 23-28).

Fine, S., Singer, Y., & Tishby, N. (1998). The hierarchical hidden markov model: Analysis and applications. *Machine Learning, 32*(1), 41–62. doi:10.1023/A:1007469218079

Forsyth, D. A., & Ponce, J. (2003). *Computer Vision—A Modern Approach.* Upper Saddle River, NJ: Prentice Hall Inc.

Fossati, A., Dimitrijevic, M., Lepetit, V., & Fua, P. (2007). Bridging the gap between detection and tracking for 3d monocular video-based motion capture. In *Proceedings of the CVPR.*

Franc, V. (2000). Pattern Recognition Toolbox for Matlab. *Centre for Machine Perception, Czech Technical University.*

Franc, V., & Hlavac, V. (2003). Greedy Algorithm for a Training Set Reduction in the Kernel Methods. *Int. Conf. on Computer Analysis of Images and Patterns* (pp. 426-433).

Freeman, W. T., Jones, T. R., & Pasztor, E. C. (2002). Example-Based Super-Resolution. *IEEE Computer Graphics and Applications, 22*(2), 56–65. doi:10.1109/38.988747

Freeman, W. T., Pasztor, E. C., & Carmichael, O. T. (2000). Learning Low-Level Vision. *International Journal of Computer Vision, 40*(1), 25–47. doi:10.1023/A:1026501619075

Friedman, J. H. (1996). *Another approach to polychotomous classification.* Statistics department, Stanford University, Stanford, CA.

Friedman, J., Hastie, T., & Tibshirani, R. (2000). Additive logistic regression: a statistical view of boosting. *Annals of Statistics, 38*(2), 337–374. doi:10.1214/aos/1016218223

Fujiyoshi, H., & Lipton, A. (1998). Real-time human motion analysis by image skeletonization. In *Proc. fourth IEEE workshop on applications of computer vision* (pp. 15-21).

Fukushima, K. (1980). Neocognitron: a self-organizing neural network model for mechanisms of pattern recognition unaffected by shift in position. *Biological Cybernetics, 36*, 193–202. doi:10.1007/BF00344251

Galata, A., Johnson, N., & Hogg, D. (2001). Learning variable-length Markov models of behaviour. *Computer Vision and Image Understanding, 81*, 398–413. doi:10.1006/cviu.2000.0894

Gao, J., Hauptmann, A. G., & Wactlar, H. D. (2004). Combining motion segmentation with tracking for activity analysis. In *The Sixth International Conference on Automatic Face and Gesture Recognition (FGR'04)*, Seoul, Korea (pp. 699-704).

Gavrila, D. (2000). Pedestrian Detection from a Moving Vehicle. In *Europe Conference on Computer Vision (ECCV'00).*

Gavrila, D. M. (1999). The visual analysis of human movement: A survey. *Computer Vision and Image Understanding, 73*(1), 82–98. doi:10.1006/cviu.1998.0716

Gawne, T. J., & Martin, J. (2002). Response of primate visual cortical V4 neurons to two simultaneously presented stimuli. *Journal of Neurophysiology, 88*, 1128–1135. doi:10.1152/jn.00151.200

Ghahramani, Z., & Jordan, M. (1996). Factorial hidden markove models. In *Advances in Neural Information Processing Systems* (Vol. 8).

Giese, M. A., & Poggio, T. (2003). Neural mechanisms for the recognition of biological movements. *Nature Neuroscience, 4*, 179–192. doi:10.1038/nrn1057

Gigerenzer, G., Todd, P. M., & ABC Research Group. (1999). *Simple Heuristics That Make Us Smart.* Oxford, UK: Oxford University Press.

Gilbert, A., Illingworth, J., & Bowden, R. (2008). Scale Invariant Action Recognition Using Compound Features Mined from Dense Spatio-temporal Corners. In *Proceedings European Conf. on Computer Vision (ECCV '08)* (pp. 222–233).

Goldenberg, R., Kimmel, R., Rivlin, E., & Rudzsky, M. (2005). Behavior classification by eigendecomposition of periodic motions. *Pattern Recognition, 38*, 1033–1043. doi:10.1016/j.patcog.2004.11.024

Gorelick, L., Blank, M., Shechtman, E., Irani, M., & Basri, R. (2007). Actions as space-time shapes. *IEEE Trans. PAMI, 29*(12), 2247–2253.

Gorelick, L., Galun, M., & Brandt, A. (2006). Shape representation and classification using the poisson equation. [PAMI]. *IEEE Transactions on Pattern Analysis and Machine Intelligence, 28*(12), 1991–2005. doi:10.1109/TPAMI.2006.253

Grabner, H., & Bischof, H. (2006). Online Boosting and Vision. In *IEEE Conference on Computer Vision and Pattern Recognition (CVPR'06)*

Grauman, K., & Darrell, T. The Pyramid Match Kernel: Discriminative Classification with Sets of Image Features. *International Conference on Computer Vision* (pp. 1458-1465).

Grauman, K., Shakhnarovich, G., & Darrell, T. (2003). Inferring 3D Structure with a Statistical Image-Based Shape Model. *International Conference on Computer Vision* (pp. 641-648).

Green, M. (1999). *The appropriate and effective use of security in schools.* US Department of Justice, Report NJC178265.

Green, R. D., & Guan, L. (2004). Quantifying and recognizing human movement patterns from monocular video images part i: A new framework for modeling human motion. *IEEE Transactions on Circuits and Systems for Video Technology, 14*(2), 179–190. doi:10.1109/TCSVT.2003.821976

Grubb, G. (2004). *3D vision sensing for improved pedestrian safety.* Master's thesis, Australian National University.

Guyon, I., & Elisseeff, A. (2003). An introduction to variable and feature selection. [JMLR]. *Journal of Machine Learning Research, 3,* 1157–1182. doi:10.1162/153244303322753616

Hampapur, A., Brown, L., Connell, J., Ekin, A., Haas, N., & Lu, M. (2005). Smart video surveillance: exploring the concept of multiscale spatiotemporal tracking. *IEEE Signal Processing Magazine, 22*(2), 38–51. doi:10.1109/MSP.2005.1406476

Han, F., Shan, Y., Cekander, R., Sawhney, H., & Kumar, R. (2006). A Two-Stage Approach to People and Vehicle Detection With HOG-Based SVM. In *Performance Metrics for Intelligent Systems Workshop,* National Institute of Standards and Technology.

Hardie, R. C., Barnard, K. J., & Armstrong, E. E. (1997). Joint MAP registration and high-resolution image estimation using a sequence of undersampled images. *IEEE Transactions on Image Processing, 6,* 1621–1633. doi:10.1109/83.650116

Harnad, S. (Ed.). (1987). *Categorical perception: the groundwork of cognition.* Cambridge, MA: Cambridge University Press.

Harris, C., & Stephens, M. (1998). A combined corner and edge detector. In *Proceedings of the 4th Alvey Vision Conference* (pp. 147-151).

Hastie, T., & Tibshirani, R. (1998). Classification by pairwise coupling. *Annals of Statistics, 26*(2), 451–471. doi:10.1214/aos/1028144844

Hathaway, R., & Bezdek, J. (1994). NERF C-means: non-Euclidean relational fuzzy clustering. *Pattern Recognition, 27,* 429–437. doi:10.1016/0031-3203(94)90119-8

Hershey, J. R., & Olsen, P. P. A. (2007). Approximating the Kullback Leibler divergence between Gaussian mixture models. In *Proc ICASSP 2007* (Vol. 4, pp. 317-320).

Hillier, F. S., & Lieberman, G. J. (1990). Introduction to mathematical programming. New York: McGraw-Hill.

Hjelmas, E., & Low, B. K. (2001). Face detection: a survey. *Computer Vision and Image Understanding, 83,* 236–274. doi:10.1006/cviu.2001.0921

Hofmann, T. (1999). Probabilistic latent semantic indexing. In *Proceedings Intl. ACM SIGIR Conf. on Research and Development in Information Retrieval* (pp. 50–57).

Hongeng, S., & Nevatia, R. (2003). Large-scale event detection using semi-hidden markov models. In *International Conference on Computer Vision* (Vol. 2, pp. 1455).

Hsieh, J.-W., Hsu, Y.-T., Liao, H.-Y. M., & Chen, C.-C. (2008). Video-based human movement analysis and its application to surveillance systems. *IEEE Transactions on Multimedia, 10*(3), 372–384. doi:10.1109/TMM.2008.917403

Hu, M. (1962). Visual pattern recognition by moment invariants. *I.R.E. Transactions on Information Theory, 8*(2), 179–187. doi:10.1109/TIT.1962.1057692

Hu, W., & Hu, W. (2006). HIGCALS: a hierarchical graph-theoretic clustering active learning system. *IEEE International Conference on Systems, Man and Cybernetics (SMC '06)* (vol. 5, pp.3895-3900).

Hu, W., Tan, T., Wang, L., & Maybank, S. (2004). A survey on visual surveillance of object motion and behaviors. *IEEE Trans. SMC-C, 34*(3), 334–351.

Huang, C., Ai, H., Li, Y., & Lao, S. (2005). Vector boosting for rotation invariant multi-view face detection. In *IEEE International Conference on Computer Vision (ICCV'05),* Beijing, China.

Huang, X., Acero, A., & Hon, A.-W. (2001). *Spoken language processing: A guide to theory, algorithm and system development.* Prentice Hall.

Hubel, D. H., & Wiesel, T. N. (1962). Receptive fields, binocular interaction and functional architecture in the cat's visual cortex. *The Journal of Physiology, 160,* 106–154.

Ikizler, N., & Duygulu, P. (2007). Human action recognition using distribution of oriented rectangular patches. In *Human Motion: Understanding, Modeling, Capture and*

Animation (HUMO'07), Rio de Janeiro, Brazil (LNCS 4814, pp. 271–284).

Intille, S. S., & Bobick, A. F. (2001, March). Recognizing planned, multiperson action. [CVIU]. *Computer Vision and Image Understanding*, *81*(3), 414–445. doi:10.1006/cviu.2000.0896

Isard, M., & Blake, A. (1998). Condensation - conditional density propagation for visual tracking. *International Journal of Computer Vision*, *29*(1), 5–28. doi:10.1023/A:1008078328650

Javed, O., Ali, S., & Shah, M. (2005). Online Detection and Classification of Moving objects Using Progressively Improving Detectors. In *IEEE Conference on Computer Vision and Pattern Recognition (CVPR'05)*.

Jhuang, H., Serre, T., Wolf, L., & Poggio, T. (2007). A biologically inspired system for action recognition. In *Proc. 11th International Conference on Computer Vision*, Rio de Janeiro.

Jia, K., & Yeung, D. (2008). Human action recognition using Local Spatio-Temporal Discriminant Embedding. In *IEEE Conference on Computer Vision and Pattern Recognition (CVPR 2008)* (pp.1-8, 23-28).

Jiang, H., & Martin, D. R. (2008). Finding Actions Using Shape Flows. *ECCV.*

Jiang, H., Drew, M.S., & Ze-Nian Li (2006). Successive convex matching for action detection. In *Proceedings of the 2006 IEEE Computer Society Conference on Computer Vision and Pattern Recognition* (Vol. 2, pp. 1646-1653).

Jitendra, M., & Jan, P. (2001). Matching shapes. *Proceedings. Eighth IEEE International Conference on Computer Vision (ICCV 2001)* (vol.1, pp.454-461).

Jolliffe, I. T. (1986). *Principal Component Analysis*. New York: Springer-Verlag.

Junejo, I., & Foroosh, H. (2008). Euclidean path modeling for video surveillance. *IVC*, *26*(4), 512–528.

Kadir, T., & Brady, M. (2003). Scale saliency: a novel approach to salient feature and scale selection. In *Proceedings Intl. Conf. on Visual Information Engineering (VIE '03)* (pp. 25–28).

Kale, A., Sundaresan, A., Rajagopalan, A. N., Cuntoor, N. P., Roy-Chowdhury, A. K., Kruger, V., & Chellappa, R. (2004). Identification of humans using gait. *IEEE Transactions on Image Processing*, *13*(9), 1163–1173. doi:10.1109/TIP.2004.832865

Kalman, R. E. (1961). A New Approach to Linear Filtering and Prediction Problems. *Transactions on the ASME - . Journal of Basic Engineering*, 95–107.

Kanade, T., Collins, R., & Lipton, A. (2000). Special Issue on Video Surveillance. *IEEE Transactions on Pattern Analysis and Machine Intelligence*, *22*(8).

Kannan, A., Jojic, N., & Frey, B. J. (2008). Fast Transformation-Invariant Component Analysis. *International Journal of Computer Vision*, *77*(1-3), 87–101. doi:10.1007/s11263-007-0094-4

Ke, Y., Sukthankar, R., & Hebert, M. (2005). Efficient visual event detection using volumetric features. In *Proceedings IEEE Intl. Conf. on Computer Vision (ICCV '05)*, (Vol. 1, pp. 166–173).

Ke, Y., Sukthankar, R., & Hebert, M. (2007). Event Detection in Crowded Videos. In *IEEE 11th International Conference on Computer Vision. ICCV 2007* (pp.1-8, 14-21).

Kellokumpu, V., Pietikainen, M., & Heikkila, J. (2005). Human activity recognition using sequences of postures. In *Proc IAPR conf. machine vision applications* (pp. 570-573).

Kellokumpu, V., Zhao, G., & Pietikäinen, M. (2008). Texture based description of movements for activity analysis. In *Proceedings Third International Conference on Computer Vision Theory and Applications* (Vol. 1, pp. 206-213).

Kendall, D., Barden, D., Carne, T., & Le, H. (1999). *Shape and shape theory*. New York: Wiley.

Kim, K. I., Franz, M. O., & Scholkopf, B. (2004). Kernel Hebbian Algorithm for single-frame super-resolution. In A. Leonardis & H. Bischof (Eds.), *Statistical Learning in Computer Vision* (pp. 135-149).

Kim, M., & Kumar, S. Pavlovic, & Rowley, H. V. (2008). Face tracking and recognition with visual constraints in real-world videos. In *IEEE Conference on Computer Vision and Pattern Recognition*.

Kim, M., & Pavlovic, V. (2007). Conditional state space models for discriminative motion estimation. In . *Proceedings of the, ICCV*, 1–8.

Koenderink, J. J., & van Doom, A. J. (1987). Representation of local geometry in the visual system. *Biological Cybernetics, 55*(6), 367–375. doi:10.1007/BF00318371

Kohavi, R., & John, G. H. (1997). Wrappers for feature selection. *Artificial Intelligence, 97*(1), 273–324. doi:10.1016/S0004-3702(97)00043-X

Kovar, L., Gleicher, M., & Pighin, F. (2002). Motion graphs. *SIGGRAPH: Proceedings of the 29th annual conference on Computer graphics and interactive techniques* (pp. 473-482).

Krueger, V. (2001). *Gabor wavelet networks for object representation*. PhD thesis, Christian-Albrecht University, Kiel, Germany.

Kumar, P., Mittal, A., & Kumar, P. (2008). Study of robust and intelligent surveillance in visible and multimodal framework. In *Informatica, 32*, 63-77.

Kumar, S., & Hebert, M. (2003). Discriminative random fields: A discriminative framework for contextual interaction in classification. In . *Proceedings of the, ICCV*, 1150–1157.

Kursun, O., & Favorov, O. (2002). Single-frame super-resolution by a cortex based mechanism using high level visual features in natural images. In *Workshop on Application of Computer Vision* (pp. 112-117).

Kwok, J. T., & Tsang, I. W. (2003). The pre-image problem in kernel methods. *International Conference on Machine Learning* (pp. 408-415).

Lafferty, J., McCallum, A., & Pereira, F. (2001). Conditional random fields: Probabilistic models for segmenting and labeling sequence data. In *Proceedings of the ICML* (pp. 282-289).

Lampl, I., Ferster, D., Poggio, T., & Riesenhuber, M. (2004). Intracellular measurements of spatial integration and the max operation in complex cells of the cat primary visual cortex. *Journal of Neurophysiology, 92*, 2704–2713. doi:10.1152/jn.00060.2004

Lan, X., & Huttenlocher, D. P. (2005). Beyond Trees: Common Factor Models for 2D human Pose Recovery. *IEEE International Conference on Computer Vision.*

Lander, J. (1998). Working with Motion Capture File Formats. *Game Developer*, 30-37.

Laptev, I., & Lindeberg, T. (2003). Local descriptors for spatio-temporal recognition. In *Proc. 9th International Conference on Computer Vision*, Nice.

Laptev, I., & Lindeberg, T. (2003). Space-time interest points. In *Proceedings. Ninth IEEE International Conference on Computer Vision, 2003* (pp. 432-439).

Laptev, I., & Perez, P. P. (2007). Retrieving actions in movies. In *Proc. Intl. Conf. on Computer Vision (ICCV 2007)* (pp. 1-8).

Laptev, I., Marszalek, M., Schmid, C., & Rozenfeld, B. (2008). learning realistic human actions from movies. In *IEEE Computer Vision and Pattern Recognition, 2008. CVPR 2008* (pp. 1-8).

Leibe, B., Schindler, K., & Van Gool, L. (2007). Coupled Detection and Trajectory Estimation for Multi-Object Tracking. In *International Conference on Computer Vision (ICCV'07).*

Leibe, B., Seemann, E., & Schiele, B. (2005). Pedestrian Detection in Crowded Scenes. In *IEEE Conference on Computer Vision and Pattern Recognition (CVPR'05).*

Lepetit, V., & Fua, P. (2006). Keypoint recognition using randomized trees. [PAMI]. *IEEE Transactions on Pattern Analysis and Machine Intelligence, 28*(9), 1465–1479. doi:10.1109/TPAMI.2006.188

Li, H., & Greenspan, M. (2005). Multi-scale gesture recognition from time-varying contours. *Tenth IEEE International Conference on Computer Vision, 2005 (ICCV 2005), 1*, 236-243.

Li, W., Zhang, Z., & Liu, Z. (2008a). Expandable data-driven graphical modeling of human actions based on salient postures. *IEEE Transactions on Circuits and Systems for Video Technology, 18*(11), 1499–1510. doi:10.1109/TCSVT.2008.2005597

Li, W., Zhang, Z., & Liu, Z. (2008b). Graphical modeling and decoding of human actions. In *Proc. IEEE 10th international workshop on multimedia signal processing (MMSP'08)*.

Li, Y., Ai, H., Yamashita, T., Lao, S., & Kawade, M. (2007). Tracking in low frame rate video: A cascade particle filter with discriminative observers of different lifespans. In *IEEE Conference on Computer Vision and Pattern Recognition*.

Liddell, S., & Johnson, R. (1989). American Sign Language: The phonological base. *Sign Language Studies*, *64*, 195–277.

Lin, Z. C., He, J. F., Tang, X., & Tang, C. K. (2007). Limits of Learning-Based Superresolution Algorithms. In *IEEE International Conference on Computer Vision*, Rio de Janeiro, Brazil (pp. 1-8).

Lin, Z., & Davis, L. S. (2008). A pose-invariant descriptor for human detection and segmentation. In *Proceedings of the European Conference on Computer Vision (ECCV'08) - part 4*, Marseille France (LNCS 5305, pp. 423–436).

Lin, Z., & Shum, H. Y. (2004). Fundamental Limits of Reconstruction-Based Superresolution Algorithms under Local Translation. *IEEE Transactions on Pattern Analysis and Machine Intelligence*, *26*(1), 83–97. doi:10.1109/TPAMI.2004.1261081

Ling, H., & Jacobs, D. W. (2007). Shape Classification Using the Inner-Distance. *IEEE Transactions on Pattern Analysis and Machine Intelligence*, *29*(2), 286–299. doi:10.1109/TPAMI.2007.41

Little, J. J., & Boyd, J. (1998). Recognizing people by their gait: the shape of motion. *Videre*, *1*(2), 2–32.

Liu, C., & Ahuja, N. (2004). A model for dynamic shape and its applications. In *Proceedings of the 2004 IEEE Computer Society Conference on Computer Vision and Pattern Recognition (CVPR 2004)* (Vol. 2, pp. 129-134).

Liu, C., & Shum, H. (2003). Kullback-leibler boosting. In *IEEE Conference on Computer Vision and Pattern Recognition (CVPR'03)*, Madison, Wisconsin.

Liu, J., & Shah, M. (2008). Learning human actions via information maximization. In *IEEE conf. on Computer Vision and Pattern Recognition (CVPR 2008)* (pp. 1-8).

Liu, J., Ali, S., & Shah, M. (2008). Recognizing human actions using multiple features. In *IEEE conf. on Computer Vision and Pattern Recognition (CVPR 2008)* (pp. 1-8).

Liu, X., & Chua, C. S. (2006, January). Multi-agent activity recognition using observation decomposed hidden Markov models. *Image and Vision Computing*, *2626*(1), 247–256.

Lowe, D. (2004). Distinctive image features from scale-invariant keypoints. *International Journal of Computer Vision*, *60*(2), 91–110. doi:10.1023/B:VISI.0000029664.99615.94

Lowe, D. G. (1999). Object recognition from local scale-invariant features. In *Proceedings IEEE Intl. Conf. on Computer Vision (ICCV '99)* (pp. 1150–1157).

Lowe, D. G. (2004). Distinctive image features from scale-invariant keypoints. *International Journal of Computer Vision*, *60*(2), 91–110. doi:10.1023/B:VISI.0000029664.99615.94

Lu, P., Nocedal, J., Zhu, C., & Byrd, R. H. (1995). A limited memory algorithm for bound constrained optimization. *SIAM Journal on Scientific Computing*, *16*, 1190–1208. doi:10.1137/0916011

Lu, W., & Little, J. J. (2006). Simultaneous Tracking and Action Recognition using the PCA-HOG Descriptor. In *The 3rd Canadian Conference on Computer and Robot Vision, 2006* (pp. 6-6).

Lucas, B. D., & Kanade, T. (1981). An iterative image registration technique with an application to stereo vision. In *DARPA Image Understanding Workshop*.

Lucena, M., Fuertes, J. M., & de la Blanca, N. P. (2004). Evaluation of three optical flow based observation models for tracking. In *International Conference on Pattern Recognition* (pp. 236–239).

Luna, F. (2004). Skinned Mesh Character Animation with Direct3D 9.0c. Retreived from http://www.moons-lab.com.

Lv, F., & Nevatia, R. (2007). Single View Human Action Recognition using Key Pose Matching and Viterbi Path

Searching. In *IEEE Conference on Computer Vision and Pattern Recognition (CVPR '07)* (pp.1-8, 17-22).

Lv, F., & Nevatia, R. (2007). Single view human action recognition using key pose matching and viterbi path searching. In *IEEE conf. on Computer Vision and Pattern Recognition (CVPR 2007)*.

MacCormick, J., & Isard, M. (2000). Partitioned sampling, articulated objects, and interface-quality hand tracking. *European Conference on Computer Vision*.

Madabhushi, A., & Aggarwal, J. K. (1999). A Bayesian approach to human activity recognition. In *Proceedings Second IEEE Workshop on Visual Surveillance*, Fort Collins (pp. 25-32).

Manning, C. D., & Schtze, H. (1999). *Foundations of statistical natural language processing*. Cambridge, MA: MIT Press.

Martinez, A. M., & Kak, A. C. (2001). PCA versus LDA. *IEEE Transactions on Pattern Analysis and Machine Intelligence*, *23*(2), 228–233. doi:10.1109/34.908974

Masoud, O., & Papanikolopoulos, N. (2003). A method for human action recognition. *Image and Vision Computing*, *21*, 729–743. doi:10.1016/S0262-8856(03)00068-4

Matas, J., Chum, O., Urban, M., & Pajdla, T. (2002). Robust Wide Baseline Stereo from Maximally Stable Extremal Regions. In *Proc. 13th British Machine Vision Conf.* (pp. 384-393).

Matthews, I., Ishikawa, T., & Baker, S. (2004). The template update problem. *IEEE Transactions on Pattern Analysis and Machine Intelligence*, *26*(6), 810–815. doi:10.1109/TPAMI.2004.16

Mccallum, A., Freitag, D., & Pereira, F. (2000). Maximum entropy markov models for information extraction and segmentation. In *Proceedings of the ICML* (pp. 591-598).

Mendoza, M. A., & de la Blanca, N. P. (2008). Applying space state models in human action recognition: A comparative study. In *Articulated motion and deformable objects* (LNCS 5098, pp. 53-62).

Meng, H., Freeman, M., Pears, N., & Bailey, C. (2008). Real-time human action recognition on an embedded, reconfigurable video processing architecture. *Journal of Real-Time Image Processing*, *3*(3), 163–176. doi:10.1007/s11554-008-0073-1

Miezianko, R., & Pokrajac, D. (2008). People detection in low resolution infrared videos. In *IEEE International Workshop on Object Tracking and Classification in and Beyond the Visible Spectrum (OTCBVS'08)*.

Mikolajczyk, K., & Schmid, C. (2002). An affine invariant interest point detector. In *Proceedings European Conf. on Computer Vision (ECCV '02)* (pp. 128–142).

Mikolajczyk, K., & Schmid, C. (2003). A performance evaluation of local descriptors. In *Proceedings. 2003 IEEE Computer Society Conference on Computer Vision and Pattern Recognition* (vol. 2, pp. 257-263).

Mikolajczyk, K., & Uemura, H. (2008). Action recognition with motion-appearance vocabulary forest. In *CVPR 2008. IEEE Conference on Computer Vision and Pattern Recognition, 2008* (pp. 1-8, 23-28).

Moeslund, T. B., & Granum, E. (2000). 3D Human Pose Estimation using 2D-Data and An Alternative Phase Space Representation. In *Proceedings of the IEEE Workshop on Human Modeling, Analysis and Synthesis* (pp. 26-33).

Moeslund, T. B., & Granum, E. (2001). A survey of computer vision-based human motion capture. *Computer Vision and Image Understanding*, *81*, 231–268. doi:10.1006/cviu.2000.0897

Moeslund, T. B., Hilton, A., & Kruger, V. (2006). A survey of advances in vision-based human motion capture and analysis. *Computer Vision and Image Understanding*, *104*(2-3), 90–126. doi:10.1016/j.cviu.2006.08.002

Moeslund, T., & Granum, E. (2001). A survey of computer vision-based human motion capture. *Computer Vision and Image Understanding*, *81*(3), 231–268. doi:10.1006/cviu.2000.0897

Mokhber, A., Achard, C., & Milgram, M. (2008). Recognition of human behavior by space-time silhouette characterization. *Pattern Recognition*, *29*(1), 81–89. doi:10.1016/j.patrec.2007.08.016

Moon, K., & Pavlovic, V. (2005). Estimation of Human Figure Motion Using Robust Tracking of Articulated Layers. *CVPR*.

Moore, D., & Essa, I. (2002). Recognizing multitasked activities from video using recognizing multitasked activities from video using stochastic context-free grammar. In *American Association of Artificial Intelligence (AAAI) Conference*.

Morency, L.-P., Quattoni, A., & Darrell, T. (2007). Latent-dynamic discriminative models for continuous gesture recognition. In *Proceedings of the CVPR*.

Mori, G., & Malik, J. (2002). Estimating human body configurations using shape context matching. In *European Conference on Computer Vision*.

Müller-Gerking, J., Pfurtscheller, G., & Flyvbjerg, H. (1999). Designing optimal spatial filters for single-trial EEG classification in a movement task. *Clinical Neurophysiology*, *110*(5), 787–798. doi:10.1016/S1388-2457(98)00038-8

Munder, S., & Gavrila, D. (2006). An experimental study on pedestrian classification. *IEEE Transactions on Pattern Analysis and Machine Intelligence*, *28*(11), 1863–1868. doi:10.1109/TPAMI.2006.217

Murphy, K. (1998). Fitting a constrained conditional linear Gaussian distribution. *Technical report*.

Murphy, K. (2002). *Dynamic Bayesian Networks: Representation, Inference and Learning*. PhD Thesis, UC Berkeley, Computer Science Division.

Murphy, K. P. (2002). Dynamic Bayesian networks. In *Probabilistic Graphical Models*.

Murphy, K. P., & Paskin, M. A. (2001). Linear time inference in hierarchical HMMs. In *Proceedings of the NIPS*.

Murphy, K. P., Weiss, Y., & Jordan, M. I. (1999). "Loopy belief propagation for approximate inference: An empirical study," in *In Proceedings of Uncertainty in AI*, 467–475.

NASA. (2000). *NASA-STD-3000: Man-systems integration standards*. Retrieved from http://msis.jsc.nasa.gov/sections/section03.htm

Natarajan, P., & Nevatia, R. (2007a). Hierarchical multi-channel hidden semi markov models. In *Proceedings of the IJCAI* (pp. 2562-2567).

Natarajan, P., & Nevatia, R. (2007b). Coupled hidden semi markov models for activity recognition. In *Proceedings of the WMVC*.

Natarajan, P., & Nevatia, R. (2008). Online, real-time tracking and recognition of human actions. In *IEEE workshop on motion and video computing (WMVC)* (pp. 1-8).

Natarajan, P., & Nevatia, R. (2008). View and scale invariant action recognition using multiview shape-flow models. In *CVPR 2008. IEEE Conference on Computer Vision and Pattern Recognition, 2008* (pp.1-8, 23-28).

Natarajan, P., & Nevatia, R. (2008a). View and scale invariant action recognition using multiview shape-flow models. In *Proceedings of the CVPR*.

Natarajan, P., & Nevatia, R. (2008b). Online, real-time tracking and recognition of human actions. In *Proceedings of the WMVC*.

Navaratnam, R., Thayananthan, A., Torr, P. H. S., & Cipolla, R. (2005). Heirarchical Part-Based Human Body Pose Estimation. *British Machine Vision Conference* (pp. 479-488).

NCSH. (1994). *Anthropometric Reference Data, United States, 1988-1994*. Retrieved from http://www.cdc.gov/nchs/

Ng, A. Y., & Jordan, M. I. (2001). On discriminative vs. generative classifiers: A comparison of logistic regression and naive bayes. In *Proceedings of the NIPS* (pp. 841-848).

Nguyen, N.T., Phung, D.Q., Venkatesh, S., & Bui, H. (2005). Learning and detecting activities from movement trajectories using the hierarchical hidden Markov model. *Computer Vision and Pattern Recognition, 2005* (vol. 2, pp. 955-960).

Niebles, J. C., & Fei-Fei, L. (2007). A hierarchical model of shape and appearance for human action classification. In *Proc. IEEE Conference on Computer Vision and Pattern Recognition*, Minneapolis, MN.

Niebles, J. C., Wang, H., & Fei-Fei, L. (2008). Unsupervised learning of human action categories using spatial-temporal words. *International Journal of Computer Vision, 79*(3), 299–318. doi:10.1007/s11263-007-0122-4

Ning, H., Xu, W., Gong, Y., & Huang, T. (2008). Latent Pose Estimator for Continuous Action Recognition. *ECCV.*

Noriega, P., & Bernier, O. (2007). Multicues 3D Monocular Upper Body Tracking Using Constrained Belief Propagation. *British Machine Vision Conference.*

Oikonomopoulos, A., Patras, I., & Pantic, M. (2006). Spatiotemporal salient points for visual recognition of human actions. *IEEE Transactions on Systems, Man, and Cybernetics . Part B, 36*(3), 710–719.

Okuma, K., Taleghani, A., & Freitas, N. (2004). Little J., & Lowe, D. A boosted particle filter: multi-target detection and tracking. In *European Conference on Computer Vision (ECCV'04).*

Oliver, N. M., Rosario, B., & Pentland, A. (1998). Graphical models for recognizing human interactions. In *Proc. of Intl. Conference on Neural Information and Processing Systems (NIPS).*

Oliver, N. M., Rosario, B., & Pentland, A. P. (2000). A Bayesian computer vision system for modeling human interactions. *IEEE Transactions on Pattern Analysis and Machine Intelligence, 22*(8), 831–843. doi:10.1109/34.868684

Oliver, N., Garg, A., & Horvits, E. (2004). Layered representations for learning and inferring office activity from multiple sensory channels. *Computer Vision and Image Understanding, 96*, 163–180. doi:10.1016/j.cviu.2004.02.004

Oshin, O., Gilbert, A., Illingworth, J., & Bowden, R. (2008). Spatio-temporal Feature Recogntion using Randomised Ferns. In *Proceedings Intl. Workshop on Machine Learning for Vision-based Motion Analysis (MLVMA '08)* (pp. 1-12).

Ozuysal, M., Fua, P., & Lepetit, V. (2007). Fast keypoint recognition in ten lines of code. In *Proceedings IEEE Conf. on Computer Vision and Pattern Recognition (CVPR '07)* (pp. 1–8).

Patil, R., Rybski, P., Veloso, M., & Kanade, T. (2004). People Detection and Tracking in High Resolution Panoramic Video Mosaic. In *Proceedings of the 2004 IN IEEE/RSJ International Conference on Intelligent Robots and Systems* (pp. 1323-1328).

Pavan, M., & Pelillo, M. (2003). A new graph-theoretic approach to clustering and segmentation. In *Proceedings. 2003 IEEE Computer Society Conference on Computer Vision and Pattern Recognition, 2003* (vol.1, pp. 18-20).

Pavan, M., & Pelillo, M. (2004). Efficient out-of-sample extension of dominant-set clusters. In *Proceedings of Neural Information Processing Systems.*

Pavan, M., & Pelillo, M. (2007). Dominant sets and pairwise clustering. *IEEE Trans. PAMI, 29*(1), 167–172.

Pavlovic, V., Rehg, J. M., & MacCormick, J. (2000). Learning switching linear models of human motion. In *Proceedings of the NIPS* (pp. 981-987).

Pavlovic, V., Rehg, J. M., Cham, T.-J., & Murphy, K. P. (1999). A Dynamic Bayesian Network Approach to Figure Tracking Using Learned Dynamic Models. In *IEEE International Conference on Computer Vision.*

Pearl, J. (1988). *Probabilistic Reasoning in Intelligent Systems: Networks of Plausible Inference.* San Francisco: Morgan Kaufmann.

Peixoto, P., Goncalves, J., & Araujo, H. (2002). Real-time gesture recognition system based on contour signatures. In *Proceedings. 16th International Conference on Pattern Recognition, 2002* (vol.1, 447-450).

Perez, P., Hue, C., Vermaak, J., & Gangnet, M. (2002). Color-based probabilistic tracking. In *European Conference on Computer Vision* (pp. 661–675).

Perse, M., Kristan, M., Pers, J., & Kovacic, S. (2006, May). A template-based multi-player action recognition of the basketball game. In J. Pers & D. R. Magee (Eds.), *ECCV Workshop on Computer Vision Based Analysis in Sport Environments,* Graz, Austria (pp. 71–82).

Peursum, P., Venkatesh, S., & West, G. A. W. (2007). Tracking-as-recognition for articulated full-body human motion analysis. In *Proceedings of the CVPR.*

Pham, M., & Cham, T. (2007). Fast training and selection of Haar features using statistics in boosting-based face detection. In *IEEE International Conference on Computer Vision (ICCV'07)*, Rio de Janeiro, Brazil.

Pickup, L. C., Capel, D. P., Roberts, S. J., & Zisserman, A. (2006). Bayesian Image Super-Resolution, Continued. In *Advances in Neural Information Processing Systems*, Vancouver, Canada.

Pickup, L. C., Roberts, S. J., & Zisserman, A. (2006). Optimizing and Learning for Super-resolution. In *Proceedings of the British Machine Vision Conference.*

Pierobon, M., Marcon, M., Sarti, A., & Tubaro, S. (2005). Clustering of human actions using invariant body shape descriptor and dynamic time warping. In *Proc. IEEE AVSS 2005* (pp. 22-27).

Pontil, M., & Verri, A. (1998). Support vector machines for 3d object recognition. *IEEE Transactions on Pattern Analysis and Machine Intelligence, 20*(6), 637–646. doi:10.1109/34.683777

Poppe, R., & Poel, M. (2008). Discriminative human action recognition using pairwise CSP classifiers. In *Proceedings of the International Conference on Automatic Face and Gesture Recognition (FGR'08)*, Amsterdam, The Netherlands.

Quattoni, A., Collins, M., & Darrell, T. (2004). Conditional random fields for object recognition. In *Proceedings of the NIPS.*

Quattoni, A., Wang, S. B., Morency, L.-P., Collins, M., & Darrell, T. (2007). Hidden conditional random fields. [PAMI]. *IEEE Transactions on Pattern Analysis and Machine Intelligence, 29*(10), 1848–1852. doi:10.1109/TPAMI.2007.1124

Rabiner, L. R. (1989). A tutorial on hidden Markov models and selected applications in speech recognition. *Proceedings of the IEEE, 77*(2), 257–286. doi:10.1109/5.18626

Ramanan, D., & Forsyth, D. A. (2003). Finding and Tracking People from the Bottom Up. *Computer Vision and Pattern Recognition.*

Ramanan, D., Forsyth, D. A., & Zisserman, A. (2005). Strike a Pose: Tracking People by Finding Stylized Poses. *Computer Vision and Pattern Recognition.*

Ramanan, D., Forsyth, D. A., & Zisserman, A. (2007). Tracking people by learning their appearance. *IEEE Transactions on Pattern Analysis and Machine Intelligence, 29*, 65–81. doi:10.1109/TPAMI.2007.250600

Ramesh, P., & Wilpon, J. G. (1992). Modeling state durations in hidden markov models for automatic speech recognition. In *Proceedings of the ICASSP* (pp. 381-384).

Rao, C., Yilmaz, A., & Shah, M. (2002). View-invariant representation and recognition of actions. *International Journal of Computer Vision, 50*(2), 203–226. doi:10.1023/A:1020350100748

Rehg, J. M., & Kanade, T. (1995). Model-Based Tracking of Self-Occluding Articulated Objects. *ICCV.*

Ren, L., Shakhnarovich, G., Hodgins, J. K., Pfister, H., & Viola, P. (2005). Learning Silhouette Features for Control of Human Motion. *ACM Transactions on Graphics, 24*(4). doi:10.1145/1095878.1095882

Ren, X., Berg, A. C., & Malik, J. (2005). Recovering Human Body Configurations using Pairwise Constraints between Parts. In *IEEE International Conference on Computer Vision.*

Ribeiro, P., & Santos-Victor, J. (2005, September). Human activities recognition from video: modeling, feature selection and classification architecture. In *Workshop on Human Activity Recognition and Modelling (HAREM 2005 - in conjunction with BMVC 2005)*, Oxford (pp. 61–70).

Riesenhuber, M., & Poggio, T. (1999). Hierarchical models of object recognition in cortex. *Nature Neuroscience, 2*, 1019–1025. doi:10.1038/14819

Robertson, N. M. (2006, June). *Automatic Causal Reasoning for Video Surveillance.* PhD thesis, Hertford College, University of Oxford.

Rodriguez, M. D., Ahmed, J., & Shah, M. (2008). Action MACH a spatio-temporal Maximum Average Correlation Height filter for action recognition. In *IEEE Conference on Computer Vision and Pattern Recognition (CVPR 2008)* (pp.1-8, 23-28).

Rodriguez, M., Ahmed, J., & Shah, M. (2008). Action mach a spatio-temporal maximum average correlation height filter for action recognition. In *IEEE conf. on Computer Vision and Pattern Recognition (CVPR)* (pp. 1-8).

Ronfard, R., Schmid, C., & Triggs, B. (2002). Learning to parse pictures of people. In *ECCV* (pp. 700-714).

Rosario, B., Oliver, N., & Pentland, A. (1999). A synthetic agent system for Bayesian modeling human interactions. In *Proceedings of the Third International Conference on Autonomous Agents (Agents'99)* (pp. 342-343).

Ross, D., Lim, J., Lin, R., & Yang, M. (2008). Incremental learning for robust visual tracking. *International Journal of Computer Vision*, *77*(1-3), 125–141. doi:10.1007/s11263-007-0075-7

Rowley, H., Baluja, S., & Kanade, T. (1998). Neural network-based face detection. *IEEE Transactions on Pattern Analysis and Machine Intelligence*, *20*(1), 23–38. doi:10.1109/34.655647

Rubner, Y., Tomasi, C., & Guibas, L. J. (1998). A metric for distributions with applications to image databases. In *IEEE International Conference on Computer Vision* (pp. 59–66).

Ryoo, M., & Aggarwal, J. (2006). Recognition of composite human activities through context-free grammar based representation. In *Proceedings of the 2006 IEEE Computer Society Conference on Computer Vision and Pattern Recognition - Volume 2 (CVPR'06)* (pp. 1709-1718).

Sabzmeydani, P., & Mori, G. (2007). Detecting Pedestrians by Learning Shapelet Features. In *IEEE Conference on Computer Vision and Pattern Recognition (CVPR'07)*.

Safonova, A., Hodgins, J. K., & Pollard, N. S. (2004). Synthesizing physically realistic human motion in low-dimensional. *ACM Transactions on Graphics*, *23*(3), 514–521. doi:10.1145/1015706.1015754

Saul, L. K., & Roweis, S. T. (2000). Nonlinear dimensionality reduction by locally linear embedding. *Science*, *290*, 2323–2269. doi:10.1126/science.290.5500.2323

Saul, L. K., & Roweis, S. T. (2003). Think globally, fit locally: unsupervised learning of low dimensional manifolds. *Journal of Machine Learning Research*, *4*, 119–155. doi:10.1162/153244304322972667

Saul, M. J. L. (1999). Mixed memory markov models: decomposing complex stochastic processes as mixtures of simpler ones. *Machine Learning*, *37*(1), 75–87. doi:10.1023/A:1007649326333

Savarese, S., DelPozo, A., Niebles, J., & Fei-Fei, L. (2008). Spatial-temporal correlations for unsupervised action classification. In *IEEE workshop on motion and video computing (WMVC)* (pp. 1-8).

Schapire, R., & Singer, Y. (1999). Improved boosting algorithms using confidence-rated predictions. *Machine Learning*, *37*, 297–336. doi:10.1023/A:1007614523901

Schindler, K., & van Gool, L. (2008). Action snippets: How many frames does human action recognition require? In *IEEE Conference on Computer Vision and Pattern Recognition (CVPR 2008)* (pp.1-8, 23-28).

Schlenzig, J., Hunter, E., & Ishii, K. (1994). Recursive identification of gesture inputs using hidden Markov models. In *Proc. Second Annual Conference on Applications Computer Vision* (pp. 187-104).

Schmid, C., & Mohr, R. (1997). Local grayvalue invariants for image retrieval. [PAMI]. *IEEE Transactions on Pattern Analysis and Machine Intelligence*, *19*(5), 530–534. doi:10.1109/34.589215

Schölkopf, B., & Smola, A. J. (2002). *Learning with Kernels: Support Vector Machines, Regularization, Optimization and Beyond*. Cambridge, MA: MIT Press.

Schölkopf, B., Knirsch, P., Smola, C., & Burges, A. (1998). Fast approximation of support vector kernel expansions, and an interpretation of clustering as approximation in feature spaces. *Mustererkennung*, 124-132.

Schölkopf, B., Mika, S., Smola, A. J., Rätsch, G., & Müller, K. R. (1998). Kernel PCA pattern reconstruction via approximate pre-images. *International Conference on Artificial Neural Networks* (pp. 147-152).

Schölkopf, B., Smola, A. J., & Müller, K. R. (1997). Kernel principal component analysis. *Internation Conference on Artificial Neural Networks* (pp. 583-588).

Schölkopf, B., Smola, A. J., & Müller, K. R. (1999). Kernel PCA and De-noising in feature spaces. *Advances in Neural Information Processing Systems*, 536–542.

Schraudolph, N. N., Günter, S., & Vishwanathan, S. V. N. (2007). Fast Iterative Kernel PCA. *Advances in Neural Information Processing Systems.*

Schüldt, C., Laptev, I., & Caputo, B. (2004). Recognizing human actions: a local SVM approach. In *Proc. International Conference on Pattern Recognition,* Cambridge.

Schuldt, C., Laptev, I., & Caputo, B. (2004). Recognizing human actions: A local SVM approach. In *Proceedings Intl. Conf. on Pattern Recognition (ICPR '04)* (pp. 32–36).

Schultz, R. R., & Stevenson, R. L. (1994). A Bayesian approach to image expansion for improved definition. *IEEE Transactions on Image Processing, 3*(3), 233–242. doi:10.1109/83.287017

Scovanner, P., Ali, S., & Shah, M. (2007). A 3-dimensional sift descriptor and its application to action recognition. In *Proceedings Intl. Conf. on Multimedia* (pp. 357–360).

Senior, A., Brown, L., Shu, C., Tian, Y., Lu, M., Zhai, Y., & Hampapur, A. (2007). Visual person searches for retail loss detection. *International Conference on Vision Systems.*

Senior, A., Hampapur, A., Tian, Y., Brown, L., Pankanti, S., & Bolle, R. (2001). Appearance models for occlusion handling. *International Workshop on Performance Evaluation of Tracking and Surveillance.*

Senior, A., Pankanti, S., Hampapur, A., Brown, L., Tian, Y., & Ekin, A. (2005). Enabling video privacy through computer vision. *IEEE Security & Privacy, 3*(3), 50–57. doi:10.1109/MSP.2005.65

Serge, B., Jitendra, M., & Jan, P. (2002). Shape matching and object recognition using shape contexts. *IEEE Transactions on Pattern Analysis and Machine Intelligence, 24*(4), 509–522. doi:10.1109/34.993558

Serre, T., Wolf, L., & Poggio, T. (2005). Object recognition with features inspired by visual cortex. In *Proc. IEEE Conference on Computer Vision and Pattern Recognition,* San Diego, CA.

Serre, T., Wolf, L., Bileschi, S., Riesenhuber, M., & Poggio, T. (2007). Object recognition with cortex-like mechanisms. *IEEE Transactions on Pattern Analysis and Machine Intelligence, 29*(3), 411–426. doi:10.1109/TPAMI.2007.56

Shawe-Taylor, J., & Christianini, N. (2000). *Support Vector Machines.* Cambridge, MA: Cambridge University Press.

Shechtman, E., & Irani, M. (2005). Space-time behavior based correlation. In *CVPR 2005. IEEE Computer Society Conference on Computer Vision and Pattern Recognition, 2005* (Vol. 1, pp. 405-412).

Shechtman, E., & Irani, M. (2005). Space-time behavior based correlation. In *IEEE conf. on Computer Vision and Pattern Recognition (CVPR 2005)* (Vol. 1, pp. 405-412).

Shechtman, E., & Irani, M. (2007). Space-time behavior-based correlation. [PAMI]. *IEEE Transactions on Pattern Analysis and Machine Intelligence, 29*(11), 2045–2056. doi:10.1109/TPAMI.2007.1119

Shechtman, E., Caspi, Y., & Irani, M. (2002). Increasing Space-Time Resolution in Video. In [Berlin: Springer-Verlag.]. *Proceedings of the European Conference on Computer Vision-Part, I,* 753–768.

Shi, J., & Malik, J. (2000). Normalised cuts and image segmentation. *IEEE Trans. PAMI, 22*(8), 888–905.

Shi, Q., Li, W., Li, C., & Smola, A. (2008). Discriminative human action segmentation and recognition using semi-Markov model. In *IEEE Conference on Computer Vision and Pattern Recognition, CVPR 2008* (pp. 1-8). Retrieved January 28, 2009, from http://sml.nicta.com.au/~licheng/aSR/

Shirdhonkar, S., & Jacobs, D. W. (2008). Approximate Earth mover's distance in linear time. In *IEEE Conference on Computer Vision and Pattern Recognition.*

Sidenbladh, H., Black, M. J., & Fleet, D. J. (2000). Stochastic Tracking of 3D Human Figures Using 2D Image Motion. In *European Conference on Computer Vision* (pp. 702-718).

Sigal, L., & Black, M. J. (2006). Measure Locally, Reason Globally: Occlusion-sensitive Articulated Pose Estimation. *Computer Vision and Pattern Recognition.*

Sigal, L., Bhatia, S., Roth, S., Black, M. J., & Isard, M. (2004). Tracking Loose-limbed People. *Computer Vision and Pattern Recognition.*

Sigal, L., Zhu, Y., Comaniciu, D., & Black, M. (2004). Tracking Complex Objects using Graphical Object Models.

In *1st International Workshop on Complex Motion* (LNCS 3417, pp. 227-238).

Sivic, J., Russell, B. C., Efros, A. A., Zisserman, A., & Freeman, W. T. (2005). Discovering objects and their location in images. In *Proceedings IEEE Intl. Conf. on Computer Vision (ICCV'05)* (pp. 370–377).

Sminchisescu, C. Kanaujia, A. Li, Z. & Metaxas, D. (2005). Conditional models for contextual human motion recognition. In *International Conference on Computer Vision* (Vol. 2, pp. 1808-1815).

Sminchisescu, C., & Triggs, B. (2001). Covariance Scaled Sampling for Monocular 3D Body Tracking. *Computer Vision and Pattern Recognition.*

Sminchisescu, C., Kanaujia, A., & Metaxas, D. N. (2006). Conditional models for contextual human motion recognition. [CVIU]. *Computer Vision and Image Understanding, 104*(2-3), 210–220. doi:10.1016/j.cviu.2006.07.014

Sminchisescu, C., Kanaujia, A., Li, Z., & Metaxas, D. (2005). Conditional random fields for contextual human motion recognition. In . *Proceedings of the, ICCV,* 1808–1815.

Smith, L. I. (2002). *A Tutorial on Principal Components Analysis.* Vicon Peak: Vicon MX System. (n.d.). Retrieved from http://www.vicon.com/products/systems.html

Starner, T., & Pentland, A. (1995). Real-time american sign language recognition from video using hidden Markov models. In *Proceedings of the ISCV.*

Stauffer, C., & Grimson, W. E. L. (1999). Adaptive background mixture models for real-time tracking. *IEEE Computer Society Conference on Computer Vision and Pattern Recognition* (vol.2, pp. 252).

Stauffer, C., Eric, W., & Grimson, L. (2000). Learning patterns of activity using real-time tracking. *PAMI 2000.*

Sudderth, E. B., Mandel, M. I., Freeman, W. T., & Willsky, A. S. (2004). Distributed Occlusion Reasoning for Tracking with Nonparametric Belief Propagation. *Advances in Neural Information Processing Systems (NIPS).*

Sugimoto, A., Yachi, K., & Matsuyama, T. (2003). Tracking human heads based on interaction between hypotheses with certainty. In *The 13th Scandinavian Conference on Image Analysis.*

Sutton, C., Rohanimanesh, K., & McCallum, A. (2004). Dynamic conditional random fields: factorized probabilistic models for labeling and segmenting sequence data. In *Proceedings of the ICML* (p. 99).

Suzuki, S., & Abe, K. (1985). Topological structural analysis of digitized binary images by border following. *Computer Vision Graphics and Image Processing, 30,* 32–46. doi:10.1016/0734-189X(85)90016-7

Tangkuampien, T. (2007). *Kernel subspace mapping: robust human pose and viewpoint inference from high dimensional training sets.* PhD thesis, Monash University.

Tangkuampien, T., & Suter, D. (2006). Human Motion Denoising via Greedy Kernel Principal Component Analysis Filtering. *International Conference on Pattern Recognition* (pp. 457-460).

Tangkuampien, T., & Suter, D. (2006). Real-Time Human Pose Inference using Kernel Principal Components Pre-image Approximations. *British Machine Vision Conference* (pp. 599-608).

Tayche, L., Shakhnarovich, G., Demirdjian, D., & Darrell, T. (2006). Conditional Random People: Tracking Humans with CRFs and Grid Filters. *Computer Vision and Pattern Recognition.*

Taycher, L., & Darrell, T. (2003). Bayesian Articulated Tracking Using Single Frame Pose Sampling Constraints. In *3rd Int'l Workshop on Statistical and Computational Theories of Vision.*

Taycher, L., Demirdjian, D., Darrell, T., & Shakhnarovich, G. (2006). Conditional random people: Tracking humans with crfs and grid filters. In *Proceedings of the CVPR (1)* (pp. 222-229).

Thurau, C. (2007). Behavior histograms for action recognition and human detection. In *Human Motion: Understanding, Modeling, Capture and Animation (HUMO'07),* Rio de Janeiro, Brazil (LNCS 4814, pp. 271–284).

Tian, T.-P., Li, R., & Sclaroff, S. (2005). Articulated Pose Estimation in a Learned Smooth Space of Feasible Solutions.

In *Computer Vision and Pattern Recognition - Workshops* (pp. 50).

Tian, Y., Feris, R., & Hampapur, A. (2008). Real-time Detection of Abandoned and Removed Objects in Complex Environments. In *The 8th Int'l Workshop on Visual Surveillance (VS)*.

Tian, Y., Lu, M., & Hampapur, A. (2005). Robust and Efficient Foreground Analysis for Real-time Video Surveillance. In *IEEE Conference on Computer Vision and Pattern Recognition (CVPR'05)*, San Diego.

Tipping, M. E. (2001). Sparse Bayesian Learning and the Relevance Vector Machine. *Journal of Machine Learning Research, 1*, 211–244. doi:10.1162/15324430152748236

Tipping, M. E., & Bishop, C. M. (2002). Bayesian Image Super-resolution. In *Advances in Neural Information Processing Systems*, Vancouver, Canada.

Tola, E., Lepetit, V., & Fua, P. (2008). A fast local descriptor for dense matching. In *IEEE Conference on Computer Vision and Pattern Recognition*.

Tomasi, C., & Kanade, T. (1991). *Detection and tracking of point features*. Technical Report CMU-CS-91-132, Carnegie Mellon University.

Toyama, K., Krumm, J., Brumitt, B., & Meyers, B. (1999). Wallflower: Principles and practice of background maintenance. In *Proceedings of the Seventh IEEE International Conference on Computer* (Vol. 1, pp. 255-261).

Tran, D., & Sorokin, A. (2008). Human Activity Recognition with Metric Learning. *ECCV 2008*.

Tseng, D., & Chang, C. (1994). Color segmentation using UCS perceptual attributes. In *Proc. Natl. Sci. Counc. ROC(A), 18*(3), 305-314.

Turaga, P. K., Veeraraghavan, A., & Chellappa, R. (2007). From videos to verbs: Mining videos for activities using a cascade of dynamical systems. In *Proceedings of the CVPR*.

Turaga, P., Chellappa, R., Subrahmanian, V., & Udrea, O. (2008). Machine recognition of human activities: A survey. *IEEE Transactions on Circuits and Systems for Video Technology, 18*(11), 1473–1488. doi:10.1109/TCSVT.2008.2005594

Uemura, H., Ishikawa, S., & Mikolajczyk, K. (2008). Feature Tracking and Motion Compensation for Action Recognition. In *Proceedings British Machine Vision Conference (BMVC '08)* (pp 1-10).

Ukrainitz, Y., & Irani, M. (2006). Aligning Sequences and Actions by Maximizing Space-Time Correlations. *European Conference on Computer Vision (ECCV)*.

Urtasun, R., Fleet, D. J., Hertzmann, A., & Fua, P. (2005). Priors for People Tracking from Small Training Sets. *International Conference on Computer Vision* (pp. 403-410).

Van Vu, T., Bremond, F., & Thonnat, M. (2003). Automatic video interpretation: A recognition algorithm for temporal scenarios based on precompiled scenario models. In *International Conference on Computer Vision Systems* (Vol. 1, pp. 523-533).

Vapnik, V. (1995). *The nature of statistical learning theory*. New York: Springer.

Vapnik, V., Golowich, S. E., & Smola, A. (1997). Support vector method for function approximation, regression estimation, and signal processing. []. Cambridge, MA: MIT Press.]. *Advances in Neural Information Processing Systems, 9*, 281–287.

Veeraraghavan, A., Chellappa, R., & Roy-Chowdhuryh. (2006). The function space of an activity. In *IEEE conf. on Computer Vision and Pattern Recognition (CVPR 2006)*.

Veeraraghavan, A., Chowdhury, A. R., & Chellappa, R. (2004). Role of shape and kinematics in human movement analysis. In *IEEE conf. on Computer Vision and Pattern Recognition (CVPR 2004)* (Vol. 1, pp. 730-737).

Veeraraghavan, A., Roy-Chowdhury, A. K., & Chellappa, R. (2005). Matching shape sequences in video with applications in human movement analysis. *Pattern Analysis and Machine Intelligence, 27*(12), 1896–1909. doi:10.1109/TPAMI.2005.246

Veit, T., Cao, F., & Bouthemy, P. (2004). Probabilistic parameter-free motion detection. In *Proceedings Conf. Computer Vision and Pattern Recognition (CVPR'04)*, Washington, DC.

Verma, R. C., Schmid, C., & Mikolajczyk, K. (2003). Face detection and tracking in a video by propagating detection probabilities. *IEEE Transactions on Pattern Analysis and Machine Intelligence, 25*(10), 1215–1228. doi:10.1109/TPAMI.2003.1233896

Viola, P., & Jones, M. (2001). Rapid object detection using a boosted cascade of simple features. In *Proceedings IEEE Conf. on Computer Vision and Pattern Recognition (CVPR '01)* (pp. 511–518).

Viola, P., Jones, M., & Snow, D. (2003). Detecting Pedestrians Using Patterns of Motion and Appearance. In *IEEE International Conference on Computer Vision (ICCV'03)* (Vol. 2, pp. 734-741).

Vitaladevuni, S. N., Kellokumpu, V., & Davis, L. S. (2008). Action recognition using ballistic dynamics. In *IEEE Conference on Computer Vision and Pattern Recognition, 2008 (CVPR 2008)* (pp.1-8, 23-28).

Vogler, C., & Metaxas, D. (1999). Parallel hidden markov models for american sign language recognition. In *International Conference on Computer Vision* (pp. 116-122).

Vogler, C., Sun, H., & Metaxas, D. (2001). A framework for motion recognition with applications to American Sign Language and gait recognition. In *Proc. Workshop on Human Motion.*

Wainwright, M. J., Jaakkola, T., & Willsky, A. S. (2001). Tree-based reparameterization for approximate inference on loopy graphs, In *Proceedings of the NIPS* (pp. 1001-1008).

Wallach, H. M. (2004). *Conditional random fields: An introduction.* Technical report, University of Pennsylvania, CIS Technical Report MS-CIS-04-21.

Wang, J., Chen, X., & Gao, W. (2005). Online selecting discriminative tracking features using particle filter. *IEEE Conference on Computer Vision and Pattern Recognition, 2*, 1037-1042.

Wang, L., & Suter, D. (2007). Learning and matching of dynamic shape manifolds for human action recognition. *IEEE Transactions on Image Processing, 16*, 1646–1661. doi:10.1109/TIP.2007.896661

Wang, L., & Suter, D. (2007). Recognizing human activities from silhouettes: motion subspace and factorial discriminative graphical model. In *Proc. IEEE Conference on Computer Vision and Pattern Recognition,* Minneapolis, MN.

Wang, L., Tan, T., Ning, H., & Hu, W. (2003). Silhouette analysis-based gait recognition for human identification. *IEEE Transactions on Pattern Analysis and Machine Intelligence, 25*(12), 1505–1518. doi:10.1109/TPAMI.2003.1251144

Wang, P., & Ji, Q. (2005). Learning discriminant features for multiview face and eye detection. In *IEEE Conference on Computer Vision and Pattern Recognition (CVPR'05).*

Wang, S. B., Quattoni, A., Morency, L.-P., Demirdjian, D., & Darrell, T. (2006). Hidden conditional random fields for gesture recognition. In *Proceedings of the CVPR (2)* (pp. 1521-1527).

Wang, Y., & Ji, Q. (2005). A dynamic conditional random field model for object segmentation in image sequences. In *Proceedings of the CVPR (1)* (pp. 264-270).

Wang, Y., Jiang, H., Drew, M. S., Li, Z. N., & Mori, G. (2006). Unsupervised Discovery of Action Classes. In *IEEE Computer Society Conference on Computer Vision and Pattern Recognition, 2006* (vol.2, pp. 1654-1661).

Wang, Y., Jiang, H., Drew, M. S., Li, Z.-N., & Mori, G. (2006). Unsupervised discovery of action classes. In *IEEE conf. on Computer Vision and Pattern Recognition (CVPR 2006)* (pp. 1-8).

Wei, Q., Hu, M., Zhang, X., & Luo, G. (2007). Dominant sets-based action recognition using image sequence matching. In *Proc. Intl. Conf. on Image Processing (ICIP 2007)* (Vol. 6, pp. 133-136).

Weinland, D., & Boyer, E. (2008).Action recognition using exemplar-based embedding. In *IEEE Conference on Computer Vision and Pattern Recognition (CVPR 2008)* (pp.1-7, 23-28).

Wilson, A., & Bobick, A. (1998). Recognition and interpretation of parametric gesture. In *Proc. Intl. Conf. on Computer Vision (ICCV 1998)* (pp. 329-336).

Wong, S., & Cipolla, R. (2007). Extracting spatiotemporal interest points using global information. In *Proceedings IEEE Intl. Conf. on Computer Vision (ICCV '07)* (pp. 1–8).

Wu, B., & Nevatia, R. (2005). Detection of Multiple, Partially Occluded Humans in a Single Image by Bayesian Combination of Edgelet Part Detectors. In *IEEE International Conference on Computer Vision (ICCV'05)* (Vol. 1, pp. 90-97).

Wu, B., & Nevatia, R. (2006). Tracking of Multiple, Partially Occluded Humans based Static Body Part Detection. In *IEEE Conference on Computer Vision and Pattern Recognition (CVPR'06)*.

Wu, B., & Nevatia, R. (2007). Detection and tracking of multiple, partially occluded humans by bayesian combination of edgelet based part detectors. [IJCV]. *International Journal of Computer Vision, 75*(2), 247–266. doi:10.1007/s11263-006-0027-7

Wu, Y., Hua, G., & Yu, T. (2003). Tracking Articulated body by Dynamic Markov Network. *Computer Vision and Pattern Recognition*.

Wu, Y.-C., Chen, H.-S., Tsai, W.-J., Lee, S.-Y., & Yu, J.-Y. (2008). Human action recognition based on layered-hmm. In *Proc. IEEE Intl. Conf. on Multimedia and Expo (ICME 2008)* (pp. 1453-1456).

Xiang, T., & Gong, S. (2003, October). Recognition of group activities using a dynamic probabilistic network. In *IEEE International Conference on Computer Vision* (Vol. 2, pp. 742–749).

Yacoob, Y., & Black, M. J. (1999). Parameterized modeling and recognition of activities. *Computer Vision and Image Understanding, 72*(2), 232–247. doi:10.1006/cviu.1998.0726

Yamato, J., Ohya, J., & Ishii, K. (1992). Recognizing human action in time-sequential images using hidden Markov model. In *IEEE conf. on Computer Vision and Pattern Recognition (CVPR 1992)* (pp. 379-385).

Yang, P., Shan, S., Gao, W., Li, S., & Zhang, D. (2004). Face recognition using ada-boosted gabor features. In *International Conference on Automatic Face and Gesture Recognition*, Seoul, Korea.

Yedidia, J. S., Freeman, W. T., & Weiss, Y. (2000). Generalized belief propagation. In *Proceedings of the NIPS* (pp. 689-695).

Yilmaz, A., & Shah, M. (2005). Actions sketch: a novel action representation. In *IEEE conf. on Computer Vision and Pattern Recognition (CVPR 2005)* (Vol. 1, pp. 984-989).

Yilmaz, A., Javed, O., & Shah, M. (2006). Object tracking: A survey. *ACM Computing Surveys, 38*(4). doi:10.1145/1177352.1177355

Zatsiorsky, V. M. (1997). *Kinematics of human motion.* Champaign, IL: Human Kinetics Publishers.

Zhai, Y., Tian, Y., & Hampapur, A. (2008). Composite Spatio-Temporal Event Detection in Multi-Camera Surveillance Networks. In *Workshop on Multi-camera and Multi-modal Sensor Fusion Algorithms and Applications (M²SFA²)*.

Zhang, D., Li, S., & Gatica-Perez, D. (2004). Real-time face detection using boosting in hierarchical feature spaces. In *International Conference on Pattern Recognition (ICPR'04)*.

Zhang, Q. (1997). Using wavelet network in nonparametric estimation. *IEEE Transactions on Neural Networks, 8*(2), 227–236. doi:10.1109/72.557660

Zhang, Z., Hu, Y., Chan, S., & Chia, L. (2008). Motion Context: A New Representation for Human Action Recognition. *ECCV 2008*.

Zhang, Z., Huang, K., & Tan, T. (2008). Multi-thread Parsing for Recognizing Complex Events in Videos. *ECCV 2008*.

Zhao, L., & Thorpe, C. E. (2000). Stereo- and neural network-based pedestrian detection. *IEEE Transactions on Intelligent Transportation Systems, 1*(3), 148–154. doi:10.1109/6979.892151

Zhao, T., & Nevatia, R. (2002). 3D tracking of human locomotion: a tracking as recognition approach. In *Proceedings. 16th International Conference on Pattern Recognition* (vol. 1, pp. 546-551).

Zhao, T., & Nevatia, R. (2002). 3d tracking of human locomotion: A tracking as recognition approach. *ICPR, 1*, 541–556.

Zheng, G., Li, W., Ogunbona, P., Dong, L., & Kharitonenko, I. (2006). Simulation of human motion for learning and recognition. In A. Sattar & B. Kang (Eds.), *LNAI 4304* (pp. 1168-1172). New York: Springer.

Zheng, G., Li, W., Ogunbona, P., Dong, L., & Kharitonenko, I. (2007). Human motion simulation and action corpus. In V. Duffy (Ed.), *Digital human modeling,* (LNCS 4561, pp. 314-322). New York: Springer.

Zhong, J. G. S. (2002). HMMs and coupled HMMs for multi-channel eeg classification. In *IEEE Int. Joint Conf. on Neural Networks* (pp. 1154-1159).

Zhu, Q., Avidan, S., Yeh, M.-C., & Cheng, K.-T. (2006). Fast human detection using a cascade of histograms of oriented gradients. In *Proceedings of the Conference on Computer Vision and Pattern Recognition (CVPR'06)*, New York, NY (Vol. 2, pp. 1491–1498).

About the Contributors

Liang Wang received the PhD degree from the Institute of Automation, Chinese Academy of Sciences (CAS), P. R. China, in 2004. From 2004 to 2009, he worked as a Research Assistant at Imperial College London, United Kingdom and Monash University, Australia, and a Research Fellow at University of Melbourne, Australia, respectively.Â Currently, he is a Lecturer with the Department of Computer Science, University of Bath, United Kingdom. His major research interests include machine learning, pattern recognition, computer vision, multimedia processing, and data mining.Â He has widely published at highly-ranked international journals such as IEEE TPAMI, IEEE TIP and IEEE TKDE and leading international conferences such as CVPR, ICCV and ICDM. He has obtained several honors and awards such as the Special Prize of the Presidential Scholarship of Chinese Academy of Sciences. He is currently a Senior Member of IEEE (Institute of Electrical and Electronics Engineers), as well as a member of IEEE Computer Society, IEEE Communications Society and BMVA (British Machine Vision Association). He is serving with more than 20 major international journals and more than 30 major international conferences and workshops. He is an associate editor of IEEE Transactions on Systems, Man and Cybernetics â€" Part B, International Journal of Image and Graphics (WorldSci), International Journal of Signal Processing (Elsevier), and Neurocomputing (Elsevier). He is a leading guest editor of 3 special issues appearing in PRL (Pattern Recognition Letters), IJPRAI (International Journal of Pattern Recognition and Artificial Intelligence) and IEEE TSMC-B, as well as a co-editor of 5 edited books. He has also co-chaired 1 invited special session and 5 international workshops.

Li Cheng received the BS degree from Jilin University, China, the ME degree from Nankai University, and the PhD degree from University of Alberta, Canada, in 1996, 1999, and 2004, respectively. he was with the Statistical Machine Learning group, NICTA Australia. he is now with TTI-Chicago, USA. He has published about 30 research papers. Together with A. Smola and M. Hutter, he co-organized a machine learning summer school (MLSS08 @ mlss08.rsise.anu.edu.au, also see www.mlss.cc). His research interests are mainly on computer vision and machine learning.

Guoying Zhao received the Ph. D. degree in computer science from the Institute of Computing Technology, Chinese Academy of Sciences, Beijing, China in 2005. Since July 2005, she has been a Senior Researcher in Machine Vision Group at the University of Oulu. Her research interests include gait analysis, dynamic texture recognition, facial expression recognition, human motion analysis, and person identification. She has authored over 50 papers in journals and conferences, and has served as a reviewer for many journals and conferences. She gave an invited talk in Institute of Computing Technology, Chinese Academy of Sciences, July 2007. With Prof. Pietikäinen, she gave a tutorial: "Local binary pattern approach to computer vision" in 18th ICPR, Aug. 2006, Hong Kong, and another tutorial "Local texture descriptors in computer vision" in ICCV, Sep. 2009, Kyoto, Japan. She is authoring/ editing three books and a special issue on IEEE Transactions on Systems, Man, and Cybernetics—Part B: Cybernetics. She was a co-chair of ECCV 2008 Workshop on Machine Learning for Vision-based Motion Analysis (MLVMA), and MLVMA workshop at ICCV 2009.

***

Scott Blunsden completed his PhD at Edinburgh University in 2009 in the field of computer vision. Specific interests include the investigation of human based motion and its interpretation by computer. Currently he is working at the European Commission's joint research center in the area of video summarisation.

Richard Bowden is a Reader at the University of Surrey and leads the Cognitive Vision Group within the Centre for Vision Speech and Signal Processing (CVSSP). His award-winning research centres on the use of computer vision to locate, track and understand humans and has received world-wide media coverage, with exhibitions at the British Science Museum and the Minnesota Science Museum, USA. He has won a number of awards including paper prizes for his work on Sign language recognition (undertaken as a visiting Research Fellow at the University of Oxford under subcontract from INRIA), as well as the Sullivan Doctoral Thesis Prize in 2000 for the best UK PhD thesis in vision. He was a member of the British Machine Vision Association (BMVA) executive committee and company director for 7 years, has organised 17 conferences/workshops in related areas and has published over 70 peer reviewed publications. He is a London Technology Network Business Fellow, a member of the British Machine Vision Association, a Senior Member of the Institute of Electrical and Electronic Engineers and a fellow of the Higher Education Academy.

Lisa Brown received her Ph.D. in Computer Science from Columbia University in 1995. She wrote her thesis on medical image registration while working in the Computer Assisted Surgery Group at the IBM T.J Watson Research Center. For the past 14 years she has been a Research Staff Member at IBM. She worked for three years in the Education Group creating software which enables students to take measurements on images and videos. She is currently in the Exploratory Computer Vision Group. She is well known for her ACM survey paper in image registration, which was extensively cited and translated into several languages. She has published extensively, been an invited speaker and panelist to various workshops and has filed numerous patents. Her primary interests are in head tracking, head pose estimation and more recently in object and color classification and performance evaluation of tracking in surveillance.

Jixu Chen is currently a Ph.D. Student in the Department of Electrical, Computer and Systems Engineering at Rensselear Polytechnic Institute. He got his Bachelor (2004) and Master degree (2006) in Electrical Engineering from University of Science and Technology of China (USTC). His research focuses on machine learning and its application to computer vision. He has applied various machine learning techniques, such as Bayesian Network, Dynamic Bayesian Network, and Gaussian Process in computer vision problems, including facial feature tracking, facial expression recognition and human body tracking.

Dong Seon Cheng is a postdoctoral fellow at the Dipartimento di Informatica of the University of Verona (Italy), working with the Vision, Image Processing and Sounds (VIPS) Lab. Cheng did his undergraduate degree at the University of Verona in the Computer Science program and earned his doctoral degree in 2008. As a Ph.D. student, he has been Visiting Research Fellow at the Instituto Superior Tecnico of Lisbon (Portugal), in 2006. His main research interests include graphical probabilistic models, statistical pattern recognition and image processing methods with applications on image and video segmentation, video analysis and biomedical image processing.

Marco Cristani received the Laurea degree in 2002 and the Ph.D. degree in 2006, both in computer science from the Università di Verona, Italy. He was a visiting Ph.D. student at the Computer Vision Lab, Institute for Robotics and Intelligent Systems School of Engineering (IRIS), University of Southern California, Los Angeles, in 2004–2005. He is now a Assistant Professor with the Dipartimento di Informatica, Università di Verona, working with the Vision, Image Processing and Sounds (VIPS) Lab. His main research interests include statistical pattern recognition, generative modeling via graphical models, and nonparametric data fusion techniques, with applications on surveillance, segmentation, image and video retrieval and social signaling. He is the author of several papers in the above subjects and a reviewer for several international conferences and journals.

Rogerio Schmidt Feris received his Ph.D. degree in Computer Science from University of California, Santa Barbara. He joined IBM T. J. Watson Research Center in 2006 where he is currently a Research Staff Member. He is an Affiliate Assistant Professor at the University of Washington and has also worked as Adjunct Professor at the Computer Science Department of Columbia University. His research interests span a wide range of topics in computer vision, graphics, and machine learning, with emphasis on visual surveillance, intelligent user interfaces, and digital photography applications. He has published about 40 papers in peer-reviewed conference and journals, including papers in SIGGRAPH, ICCV, and CVPR. He received several awards and distinctions including IBM Emerging Leader in Multimedia in 2005 and Best Computer Science MSc Thesis in Brazil-2nd Prize in 2002. For more information see http://rogerioferis.com

Robert B. Fisher received a B.S. with Honors (Mathematics) from California Institute of Technology (1974) and a M.S. (Computer Science) from Stanford University (1978) and his PhD from University of Edinburgh (1987). Since then, he has been an academic at Edinburgh University, now in the School of Informatics, where helped found the Institute of Perception, Action and Behaviour. His research covers various topics in 3D computer vision. More recently, he has been researching video sequence understanding, in particular attempting to understand observed behaviour. He also has a passion for on-line teaching and research resources for the computer vision community, leading to several well-used text and interactive exploration resources. He has published or edited 9 books and over 200 peer-reviewed scientific articles, including 40 journal papers. He is a Fellow of the Int. Association for Pattern Recognition (2008).

Andrew Gilbert received the BEng (Hons) degree in Electronic Engineering from the University of Surrey, United Kingdom in 2005. He received the PhD degree from Centre for Vision Speech and Signal Processing at the University of Surrey in 2009. His current research interests include real time visual tracking, human activity recognition, and Intelligent Surveillance. He is currently a Research Fellow at the University of Surrey.

Arun Hampapur is an IBM Distinguished Engineer. He is currently leading the integrated security research effort at IBM Research. Additionally, he works with IBM's Global Technology Services Division on Physical Security projects. In 2008 Arun served as the CTO for Physical Security in IBM's GTS division. He led the creation of advanced technologies and new solution offerings in the physical security space, including Digital Video Surveillance, Video Analytics Biometrics, Access Control and related technologies. Dr Hampapur led the research team which invented IBM Smart Surveillance System (S3) at IBM T.J Watson Research Center. He has led the S3 effort from its inception as an exploratory research effort, thru the building of the first lab prototype, first customer pilot engagement, to the commercialization as a services offering. He has developed several algorithms for video analytics and video indexing. He has published more than 40 papers on various topics related to media indexing, video analysis, and video surveillance and holds 9 US patents and more than 50 patent applications. He is also active in the research community and serves on the program committees of several IEEE International conferences. Dr Hampapur is an IEEE Senior Member. He is one of the early researchers in the field of Applied Computer Vision and Multimedia Database Management. Dr Hampapur obtained his PhD from the University of Michigan in 1995. Before moving to IBM he was leading the video effort at Virage Inc (1995 – 1997).

Weiming Hu received the PhD degree from the Department of Computer Science and Engineering, Zhejiang University. From April 1998 to March 2000, he was a postdoctoral research fellow with the Institute of Computer Science and Technology, Founder Research and Design Center, Peking University. Since April 1998, he has been with the National Laboratory of Pattern Recognition, Institute of Automation, Chinese Academy of Sciences. Now, he is a professor and a PhD student supervisor in the lab. His research interests are in visual surveillance, neural networks, filtering of Internet objectionable information, retrieval of multimedia, and understanding of Internet behaviors. He has published more than 70 papers on national and international journals and international conferences.

John Illingworth has been active in computer vision and image processing for over 25 years and has co-authored nearly 200 papers in refereed journals and conferences. He has been active in professional society work and is a former Chairman of the British Machine Vision Association. He has been a senior editor on two international journals. He has made contributions to low level image processing, feature and shape detection, the analysis of dense range imagery, 3D face recognition, document analysis and high level vision. His research has been funded from many diverse government and industrial sources.

Qiang Ji received his Ph.D degree in Electrical Engineering from the University of Washington. He is currently a Professor with the Department of Electrical, Computer, and Systems Engineering at Rensselaer Polytechnic Institute (RPI). He is also a program director at the National Science Foundation, managing part of NSF's computer vision and machine learning programs. He has also held teaching and research positions with the Beckman Institute at University of Illinois at Urbana-Champaign, the

Robotics Institute at Carnegie Mellon University, the Dept. of Computer Science at University of Nevada at Reno, and the US Air Force Research Laboratory. Prof. Ji currently serves as the director of the Intelligent Systems Laboratory (ISL) at RPI. Prof. Ji's research interests are in computer vision, pattern recognition, and probabilistic graphical models. He has published over 100 papers in peer-reviewed journals and conferences. His research has been supported by major governmental agencies including NSF, NIH, DARPA, ONR, ARO, and AFOSR as well as by major companies including Honda and Boeing. Prof. Ji is an editor on several computer vision and pattern recognition related journals and he has served as a program committee member, area char, and program chair in numerous international conferences/workshops. Prof. Ji is a senior member of the IEEE.

Wanqing Li received his B.Sc. in physics and electronics in 1983, M.Sc. in computer science in 1987, both from Zhejiang University, China, and PhD in electronic engineering in 1997 from The University of Western Australia. He was a Lecturer (87-90) and Associate Professor (91-92) at the Department of Computer Science, Zhejiang University of China. He joint Motorola Lab in Sydney (98-03) as a Senior Researcher and later a Principal Researcher. From Dec. 2007 to Feb. 2008, he was a visiting researcher at Microsoft Research, Redmond, WA. He is currently with SCSSE, University of Wollongong. His research interests include human motion analysis, audio and visual event detection and object recognition. Dr. Li has served as a publication chair of MMSP'08, General Co-Chair of ASIACCS'09 and DRMTICS'05, and technical committee members of many international conferences including ICIP'03-07. Dr Li is a member of the IEEE.

Zicheng Liu received the B.S. degree in mathematics from Huazhong Normal University, China, the M.S. degree in operational research from the Institute of Applied Mathematics, Chinese Academy of Sciences, Beijing, China, and the Ph.D. degree in computer science from Princeton University, Princeton, NJ. He is a Researcher at Microsoft Research, Redmond, WA. Before joining Microsoft, he was a Member of Technical Staff at Silicon Graphics, focusing on trimmed NURBS tessellation for CAD model visualization. His research interests include linked figure animation, face modeling and animation, face relighting, image segmentation, and multimedia signal processing. Dr. Liu is an Associate Editor of Machine Vision and Applications. He was a Co-Chair of the 2003 IEEE International Workshop on Multimedia Technologies in E-Learning and Collaboration, a Program Co-Chair of the MMSP'06, an Electronic Media Co-Chair of ICME'07. Dr Liu is a Senior Member of the IEEE.

Takashi Matsuyama received B. Eng., M. Eng., and D. Eng. degrees in electrical engineering from Kyoto University, Japan, in 1974, 1976, and 1980, respectively. He is currently a professor in the Department of Intelligence Science and Technology, Graduate School of Informatics, and a vice president of Kyoto University. His research interests include knowledge-based image understanding, computer vision, 3D video, and human-computer interaction. He wrote about 100 papers and books including two research monographs, A Structural Analysis of Complex Aerial Photographs, PLENUM, 1980 and SIGMA: A Knowledge-Based Aerial Image Understanding System, PLENUM, 1990. He won over ten best paper awards from Japanese and international academic societies including the Marr Prize at ICCV'95. He is on the editorial board of Pattern Recognition Journal. He was given Fellowships from International Association for Pattern Recognition, Information Processing Society Japan, and Institute for Electronics, Information, and Communication Engineers Japan.

Vittorio Murino is full professor at the University of Verona, Italy. He took the Laurea degree in Electronic Engineering in 1989 and the Ph.D. in Electronic Engineering and Computer Science in 1993 at the University of Genoa. He was chairman of the Department of Computer Science of the University of Verona from 2001 to 2007. His main research interests include computer vision and pattern recognition, in particular, probabilistic techniques for image and video processing, with applications on video surveillance, biomedical image analysis and bioinformatics. Prof. Murino is author or co-author of more than 150 papers published in refereed journals and international conferences, reviewer for several international journals, and member of the committes of important conferences (CVPR, ICCV, ECCV, ICPR). He is member of the editorial board of the Pattern Recognition, IEEE Trans. on Systems, Man, and Cybernetics, Pattern Analysis and Applications, Machine Vision & Applications, and ELCVIA journals. He is also senior member of the IEEE and Fellow of the IAPR.

Pradeep Natarajan received his B.Tech degree in Computer Science and Engineering from the Indian Institute of Technology,Madras at Chennai, India in 2003, and M.S. degree in Computer Science from University of Southern California (USC), Los Angeles in 2005. He finished his PhD in Computer Science at USC in 2009, where he was a member of the Computer Vision Laboratory lead by Prof. Ramakant Nevatia. Currently, he is a Scientist at BBN Technologies in Cambridge, MA. His general research interests are at the intersection of Computer Vision and Artificial Intelligence. More specifically, he has focussed on the problem of Action Recognition in videos and has made novel contributions in all aspects of the problem, ranging from high-level event representation, to low-level feature extraction, to efficient algorithms for inference and parameter learning. He has published his work in leading Computer Vision and AI conferences including IJCAI and CVPR.

Ram Nevatia received his PhD from Stanford University and is currently a Professor of Computer Science and Electrical Engineering at the University of Southern California, where he is the founding director of the Institute for Robotics and Intelligent Systems (IRIS). Prof. Nevatia has more than 30 years of experience in computer vision research, and has published more than 100 refered techincal papers. Prof. Nevatia is a fellow of the Institute of Electrical and Electronics Engineers (IEEE) and the American Association of Artificial Intelligence (AAAI). In recent years, his research has been focused on detecting and tracking humans and vehicles in video and on techniques for representation and recognition of events.

Philip O. Ogunbona received the B.Sc. degree (with first class honors) in electronics and electrical engineering in from the University of Ife, Nigeria (1981), and the Ph.D. degree in electrical engineering from Imperial College, London, U.K.(1987). After post-doctoral work in the Department of Computing, Imperial College, and a stint at STC Research Labs, Harlow, U.K. he joined the Department of Electrical and Computer Engineering, University of Wollongong, Australia, as a Lecturer in 1990. Between 1998 and 2004 he was with Motorola Labs, Australian Research Centre, Australia, where he developed multimedia algorithms and systems for mobile devices. He is currently a professor and Dean of the Faculty of Informatics, University of Wollongong, Australia. His research interests include signal and image processing, pattern recognition and machine learning. Professor Ogunbona is a Senior Member of the IEEE.

Olusegun T. Oshin received the BEng (Hons) degree in Electronics and Computer Engineering from the University of Surrey, United Kingdom, in 2007, where he is currently working towards the PhD degree in Computer Vision under the supervision of Richard Bowden. His interests include Computer Vision with emphasis on Action Recognition and Machine Learning.

Ronald Poppe received his MS (2004) and PhD (2009) degrees in computer science from the University of Twente, The Netherlands. He has worked on vision-based human pose recovery and human action recognition. His other interests include the modeling and understanding of human behavior from various cues, the human perception of these cues and the use of novel ways to label large amounts of multimodal data. He is currently a postdoctoral researcher at the Delft University of Technology.

Konrad Schindler received the PhD degree in computer science from Graz University of Technology in 2003 with work an image-based 3D reconstruction. He has worked as a photogrammetric engineer in the private industry (1999-2000), and has held research assistant positions at Graz University of Technology (2001-2003), Monash University (2004-2006), and ETH Zurich (2007-2008). Since 2009, he is an assistant professor of computer science at TU Darmstadt, where he heads the image understanding group. He has authored or co-authored over 50 papers in refereed journals and conferences. His research interests include image-based 3D modeling, analysis and reconstruction of dynamic scenes, visual object detection and tracking.

Vassilis Syrris has studied Mathematics at the Aristotle University of Thessaloniki, Greece (B.A.), Business Management at the Hellenic Management Association (Postgraduate studies) and Artificial Intelligence: Knowledge-based Systems at the University of Edinburgh, U.K. (M.Sc.). He is currently completing his Ph.D. in the Automation and Robotics Lab, Faculty of Electrical and Computers Engineering, Aristotle University of Thessaloniki, Greece. He is also working as assistant tutor in the Aristotle University of Thessaloniki, as laboratorial instructor in the Technological Educational Institute of Thessaloniki and as a high-school teacher with a private college in Thessaloniki. He has participated in and run European Community Programs related to education, informatics and professional occupation. His research interests are: machine learning, robotics, computer vision, automation, evolutionary algorithms, fuzzy logic, e-learning, intelligent tutoring systems, symbolic representation, data manipulation and statistical analysis.

YingLi Tian received her PhD from the Chinese University of Hong Kong. She is an associate professor in the Electrical Engineering Department of CCNY and head of the Media Lab. Prior to joining CCNY, she was a Research Staff Member in Exploratory Computer Vision Group at the IBM T.J. Watson Research Center. As one of the inventors of the IBM Smart Surveillance Solutions (SSS), she led the video analytics team and received the IBM Outstanding Innovation Achievement Award. She was also one of the key contributors to DARPA ECASSIST project. She obtained the Best System Paper award on IEEE Workshop on Multi-modal Sentient Computing: Sensors, Algorithms, and Systems, 2007. Dr. Tian focused on automatic facial expression analysis when she worked at the Robotics Institute in Carnegie Mellon University. Dr. Tian has published more than 70 papers in journals and conferences and has filed more than 30 patents. Her research experience includes target detection and tracking, event and activity analysis, scene understanding, facial expression recognition, human computer interaction, multi-sensor fusion, and machine learning. She is a senior member of IEEE.

Tony Tung received the M.Sc. degree in physics and computer science from the Ecole Nationale Superieure de Physique de Strasbourg in 2000, and the Ph.D. degree in Signal and Image processing from the Ecole Nationale Superieure des Telecommunications de Paris in 2005. He is currently a research fellow in the Department of Intelligence Science and Technology, Graduate School of Informatics, at Kyoto University, Japan. His research interests include computer vision, 3D video, shape modeling, and human motion analysis. He was awarded Fellowships from the Japan Society for the Promotion of Science in 2005 and 2008. He is a member of the IEEE.

Luc van Gool received the PhD degree in electrical engineering from KU Leuven in 1991 with work on visual invariants. He is currently a full professor of computer vision at KU Leuven and at ETH Zurich. His main interests include 3D reconstruction and modeling, object recognition, tracking, and their integration, as well as computer vision for archaeology. Over the years, he has authored and co-authored over 250 papers in this field and received best paper awards at ICCV 1998 and CVPR 2007. He has been a program committee member and area chair of several major vision conferences and was program co-chair of ICCV05. He is a co-founder of the companies Eyetronics, kooaba, GeoAutomation, Procedural, and eSaturnus.

Daniel Vaquero received the BS degree in computer science from the University of Sao Paulo, Brazil, in 2003. Two years later, he received the MS degree, also in computer science from the University of Sao Paulo, for his research on image processing and optical character recognition. He is now a PhD candidate at the University of California, Santa Barbara, working with Prof. Matthew Turk in the Four Eyes Laboratory. Throughout his PhD studies, Daniel held research internship positions at Mitsubishi Electric Research Labs, where he worked on computational illumination techniques, and IBM Research, where he developed visual surveillance algorithms. His current research interests span topics in computer vision, graphics and machine learning, with applications in surveillance and digital photography.

Qingdi Wei received the BSc degree in Mechanical Engineering and Automation from the South China University of Technology, China, in 2004. He is currently a PhD student in the pattern recognition, the National Laboratory of Pattern Recognition, Institute of Automation, Chinese Academy of Sciences. His research interests include motion analysis, and action recognition.

Yun Zhai received his Ph.D in computer science from the University of Central Florida in 2006, and his B.S. degree from the Bethune-Cookman College in 2001. He joined IBM T.J. Watson Research Center in 2006 as a post-doctoral researcher. He is currently a senior digital video research engineer in a joint department of IBM Research and GTS. His research interests include computer vision, multimedia signal processing, content-based video retrieval and computational attention models. He has publications in leading conferences and journals including ICCV, CVPR, Sig-Multimedia, CVIU and IEEE T-MM. He has over 20 patents granted or pending. He has served in the program committees of ACM Multimedia, AVSS, ICPR, CGIV, CHI and ICIP, and in the review panels of MVA, IEEE T-MM, IEEE T-CVST, CVIU, IJPRAI and IEEE SPL. He is currently a key member of the IBM Smart Surveillance Solution (SSS) development team. He is a member of ACM and IEEE.

Lei Zhang received his B.S. degree and M.S. degree in Electrical Engineering from Tsinghua University, China, in 1999 and 2002 respectively. He recently received his PhD degree in Electrical Engineering from Rensselaer Polytechnic Institute in May 2009. His research focuses on machine learning and its application to computer vision problems. His current research is primarily about developing probabilistic graphical models such as Bayesian Network, Dynamic Bayesian Network, Condition Random Field, Factor Graph, Chain Graph, etc. He has applied different graphical models to several computer vision problems, including image segmentation, upper body tracking, facial expression recognition, etc. He is a student member of the IEEE.

Xiaoqin Zhang received the BSc degree in Electronic Engineering from Central South University, China, in 2005. He is currently a PhD student in the pattern recognition, the National Laboratory of Pattern Recognition, Institute of Automation, Chinese Academy of Sciences. His current research interests include visual tracking, motion analysis, and action recognition.

Zhengyou Zhang received the B.S. degree in electronic engineering from the University of Zhejiang, China, in 1985, the M.S. degree in computer science from the University of Nancy, Nancy, France, in 1987, the Ph.D. degree in computer science (specializing in computer vision) from the University of Paris XI, Paris, France, in 1990, and the Dr. Sci. (Habil. diriger des recherches) diploma from the University of Paris XI in 1994. He is a Principal Researcher with Microsoft Research, Redmond,WA. He has been with INRIA for 11 years and was a Senior Research Scientist from 1991 to 1998. During 1996-1997, he spent a one-year sabbatical as an Invited Researcher at the Advanced Telecommunications Research Institute International (ATR), Kyoto, Japan. He has published over 150 papers in refereed international journals and conferences, and has co-authored three books in Computer Vision. Dr. Zhang is an Associate Editor of the IEEE Trans. on Multimedia, an Associate Editor of the International Journal of Computer Vision (IJCV), an Associate Editor of the International Journal of Pattern Recognition and Artificial Intelligence (IJPRAI), and an Associate Editor of Machine Vision and Applications (MVA). He served on the Editorial Board of the IEEE Trans. on Pattern Analysis and Machine Intelligence (PAMI) from 2000 to 2004, and of two other journals. He has been on the program committees for numerous international conferences, and was an Area Chair and a Demo Chair of ICCV'03, a Program Co-Chair of ACCV'04, a Demo Chair of ICCV'05, a Program Co-Chair of MMSP'06, and a Program Co-Chair of International Workshop on Motion and Video Computing, 2006. He has given a number of keynotes in international conferences. Dr Zhang is a Fellow of the IEEE.

Zhi Zeng is currently a Ph.D. student in Department of Electrical, Computer and Systems Engineering at Rensselaer Polytechnic Institute. Before coming to Rensselaer, he received his M.S. degree from Tsinghua University, Beijing, China, and B.S. degree from Fudan University, Shanghai, China, both majoring in Electronic Engineering. His research mainly focuses on the joint field of machine learning and computer vision, more specifically, the parameter and structure learning of Bayesian network (Dynamic Bayesian Network), and their applications in human body tracking and human activity recognition.

Index

Symbols